THE PATTONS

THE PATTONS

A Personal History of an
American Family

ROBERT H. PATTON

BRASSEY'S
WASHINGTON • LONDON

For Vicki, with love

Copyright © 1994 by Robert H. Patton

Reprinted by arrangement with Crown Publishers, Inc.

Manufactured in the United States of America

Library of Congress Cataloging-in-Publication Data

Patton, Robert H. (Robert Holbrook), 1957–
   The Pattons : a personal history of an American Family / Robert H.
Patton. — 1st Brassey's Five-star paperback ed.
      p.   cm.
   Originally published : New York : Crown Publishers, © 1994.
   Includes bibliographical references and index.

   ISBN 1-57488-127-2 (pbk.)

   1. Patton Family 2. Patton, George S. (George Smith). 1885–1945—Family
   3. Generals—United States—Biography. 4. United States—Army—Biography
   5. United States—Biography.   I. Title.

CT274.P384P38   1996
355'.0092'273—dc20
   [B]   96-9585
                                                                                   CIP

CONTENTS

INTRODUCTION

"The Pattons"

IN JANUARY 1746, Sir Robert Munro of Foulis, Scotland, fought his own grandson at the battle of Falkirk and was defeated and killed in action. His grandson was a young volunteer in the rebel army of Bonnie Prince Charlie; Sir Robert was a Scottish general loyal to the king of England. The image of these kinsmen meeting at sword point underscores the sorrow of war and especially of civil war. It would make an interesting historical footnote if only it were true.

Sir Robert Munro fought and died at Falkirk. Against him on the other side was a nineteen-year-old medic named Hugh Mercer, whose descendants in America include, seven generations later, me. Though Mercer was long believed to be Sir Robert's grandson, in 1981 a Scottish genealogist confirmed that the two were not related. This discovery struck me as less than trivial at first—they'd been dead a long time, after all. But since researching this family history I've come to a different opinion. I know now that there have been those among Mercer's descendants who for various reasons attached great significance to his supposed relation to Sir Robert Munro. It offered them a link to Scots nobility. It testified, given their clash on the battlefield, to the younger man's commitment to follow his heart and the older man's commitment to duty, qualities any heir would admire. And it seemed to suggest a prevailing family destiny: to fight and if need be, to die in honorable battle.

Not all Hugh Mercer's descendants took note of, or read anything into, his relation to Sir Robert. Of those who did, two in particular believed emphatically that the battle of Falkirk was the opening scene, like daybreak in Eden, of the true story of our family. Those two were my grandfather, General George S. Patton, Jr., "Old Blood and Guts" of World War II fame and legend, and his father, George S. Patton II, an orange grower and failed politician from Southern California. With Falkirk as one ingredient, these men concocted an idea of themselves and their heritage to stroke their vanity, soothe their insecurity, and inspire them to strive for greatness.

That idea, called "The Pattons," had less to do with family than with individual conduct. Its origins, its rules, its effect on the lives of family members, is the story I have to tell. It is part history and part fable: witness the mythical clash at Falkirk. But the idea of "The Pattons," and the tales that founded it, cast a powerful spell on the family's most prominent member, George S. Patton, Jr. It also influenced, often darkly, many of the rest of us.

Scattered about the room where I'm writing are half a dozen cardboard crates full of family letters and documents, some more than two hundred years old, all of them helping me to comprehend my family, my grandfather, myself. These letters are not part of Patton's collected private papers now housed at the Library of Congress. They were written by other relatives and saved, I suppose, for reasons of neurosis. The Pattons could not bear to throw anything away, lest when they died there would be nothing, not a letter, not a grocery list, for their descendants to remember them by. And to be forgotten was to be condemned.

Reading such old letters has been a strange experience for me, at times a rather morbid one. Not for their content, which even when recounting bad news conveys the chatty vitality of overheard telephone conversations. The morbidity lies in the letters themselves, cracked in the folds, gone brown at the edges, and redolent of the attics and steamer trunks where they have been stored for decades. My ancestors' penmanship is often as poor as my own, with ink blots and misspellings and breathless PS's, the writing scrunched at the end of a line, the lines turning vertically up one side in order to save paper. I unfold the letters carefully. Several have contained flower petals pressed inside them a century ago, now drab and fragile as the wing of a moth. My great-grandfather once mailed his fiancée a four-leaf clover he'd found. It fell from the envelope into my lap along with his accompanying love letter, mementos treasured in my great-grandmother's bureau since 1882. These people lived and then they died. But their voices speak clearly through the words they wrote, as do, I've found, their hearts.

In addition to unpublished family letters and journals, I have the testimony of my father, George, and my aunt Ruth Ellen, General Patton's son and daughter, to help me understand "The Pattons" and, in particular, the general himself. Because of the fame their father gained in World War II, and because of his sheer vividness in person, he reigns as the family's exemplary figure, a goal he sought from childhood. "It is my sincere hope," he wrote in his journal, "that any of my blood who read these lines will be similarly inspired and ever true to the heroic traditions of their race."

There is a Greek myth in which the god Zeus is asked by one of his mortal mistresses to reveal himself to her in his true Olympian form rather than as a mere man. Zeus grants the request, and at the blazing sight of him the woman is burned to a crisp. I might wonder, given the general's charisma, narcissism, charm, and swagger, how George and Ruth Ellen were not reduced to smoldering cinders for having viewed their father at close range. A third sibling, named Beatrice for her mother, died in 1952 at the age of forty-one. "Daddy broke her spirit," Ruth Ellen says today. Her brother doesn't disagree. Do I smell smoke in the room after all?

My father is seventy now, ten years older than General Patton was at the time of his death in 1945. Like the general, my father attended the U.S. Military Academy at West Point and had a long army career. His sister Ruth Ellen, seventy-nine, married a West Pointer; her two sons became military officers. Beatrice also married a West Pointer; her sons were officers in the army and navy. Likewise the sons of General Patton's sister: army and naval officers. As for my father, he married the daughter of a brigadier general. She, my mother, is descended through both parents from multiple generations of West Pointers, multiple generations of generals, in fact. Her sister married an army officer. Her brother was a West Pointer. His son is an army lieutenant. My own sons are seven and three years old. Civilians, as yet.

And what of me, my two sisters, and two brothers, who, for what it's worth, are the only direct descendants of the famed World War II general to carry his last name? None of us is involved either by profession or through marriage with the military. My own career might charitably be called fluid; I've worked as a reporter, a carpenter, a commercial fisherman, and a small-town real estate developer. Strangers often ask my parents why their kids aren't in the service. I'd like to know their answer, for there have been times in my life, and not so long ago, when I've asked myself the same question. I figured I was an independent person who came of age in the muddled aftermath of an independent era: the 1960s. It didn't honestly feel that way, however.

Deciding not to apply for admission to West Point was the pivotal decision of my youth. I say this not because I struggled through painful deliberations (I didn't), but because since opting for a civilian life I've been periodically dogged by the sense that I made a basic error. Not often did I think this; maybe three or four times in the seventeen years since I told my parents that the military wasn't for me. But often enough to suggest that something inside me—something to do with heritage, upbringing, my father and grandfather—remained in almost childlike thrall to that notion called "The Pattons." I thought to myself in undertaking this history, it will be good to find out why.

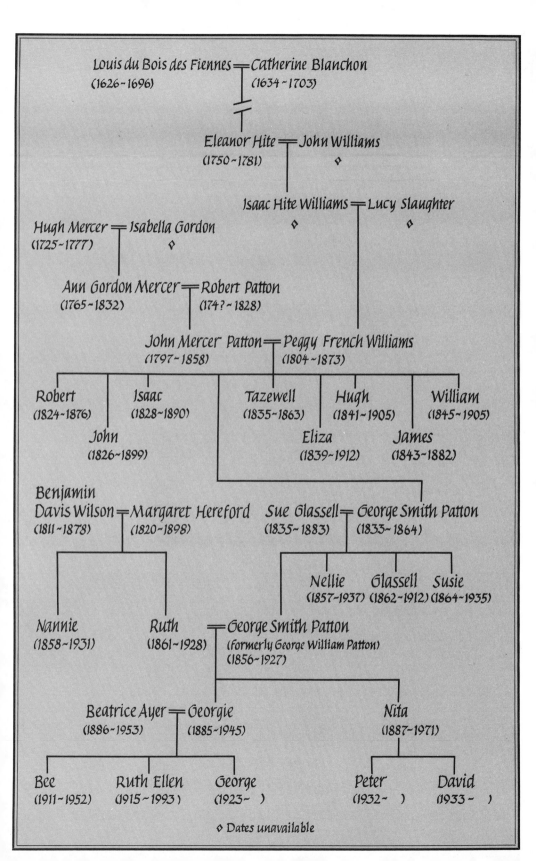

PROLOGUE

September 1918: A Good Honorable Wound

IN ANOTHER WAR it might have been called a million-dollar wound, one serious enough to warrant transfer to the rear and perhaps all the way home, but not terrible in any permanent way that could potentially ruin your life. Fired from a distance of forty yards, the German bullet passed through Georgie's upper left thigh just below the groin and exited two inches to the left of his rectum, taking a teacup-size piece of flesh out of his backside. The surgeon was amazed that it had neither shattered the pelvis, struck the sciatic nerve, nor nicked the femoral artery; had he tried to pass a probe along the bullet's path, he could not have avoided all three. "My guardian spirits," Georgie wrote his father, who knew exactly what Georgie meant.

A general said Patton's "good honorable wound ... will be the envy of everybody!" A French colonel was surprised that the young officer had survived. "You are one of those gallant men who always gets killed. But you will get it yet." This last pleased Georgie, for it implied there was more fighting to do. There wasn't. His wound developed sepsis. By the time it had healed, World War I was over.

Armistice was declared on November 11, two days before he was scheduled to return to the front with a new brigade. It was his thirty-third birthday. He hated getting older; the prospect of his future in a peacetime army darkened his mood still further. After training in France for more than a year, after dreaming of it nearly all his life, he would return to America having experienced only two days of actual combat. All the dearer to him, then, were his battle scar and Distinguished Service Cross. He'd received the DSC for valor during the Meuse-Argonne offensive. The medal confirmed that he'd overcome his youthful fear of proving cowardly under fire. The scar confirmed that his combat experience had been perilous, if brief.

The scar and the medal made his exploits in France self-evident. Yet from the moment he returned in March 1919, he felt compelled to dramatize them. He was playing touch football and walking without a limp within two months of his wounding in 1918. Yet rejoining his wife after nearly two years apart, he made his entrance carrying a cane in one hand. Beatrice was waiting on shore when Georgie's troopship docked in New York harbor. Her husband so thin, his blond hair graying, was proof enough of the stories she'd heard of war aging men past their years; to see him leaning on a cane made the truth of those stories sting. At the top of the gangplank Georgie hesitated. He waved down to her, then grandly set aside the cane and strode into her arms unaided, as if only this miracle vision of Beatrice could heal his pain completely.

He fought the urge to trumpet his exploits. It ought to have been gratifying enough that the army had recognized him and that his family, having long indulged his grandiose dreams, had seen its faith in him rewarded. But as World War I faded into the past, Georgie began telling the story of his battle wound every chance he got. It evolved into a performance piece interspersed with recited bits of *The Iliad* or *Henry V.* Many of his wife's high society relatives had little interest in these monologues. They didn't consider the military a gentleman's profession, and though sometimes amused and charmed by Georgie, they preferred him in small doses, forgiving his lapses of gauche behavior for Beatrice's sake. He in turn mocked them as pampered ingrates who had never been near a combat zone, who cowered behind their armed forces in wartime and neglected them in peace. If they thought him loud and uncouth then by God he would *give* them loud and uncouth. At certain dull formal gatherings on Boston's North Shore, Georgie imbibed the Prohibition liquor and then loosened his trousers before the guests that they might view his scarred buttock. Often at such parties he took position by the drawing room fireplace declaiming Kipling's "Barrack Room Ballads" to whoever would listen. Often the children of the household proved his most appreciative audience, let stay up late to ogle Uncle Georgie while the grown-ups slipped discreetly away.

In the late 1920s Georgie was thrown off a public beach at Narragansett, Rhode Island, for indecent exposure. With a pair of shears he'd scalloped a high wide cut in the back of his bathing suit to better display his scar to innocent vacationers. Banished to the parking lot by beach officials while his companions went on with their swim, Georgie and his good honorable wound were finally recast into caricature. In the years ahead that caricature would by turns grow pathetic and bitter, self-pity becoming his sharpest emotion and alcohol its consistent spur. His continued infatuation with all things martial began to seem like a boyish eccentricity gone irretrievably dark and disturbed. As Georgie himself had acknowledged in his 1918 poem, "Peace," he was the kind of man who could only "moulder in the virtuous vice/Of futile peaceful life."

Still he prepared, drilling his paltry units of an army in mothballs for battle with a nameless foe. At night he read volumes of military history, annotating the margins with fervid comment, as if someday someone might care. He pounded the dinner table with each pronouncement of personal destiny while his children rolled their eyes. The war to end all wars had been won in 1918. Georgie's eager talk of a great war to come seemed little more than a diseased dream. Until fortune blessed him with an enemy, however, the dream seemed better by far than the embarrassment his life had become.

A NAME IN AMERICA

By heaven, methinks it were an easy leap
To pluck bright honor from the pale-faced moon.

—William Shakespeare
Henry IV (Part One)

The Contempt of the Proud

L EGEND holds that on August 24, 1572, Catherine de Medici gave the signal to begin the massacre of St. Bartholomew's Day by casually dropping a silk handkerchief off her balcony at the Tuileries palace. Soldiers in the service of Catherine's son, King Charles IX of France, dispersed through the city of Paris to the homes of various Huguenot leaders and murdered them. The Huguenots were French Calvinists whose political and spiritual independence undermined King Charles's Roman Catholic regime; St. Bartholomew's Day marked a brutal betrayal of the recent truce between them. The killing spread to the provinces and went on for weeks, the death toll rising into the thousands. In Rome the jubilant pope had a commemorative medal struck in celebration.

The massacre accelerated the exodus of French Huguenots to Holland, Germany, and eventually to the New World across the sea. Among the refugees were Louis du Bois des Fiennes and his wife, Catherine Blanchon. Descended from Huguenot aristocrats, educated and well-to-do, Louis and Catherine shortened their last name to the more anonymous DuBois and sailed for America with their two young sons in 1660. They expected not merely to survive there, but to prevail, an expectation promoted by their privileged upbringing and by the memory of the Huguenot leaders slain in the massacre of Saint Bartholomew's Day, whom they exalted as heroes of misfortune. In America the DuBoises would reclaim what they considered their birthright: an honored position on society's upper level. If they held true to their principles—pride, hard work, faith in the heroic traditions of the past, and faith in the Calvinist God—Louis and Catherine believed that triumph was assured.

The arrival of European settlers on the shores of the New World was the first blow in the long cycle of violence between the settlers and the land's Native Americans. Early on, however, there were periods when relations between white men and Indians were accommodative and even mutually profitable. In the early settlements of eastern New York, beaver pelts were a valued commodity used to make clothing and hats. (Beaver testicles also were highly prized. A Dutch naturalist wrote that the organs, dried, crushed to powder, and taken in water, cured toothaches, restored sight, and reversed the effects of idiocy.) In 1655 a band of Mohicans entered the Dutch village of Manhattan bringing pelts and corn as barter for trade goods and gunpowder. An Indian woman idly picked a peach off a nearby tree and for the offense was shot dead by a Dutchman. The incident touched off the so-called Peach War, which continued sporadi-cally for a decade. Indians and settlers answered injury with injury, massa-cre with massacre. This was the environment into which the DuBois family disembarked in 1660.

They traveled up the Hudson River to a French Huguenot settlement called New Village, near Kingston, New York. The settlers there were trying to keep clear of the ongoing Peach War. They condemned the thuggish behavior of their Dutch neighbors, accusing these "low Holland-ers" of cheating the Indians, chasing their women, and selling them liquor, and by these acts inciting Indian retaliation, putting everyone at risk. But in 1663 the Huguenots were irrevocably drawn into the conflict.

At midday on June 7, when most of the men were out working the fields, an Indian war party attacked the village and set it on fire. Hearing the cries, seeing the smoke, the men grabbed their muskets and came running but arrived too late. Twenty villagers, mostly children and women (several of them pregnant), had been killed. "The burnt and roasted corpses," one witness wrote, lay "like sheaves behind the mower." Six women and sixteen children had been taken captive, among them Catherine DuBois and her (now) four children, including a baby daughter, Sara, still nursing at Cath-erine's breast.

Louis had become a village leader (later he would cofound New Palz, New York), and quickly he organized an armed posse to go after the

Indians. The pursuit was delayed by the refusal of neighboring Dutch settlers to loan horses to the rescue effort without first securing collateral. The Dutch resented the snobby French Huguenots and were not inclined to do them any favors; in a few hours a deal for the horses was struck, though not without a considerable exchange of "foul and unbecoming language not to be repeated." By then the Indians and their captives had vanished into the forest. In the following days, the Dutch governor of the region, Peter Stuyvesant, tried to raise troops to crush decisively the Indians. Few beyond the men of New Village volunteered. "We are first obliged to take care of ourselves and not get otherwise involved," was the prevailing attitude. Nearly two months after the attack, however, one of the captured women appeared back home, having escaped from the Indians. She guided a party of seventy men to an Indian village thirty miles away. They attacked the village and killed its chief and fourteen braves. But the captives were nowhere to be found, and in frustration the men torched the village and slaughtered its women and children, throwing the corpses into a nearby creek.

The original Indian raiders learned of these atrocities and as revenge decided to burn one of their prisoners to death. No deliberation was needed as to which one it would be. Catherine DuBois, as later described, was "short, high bosomed, with blue eyes, bright brown hair, and a formidable temper." She'd been a holy terror from the moment of her kidnapping back in June, complaining and scratching and hitting without end, and the Indians were heartily sick of her. They built a log pyre and set her atop it with her baby, Sara, in her arms. Just as the torch was about to be applied, Catherine broke into a soaring Huguenot hymn and followed it with the 123rd psalm. The Indians paused to listen. Some distance away in the woods, the pursuing band of settlers followed the sound of Catherine's voice and burst upon her captors, whom they "terribly punished." Several captive women and six of the children were killed in the ensuing battle. The rest returned to New Village except a Miss Slecht, who'd fallen in love with an Indian brave and remained behind to marry him.

On the fortieth anniversary of her rescue, Catherine DuBois freed her seventeen-year-old Negro slave, named Rachel, as "testimony of her everliving gratitude for deliverance." The event is believed by some to be the first voluntary freeing of a slave in North America. But Catherine's legacy to her descendants was hardly altruistic; at forty years after the fact, her gesture was tardy at best. Rather, she was a symbol of gutsy pride, a character trait that in excess may become a character flaw, as the 123rd psalm would seem to attest:

Have mercy upon us, O Lord . . . Our soul is exceedingly filled with the scorning of those that are at ease, and with the contempt of the proud.

No doubt in her view it was her Indian captors whose pride had been contemptuous. Yet it was Catherine's own pride that had got her through the ordeal. This was the lesson her descendants took from her story, which became a kind of formative family myth as it was passed down through the generations, beginning with her babe in arms, Sara.

As in the arranged political marriages of old Europe, the marriage of Sara DuBois and Joost Jans Van Metre, whose first wife and two children had been killed by Indians, bound together two bickering factions of French and Dutch settlers. Sara's granddaughter Eleanor, upon marrying Isaac Hite in 1745, moved from Pennsylvania to northern Virginia. Isaac's father had acquired 140,000 acres in the fertile valley of the Shenandoah River. When Isaac was still a young boy, his father let him choose a parcel of land for himself. Isaac picked a three-mile stretch along the Shenandoah, and in the year of his marriage he built the Long Meadow plantation for himself and his new bride.

Isaac was handy with horses and firearms. His wife was known as a beauty and as a good shot. She was strict with her children, once chiding her daughter, also named Eleanor, "for stepping too high in the minuet" as she danced with her bridegroom on her wedding day. Her daughter's husband, John Williams, was of English descent; he would initiate the family's shift from Calvinist Protestantism to the more traditional, more elitist Episcopalian church. Isaac gave his daughter and new son-in-law a large tract of land on which to build their own plantation. He did the same when his son married Nelly Madison (sister of the nation's eventual fourth president). To complement Isaac's generous wedding gift, Nelly's father gave the newlyweds "the following slaves, namely, Jemmy, Jerry, Eliza and her five children, to wit, Joanna, Diana, Demas, Pendar, and Webster; also Truelove and her four children, to wit, Peggy, Priscilla, Henry, and Katey; also Sally and Milley; to have and to hold the said fifteen slaves . . . and all their future increase to the said Isaac Hite junior and his heirs forever."

By the mid-1700s, the Hites, Williamses, and Madisons were among the wealthiest families in Virginia. The marriages of their sons and daughters were excellent matches for all sides. It seemed that nothing could disrupt their happiness or the elegant society in which they and their relatives thrived. The prize of status and wealth that Louis and Catherine DuBois had sought long ago had been won. Their descendants were beyond the brutal whims of powers above them. They were on top again. It had taken 150 years, but surely now that prize, like the plantations they'd built and the slaves they'd bought, would belong to them forever.

To Die As I Had Lived

T HE HISTORY of Scotland is full of examples of lives pledged to romantic causes. From its poets to its would-be kings, from Lord Byron to Mary, Queen of Scots, the land has bred passion at the expense of prudence, inspiring lovely commemorative songs and poems but often bringing only trauma to those actually involved. The traditional seedbed of this romanticism is the Scottish Highlands. Home to the violent Gaelic clans of such storied names as Mackintosh, Fraser, and Campbell, the harsh craggy region is synonymous with fierce independence. In the Highland valley of Glenfinnen in August 1745 a young prince wearing gold lace and tartan raised up a treasonous flag and declared himself born to be king. The colors of the flag were red, white, and blue. It was the emblem of the outlaw Stuarts, former rulers of Scotland and England.

Within the crowd of cheering clansmen stood a young medical student. These Highlanders seemed like wild mountain men to him, their Gaelic language and hefty swords and axes setting them far apart from the urbane citizens of Aberdeen, where he'd been raised in comfort and sophistication.

He'd traveled here to see for himself this charismatic Stuart prince, who at twenty-four was the talk of Scotland. The prince's name was Charles Edward Stuart. He was Bonnie Prince Charlie, and he'd pledged his life to Scotland's freedom. The student was Hugh Mercer, a Presbyterian minister's son. In the past Hugh's family had suffered religious persecution under the Roman Catholic Stuart regimes; and having grown up in largely Anglican Aberdeen, he carried no ingrained hatred of the English monarch, King George II. Yet on a whim, he exchanged his breeches for a Highland kilt and joined Stuart's rebel army as an assistant surgeon. Nineteen years old, fresh out of college, he was game for a grand adventure.

Under the prince's command, the Highlanders captured Edinburgh, firing scarcely a shot. They defeated a government force in a coastal field called Prestonpans. After the battle, Hugh and the other surgeons made their way to the field to gather the wounded onto horsedrawn wagons, beholding there "a spectacle of horror . . . heads, legs, arms, and mutilated bodies." It was Hugh's first glimpse of war. He would see it often again.

In November Charles invaded England, driving to within two hundred miles of London. It would mark the rebellion's pinnacle. Desertions began to plague the army. Winter was coming. And a new adversary loomed: King George's son William Augustus, Duke of Cumberland, and his army of 10,000 crack British regulars. Charles retreated to Scotland.

Early the next spring Cumberland attacked Charles at Culloden, ten miles east of Inverness. Being on the defensive was an uncomfortable change for the rebel army. An aborted plan for a surprise attack had meant an exhausting all-night march. Early the next morning, April 26, the weary Highlanders formed battle ranks on Culloden moor. They were outnumbered, with little cavalry or artillery. The wind whipped rain and sleet in their faces, along with the smoke from the British cannonade that slowly killed them where they stood.

The Highlanders' strength was in attack, overwhelming the enemy as much with their yelling and wild appearance as with their weapons. In previous battles, panicked government soldiers had ineffectually thrust their bayonets at the bodies of the onrushing rebels, who deflected the thrusts with their small forearm shields and then slashed back with their swords. But over the winter Cumberland had drilled his men in a countermeasure—his soldiers would work in pairs, one sweeping aside the enemy's shield with his musket, the other plunging his bayonet into the enemy's exposed ribs. Hugh and the other surgeons had set up facilities in the houses and churches of Culloden. Finally the distant thudding of cannon fire was broken by the Highlanders' howls of attack. As the fighting wore on, the first of the wounded were brought to the rear, many bearing the same single puncture wound deep in the sides of their chests, the fruit of Cumberland's bayonet drill.

The sounds of battle subsided. The surgeons drove their hospital wagons to the moor to tend the injured. There they found hundreds and hundreds of Highland corpses, piles of them three and four deep, some of the bodies stripped of their bonnets and tartan finery. Meanwhile, Cumberland's men methodically continued the slaughter. The duke had decreed that no prisoners were to be taken, no mercy shown. The rebel wounded were bayoneted and clubbed where they lay. Local women and children barricaded themselves inside their homes lest they fall to the sabers of English dragoons galloping through the streets. The surgeons, too, against every rule of war, were hunted down and murdered—executed rather, for all were deemed traitors, all were fugitives. The Stuart rebellion was crushed forever. The winners were making the rules.

Hugh fled Scotland in 1746 on a ship bound for Philadelphia. In a last gesture of defiance, he boarded the vessel—departing his homeland, his family, his past—wearing a rebel kilt. He disembarked in the breeches and stockings of an anonymous young physician. His manner was shy. His smooth round face conveyed a guileless, diligent character. Chastened by the bitter result of his adventure with Charles Stuart, Hugh spoke little and listened a great deal. He would choose his passions carefully in the future. And he would never forget the horror of Culloden.

Fearing discovery as a political fugitive, he left Philadelphia soon after his arrival, settling near Greencastle, just north of the Maryland border; thickly forested and sparcely settled, it was the westernmost edge of secured territory under British dominion. He reluctantly accepted command of the local militia of tradesmen and farmers in defense against menacing Indians. So began a long period during which he blended his intended vocation in medicine with the necessity of soldiering. Often he worked at both together, one day a country doctor serving settler families, the next day his poultices set aside for the sword and flintlock pistol of an officer of the realm.

In the spring of 1755 he participated in a British Army expedition against the French stronghold Fort Duquesne, located where the Allegheny and Monongahela join to form the Ohio River. Among other colonials who had joined up, George Washington, a Virginian, served as an aide to General Edward Braddock, the expedition's commander. Braddock considered the French and their Indian allies no match for the disciplined firepower of His Majesty's regular army. Overburdened with heavy artillery and undersupplied with wagons and food, his 2,500 men trudged across the Allegheny Mountains. A lack of native scouts fanning out ahead invited surprise attack. Four miles from its destination at what is today

Pittsburgh, the army's advance party was ambushed from three sides. The soldiers ran in panic, barreling headlong into reinforcements coming up from behind. The French and Indians hidden unseen in the trees poured bullets into the clustered redcoat ranks.

Nearly a thousand British soldiers were killed in the three-hour engagement. Officers on their mounts were most exposed; sixty-three out of a total of eighty-six fell to enemy marksmen. Braddock was shot through the lung. George Washington's coat was torn by four bullets. Nightfall brought the added terror of Indians seeking scalps. As survivors dispersed through the woods, injured stragglers were set upon and killed; those taken alive were burned to death at camps outside the French fort. Washington rode ahead to alert British reserves to the south. Around him the night-darkened forest filled with the cries of dying men. Somewhere in the woods through which Washington rode that long night, Hugh Mercer lay severely wounded. Six other future generals of the American Revolution were out there as well. The friendships made during the expedition were cemented by its terrible result.

Hugh fought in the French and Indian War for the next three years. He was thirty-four. He wanted a home, a settled life. He wanted to be a doctor again. So he resigned his commission and headed south for Fredericksburg, Virginia, a center for Scotch-Irish colonists and a hotbed of antigovernment fervor.

Mercer's friends were men he socialized with in the early 1770s at Fredericksburg's Rising Sun tavern. George Weedon ran the tavern, pouring his rum punch from a hollow gourd; he would be nicknamed "Old Joe Gourd" by the troops he commanded as a Continental Army colonel. John Marshall, later chief justice of the United States, was a regular customer. Spence Monroe sometimes brought his son James, the new nation's eventual fifth president. George Washington patronized the Rising Sun, as did Patrick Henry, the young firebrand from Richmond, and John Paul Jones, a Scotsman whose rumored past included piracy and murder.

Mercer had established himself in Fredericksburg as a physician and pharmacist. His apothecary shop on Caroline Street was the place to buy rosewater and decoctions of tree bark. One of his patients was Mary Washington, the future president's mother. Her son George feared she was developing a drinking problem and so referred her to Mercer. An examination revealed that she was suffering from cancer and that she tippled to ease the pain. Hugh suggested that Mary drive with her coachman to his shop each day to share an afternoon toddy in private. He spiked her drink with a mild opiate. Mary told her son George that Dr. Mercer's prescription had "much improved her health and her feeling of beatitude."

At age thirty-nine, Hugh married George Weedon's sister-in-law, Isabella Gordon; they had five children. He became a church vestryman, though he cared little for religion and certainly could never, he told a friend, join in any prayer for the king of England. He wasn't alone in that sentiment.

In the spring of 1775 war fever heightened. Patrick Henry declared at the Virginia Revolutionary Convention, "Give me liberty or give me death!" British marines removed the colonials' stored gunpowder at Williamsburg on the night of April 21. Hugh wrote George Washington urging retaliation against this "public insult." Confrontation was defused when news arrived of the bloody battles at Concord and Lexington. With war threatening everywhere, Virginia's royal governor relented, returning the stolen powder.

The Virginians appointed a committee of safety to defend their rights. Three regiments were mustered, Patrick Henry commanding one, Hugh Mercer another. Hugh said in accepting, "We are not engaged in a war of ambition or I should not have been here. For my part, I have but one object in view, and that is the success of the cause; and God can witness how cheerfully I would lay down my life to secure it." He bid good-bye to his young wife and family and left for Williamsburg with his men. There he would begin the transformation of enthusiasm into capability, of raw militia into disciplined troops. It was all an echo to Hugh, a circle closing around. To fight the king in freedom's name? He'd walked this road before.

It was rare that a man patronizing the Rising Sun tavern should not be consumed with the political unrest of the period. Such a man was regarded dubiously at best, and more typically with frank distrust. That was people's feeling about Robert Patton, a young businessman who'd come to Fredericksburg from South Carolina in 1770. A tobacco exporter, Patton carried himself with an off-putting mix of flash and furtiveness. He swept his reddish hair back in a pompadour, had a sly, self-aware smile, and sported tight waistcoats with high frilly collars. From Scotland originally, he was coy about his past. He liked to drop hints about a possible royal lineage, about his involvement with Bonnie Prince Charlie's Rebellion of 1745. He knew better than to push that story at the Rising Sun. Hugh Mercer, for one, had actually fought with Charles Stuart. And any fool could tell that

Robert was barely thirty, and so had been a mere toddling baby when the Highland patriots were slaughtered at Culloden.

The young man had good reason to keep his past obscure. Back in Scotland he was a wanted criminal. He'd fled the country in the mid-1760s with a price of five hundred pounds on his head, changing his name to Robert Patton to better lose himself in America. The name Patton was a popular alias of Scots emigrants. In Gaelic it means king's pensioner, *pensioner* in its original usage being a gentleman-at-arms. Taking the name was a declaration of service to the king. The *true* king, that is, who in the opinion of many in the southern colonies was not the king of England but Charles Stuart. The Patton alias was an emblem of mutual identification among former rebels on the run from British authorities. In its crafty expedience, the choice of Patton was typical of Robert. There were advantages to claiming solidarity with the cause of Charles Stuart in a society of so many like-minded colonists. And since King George had offered a blanket pardon of Charles's rebels in 1747, those advantages were no longer offset by the risk of government arrest.

When the call to revolt sounded in 1775, Robert declined to serve in the Continental Army whereas most other local gentlemen, Hugh Mercer included, set aside their private careers for the duration. Robert always had looked out for himself alone; he wasn't about to risk his life for a cause as shaky as American independence. He stayed neutral, continuing his tobacco business during the early part of the war while amiably (and profitably) socializing with patriots and redcoats alike. The arrangement didn't last. At an evening banquet with some British officers in the cavalry of Banastre Tarleton (later known as "Bloody Tarleton" for his history of yielding no quarter to surrendering Continentals), Robert flung a glass of wine in the face of an officer who had been "very free in his use of abusive terms" regarding some Fredericksburg ladies. The officer reacted in "a storm of fury," according to one record of the incident. Robert's temper was likewise ignited. "Patton said the affair must be then and there settled, and going to the door, locked it and put the key in his pocket. They fought with pistols across the table and the officer was killed."

Robert became a fugitive. His impetuous act had placed him in the patriots' camp when in truth he felt no particular allegiance toward them. During the war his whereabouts remained unknown. His business collapsed, but he would survive and someday thrive again. He always had before.

*   *   *

As a general in George Washington's Continental Army, Hugh Mercer's destiny had entirely aligned with that of his adopted nation. The fortunes of war became something shared, something endured, by compatriots in the cause. Easy victory at Boston in March 1776; humiliating defeat at New York four months later; then new life and hope in Washington's daring Christmas campaign at Trenton and Princeton, New Jersey. But in that autumn of retreat from New York, the revolution seemed near collapse. Public support, military recruitment and desertion, the availability of food and supplies, all hinged on the news, good or bad, of how the Continental Army fared. Washington was pessimistic. "I think the game is pretty near up," he wrote as he drove his beaten army across the Delaware River to Pennsylvania in November 1776.

No one knows who originally proposed the army's dramatic counter-attack *back* across the Delaware on Christmas Day. Rumors of the plan were circulating among the general staff as early as December 18. On December 21, one general wrote of "giv[ing] the enemy a stroke in a few days." Washington hinted in a letter on December 23 that something big was afoot. General John Armstrong recalled overhearing on December 16 a private discussion between two men about a possible Delaware crossing and surprise attack on the enemy garrison at Trenton on the river's east bank. It is the earliest recorded mention of the plan's consideration. Having the discussion were generals Washington and Mercer.

The plan called for a night crossing, then a three-pronged assault. Two of the prongs turned back because of rough water and a harsh winter storm. General Mercer was with the third element directly under Washington. The patriots encircled the town. At dawn they struck from all sides.

Trenton was garrisoned by 1,200 Hessions, German mercenaries under the command of Colonel Johann Rall. Rall was sleeping off a hangover when the attack began. More than one hundred Hessians were killed, more than a thousand captured. The patriots suffered four wounded. The victory was important mainly for its psychological lift. Troops who'd been counting the days till their tours of duty ended at the end of the year were encouraged to reenlist. At 5,200 strong, the army was back in business.

Washington kept up the momentum, setting his sights on a British supply depot at nearby Princeton. But the enemy now was alerted. Eight thousand redcoats under Charles Cornwallis were approaching from New York intending to pin the Continentals against the Delaware and crush them once and for all. By evening, January 2, American campfires flickered in view of Cornwallis's forward sentries. The British prepared for a morning attack. The campfires burned all night. At daybreak they were still burning, but the Continental Army, in an old Indian trick, had slipped around Cornwallis's flank and was marching fast for Princeton.

The weather the next morning was bitterly cold. Washington based his plan on a spy's sketched map, which showed a little-used trail passing around the British defense works along the Post Road into Princeton. As the main body of troops followed the trail northeast into town, four hundred men under General Mercer would proceed north along Stony Brook creek to the Post Road bridge. Destroying the bridge would prevent the British from reinforcing Princeton from Trenton.

A large unit of redcoats was leaving town over the bridge as Hugh's soldiers came upon it. Both armies rushed for the high ground nearby, today known as Mercer Heights. Unable to gain it, Mercer, on horseback, led his men across William Clark's orchard to rejoin the main column marching to Princeton via the spy's sketched trail. In the orchard he was shot at by enemy infantry positioned behind a fence. The large British force that had been crossing the bridge had doubled back and was closing fast. Hugh's men fired a volley, but their reloading was slow. In the delay the British got off three volleys and then charged with bayonets. Hugh's horse tumbled down, its foreleg snapped by a musketball. On foot he tried to rally his men, who were faltering before the attack. The men broke ranks and took off in retreat. The general was not among them.

Washington, drawn by the sound of gunfire, confronted the retreating soldiers. "Parade with us, my brave fellows! There is but a handful of enemy, and we will have them directly!" The New England brigade arrived in reinforcement. Washington rode out alone between his troops and the approaching British thirty yards away. He turned his back on the enemy and bid his troops prepare to fire. Volleys were exchanged. The British fled the field.

Washington had no time to delay. Cornwallis was in hard pursuit from Trenton. When he reached Princeton two hours later, the Continentals were well on their way north to Morristown. That location offered a strong defensive position, a protected line of communication to Philadelphia, and superior access to any British troop movements across the state. Cornwallis withdrew to New York. The patriots held New Jersey. Hugh Mercer, it was reported, lay dead in William Clark's orchard.

He was not dead. He'd been shot at least once, bludgeoned severely about the head with a musket butt, and bayoneted between five and seven times. When found to be breathing, he was taken to the Clark house and nursed by Clark's wife and daughter. British soldiers burst into the house. "Would you believe," wrote a young Continental wounded alongside Mercer, "that the inhuman monsters robbed the general as he lay unable to resist on the bed, even to taking his cravat from his neck, insulting him all the time?"

Hugh's blood had soaked through his straw mattress and dripped onto the wood floor. He told the British soldiers he'd been paroled in 1747, that he was no longer a fugitive from Charles Stuart's rebellion. He was delirious, in shock. He thought the redcoats were Cumberland's men come to finish the massacre started at Culloden, thirty-one years before.

When word reach Washington that his friend was alive, he dispatched his nephew George Lewis under a flag of truce to see what could be done. Rumors spread that the British had given Mercer no quarter, that they'd stabbed him as he tried to surrender. Within a week Philadelphia was buzzing with outrage; recruits joined the army in vengeance. To make amends, Cornwallis sent his personal surgeon to join the colonial doctors already on the scene. Hugh regained his senses. His condition improved.

On hearing from Lewis the rumors of atrocity perpetrated against him, Hugh set the record straight.

I was on foot endeavoring to rally my men who had given way before the superior discipline of the enemy, when I was brought to the ground by a blow from a musket. At the same moment the enemy discovered my rank, exalted in having taken a rebel general, as they termed me, and bid me ask for quarter. ... Without begging my life or making a reply, I lunged with my sword at the nearest man. They then bayoneted and left me.

As he lay in bed tended by doctors from both sides of the conflict, he rejected their diagnosis that the head blows he'd suffered posed the greatest threat to his life. Hugh told George Lewis to raise Hugh's left arm. "There discover the smallest of my wounds, but which will prove the most fatal. Yes, sir, that is the fellow that will very soon do my business." A deep puncture through his ribs and lung, it was the same wound that had felled so many of Hugh's fellow rebels long ago on Culloden moor. To have received it at Princeton thirty-one years later seemed more than coincidence. Surely it was destiny's signature.

Since fleeing the horror of Culloden, he'd repeatedly been drawn back into war despite his wish for a gentler life. Now, instead of resisting his fate, Hugh accepted it as fulfillment. Though many years of fighting remained for his Continental compatriots, the victories at Trenton and Princeton were glimpses of triumph to come. "My death is owing to myself," he told George Lewis. He had determined, he said, "To die as I had lived, an honored soldier in a just and righteous cause." It was Hugh's own epitaph on the life he had lived, the last words of a contented man. On January 12, nine days after the battle, he died in George Lewis's arms.

Thirty thousand mourners attended his funeral in Philadelphia in 1777, where a large monument was erected in his honor. Shortly after the war, several paintings were done of Mercer at the battle of Princeton. The most famous one, by the Revolutionary War artist John Trumbull, hangs today at Yale University. Another painting, this one by Washington's adopted step-grandson, George Washington Parke Custis, reflects the outrage Mercer's supposed murder (as he attempted to surrender) sparked throughout the colonies during the war. Portraying Hugh sprawled on the ground in a grotesque contortion as a pair of hatchet-faced redcoats plunge their bayonets into him, Custis sought to chronicle an atrocity that never actually happened. A third version of the general's wounding at Princeton was painted by one of his sons, William.

After the war Hugh's brother-in-law George Weedon, "Old Joe Gourd" of the Rising Sun tavern, became as a father to Hugh's five children. Hugh's youngest son was educated free at Princeton University by act of Congress. Ann, the oldest child, married the tobacco merchant Robert Patton. Suspicions about Robert's character had only slightly diminished since the war. He dressed foppishly and had hooded, quick eyes. He looked like a man with a price on his head.

William Mercer was a boy at the time of his father's death, and he was a deaf-mute. His painting style was spare, purposely crude, like a child's crayon drawing. In rendering the scene of his father's last battle, William put him in the background. The story of that day was Washington's heroic entrance. So Washington is the dominant figure, riding a prancing steed with his saber drawn and his gaze fixed far beyond the painting's field, as if already envisioning the next day's struggle. Hugh Mercer is a distant figure lying limp on the ground. The bayoneting is over. The redcoats have left him. He is part of the painting's past.

Hugh's last words suggest that he felt the influence of destiny as he lay dying in that New Jersey farmhouse. His son's painting suggests that William shared this feeling. Hugh's death was no tragedy. The path from Culloden to Princeton bespoke a special providence. For that reason, in the skies above his dying father, William painted a rainbow.

*   *   *

Having laid low for the duration of the Revolutionary War, Robert Patton's name appeared on official records only in 1793, when he became superintendent of the Fredericksburg Bank. Whatever his doings in the interim period, he'd gotten by just fine. Now in his late forties, he married Ann Gordon Mercer, a woman described as "amiable and accomplished" in the Virginia *Herald*, as "infinitely lovely" by a family friend, and as "often exercised with spiritual troubles" in a biographical sketch of the town written several years after their marriage. That same sketch described her husband as dignified and majestic. A rich merchant and banker, Robert Patton was by all appearances a New World success story. He had a sad secret, however.

For the last thirty years of his life, he concealed in his desk a ten-page journal written several years before his marriage to Ann Mercer. The journal's author was a man named Davenport. It covered a ten-week period between December 1789 and February 1790 and was accompanied by a long letter from Davenport to his wife. When both documents were found among Robert Patton's papers after his death, Robert's family gained insights into his elusive character that he'd never revealed when alive.

He'd always lived for himself. But with the war over and his business booming again, he fell in love with a young woman named Nelly Davenport in 1789. Robert proposed, Nelly accepted—but six months before their wedding date she was stricken with consumption. Her doctor suggested she spend the winter in the Caribbean, where the warm climate would restore her health.

When sailing to America thirty years earlier, Robert had disembarked at an intermediate port of call in Antigua, in the British West Indies, and briefly settled there. He'd established contacts in the seafaring trade that later benefited his export business; it was on Antigua that he'd changed his name. He still had friends in the island town of St. John's, and he recommended that Nelly reside with them until the time came for their spring wedding.

Nelly sailed from Virginia with her father, who excitedly began a journal of the trip. "Trip to the West Indies and home again," was his first entry, "on board the [ship] *Success*." He recorded each day's weather, meals, and dinner company, setting down these details beside impressions of his daughter's medical condition. Her condition was poor. Davenport described its daily fluctuation in precise, reserved prose, noting Nelly's persistent coughing and discomfort as detachedly as he noted the color of the sky and the temperature of the sea air.

The Davenports made landfall at St. John's, Antigua, on February 7, 1790, and were received by Robert's friends. Almost immediately, Nelly's conditioned turned critical. Her father no longer had the time nor the fortitude periodically to pause in his care of her to record each instance of spit blood or incontinence. Things were too hectic at the last, too obviously dire. Taking up his pen afterward to write a letter to his wife, he affected none of his earlier emotional armor, none of the brusque observance that had threatened to convert his journal into a passionless log of a young woman's suffering. Instead, he took a tone both direct and heartfelt. There were sad facts to tell and inner feelings to unclench.

Davenport mailed the letter to his wife by ship the next morning. He remained on Antigua several more days to settle his affairs. But sailing north to Virginia, Davenport's ship overtook and passed the ship bearing his letter. He arrived home without warning. When his wife rushed to meet him she swooned in horror to see him alone, without their daughter, and collapsed stone dead on the spot.

The dreadful turn of events stunned Robert Patton. It had been on his advice that Nelly had gone to Antigua; now she lay buried in a churchyard there, far from her family and home. When Nelly's father offered him the journal and letter as mementos of her, Robert accepted. Reading the story of his fiancée's last days no doubt pricked him with sorrow and guilt. But perhaps he didn't want to get over her memory, didn't want to feel better one day.

Robert married Ann Mercer three years later and had six children with her. He and Ann were not particularly compatible. His outward temperament was remote and cynical. His eldest son, John, threatened to kill himself if Robert didn't let him quit medical school for law school. In reply, Robert sent him a boxed pair of premium straight razors made in Edinburgh, with a message to the effect that if his son indeed intended to cut his own throat, why not use the best.

Robert's wife was frail and flighty in her convictions. Her "spiritual troubles" led her to seek solace in religion, not Robert's interest at all. Presbyterian originally, Ann and many other Fredericksburg ladies came under the spell of a Baptist minister recently returned from missionary work in the Far East. With "eloquence like a torrent that bears down all before it," the fellow soon was dipping middle-aged women right and left in the Rappahannock River. One irate gentleman "caned" the preacher for baptizing his sisters. A local doctor locked up his wife until she regained her senses to his satisfaction. But Robert stood by indifferently as Ann converted to the Baptist faith. Her salvation was her own business.

Some estrangement between them was inevitable, given Ann's unsteady passions. It was in fitful moments alone, his wife out somewhere testifying of her experience of rebirth, that Robert, perhaps while reading in his library or working at night at his desk, would retrieve Davenport's old journal and letter from their place of safekeeping and read through the pages again.

Years might go by between these readings. Eventually the pangs they stirred in Robert widened to an encompassing reverie of all the choices he'd taken in life, the crimes committed, the regrets he carried, the consequences dodged or suffered. The journal of his former fiancée's dying sparked his self-reflection like an old song or an evocative scent. By the time his gaze crossed the last lines of Davenport's mournful letter, the tears he cried were less for Nelly than for himself.

Saturday morning Nelly was very weak and fatigued . . . talked cheerful . . . little appetite . . . sweat copiously . . . to calm my feelings, I sent for the doctor . . . very cold and very pale . . . we bathed her feet several times in the night . . . wished that she should remain easy to the last . . . complained of no pain . . . breathing greatly obstructed . . . dissolution approaching . . . my business was to cherish her . . . my distress so great I wished to see her no more . . . she asked for me and I always went . . . her face as cold as clay . . . she retained her perfect senses . . . turned faint and said, "God bless you," and died immediately . . . so good and fine a girl . . . my dear child . . . on Monday, I said good-bye . . . never heard her complain . . . always willing and wishing to obtain the desirable end.

Davenport's postscript noted the medicine given to Nelly when her suffering was at its worst: horseradish, asparagus root, pine tops, grapevine ashes, mustard seed, and anvil dust, "equal quantities infused in hard cider, taken in a wineglass three times a day." A futile prescription, Robert knew too well now.

Discontent that long had simmered inside him erupted at the end of his life. Married more than thirty years, a prosperous father and grandfather, nearly six decades an inhabitant of America, Robert nonetheless lamented bitterly that he was fated to die far from his homeland, among these strangers who called themselves family. Old and bedridden, he began to murmur and rave about his foresaken Scottish roots. He recounted a childhood memory of his grandfather's funeral. There was feasting at the castle. The funeral games lasted three days. His grandfather's coffin was carried to its gravesite "by the lords of the isles."

Robert's wife and children sat in vigil at his bedside. Ann begged her husband finally to reveal the original surname he'd shed decades ago on Antigua—it was their name as well, after all. But Robert would not. His last words were a kind of sigh. "A Patton I have lived, and a Patton I will die. Better a new name in a new country." He died that day in 1828. Later, the papers describing Nelly Davenport's death were found in his desk. No one knew who she was. Searching out the facts, plumbing this private history, awakened Robert's family to his mystery.

That he kept secret through thirty-five years of marriage the memoir of his first love's illness revealed something about Robert's heart. That his descendants kept the memoir safe through six generations said something about them. They were touched by Nelly Davenport's fate, though she wasn't a blood relation; they couldn't bear to discard the memoir and in effect discard Nelly, leave her to the oblivion of a churchyard on a faraway island. As for the elusive Robert, the only thing certain about him was that he died full of regret. He was their patriarch, the original Patton. He was someone nobody knew.

A Torchlight Procession

IN 1775, sixteen-year-old Philip Slaughter rushed with squirrel gun in hand to his grandfather's farm near Culpeper, Virginia, to drill with the newly formed Culpeper Minutemen in preparation for war with the British. Philip fought with the Continental Army until victory was won in 1783. Late in life he began writing the memoirs of his war experience. The document ran to hundreds of pages; all but a few pages were destroyed in 1863, when the Yankees came to Culpeper. Philip's description of his Revolutionary War uniform survived: a linen hunting shirt "dyed with leaves, and the words 'Liberty or Death' worked in large letters on the breast." One day his descendants would proudly invoke those words, "Liberty or Death," in another context, in another war.

Serving with Philip Slaughter through the Revolution was John Williams, a Continental Army major and later a general in the War of 1812. John's wife was the former Eleanor Hite of the famous Long Meadow plantation, great-great-granddaughter of the French Huguenot Catherine DuBois. His and Eleanor's plantation was Spring Farm, outside Culpeper. Their son married Philip Slaughter's daughter in 1800, and soon a granddaughter was born, Peggy French Williams.

Peggy was born into the Virginia plantation society later romanticized in Margaret Mitchell's *Gone with the Wind,* with such family estates as

Spring Farm, Long Meadow, and Belle Grove as the inspiration for Mitchell's Tara and Twelve Oaks. Sons and daughters were matched in marriage with all the careful attention to pedigree of a breeder enriching his stock. Since the families were huge and intertwined, the society was at once close-knit, provincial, and sprawling. Summer brought a swirl of reunions and lavish picnics, guests journeying by carriage from place to place and staying on for days.

While attending a gala at Spring Farm a young attorney named John Mercer Patton met Miss Peggy Williams. She was a tall, stern-looking woman who preferred her nickname, "French," because Peggy, she thought, lacked dignity. She tended to lord it a bit over young gentlemen whose family prestige did not measure up to her own. Though John Patton was well fixed (his family owned an estate called The Meadows in Albemarle County), he couldn't match the Williamses' wealth. But he was the grandson of General Hugh Mercer, a credential that couldn't be topped in these parts. He and Peggy married in 1824 and settled in Fredericksburg, where he began his law practice. The first of their children was born nine months later. Child number four was born there on June 26, 1833, and was christened George Smith Patton.

Peggy and John Patton would have twelve children in all. Three died in infancy; of the nine surviving to adulthood, eight were sons. Seven of those eight would fight for the Confederacy against the North in the American Civil War. They would fight, as the historian James M. McPherson says of Confederates in general, "to defend their independence, their institutions (mainly slavery), their way of life, from the annihilation they feared would result from defeat." They would fight out of love for Virginia. And they would fight for their mother, who instilled in them the values of pride and grit as exemplified in their forebear Catherine DuBois. Northern condemnation of the institution of slavery translated to contempt for the institution's defenders. Peggy Patton was a southern grande dame who knew only to answer such contempt with contempt. Her sons would fight and, if necessary, die for the Confederacy because Peggy expected it of them.

In 1830, her husband, John, was elected as a Democrat to the United States Congress. Through three terms in Washington, he was initially an unbending supporter of states' rights and of the commercial interests of southern planters: he was pro slavery. He shared the view of other secessionists that the North and South had become two distinct countries whose differences could not be bridged. Later he softened his stance, and after leaving Congress briefly to serve as acting governor of Virginia and then, for the last twenty years of his life, as an appellate judge in Richmond, John became increasingly identified with the moderate Whig party of Daniel Webster and Henry Clay.

In 1856, two years before his death, he ran for state attorney general on the ticket of the American Party, whose members were called the Know Nothings because they were purposely vague about their beliefs; in fact their intent was to defend the supremacy of Protestantism over other religions, to tighten national immigration laws, and to deprive foreign-born citizens of the ballot. He lost the election and retired from public life.

His affiliation with the xenophobia and religious bigotry of the Know Nothings did not entirely sound the last note of John Patton's life. He'd expressed hope that the Union would resolve through compromise its regional disputes, over slavery particularly, and thereby stay intact. Yet in his heart he feared that secession and war were inevitable. When his sons came of age, he sent them to military colleges—West Point, Annapolis, the Virginia Military Institute—so that they would be well prepared to help the cause. Now, terminally ill at the age of sixty, he gave his sons a curious directive: should war come, they must free their slaves before taking up arms. There was no honor in fighting for slavery. The honor lay in defending Virginia.

Combative in the courtroom, John Patton was mild-mannered in private. "French," he would tell his wife when their sons acted up, "if those were my children I'd spank them." He never punished them himself. His wife did that duty, by whipping them or tying them to the bedpost for the day. Peggy Patton was very conscious of keeping up appearances. One household slave's entire job was to stand outside their Richmond home and polish the brass finials on the iron railing of the front steps. Peggy once was humiliated when, without warning, her husband brought home some friends for dinner on an evening when leftovers were on the menu. She added more place settings and served the food with a frozen smile. At the end of the meal she stood and announced that tonight the men had been Mr. Patton's guests. "Tomorrow you and your wives shall be *my* guests." True to her word, she laid out a spread so lavish as to smother all rumor that things were slipping a little at the Patton house.

Finally, a story is told about Daniel Webster's visit with the Pattons during a junket through Virginia toward the end of his Senate career. Webster, who had come to know John Patton when both served in the Congress, was a heavy drinker. At the Pattons' midday luncheon he began to nod off. Meanwhile a crowd had gathered outside on Franklin Street calling for a speech from the famed orator. Webster tried and failed to rise from his chair. But inspired by the hollering audience, he called for a tumbler of peach brandy, downed it in one gulp, then with the help of two slave boys wobbled to the front window, where he rousingly addressed the appreciative crowd, the two crouching slaves steadying his rubbery knees to keep the senator standing.

After her husband's death in 1858, Peggy Patton emerged as the major force in the family, her dominance confirmed in 1861 when she counter-manded her late husband's dying wish that the Patton boys, on the eve of the war for which they had so long prepared, set free all their slaves. Absolutely not, said Peggy. As officers and gentlemen, they must have thoroughbred mounts, custom boots, tailored uniforms—and they must have body servants to accompany them through their campaigns against the Yankee invaders. Peggy personally chose the slaves from those she owned at Spring Farm. She gave her son George, then twenty-eight, a slave named Peter. Peter accompanied his young master through all his battles, for which service, in what perhaps was a secret bow to John Patton's last wish, George paid him a regular salary.

Tall and slim like his mother, George Patton had his father's dark Mercer eyes and thick brown hair. Of his many siblings, he was closest with his next younger brother, Waller Tazewell Patton, called Tazewell or "Taz" by the family. They were drawn to each other as opposites; Tazewell was rowdy and clownish where George was restrained, responsible, and protective. With a spread of twenty-one years between the eldest and youngest, the Patton siblings were more loyal than devoted to one another, more clubby than close-knit. They were competitive. The overseer at Spring Farm complained that no work got done when the boys were home because they took all the horses out racing. That competitiveness extended to the dinner table. Since the brothers were all great talkers who enjoyed the spotlight, they agreed to speak in sequence for two minutes apiece, each impatiently eyeing his watch to be sure no one exceeded his limit.

In accordance with his father's wishes, George attended the Virginia Military Institute at Lexington. His first two years there, he placed in the middle of his class academically and was a leader in demerits received. In his fourth year, one of his professors was Thomas Jonathan "Stonewall" Jackson. The stern and pious Jackson was disliked by many cadets, perhaps unfairly. At home, George told how one day the professor was struck by a brick flung from a barracks window. Jackson refused to look up, lest if he spotted the culprit he would have to punish him.

Upon graduation in 1852, George ranked second in his class overall and first in the subjects of French, Latin, English, Chemistry, and Artillery Tactics. A classmate described him as "the charm of the social circle, where his genial wit . . . made him ever welcome." Reserved in manner, in dress he was rather a dandy. He wore his hair long and later sported a crisp mustache, for which his friends ribbingly called him "Frenchy." He left Lexington at age nineteen with a career plan fixed in his mind. He would teach for two years while studying to become a lawyer like his father. He'd always been closer to his father than to his mother, citing his father's "affectionate" letters while complaining that his mother hardly wrote to him at all.

George's best friend was his first cousin George Hugh Smith, sarcastically nicknamed "Nigger Smith" for his ice blue eyes and flaxen hair by his fellow cadets at the Institute. In the summer of 1852 the cousins simultaneously courted a petite southern girl named Susan Thornton Glassell. Sue was up visiting from Alabama where her family had moved soon after her birth, making her debut in Virginia society at the age of seventeen. Her pale fragility appealed to George's protective instincts. Both he and his cousin fell in love with her; through the round of dances and picnics the suitors competed for her favor. In September George Patton wrote Sue a letter that began without salutation.

In accordance with the current position you granted me to write you on a subject near to my heart, I now my dearest Sue will open that heart to you. I love you as you deserve to be loved . . . a love which is fanned into flame by your quality of head and heart. I could not love if I did not esteem, and I first esteemed and then I learned to love. Can you love me? . . . as you have given me the privilege of hoping, I will hope until [I receive your reply] and my imagination will run riot in building delicious castles in the air. Hoping through a speedy and favorable answer, permit me to sign myself, dearest Miss Sue,

> Your sincerely attached lover,
> George S. Patton

Sue's answer was indeed favorable. She and George were engaged, though no date was set, since he was, being as yet unlaunched on any career, "in no condition to marry. . . . It may be long years." Patton's friend George Hugh Smith withdrew like a gentleman, and evidently their friendship did not suffer. In the coming years Smith would often be asked why he remained single. "I will marry," he said, "when I find a woman like Sue Glassell."

What kind of woman was she? Her fiancé's early letters to his "dear little Sue" indicate that he liked to think of her as delicate and needful. But though her family was as well off as any of those in their circle, she'd survived some hard moments in her brief life, giving her an inner toughness, which her future husband soon recognized and came greatly to depend on.

Sue had been an infant when her family left Virginia for Alabama in 1835. During the long overland trip her mother and sister died of yellow fever, and Sue was nursed on mare's milk. Her grandmother came south to care for the family, accompanied by her younger son. Sue grew devoted to her Uncle Will Thornton, who became a doctor, and used to tease him about his studied air of melancholy. One of Will's grander pronouncements was that he would die before he turned thirty, for which the family gleefully took him to task on the day of his thirtieth birthday. He didn't join in the laughter: "The ides of March are not yet passed." That afternoon he went out hunting and accidentally shot himself in the foot. He called for his instruments and tried to amputate his own leg, bleeding to death in the process. Sue's grandmother made a mourning pin—a glass locket containing a strand of Will's hair entwined with strands of her own hair and little Sue's—as a symbol of the special bond among them. The old woman gave it to Sue because Sue had been fond of Will, and because she seemed to possess something of his same nature—sad, prescient, and fated.

The Glassells were staunch Christians, which stood them in good stead through their constant acquaintance with death. One of Sue's brothers died of typhoid at eighteen. Another, William T. Glassell, called "Willie," took that brother's appointment to Annapolis, leaving home at sixteen. When Andrew Jr., the eldest, went west to seek his fortune, Sue's closest companion became her remaining sibling, Hobart.

In 1853, with Sue back at home during the first year of her engagement to George Patton, yellow fever raged in Alabama. Her father moved his family to the Gulf Coast to escape the epidemic. He permitted Sue and Hobart to mix only with the family's slaves, for Negroes were thought to be immune from the disease. When the elderly coachman came down sick, Mr. Glassell forbade his children to visit him. Hobart went anyway, shrugging, "We either get it, or we don't get it." He got it, and soon the whole household was stricken. Delirious with fever, Sue looked up from her bed to see her father wailing at her bedside, "Oh, Lord, am I to lose all my children?" Recovered, she wrote a cousin in Virginia,

> My nerves are in an awful state. . . . How can I tell you of the last end of my Hobart, my brother, my companion, the sharer of all my griefs and pleasures? . . . He told Dr. Massey that he was perfectly willing to die but for leaving his friends in distress. . . . Once he raised his hands and exclaimed, "Soon the great mystery will be disclosed." He retained his reason to the last and went off like an infant going to sleep.

She was eighteen at the time, her brother Hobart twenty. With nothing left for her at home, she might have proceeded with her wedding to George Patton but for the continued uncertainty of his professional situation. He'd found himself a teaching post only after a year of searching. Twenty now, he was one of those young men for whom any delay in their projected career timetable fills them with anxiety. He wrote Sue, "As yet I have not tried myself. . . . What if I should fail? . . . Are you afraid, too, pet? Don't you fear failure?" Needing time "to prepare myself," he told her their wedding must wait. He assumed that she would wait as well.

George was picky about what sort of teaching job suited him. He turned down several offers to tutor in private homes. "My chief and almost only object in teaching is to improve myself, and this object would be ill accomplished by teaching children their alphabet and multiplication table." Impatient to get started, in August 1853 he borrowed money from his parents to cofound with a German-born language professor a small academy for boys in Richmond. His partner would teach philosophy and languages, George mathematics and English.

Within a few months, George was soliciting his alma mater for a math teacher to replace him. He was having trouble teaching the more esoteric calculations. "As treated in the text they are by no means clear, and the so-called explanations tend to confuse rather than enlighten." Feeling "almost in despair," toward the end of his second year at the academy he began advertising for someone to buy out his share of the place. Finding no takers, his choice was to stay on there or walk away at a considerable loss of money. He chose to leave, and consequently found himself, in the summer of 1855, back living at his parents' plantation.

He'd completed his law studies and been admitted to the Richmond bar.

But he could find no job openings, and so fretted at Spring Farm while his father used his influence to get George hired by a law firm somewhere. "Time does not fly so fast with me," George wrote Sue glumly. "It is the last month in summer, and with the autumn I must commence to cast aside the green leaves of extreme youth and take my place among the men of my country." He was feeling, he said, "peculiar" about his future. "I am in daily expectation of a letter from my father which in all probability will determine my location." But whether that location would even be in Virginia, George couldn't say for sure. "I have written thus, darling, because I know that, save myself, you take a deeper interest in the matter than anyone in the wide world." Sue took an interest, all right. His letters were full of anxiety, full of languid affection for her—but they contained no mention of a wedding date. She resolved to bring the issue to a head. She told him that she was having second thoughts about the marriage, and that she soon might travel abroad with her cousin Cornelia, whom she was visiting in Fredericksburg. George's response was frantic:

> Is it possible, my darling, that you will allow the cajoling tongue of your sweet cousin to eradicate all the good principles which I have been instilling in your mind, make you forget that great moral maxim that the chief end of woman is marriage? Oh! let me warn you, pet, against listening to the siren's song, and come back to your old faith. The colour flew from my cheek and the light from my eyes when I saw that the alarming heresy had made such progress that you had promised to go to Europe next Spring with the successful missionary of this dreadful faith, and leave your husband here, for won't you have one before next Spring? . . . Providence never intended that the man should be a solitary being, nor that the woman should be her own companion through life. But in wise prescience it was ordained that the strong arm of the one should support the slender form of the other—and that the gentle eye and soft heart of woman should temper the afflictions and pour balm on the sorrows of her love partner—(tremendous applause)—Those are my sentiments, and *yours* too, you little scamp!

In her reply Sue allowed that she might be persuaded to stay in America after all. She would meet him the next week to discuss it. George was ecstatic. "What a struggle I shall have, if any one is present, to keep to the distasteful forms of civility and content myself with a shake of hands. But I shall be revenged when I can see you alone. Won't I do something that spells with a K and three other letters? Won't I?"

Two months later they were married at St. John's church in Richmond. They spent their wedding night on a riverboat heading up the Rappahannock on the first leg of their trip to Charleston, Virginia (now West Virginia), where George had been offered a partnership in a small law firm. As she boarded the vessel Sue was gripped with fright. Her father kissed her and gently nudged her into George's cabin, shutting the door behind them.

The following spring she awoke one morning with a craving for cranberries. Her husband told her none could be found, so she made a petulant joke that the baby would be born with a cranberry for a nose. On September 30, 1856, Sue gave birth to a son. The baby was in perfect condition except for a large red mole on the end of its nose; this was cross-stitched with thread and removed, leaving a faint scar. Sue named the child George William, "George" for her husband, "William" for her brother and for her late uncle, Will Thornton, who, like Sue (everyone recognized now), had possessed the gift of second sight.

Charleston was a town of 2,000 inhabitants located in the heart of the Kanawha River Valley. Its impression on visitors varied from "quite a pretty place" to "a small, dirty-looking, country town." The buildings and residences along its six dusty streets were cruder versions of the grand antebellum mansions of eastern Virginia. The Pattons lived in a one-story house called Elm Grove on the corner of Quarrier and Dunbar streets. (Since moved from its original location, it stands today in Charleston's Daniel Boone Park.) George was a partner in a law firm, served as a commissioner of the county court and on the board of directors of a local shipping company whose president, William Rosecrans, would later conquer the Kanawha Valley as a Union Army general.

Salt deposits were the area's most valuable resource (especially in wartime, when meat preservation was essential in provisioning mobile armies). The land was rich in crops and lumber, though its rolling terrain resisted cultivation on the vast scale of the state's cotton plantations. Local farmers planted for themselves alone, as George explained in a letter to his sister, Eliza, a year after his arrival in Charleston. "They literally raise nothing for sale. When a drought kills the crop, they are destitute, having nothing to fall back on. God help the poor!"

Used primarily as domestic servants rather than as field hands, there were fewer slaves in Kanawha County than elsewhere in Virginia. George followed the national slavery debate closely, however, and pridefully supported secession. In 1856 he organized a militia company of seventy-five young gentlemen (including twenty lawyers) calling themselves the Kanawha Minutemen. With the help of a manual on light infantry tactics, he drilled the men in a Charleston meadow. "He was a martinet in discipline," one of them recalled, "and had the marked bearing of the typical gentleman soldier, and of the most pleasant personality and address." The unit elected George its captain.

In the late 1850s many such militias sprang up throughout Virginia. The most renowned of these "drilling clubs" was the Richmond Light Infantry Blues, which George often had seen marching in holiday parades during his teaching stint in the capital. Formed partly in anticipation of conflict and partly as a kind of weekend hobby, the drilling clubs turned serious in the fall of 1859 when the abolitionist John Brown tried to spark a slave rebellion by seizing a government arsenal in Harper's Ferry, Virginia. George's drilling club changed its name to the Kanawha Riflemen and rewrote its bylaws with new intensity: "No provision is made for the failure of a member of this company to attend in time of war or tumult, for it is naturally supposed that every member will be present. However, should any member fail to answer roll call under such circumstances, and not show good reason therefor, he shall be dealt with as a deserter from the army." New rifles were procured from the state. George designed a flashy uniform of "dark green broadcloth, matching overcoats, broad gold stripes down the pantaloons, a fancy headgear consisting of black hats with ostrich feathers dangling from the wide brim with a gold KR on the front . . . and white gloves." A small brass band was hired to provide appropriate martial music.

To the neglect of his law practice, he devoted himself increasingly to the Riflemen. One of his son's earliest memories was of watching the unit march back and forth across the courthouse green, and afterward being hoisted atop Captain Patton's horse. Demand heightened for the Riflemen to perform at civic ceremonies throughout the area. At a Fourth of July picnic, one member recalled marching "for hours in the hot sun, in my new uniform with my rifle on my shoulder—proudly guarding the fried chicken and lemonade." The ladies of Charleston sewed the unit a special flag featuring thirteen stripes and the Virginia coat of arms. At Gallipolis across the Ohio River, however, the Riflemen were virtually run out of town by jeering, pro-Union citizens. And they were derisively called "Kid Gloves" by other area militia companies whose members were farmers and mountain men with little regard for prancing aristocrats playing soldier. What kind of fighters wore white gloves and ostrich feathers?

The Charleston men continued to drill. Captain Patton, for all his showiness, was observed to possess "a peculiar instinct" for military matters. Certainly he possessed zeal. He'd already written the governor to pledge to him the services of the Kanawha Riflemen, in whatever capacity, to whatever degree, Virginia might someday require.

Sue gave birth to a daughter, Nellie, in 1857. While her husband devoted himself to his law practice and to the Riflemen, Sue ran the household with the support of two "servants." Aunt Mary, as she was called by the Patton children, was three years younger than Sue; she'd been given to Sue when Sue was eight. The Pattons' other servant was Fanny, a slave they leased from her owner. "She has become so dishonest," Sue complained, "that she even stole some of Mary's underclothes, and she is so hardened that nothing makes the slightest impression on her. Neither of the children like her ... which shows how plainly she is not kind to them." Slavery as a moral issue was not something Sue considered. Slaves were so integrated into her life as to be noticed only when they caused inconvenience, like a faulty household appliance.

Pregnant again in 1859, Sue was a happy, pampered, shallow twenty-four-year-old mother. She made her children's clothes on a sewing machine ("Children are certainly dear darling angels but they do certainly require the most never ending attentions of every kind"). She kept up with the latest women's fashions out of Europe and New York ("You see I have no idea of being an old woman yet"). She prettied up her home ("I am quite impatient to know what you think of our house since it has been painted"). She fretted about her health ("Still complaining," George wrote his sister). And she entertained through extended visits her many relatives, of whom her favorites were her brother William Glassell and her brother-in-law Tazewell Patton.

A lieutenant in the U.S. Navy, Willie Glassell was an emotional, strikingly handsome man. On shore leave he was always falling in love, at one time developing an awkward crush on George's sister, Eliza (he proposed to her twelve times, though she was engaged to someone else). But his fondest attachment was to his sister. He once told Sue that he resented the closeness with which they'd been brought up because he "suffered so" when separated from her. While in Japan with Commodore Perry in 1854,

Willie had commissioned a portrait from a Japanese artist who was painting sailors' hometown sweethearts from the photographs they carried. Willie brought back to America an oval portrait of Sue, her blue eyes rendered in brown and her skin translucent almond.

Whereas Willie was moody and wistful, Tazewell was the proverbially jolly bachelor uncle to Sue and George's children. He was especially attached to his little nephew George William, roughhousing with him on the floor with an easy, demonstrative affection that Tazewell's more reserved older brother found difficult to express. Both Sue and George had hoped that Tazewell would settle in western Virginia after graduating from VMI in 1855. But Tazewell returned to Culpeper to establish a law practice and help his parents run the family plantation. He joined the fabled Culpeper Minutemen, the same company in which his ancestors Philip Slaughter and John Williams had served during the Revolution; soon Tazewell was named company commander. In 1859 he led the Minutemen to Harper's Ferry during John Brown's insurrection. His former VMI professor Thomas Jackson was there as well, and Tazewell asked him to let him have one of the heavy cavalry sabers from the liberated government arsenal. Jackson observed that the young captain already had a sword. Tazewell complained that it was a puny ceremonial thing left over from his days as a cadet, barely longer than a bayonet. Jackson shrugged. "Stick 'em quick, Mister Patton. Stick 'em quick."

Tazewell was elected to the state legislature in November 1860—and Abraham Lincoln was elected president. Within weeks South Carolina declared its secession from the Union and was soon followed by six other states. The Virginia legislature hesitated, though Tazewell's vote was to secede immediately. Willie Glassell was unaware of the upheaval, for he was halfway around the world on a naval mission to China. In Charleston, meanwhile, George Patton and the Kanawha Riflemen learned that Robert E. Lee, in charge of all Virginia state forces, was accepting into service any local volunteer companies that requested to join him. The dream, or perhaps the nightmare, of the old patriarch John Mercer Patton, dead since 1858, seemed near to coming true. The Patton brothers were thrilled.

"Just before Virginia seceded the family decided to visit the ancestral home," George William Patton later recalled in his memoir of the war. "The morning we started I remember the coach coming to the door and my indignation at the fact of my toy drum, of which I was very proud, being left on the mantle piece in the nursery. I cried bitterly as I was being put in the coach. . . . When the coach reached the railroad my father took me in his arms to see the locomotive, which he called the 'Iron Horse.' This was my first sight of a train."

His half-lamenting, half-amazed response to this first instance of what would be four years of upheaval, tells much about George William's nature as a boy and later as a man. He was sensitive both to the shock of experience and to its adventure; his eyes filled equally with tears and with stars at the extraordinary events he witnessed in the coming Civil War. Swept away by those events like a cork tossed on the sea, when driven to react it was usually for the sake of his family, and especially for his mother Sue—he was the eldest child, the man of the house in his father's absence. Even earlier he'd showed an instinct to take care of her. Shortly after her third child's birth in 1859, it had shut its eyes and died. Sue had wailed in her bedroom that her poor baby was gone. George William frantically had dashed through the house, returning to his mother a moment later and taking her hand with a three-year-old's proud triumph. "I found the baby! I found the baby!" Dazed with grief, Sue let him lead her to the front room where George William indeed had found the baby, at rest in its tiny open coffin between two flickering candles.

A Patton family reunion was held at Spring Farm, "a long low rambling house with a veranda in front and a detached kitchen and well beyond this the lines of slave cabins," in March 1861. The eldest of the eight brothers, Robert, was a former naval officer and now a serenely pickled alcoholic. "Old and no account" (he was thirty-seven), he lived with "a bulldog by the name of Dinkey" in one of the house's back rooms. Isaac was up from New Orleans, where he had married the daughter of a sugar planter and now served as a colonel in the Louisiana Zouaves. Then came George and Tazewell, then Hugh and James, the latter two at boarding school. William, the youngest, still living at home, feared that war might break out without his being old enough to participate. Only John, the second eldest brother, was absent from the gathering. He was with his own family at his plantation in Albemarle County, drilling with the militia there in expectation of good news of secession.

After several weeks at Spring Farm, George Patton rejoined his Kanawha volunteers; soon the unit was officially mustered into the service of the state. Tazewell went to Richmond as part of the state convention debating the ordinance of secession. Little George William amused himself at Spring Farm. Just before the much-anticipated vote on secession, he traveled to Richmond at his uncle's invitation. "On the day the ordinance was passed Uncle Tazewell held me up in his arms so that I could see, and pointing to the platform told me to always remember that I had seen this historic ordinance ratified." The city erupted in triumphant jubilation. Church bells peeled and music and whiskey flowed. Revelers spilled from their homes to continue the party outside, Tazewell whooping and whirling around with the boy on his shoulders all through the day and evening. That night the mood turned somber with foreboding. "There was a torchlight procession through the streets and all the windows were illuminated with candles. I was greatly impressed with the grandeur of the scene." It was April 17, 1861. George William was four years old.

Back in Charleston, the Kanawha Riflemen were integrated into the First Kanawha Regiment. George was commissioned as a Confederate Army colonel. The men exchanged their fancy green uniforms for "light blue jackets and gray trousers with yellow trimmings." Their spirit was euphoric, one soldier exalting that "now that our old glorious State is thoroughly aroused and armed to the teeth, heaven grant us a speedy and eternal separation from Yankeedom." As for Colonel Patton, he'd made his view clear a month earlier in a directive to his unit. He had no doubt, he wrote, "that every Rifleman will respond cheerfully and with alacrity to the call of his State, and be prepared to do his duty under the grand old flag of Virginia."

Perfectly Resigned

G EORGE PATTON'S introduction to combat occurred in July 1861 at Scary Creek, twenty miles down the Kanawha River from Charleston. The battle involved about nine hundred soldiers under George's command against elements of two Federal infantry regiments pushing up the valley as part of General George McClellan's assault into the region from Ohio. In the days leading up to the battle, several skirmishes had broken out between advance scouts of both armies. On July 16 the opposing commanders—Patton on one side, Colonel Jesse Norton on the other—met over drinks and cigars at a local farmhouse to postpone the imminent battle until local citizens could be moved to safety. The evacuation of fifty-eight people, including eighteen slaves, was completed that night.

The inevitability of the next day's bloodshed was hard on the Confederate soldiers' nerves. The glee with which so many had looked forward to fighting the Yankees gave way to dread. They held prayer meetings and sang hymns, and as they boarded the steamboat taking them to Scary Creek several young men nearly fainted from fright; others were sick over the side. On the morning of July 17, George rejected his commanding general's order to deploy his troops more to the east. He correctly gauged the terrain around Scary Creek to be better suited for defense. But his last-minute request of a subordinate for advice on where to place his unit's two field cannon suggests he was feeling a bit rattled. Hadn't he scored number one in artillery tactics at VMI?

Ultimately, his confidence in the Confederate cause carried him through these trying last moments as it had carried him through nearly four years of preparation. But just a few weeks earlier, that confidence had nearly caused him grave trouble: George had bragged to a visiting English tourist that so well fortified was his regiment's base camp, "with 600 Confederate soldiers I can defend against 10,000 Yankees for ten years." That Englishman had been Pryce Lewis, a Pinkerton spy in disguise, scouting Confederate forces for the Union Army. Only the spy's delay in reporting to his superiors prevented them from gaining a huge advantage thanks to the young colonel's careless exuberance.

The Scary Creek battle was a rather clumsy operation on both sides, which perhaps was predictable given the inexperience of everyone involved. Although the first musket shots were exchanged at 9 A.M., it was not until about five hours later that the Federal troops mounted a concerted advance upon the Confederate positions. When the Federals had closed to five hundred yards, the two Kanawha artillery batteries opened fire with rounds of grapeshot and six-pound cannonballs. One bluecoat was killed, his comrades falling back in retreat. A pair of Union cannon were wheeled into position to answer the barrage. The Confederate batteries fired shot after shot at them, but could not find the range, demolishing the trees and fences in the distance but leaving the enemy unscathed. The Union artillerymen proved the better marksmen, with their third shot scoring a direct hit on a Confederate cannon. When the cannon blew apart, a chunk of flying metal virtually decapitated James Welch, one of the original Kanawha Riflemen. The Confederates finally landed a round near an enemy battery, leaving a teenaged gunner with his hip "removed." Colonel Patton, riding up behind, ordered his remaining cannon withdrawn lest it too be destroyed. In this early round of the battle, the Federals clearly were winning.

Elsewhere, Rebels and Yankees shot at one another across Scary Creek. The exchanges were not precision volleys between standing ranks of infantry; they were haphazard potshots from soldiers hidden behind any available tree or rock, soldiers much preferring to fight "Indian style" than to stand and attack head-on. A kind of chaotic inertia settled over the battlefield, no one quite sure what to do nor much inclined to do it. Suddenly on the Rebel side an old hillbilly showed up with a double-barreled shotgun. As Confederates gaped at him from behind their cover, he stood brazenly in the open and shook his fist at the Yankees. He fired one barrel of the shotgun, paused to shout hurrahs for Jefferson Davis and curses on Abraham Lincoln, then fired the second barrel. (The old man is thought to have been Anse Hatfield of the feuding Hatfields and McCoys.) Meanwhile across the creek, the cook of the Twelfth Ohio spotted a flock of domestic geese waddling through the line of fire. A Federal soldier remembered, "he darted after the flock, chasing them hither and thither, at one time getting almost inside the enemy's works, until he secured as many as could conveniently be carried. . . . How he escaped is a matter of perplexity, for at one time no less than one hundred bushwackers directed their fire at him."

Inspired by these examples of reckless courage, soldiers on both sides began to move from their positions. At several points along the creek Yankees waded across and engaged the Rebels in hand-to-hand combat. Colonel Patton had placed a company in "the woods to the left to prevent annoyance by a flanking party," but it seemed that the enemy still had swept around him. His men defending there fired on the attackers, who answered with shots of their own. The supposed enemy were friendly reinforcements. Rebels were shooting Rebels. Several fell wounded, at least one was killed. Hearing the gunshots, Confederates at the center of the line believed they were being overrun. Hundreds turned and lit out of the woods down to the Kanawha River. George galloped out before them waving his saber to rally them. Just then his horse began to buck in fright. As George wrestled with his reins, his troops running toward him mistook his gestures for a sign to retreat. Some threw down their weapons to run still faster. In a moment George calmed his horse and managed to gather a few men around him. He might gain the victory yet.

A minié ball—an ounce of pointed lead more than half an inch wide— struck his right shoulder and pitched him off his horse. The bone of his upper arm was shattered. His arm hung limp as he was carried to safety by his men. Captain Albert Jenkins took over command, and with the help of reinforcements drove the Yankees back across Scary Creek. The Rebels lost four dead and ten wounded that day and killed fifteen of the enemy, whom they buried unmarked in a common grave. The night after the battle, it was decided that George's arm must be amputated. With his left hand he trained his pistol on the surgeon and swore he would kill him if he tried to cut off his arm. "Finally a medical student said he thought he could save the arm. He fixed a pulley on the ceiling and passing a cord through it fastened one end to the wrist and put a brick on the other to hold the arm vertical. He then arranged a tin bucket with a small hole so that water from the pump would drip constantly on it. The arm was saved."

The Confederates won the Battle of Scary Creek. But elsewhere in the Kanawha Valley, Union forces had swept around in a pincer movement, threatening to cut supply lines to eastern Virginia. The First Kanawha retreated. Charleston was captured and burned. George Patton, too severely injured to be moved, was left behind in the hands of the enemy.

George Hugh Smith, George's first cousin (and one-time rival for the hand of Sue Glassell), had fought the Yankees north of Charleston. During the Confederates' dispirited withdrawal, Smith and several fellow officers accepted the offer of a local moonshiner to join him for a pick-me-up in his mountain cabin. The moonshiner passed around mugs of hot whiskey from his still, downing plenty himself. As the man grew drunker, he climbed atop the still, unbuttoned his fly, and began to piss in it. His horrified guests threw their mugs away, gagging. The moonshiner tried to calm them. "Drink only whiskey, piss only whiskey. It's all right, boys! It's all right!" The Confederate officers were not persuaded. "This broke up the party," George Smith told his grandchildren years later. Within several months he too was wounded in action and taken prisoner.

Tazewell Patton's Culpeper Minutemen had been integrated into the Seventh Virginia Infantry Regiment. The unit was training near Manassas Junction at the time of the Scary Creek battle. Tazewell's first action occurred at Blackburn's Ford on July 18; the skirmish tipped off the Rebels to the enemy's intention to move on Richmond with an army of 35,000. Confederate General P. G. T. Beauregard moved to cut off the Yankee advance before it got started, engaging the enemy near Bull Run creek, thirty miles from Washington.

Beginning with Bull Run on July 21, Tazewell's military résumé eventually carried the names of some of the Civil War's most storied battles. He was at Yorktown during McClellan's Peninsular Campaign. He fought at Fair Oaks and in the Seven Days' Battles around Richmond. He fought at Second Bull Run and Gettysburg. Among the generals he served under were Richard Ewell, A. P. Hill, and James Longstreet. In June 1862 he was promoted to colonel and given command of the Seventh Virginia.

*   *   *

George Patton was "paroled" by his captors within a few weeks after Scary Creek and rejoined his family at The Meadows. (Charleston, George's home, was in enemy hands now.) By the rules of the conflict, a soldier released on parole was obligated not to report any military information he might have gleaned while in custody; nor could he take up arms again until officially exchanged for an enemy prisoner of comparable rank. For nearly a year George stewed at home, recuperating from his wound and awaiting news of his exchange. After years of preparing for war, he'd been knocked out of it in his first action. The memory of that action rankled him deeply. His peak moment in combat had been spent in trying not to be thrown off his horse—and then a junior officer had stepped in to lead the Virginians to victory.

His injured shoulder healed poorly. The arm was weak and he could not raise it above his head; months after the colonel was wounded, his son George William saw him pick bone splinters out of the festering wound with one of Sue's knitting needles. On the assumption that the injury would force Patton to resign from the army, the superintendent of VMI offered him a teaching position at the Institute in March 1862. George answered ambivalently:

It would ill become me at this juncture—so critical to the country—to retire to Lexington of my own accord. At the same time . . . if I am not released [from parole], nothing would be more acceptable to me than to accept your offer. . . . I fear however that my pursuits and habits of thought for the last several years have greatly unfitted me for academic duty. If I go to the Institute . . . I will endeavor to break my self to it again."

A week later, George was summoned to the War Department in Richmond to discuss "the pleasing probability of an exchange." His subsequent note to VMI's superintendent was brief and joyful: released from parole, he would rejoin his regiment at once. His emotions of the moment were summed up in his signature, whose florid plump characters and decorative underline would have done John Hancock proud.

On the eve of rejoining his regiment, George thought to consider his wife's feelings on the matter. Along with George William and Nellie, Sue had a new baby to care for, a boy called Glassell. The professorship at VMI was still open to the colonel; having been seriously wounded in battle, no stigma of cowardice would come to him if he took the job. He asked Sue to advise him but she refused; the decision must be his alone, she knew. At length he announced that he indeed would return to combat. He rationalized that his wound was in his sword arm and therefore made little difference. As a commander of infantry, his sword was more to be waved as a signal to fire than to strike the enemy. If he could control his horse with one hand on the reins, he could lead.

Before he left, Sue placed an 1847 ten-dollar gold piece that her father had sent from Alabama inside a money belt she'd made for her husband. If he were captured, it would buy him better treatment than would Confederate paper. "Don't spend your gold." It became a constant refrain in her letters to him, her adamancy on this small point almost irrationally overblown. "Don't spend your gold," she wrote again and again, as if it were deadly important.

During his eight-month absence, George's First Kanawha Regiment had been renamed the Twenty-second Virginia Infantry. In May 1862, the regiment participated in General Henry Heth's campaign against Yankee forces seeking to cut rail lines in southwestern Virginia. The Twenty-second attacked an Ohio infantry regiment at Giles Court House on May 10. It was George's first fight since returning, and after the Confederate victory he and his unit were commended for "carrying the last and probably the most determined stand of the enemy." Two Rebels were killed. George was wounded—shot in the belly, which in those days of untreatable infections meant almost certain death. After the battle he was laid under a shade tree. He leaned on the trunk and with a pencil stub and small sheet of paper began to write a last letter to Sue. General Heth rode up and asked how he was faring. George's son George William recorded the exchange as told to him later:

"It is all over with me," said the colonel. "I sent the doctor to look after men he can save."

General Heth was puzzled. "You look very well for a dying man. May I examine the wound?" George opened his shirt to reveal a huge purple splotch with a clotted bullet hole in its center. Heth "then stuck his unwashed finger in the hole and found something hard, which on being fished out proved to be a ten-dollar gold piece. The bullet had struck this and ricocheted off, driving the coin into the flesh"—but not, however, through George's abdomen. His wife later would call it "your old luck." But George credited Sue with saving his life. How many times had she told him "Don't spend your gold"? Now he understood why.

Though the wound was not serious, George developed blood poisoning and returned home to convalesce—again knocked out of action after one battle. Worse, after joining his family in Richmond, he learned that his exchange in March had never been formally completed. By honor, and to avoid being executed if captured again, he was forced to remain a noncombatant. In the months of waiting for another exchange, he could only hear about the victories, setbacks, and sacrifice of other family members. His younger brother James was a lieutenant in George's regiment. Isaac was at Vicksburg. Hugh was with Tazewell in the Seventh Virginia, while William, the youngest, would soon matriculate at VMI. Cousin George Smith, having been properly exchanged months ago, was now with John Imboden's Partisan Rangers in western Virginia. The Rangers (soon designated the Sixty-second Mounted Infantry) were a guerrilla band whose declared mission was "to hang about [enemy] camps and shoot down every sentinel, picket, courier, and wagon driver we can find." This suited Smith, who was on the way toward gaining the reputation that would lead General Imboden to describe him as "the bravest man I ever saw."

John Patton was a colonel under Stonewall Jackson. On June 2, 1862, after a particularly bloody battle, he had an exchange with Jackson in which John expressed to the general his pity for the dead enemy soldiers. "Colonel," Jackson asked, "why do you say that you saw those Federals fall with regret?" They had showed such bravery under fire, John said, that it seemed a shame to kill them. Jackson was unmoved. "Kill them all. I do not wish them to be brave." (Often cited as indicative of Jackson's implacable approach to warfare, the exchange gives a glimpse as well into John's character. He saw much action in the first years of the war; though never wounded, his clothes "were hit six times and his horse was killed under him." Before the war was over he left the army without explanation. He may have been incompetent. A colleague later described him as "but a pigeon-headed fellow with a mind as narrow as any king's that ever tormented mankind." Or he may simply have lost his stomach for "killing them all.")

While Tazewell Patton was with Longstreet's army defending the outskirts of Richmond during the Seven Days (June to July, 1862), George was reduced to constructing city defenses with a ragtag company of other injured soldiers and a collection of old men called the Home Guards. Ultimately the city was not besieged, so this too proved another hapless effort on George's part to somehow get into the fight.

His son, meanwhile, was adapting to wartime life. George William later recalled the bemused wonder with which, as a boy, he took in the sights and sounds of Richmond as it prepared for attack:

Just across the street was a female seminary converted into a field hospital. From the window of my room I could see them bringing in wounded soldiers. Most of the operations must have been amputations, for I recall seeing cart loads of arms and legs being taken away. One day I saw a nigger boy with a bundle wrapped in oil cloth. When I inquired what it was, he told me that it was a leg belonging to his master and he was burying it for him so that he would always know where it could be found when needed—I suppose the necessity was to arise on Judgement Day.

George William had become "very intimate" with Jeff and Joe Davis, sons of the Confederacy's president, Jefferson Davis, whose house was located down the block. "I was a guest at the May Pole party in the rear of this house when young Joe fell from the railing of the balcony and was killed." Violent death had come to seem an unremarkable thing to the boy: in the hospitals of the Civil War, where there were cartloads of severed limbs, there also were cartloads of corpses. "The children of Richmond gave him a very fine tombstone," was the detail George William would remember of his friend's funeral, acknowledging with an acquired precocity that most people don't even get that.

Colonel Patton's prisoner exchange at last was completed, and he went west to Lewisburg to rejoin his regiment. George William and his sister Nellie contracted scarlet fever soon thereafter. Their mother and the slave Mary nursed the children back to health. "I was especially ill," George William recalled, "and when I recovered I was very thin. The first time I went down stairs Uncle Tazewell who was home recovering from a bullet hole through the center of his right hand saw me and was so impressed with my skinniness that he called me 'Smike' after the boy in Dickens's *Nicholas Nickleby*." Tazewell, wounded at Second Manassas, was considering more than George William's physique in the comparison. George William was quiet and passive. Perhaps Tazewell fancied himself a kind of Nicholas to his nephew's Smike, caring for and befriending the boy when others didn't have time for him.

Tazewell's experiences over the past year had greatly changed him. Once boisterous and flippant, he now spoke often of religion and "reflected upon his desire to lead a pure and holy life." Of his older brother George, it was said that "divine things he reverenced"—but George carried his faith as a kind of cultural accessory befitting his image as an upstanding southern gentleman, almost never referring to it (or to his own mortality) in conversation or his personal letters; his wife, Sue, was more devout by far. Tazewell, on the other hand, was deeply haunted by the killing he'd seen and committed. While home recuperating from the wound in his hand, he was elected to the Virginia Senate, a post that would have permitted him honorably to resign his commission to serve as a full-time legislator. He chose to stay with his outfit, which in December was assigned to the division of General George Pickett in Robert E. Lee's Army of Northern Virginia.

Cited for gallantry in virtually every battle he fought in, Tazewell would be remembered as the most courageous Patton brother, because, of them all, he'd been the most afraid.

Navy Lieutenant Willie Glassell, Sue Patton's brother, returned to Philadelphia in December 1861 after nearly two years at sea on the United States steamer *Hartford*. Federal authorities came aboard the vessel and informed the crew that the nation was six months into a civil war and that each must now take an oath of allegiance to the United States. "I could not truthfully swear that I felt no human sympathy for my own family and for the friends of my childhood," Willie recalled in his memoir of the war years. "I was denounced as a traitor, thrown into prison for eight months, and then exchanged as a prisoner of war."

Upon his exchange, Willie was made a lieutenant in the Confederate Navy and appointed deck officer on the ironclad *Chicora* engaged in defense of the harbor at Charleston, South Carolina. Though his good looks were often commented on, he was an insecure, gentle, unprepossessing man with seemingly little aptitude for warfare. (In the future, George William would be said to resemble his uncle, "especially when he was unwell.") Even after proving appearances wrong, the sheer nerve Willie displayed in battle seemed somehow accidental, unconscious, as if performed in a kind of audacious sleepwalk that on waking he could scarcely remember, much less take credit for. "I never entertained a feeling of hatred or personal enmity against those who were my honorable opponents. I may have been a fool. I hardly hoped to live through the war." Yet live through it he would, more or less.

His first major action was a night attack against a squadron of Union warships blockading Charleston harbor. Willie proposed not to use the *Chicora*'s cannon, but instead to "trust to the effect of iron rams at full speed." He was overruled by his captain, and in Willie's opinion the attack consequently was "fruitless . . . only frightening the enemy and putting them on their guard for the future." Typically, he was understating matters a bit: "It was my part . . . to aim and fire one effective shell into the *Keystone State* . . . killing twenty-one men and severely wounding fifteen, [causing the Union captain] to haul down his flag as a token of surrender."

But the Union squadron as a whole was little damaged by the attack. Discouraged, Willie took notice of a recent successful experiment with an underwater torpedo developed by Major Frank Lee of the Confederate Engineers; the torpedo was a copper tube filled with gunpowder and suspended off the bow of an attack boat on the end of a long wooden pole. Willie estimated that forty torpedo boats could be "constructed secretly at one-half the cost of a clumsy ironclad." But Commodore Ingraham mocked Willie's newfangled notions and threw him out of his office. "With a feeling of grief, and almost desperation," Willie resolved to implement the plan on his own.

With a fifty-pound torpedo and a crew of six oarsmen, under cover of darkness he "started out with the ebb tide in search of a victim." At 1 A.M. he had closed to within three hundred yards of the U.S.S. *Powhatan*. "I did not expect to reach the vessel without being discovered, but my intention was, no matter what they might say or do, not to be stopped until our torpedo came in contact with the ship." Willie was hailed by Yankee watchmen, whom he answered evasively. "I trusted they would be too merciful to fire on such a stupid set of idiots as they must have taken us to be." Forty feet from the target, one of the oarsmen "from terror or treason" suddenly backed his oar and stopped the boat's headway. Armed men poured onto the deck of the enemy ship. The man who had backed his oar threw his pistol overboard and urged his mates to surrender and save their lives. The rowboat floated dead in the water. Willie weighed his options: "I never was rash, or disposed to risk my life, or that of others, without large compensation from the enemy. But to surrender thus would not do. Resolving not to be taken alive till somebody at least should be hurt, I drew a revolver and whispered to the men to cut loose the torpedo."

He ordered the men to row for home (which they did, Willie noted, with much more speed than on the journey out). Since no shots were fired after them, Willie guessed that the *Powhatan*'s crew "never [had] known how near they came to having the honor of being the first ship ever blown up by a torpedo boat." He was more convinced than ever that torpedoes could succeed in crippling the blockaders where battleships had failed, with one adjustment: "Steam was the only reliable motive power."

For over a year Willie would devote himself to what he called "my pet hobby." Then once again he would venture out past Fort Sumter across a moonless Charleston harbor, this time under steam power and carrying a hundred-pound torpedo. He would need the extra explosive. His target was the *New Ironsides,* flagship of the Yankee blockade and the most powerful vessel in the world.

In September 1862, Sue Patton's father wrote her from his home in Alabama. Having read newspaper reports of recent military operations in western Virginia, he praised "the triumphant march of your husband down the Valley where a year since he was reeling in the opposite direction." In the same letter he told Sue not to worry about reimbursing him for the few dollars in gold he'd sent her. He had plenty of money, every cent of it invested in Confederate war bonds. Mr. Glassell closed with some advice for his lonesome daughter: "Try to school yourself to submit to the want of your husband's society. You cannot keep up with him. There is no telling where he might be ordered. To have you with him will certainly embarrass him when on marching orders." But Sue had made up her mind. With conflict in an apparent lull around Lewisburg, Virginia, where the Twenty-second Virginia was encamped, she left Richmond with her three children and the slave Mary to live in the house of the mayor of Lewisburg, a Mr. Withrow and his wife.

The Twenty-second Virginia was now attached to the First Brigade in the Army of Southwest Virginia. Brigade commander Henry Heth had been fired for lack of aggressiveness and replaced by General John Echols, a competent leader who suffered from heart disease. During the general's frequent sick leaves Colonel Patton replaced him, and through most of its campaigns of the next two years the brigade was called Patton's Brigade.

Its mission that autumn was to help drive the Yankees from the Kanawha Valley and retake Charleston, an objective as much psychological as strategic. The Kanawha Riflemen, the militia company originally formed at Charleston, were given the privilege of entering the town at the head of the Confederate forces. Far away in Alabama, Sue's father exalted over this sweet revenge, wishing he could "witness the humiliation of the Tories and traitors" who'd collaborated with the Yankee occupation. His daughter, however, had more practical concerns. She wished first to know from her husband whether their house was still standing (it was) and if its contents were intact. If so, she directed George to sell the house "provided you can get four thousand dollars for it," sell the furniture and anything "ornamental," and keep only her sewing machine, the family Bible, and George's books. From town she needed gloves and "good thick walking shoes." For the children she needed calico and linen to make their clothes. She needed salt, tea, "and by all means a bag of coffee." She told him to requisition a wagon to transport these items to her, and closed with a sheepish request of her husband to "please don't laugh at me" if the situation at Charleston made her wish list ludicrously impossible to fulfill. And it was impossible. Less than a month after taking the town, the Rebels were driven back to Lewisburg where they went into winter quarters.

If Sue Patton was feeling the pinch of wartime deprivation, so was the Army of Southwest Virginia. It opened its operations in spring of 1863 with a four-hundred-mile raid through the countryside north of Lewisburg. Forty soldiers of the Twenty-second Virginia marched the whole way barefoot. The trail of the march could be traced by the birch bark pulled off the trees for food. In addition to foraging for his men, George was foraging for his family as well. Sue had requested a cooking stove, utensils, butter, and molasses. He doubted that he could find any of these, "but I will send down a wagon to haul you some wood." In June, he passed along news to her that "the Yankees have suffered another tremendous reverse and repulse at Vicksburg [where Isaac Patton was fighting]." Concerning Tazewell, however, George had heard "nothing from Lee's Army."

Finally, a new tone of impatience crept into George's letters. Receiving only one letter from Sue in a two-week period, he was "grievously disappointed." "I cannot account for your silence," he complained, though each day he was "trusting that I will get a nice sweet long letter from you . . . and I will then write you one of the same kind." Like every homesick soldier in every war, George wanted mail.

The Confederate raid through northern Virginia forced an enemy change of command. General William Averell had known George Patton socially in the years before the war, and through the rest of the summer and fall the two would become each other's victim and nemesis, circling each other with intent to kill, and yet, as well, with that unlikely courtliness (given the savagery of the fighting) so often displayed among combatants in the Civil War.

Averell advanced on Lewisburg with 3,000 men. George led his brigade to meet the threat. On August 26 the battle was joined at Dry Creek. Sue and the children were three miles away at White Sulphur Springs, a mountain vacation spot (closed during the war) where they recently had occupied one of the empty cottages at a resort hotel. During the battle Yankee and Confederate casualties were brought to the hotel and laid on blankets spread out in the lobby. Sue joined the other women of the town to help care for the wounded. George William helped, too, "following my mother around with a bucket and sponge. The smell was so awful that my mother fainted and had to be carried out."

The fighting at Dry Creek lasted two days. On the first evening, both commanders convened councils of war at which their staffs advised them to retreat—and both men rejected the advice, Patton announcing he would "continue the fight even it involved the loss of his entire command." On September 5, the United States *Army and Navy Journal* reported, "telegraphic dispatches from White Sulphur Springs, Va., under date of 27th, announcing a fight near that place between a brigade of rebel cavalry under Gen. Patton and three thousand Union Cavalry under Gen. Averill. [sic] They claim that the latter was badly beaten. . . . The whole affair is probably a canard, as not one word touching any such fight has been made public." The Confederate victory at Dry Creek had cost 170 casualties, or nearly 10 percent of the undermanned First Brigade. Despite the heavy losses, one historian wrote, "Patton could claim his most outstanding victory of the war, proof he could command an army in the field."

One afternoon two days after the battle, the colonel's son George William was out alone "gathering blackberries to increase our food." Feeling someone's gaze on him he whirled to see a tall lanky soldier mounted on his horse, which grazed quietly in the tall grass. The soldier wore a full dark beard and the ragged butternut homespun of a frontline veteran. It took a moment for George William to recognize his father, who slowly and wordlessly approached across the meadow. "He dismounted and put me on his horse which he led to the house." Only there, with his wife and other children gathered around him, did the colonel finally speak. He had news about Tazewell, he said. From Gettysburg, Pennsylvania.

General Pickett's division had been held out of the fighting during the first two days of the battle of Gettysburg. At 7 A.M. on July 3, the division marched up from the rear and assembled behind Seminary Ridge in preparation for a frontal assault upon the heart of the enemy's battle line, a heavily defended stone wall three-quarters of a mile distant across an open meadow. James Kemper's brigade was positioned on the division's right flank, Tazewell Patton's Seventh Virginia at the left center of the brigade. For five hours the Confederates baked under the hot summer sun and crushing humidity. Sometime during those anxious hours Colonel Patton made a confession to one of his subordinates. He told the man that he, Tazewell, was going to die today.

Shortly after 1 P.M. the Confederate cannonade began. For two hours 150 guns pounded twenty-seven Yankee regiments to soften them before the attack. Woven within the roar of the bombardment could be heard the sound of a Confederate band playing lighthearted polkas and waltzes. The men of the Seventh Virginia lay prone in the grass as enemy artillery returned fire. "Guns, swords, haversacks, heads, and limbs went flying as shells plowed enormous furrows in the ground." The infantry regiment suffered 15 percent casualties before its troops even shouldered their rifles.

At 3 P.M. General Pickett shouted, "Up, men, and to your posts! Don't forget today that you are from old Virginia!" Tazewell moved out with his cousin Lewis Williams beside him. (Brother Hugh Patton recently had been transferred to another unit.) The men called back to the wounded lying on the ground, "Good-bye, boys! Good-bye!"

The Union artillery leveled its sights and poured lead gusts of grapeshot and canister directly into the oncoming waves of Confederates. Blue-coated infantry rose up behind the stone wall and unleashed their volleys, weeping, it was said, as they fired and reloaded and fired again through this all-too-easy slaughter. The Seventh Virginia's color-bearer fell dead. Another took up the regimental flag until he too was hit. Before the field was crossed the flag changed hands eight times.

On reaching the stone wall, two Confederate officers were seen to clasp hands and leap atop the wall together, one of them exhorting, "It's our turn next, Tazewell!" Having gained the objective, the Rebels were too depleted and weakened to hold it. After twenty minutes of hand-to-hand fighting, they were driven back in a rout. By evening, according to Union observers, "the most profound calm" had settled over the scene. Dead bodies were everywhere. Wounded men cried into the night for water. But sniper fire was still a danger. "All labors of charity were necessarily put off till the next morning"—when, remembering the two enemy officers he'd seen leap the stone wall and then fall to the ground, a Union artillery major went out to find their bodies. They were still alive.

Over a month later, in mid-August, Peggy Patton received in Richmond two letters enclosed in the same envelope. The first was dated July 15.

Though she recognized immediately that it was not her son's handwriting, the letter began,

My dear Mother

It has now been nearly two weeks since I have been stretched out on this bed of suffering. You will doubtless have heard before this reaches you that I was badly wounded and left in the hands of the enemy. My sufferings and hardships during about two weeks that I was kept out in the field hospital were very great.

I rec'd a wound through the mouth, fracturing the face bone badly on both sides. The doctors seem to agree that the danger of losing my life is small. The wound is serious, annoying, and will necessarily be a very long time in getting well.

I can assure you that it was the greatest consolation to me, whilst lying in pain on the dark and cold ground, to look up to that God to whom you so constantly directed my infantile and puerile thoughts, and feel that I was his son by adoption. When friends are far away from you, in sickness and in sorrow, how delightful to be able to contemplate the wonderful salvation unfolded in the bible. Whilst I have been far from being a consistent christian, I have never let go my hope in Jesus, and find it inexpressibly dear now. I write these things to show you my spiritual condition, and to ask your prayers continually for me.

I am glad under such adverse circumstances to be able to write so cheerfully. I do not feel that I could do so every day. Sometimes I feel very badly and very weak. I have strong hope however that I shall get well ultimately, and be restored to the fond embraces of my friends in Virginia. To be at The Meadows, at Spring Farm, or in Richmond, with all the family around, would be the highest delight I could experience. I must however put it off for some time. As soon as I am able to travel, I will hurry homeward.

Give my love to all. I write with some difficulty. Should you wish to communicate, address me Col W T Patton, 7th Va Infy, College Hospital near Gettysburg, Pennsylvania. Poor Lewis Williams died a few days after the battle from the effects of a wound. I am very affectionately your son,

W. T. Patton

The second letter, dated July 24, was written in the same hand. Mailed from Baltimore, Maryland, it opened with an ageless clause of rote directness and eloquence: "It is my sad duty to inform you . . ." Tazewell had died at eleven in the morning on July 21, six days after his twenty-eighth birthday. No doubt hoping to uplift the bereaved if only a little, the writer went on to offer some details of the young colonel's passing:

> He was aware of the approach of death, and met it as became a soldier and a christian. He repeated often the words "in Christ alone, perfectly resigned, perfectly resigned." He spoke with great difficulty, but I could understand him repeating the first lines of the hymn "Rock of ages, cleft for me". . . . He called for the 14th chapter of Saint John, which was read to him. . . . From Miss McRea and Miss Sayer of Baltimore, who were nurses in the hospital . . . he rec'd the most devoted attention, and much kindness from several Federal officers who were stationed near the hospital.

The letter was signed by Isaac W. Smith, George Hugh Smith's brother. Himself slightly wounded in the battle, Isaac had joined Tazewell at the college hospital on July 18 and had remained with him until his death. Isaac had transcribed his cousin's feebly scrawled July 12 letter to Peggy Patton, and also had seen to Tazewell's burial. "He often requested that his body might be sent home," Isaac wrote—but any transfer south would have to wait until a permit could be obtained from Union authorities. Isaac had had Tazewell's body embalmed and placed in a cousin's burial vault in Baltimore. "He was clothed in his uniform. I have his two rings, pipe, and a lock of his hair. . . . He has some money in the Farmer's Bank. . . . After paying his just debts, he wishes all else to go to his mother."

Shortly after receiving Isaac's letter, Peggy received a note from Tazewell's nurses, Miss McRea and Miss Sayer. Inside the note was a poem cut out of a newspaper that the women said they had recited to Tazewell as he lay dying. Its imagery echoed, and perhaps had inspired, Tazewell's deathbed testimony of intimations of heavenly grace: "On the field of battle, Mother, all the night I lay,/Angels watching o'er me, Mother, 'til the break of day." The nurses closed by saying that they would never forget Tazewell's "beautiful chestnut hair on the pillow."

Her eldest son, John, later recalled that as she folded the note, Peggy broke down for the first time since learning of Tazewell's death. John asked his mother (obtusely, one might think) why she was crying. She lifted her head from her hands. "I am crying," she said, "because I have only seven sons left to fight the Yankees."

The Effects of a General Breakdown

I N CHARLESTON, South Carolina, the specially designed "little cigar boat *David*" was tied up to the waterfront pier. Thirty-five feet long and only five feet wide, the vessel was ballasted to float nearly submerged in the water. It was painted blue-gray, "the most invisible color," and powered by a small steam engine capable of making seven knots. Suspended under the water fourteen feet in front of the bow was a torpedo with a hundred-pound warhead.

A little after dark on October 5, 1863, Willie Glassell and three crewmen pushed off in the *David* and headed out "to reconnoiter the whole fleet of the enemy at anchor between me and the campfires on Morris' Island." Sighting the flagship *New Ironsides* in the center of the Union fleet, Willie "determined to pay her the highest compliment" and steered for the vessel's starboard beam. His engineer and fireman crouched in the darkness below deck, stoking the *David*'s engine, while Willie and the helmsman sat topside and double-checked their firearms in preparation for attack on the huge Yankee ironclad.

Hearing the steam gurgle of the *David*'s approach, watchmen aboard the *New Ironsides* hailed the intruders, demanding they identify themselves. Making no reply, Willie cocked the hammers of his double-barreled shotgun. The deck officer stepped to the rail. "What boat is that?" he shouted.

Willie, "being now within forty yards of the ship . . . thought it about time the fight should commence." He fired both barrels at the deck officer, then ordered the engine stopped. As the *David*'s momentum swept it toward the *New Ironsides*, the four Confederates aboard awaited with wondering expectation what would happen next.

The torpedo's explosion rocked the little boat and sent a wave of seawater over its bow and down its open hatch, dousing the fires of the steam engine. Enemy sailors beat to quarters and a general alarm sounded throughout the fleet. Unable to restart the engine, Willie and his men grabbed cork life preservers and leaped into the chilly October water. They frantically swam for shore as the enemy, "in no amiable mood, poured down upon the bubbling water a hailstorm of rifle and pistol shots." The four men were quickly separated in the darkness. After an hour in the water, Willie was numb with cold. He hailed a Yankee coal schooner and was hauled aboard by its crew, who "found, to their surprise, that they had captured a rebel."

He was given whiskey and blankets to warm himself. The next day he was transferred to the guard ship *Ottowa*, where he found that his fireman was also a prisoner. The *New Ironsides*, whose hull had four and a half inches of armor plating backed by twenty-seven inches of wood, was only slightly damaged by the *David*'s torpedo, though the psychological effect of the attack on the Yankee sailors, who previously had felt quite invulnerable aboard their battleships, was considerable. Willie speculated that it may have dissuaded the Yankee admiral from advancing his warships into Charleston harbor and shelling the city to rubble.

During his imprisonment of more than a year, Willie learned that he'd been promoted for "gallant and meritorious service." He learned that the deck officer whom he'd shot in the attack had later died of buckshot wounds. He learned, too, that the officer, named Howard, had been his friend and roommate at the U.S. Naval Academy thirteen years earlier. "Poor fellow," Willie said.

Peggy Patton was more affected by Tazewell's death than she first let on. "He was so affectionate," she lamented, "so considerate and thoughtful." Her letters to her soldier sons, formerly replete with the blithe encouragements of a château general, took on tones of real worry. Feeling "miserable" that sons George and James "have been engaged in a fight," she begged to hear from them often. Her fatalistic prayer—"Thy will Oh God not mine be done"—doubtless applied as much to her beloved Confederacy as to her children, as if Peggy were trying to absolve herself of any part in their undoing.

The family's joy over George's victory at Dry Creek was greatly tempered by Tazewell's death. George went on with his business, however, marching his men into Lewisburg and directing them to the usual tasks of setting up long-term quarters: cutting timber, harvesting produce, erecting barracks, and conducting recruitment drives. Sue packed up the children and returned to the Withrows' house in Lewisburg. In early November the Union General Averell struck back. Colonel Patton was ordered north to confront him. George protested the order, believing that it was Averell's plan to lure the Confederates from their stronghold at Lewisburg. But early in the morning of November 6 he moved out with 1,700 men to battle 5,000 Yankees at a place called Droop Mountain. He lost the battle. His son George William saw the exhausted troops of the First Brigade straggling through Lewisburg later that day.

Father had sent an ambulance with a pair of mules to the house and told my mother to take it and follow the army. . . . It was dark and raining and just as we were getting into the ambulance an artillery officer came up and took the mules in an attempt to save a gun, so we had to stay where we were. Late in the night my father stopped to tell us good bye and give my mother a letter for General Averell asking to see that we were not bothered.

The Yankees arrived the next morning. Sue delivered the letter to Averell, who detailed a sergeant to guard the house. Later, after taking "our host" Mr. Withrow into custody "as a hostage for the good behavior of the citizens," Averell sent over provisions of coffee, sugar, "and other delicacies unknown in the South," together with a note asking if he might dine with Mrs. Patton and Mrs. Withrow that evening.

The general put himself at ease on arriving, unbuckling his sword belt and setting it aside. As he sat by the fire he remarked that he had a bad cold. Mrs. Withrow offered to prepare him a home remedy of honey and vinegar. Observing in polite silence across the room, George William "at once jumped to the conclusion that she was going to poison him." General Averell received the hot potion with thanks. The boy watched excitedly for the first convulsions. His heart sank "when on swallowing the draught he failed to drop dead."

During the few days that Lewisburg was occupied, George William was befriended by the sergeant guarding the house. The man stood him on a table on the back porch and ruffled his hair. "Tell me, kid. Are you a Rebel?" The boy swallowed weakly and confessed that he was. The sergeant removed his cap and placed it on George William's head. "Now you are a Yankee!" When word came that Patton's Brigade was counterattacking, Averell retreated from Lewisburg. Only then did George William tell his mother about his sergeant friend and how he'd worn a Yankee cap. "Whereupon," he remembered, "my head was vigorously scrubbed."

A soft focus of admiring romanticism attaches easily to the memory of Colonel George Patton. His aide, Lieutenant Noyes Rand, termed him "our brave and noble commander . . . as courteous a gentleman as God ever created." His superiors recommended him for brigadier general in 1863, though the promotion never was finalized. For two convicted deserters he commuted the sentence from death to flogging, inciting "piteous screams" but sparing their lives. When some soldiers found three kegs of whiskey, he dispensed the alcohol equally among his companies. Subordinates freely visited his quarters with their suggestions or grievances, and he was said to have made every effort to help the regimental chaplains to minister to the troops. A colleague wrote that as a leader, George "enforced discipline without exciting dislike, and commanded his men without diminishing their self-respect."

All of these qualities would cast him as a fine man to know and maybe even follow into battle. But as to characterizing his conduct once the battle began, the more revealing detail is his hatred for the enemy. He never expressed this hatred in letters to his wife. However, according to the official regimental history of Twenty-second Virginia, he expressed it once in a letter of 1862 to the superintendent of VMI. Whether this hatred of Yankees was heartfelt and all-consuming, or whether it was something he whipped up inside him, like an athlete pounding his locker before a game to better ready himself for the frenzy, such an expression would have a basic implication: George understood that war means killing, and that in killing, hatred helps.

In December 1863, his brother Isaac lost his daughter to illness. Isaac's wife, Fanny, was distraught and wanted him to quit his regiment and return home—and Isaac was considering it. Sue passed along this news to George in an attempt to gauge whether he too might be persuaded to leave the army. She was pregnant and had returned to Richmond to have the baby.

George was not thrilled about becoming a father again in the midst of a desperate war. On learning from Sue that a friend of hers also was pregnant, he was "amused, and as misery loves company, pleased to see . . . that we are not the only couple to be surprised soon." As to Isaac Patton's dilemma, however, George was adamant: "I deeply sympathize with him in the painful position in which he is placed by Fanny's state of mind, and the desire manifested that he should resign. But I sincerely trust that he will not be induced to take so false a step. His conscience, I am sure, would not be clean in so doing." Without ever putting the question to him directly, Sue had her answer. Her husband would continue the fight.

Historians have suggested that for the young southern aristocrats who began the war so eagerly, any last illusions of glory died with General J.E.B. Stuart on May 12, 1864. A cavalry corps commander at thirty-one, dashing in both his bravery and dress, "Jeb" Stuart was one of the South's most popular and romantic figures. Colonel Patton was home in Richmond seeing his newborn daughter, Susie, for the first time when Stuart was mortally wounded at Yellow Tavern just outside the city.

The general's body was brought to a private home in Richmond. George put on his best uniform and went to pay his respects, taking his son with him. A hushed crowd of soldiers and citizens filed slowly into the house. Colonel Patton removed his hat and took a place at the end of the line. Mourners passed in silence before the billiard table on which Stuart was laid out. The white sheet draped over his legs and torso was as smooth as marble and contrasted vividly with his wiry red beard. He can't be dead, George William thought to himself. People like that do not die. The boy breathed the scent of flowers as he left the house. Yellow roses were in bloom outside the door, and it would be this—the scent of yellow roses in spring—that for the rest of his life would remind him of that day. As for his father, Colonel Patton could offer no more eloquent comment on the occasion than the fact that he wanted his son to witness it. But after that day, the phrase "our glorious struggle" was absent from his letters. The war, its outcome ever more apparent, became a grim obligation of honor.

Three days later, the First Brigade joined the small army of General John C. Breckinridge to attack 6,500 Federals advancing up the Shenandoah Valley northwest of Richmond. The Battle of New Market on May 15 is famous for the participation of the cadets from VMI, who were called up as last-ditch reinforcements and hurled in a successful bayonet charge against Yankee artillery. One of those cadets was William M. Patton, the youngest of the Patton brothers. To the cadets' right along the Confederate line was the Sixty-second Virginia Infantry under the command of George Hugh Smith. The Sixty-second bore the worst of the fighting, losing roughly half its men in an assault against enemy infantry positions. Patton's Brigade was at the far right of the field, defending against Union cavalry attempting to outflank the Confederates. When the cavalry punched through his line, George wheeled two regiments toward each side of the gap and raked the Yankee horsemen in a crossfire. Caught in "a deadly corridor with no end," the enemy retreated.

Afterward, George spent a moment with his cousin George Smith, whom he hadn't seen since the start of the war. Each man's horse had been killed in the fighting, so they walked together in the warm rain that had fallen all day. General Breckinridge rode up behind them. "Please, one of you gentlemen take my horse." The colonels declined. The general then dismounted and led his horse by the reins alongside them. "I will not ride when you who have borne the brunt of battle, walk."

"It was a most brilliant affair," Sue Patton said of the battle, echoing her husband's report. To the east, however, Union forces under General Ulysses S. Grant were bearing down on Richmond. Breckinridge's army was ordered to move out at once. Sue hastily traveled to The Meadows in Albemarle County in hopes of seeing her husband. Though his unit passed "within fifty paces" of her, George "could only wave his hat and throw me a note saying he could not stop. This was trying in the extreme." Skirmishing with Yankees at several points along the march, the brigade reached its destination on June 2. Digging trenches through the night with their bayonets and bare hands, George's men were still constructing rudimentary defense works when at 4:30 A.M. Grant launched the massive frontal assault at Cold Harbor in which, repulsed, he lost 7,000 men in half an hour. Said one Confederate general, "It was not war, it was murder." And George Pickett, who'd been on the other end of such slaughter at Gettysburg, could only cry, "Oh, this is all a weary, long mistake."

Patton's Brigade immediately marched west out of Cold Harbor. Franz Sigel, the Union general defeated at New Market, had been replaced by David Hunter. Hunter had regrouped his army and was advancing south. Confederate General Jubal A. Early led his II Corps to defend the Shenandoah Valley. Sue and the children were staying at The Meadows. George William remembered:

While there my mother received a letter from father saying that he was moving into the Valley with Early and would be on the first train which passed just at the foot of the yard. He got off and stayed with us for several hours during which time the old cook Aunt Susan gave him a fine dinner. Then the last train composed of flat cars loaded with artillery stopped for him. I remember seeing a soldier on a car give him a hand to get aboard and as the train moved out he was leaning against a gun and waved us good bye. I never saw him again.

Initially that summer, General Early's corps had followed success with success, rolling down the Shenandoah Valley into Maryland and ultimately to the outskirts of Washington. It was little more than a guerrilla strike, however, razing towns and destroying railroad tracks but lacking the manpower and matériel to remain in hostile territory for long. And it brought about the replacement of the ineffectual General Hunter with Philip Sheridan, who shared Grant's unrelenting determination to grind down the enemy by sheer force of numbers, crushing its army and if necessary starving its people into submission.

Soon Early's 14,000 troops were falling back before Sheridan's 40,000. The Yankees caught the Rebels at Winchester, in northern Virginia, and in the battle of September 19 Early lost one-third of his army and Patton lost half his brigade, including all its officers above the rank of captain.

He was standing in his stirrups on a Winchester street when an artillery shell exploded nearby and sent an iron fragment into his right hip. He'd been trying to rally his men, who were in full retreat before onrushing Yankee cavalry under the command of General George Custer. Patton's younger brother James, a lieutenant in the Twenty-second Infantry, wrote their mother some weeks after the battle. He called the Confederate retreat "the most disgraceful stampede I ever saw." He described General Early despairingly throwing his hands to heaven and exclaiming, "God have mercy on my sinful soul." He hadn't seen his brother fall, so couldn't characterize George's reaction to the sight of his brigade's destruction. General Early's words probably came close.

George was carried to the home of John J. Williams on Piccadilly Street in Winchester ("First room on the right of the front door as you enter . . ."). In a replay of the scene after Scary Creek, he refused the recommended amputation of his right leg, setting his pistol on the bedside table lest anyone mistake his resolve. "What would I look like stumping through life with a wooden leg?" His wound remained free of infection, and for a while it seemed he would be lucky again. His mood grew "cheerful, even buoyant." Taking his first food in days, he sat up and ate a bowl of sliced peaches.

On September 24 Sue read in "a Yankee paper" that her husband was among the wounded at Winchester. After George's battles at Scary Creek and Giles Court House, she always had rushed to join him as soon as possible, leaving her children in Mary's care. (Sue's daughter Nellie later said that her mother had always *intuited,* through her fabled sixth sense, that George had been wounded in action, having her bags packed and train ticket purchased long before she was officially notified.) But this time Sue did not rush at all. She prepared for the journey with an air of stoic resignation. "He will be dead before I get to Winchester," she said, and no one doubted it would be so.

George died on September 25. He had lain alone in his room for most of the day. When the home owner, John Williams, at last looked in on him he found "a great change" in George's condition. The wound had developed gangrene. George was burning with fever. Weakly beckoning Williams to his bedside, he tried to speak. He had something to say. Williams bent low to hear, but George's whispered words were "unintelligible . . . and his voice was hushed forever."

He was buried at Winchester shortly before Sue arrived. She had no wish to move his body to the family plots at Richmond or Fredericksburg. He was in Virginia soil, that was the main thing. And it seemed right to let him lie where he fell.

"Weep, and weep bitterly," John Patton wrote to his sister-in-law Sue:

> It does seem to be a dark and mysterious providence that [George] should be snatched away while so many of us are left behind, so far less worthy than he. . . . It is only for a little season that we ourselves will be here. A very few years at best will pass before we too must die and follow him. . . . God grant that we all may learn this lesson and receive his fitting chastisement to our eternal good.

There was little time for mourning. The enemy was advancing through Albemarle County, freeing slaves and burning property. Sue's father had managed to travel north from Alabama to join her. The trip cost him the last of his money. Having invested everything in Confederate bonds, he'd been left penniless by the South's collapse; old and nearly blind with cataracts, he henceforth would be as one of Sue's children, another life to protect. The family fled east to a cousin's plantation on the James River above Richmond and occupied an abandoned slave cabin behind the main house, "where we stayed all winter of 64 to 65 in great want of food and clothing," recalled George William. The place was prey to enemy raids. Soldiers under General George Stoneman "burned the little grist mill where we had taken our corn to be ground into meal." Fortunately, Sue's brother-in-law John Patton had given her an old steer. "By corning the beef, we managed to get along."

In the spring, the boy caught eels and perch for the family table. One day while fishing he saw a line of mule-drawn canal boats approaching up the river. A crewman "yelled to me that Richmond had been evacuated and Lee had retreated." A few nights later, a large number of soldiers approached the Pattons' cabin. At the sound of sharp knocks on the door, Sue huddled fearfully with her children. The door pushed open and Willie Glassell stepped inside. She hardly recognized her brother. He was gaunt, his hair had thinned, and his skin was covered with carbuncles—"the effects of a general breakdown resulting from his two imprisonments." Exchanged a month ago, Willie had been skippering the Confederate ironclad *Fredericksburg* operating on the James River. When Richmond had fallen on April 3, he'd been ordered to scuttle the ship. He gave his sister the latest news: Lee had surrendered to Grant at Appomattox Court House. Old Mr. Glassell stepped slowly to his son, whom he hadn't seen in eight years, and his daughter. "Then the struggle is ended," he said as his daughter nodded wordlessly.

It wasn't over for Willie. He and his men were heading for North Carolina to join the forces of General Joseph E. Johnston and continue the fight. Hearing this, Sue broke down. She'd lost so much in the war, she couldn't bear to lose her brother in the moment he'd been restored to her. But Willie was resolute. "He left my mother a twenty-dollar gold piece and told her to stay where she was until he could get back to us."

George William was fishing in the river when, a few days after April 14, another boat came by. "Did you hear?" yelled a man on board. "Abe Lincoln has been shot and killed! The South is avenged!" George William threw down his fishing pole and ran to tell his mother and grandfather this happy news. But Sue was too exhausted, too sick of it all to rejoice over the death of the man they'd called "the tyrant." And Mr. Glassell just shook his head sadly. "The South has lost her best friend," he said. George William, almost nine years old now, could not imagine what the old man meant.

☆ ☆ **6** ☆ ☆

The Tin Box

S HORTLY after Colonel Patton's death in September 1864, the family had been surprised by the arrival at The Meadows of his Negro bodyservant Peter, the slave given George by his mother at the outbreak of the war.

Hiding in the woods by day and riding at night, eluding the pickets and foragers of both armies, Peter brought back through the battle lines the colonel's horse, saddle, and saber; also a ragged strip of George's blood-soaked undershirt, the jagged shell fragment that the surgeons had removed from his fatal wound, and the 1847 ten-dollar gold piece that he'd carried for good luck ever since the battle of Giles Court House. Sue put these mementos in a tin strongbox along with her husband's letters bound in white ribbon and the well-thumbed manual on infantry tactics from his days with the Kanawha Riflemen. In the future, when her children complained of hunger or fear or boredom, Sue would sternly place the shell fragment in their hands, or the gold coin or the bloody shirt, and they would know to hush up and abide.

Willie Glassell returned to The Meadows after the surrender of General Johnston on April 26, 1865. Arriving in an old Confederate ambulance drawn by two horses, he and Peter loaded the wagon with the Pattons' belongings, then piled in with Sue, the four children, old Mr. Glassell, and the slave Mary, and drove to Madison County where they occupied a gutted colonial plantation called Woodberry Forest. There they found the corpses of two Yankee soldiers, one in the front hall, the other wedged in a second-floor window, "wedged" because it was so swollen with decay that it was necessary to pry it through the window with a crowbar. It was Peter and George William's task to haul the bodies to an outlying field and bury them. Peter dug the trench as George William stripped the bodies of their clothing, which he then burned. Should rains ever wash out the grave and expose the remains, the family might be accused of murdering Yankees. Naked, the bodies could never be identified.

Having helped the Pattons resettle, Peter said good-bye and walked out of their lives a free man. Certainly one reason he'd returned was to collect some back pay owed him by the late colonel. Since that pay was less than the value of the colonel's horse (which Peter easily might have kept), the Pattons believed that he'd returned out of loyalty to and perhaps even love for his master. The notion fit their worldview and also helped bolster it in the face of their drastic comedown. Virtual paupers now, their cherished southern society shattered and discredited, still they felt high class at heart.

They were joined at Woodberry Forest by Peggy Patton and her son Hugh, the latter badly wounded in the war and not capable of physical work. Willie Glassell was scarcely in better shape, but to him fell the duty of providing food for the family. A seaman most of his life, he knew nothing about farming; his meticulous journal of his seeding and harvesting of a meager patch of bottom land bespoke a beginner trying his best. The two ambulance horses pulled his plow. His nephew walked behind, "dropping corn in the furrows and covering it up with my bare feet."

Willie was a savior during the next eighteen months at Woodberry Forest. Feeding the family in the Civil War's desolate aftermath would be his life's last great endeavor, a fact he had to concede when "two mysterious strangers" arrived one day and spoke to him in private. They were representatives of the government of Chile, then at war with Spain. They offered Willie the command of a new Chilean warship and the rank of admiral in their navy. He turned down the offer, citing family obligations—but he was in no condition to fight. In addition to skin rot and nervous exhaustion he was suffering from the early stages of tuberculosis contracted in prison. When in the fall of 1866 his brother Andrew mailed Willie six hundred dollars to pay for the family's journey to California, where Andrew lived, Willie put the money in his sister's hands. She'd headed the family in her husband's absence and would head it from now on; her brother, increasingly frail and sick, became another of her responsibilities along with her father and four children. But to acknowledge his effort in saving them all from starvation, Sue placed Willie's farm journal in the tin box beside her husband's mementos.

Peggy and Hugh Patton did not leave Virginia with Sue and the family. Peggy, who'd never been close to her daughter-in-law, gave Sue a parting gift that seemed to admit this lapse: Peggy gave Sue Tazewell's deathbed letter. It went into the tin box, which by now had become much more than the family reliquary; it was like one of those cases of portable implements of worship that clergymen bring on housecalls to bedridden congregants. The family's whole idea of itself was contained in the tin box. Locked tight and safe in Sue's steamer trunk, that idea would be carried intact from out of the wreckage of the Confederate South to the new land of California, where it would be released like a genie from its bottle to make somebody's dream come true.

Sue's hardest farewell was for the slave Mary. They'd been together since childhood, when Mary had been given to Sue as a playmate and also her property. Invited to accompany the family west after the war, Mary declined. Sue gave her some of the money her brother Andrew had sent from California. The women embraced. Later, as the Pattons and Glassells were leaving for the train station, Mary ran up with a box of toys purchased for the children with the money Sue had just given her. For the rest of her life Sue would have a recurrent dream where Mary was hurriedly packing Sue's bags in preparation for Sue's leaving to join her wounded husband, whom Sue never caught up with and so never, not even in dreams, saw his face again.

The family left New York aboard the *Arizona* in November 1866. En route to California, dinners at the captain's table were full of tension between "we Southerners" and two Union generals and their wives. One general, according to Sue, had a face of "relentless cruelty" and a personality to match, while the other was "more magnanimous." The latter's wife tried to befriend George William, asking if he would let her kiss him. The boy "refused most positively and said he would never kiss a Yankee, at which she seemed highly amused, and asked if all Southern boys were as smart as he." George William was angry. The Yankees had killed his father and uncle. He wouldn't soon forgive them.

Those deaths were two of many childhood blows that had indoctrinated

George William to the power of fate over life. Buffeted by all the reloca-
tions from town to town and county to county as battles had swept across
northern Virginia, numbed by all the indiscriminate death he'd seen in the
hospitals and along the roadsides, the boy had become passive before life's
blows. This passivity clashed with the example of his father, whose action
and dash he desired to emulate. Even in life the colonel had seemed a
romantic figure; his death by a Yankee cannonball added glorious tragedy
to that impression, making him, as his son wrote later, "one of our martyrs
of the lost cause." Just as that cannonball forever froze the colonel at age
thirty-one, so did it freeze George William, at least in part, in the role of
a starry-eyed boy.

His introduction to California wasn't promising. He nearly died of
typhoid soon after arriving at his uncle's house in Los Angeles. When well
enough to venture out for the first time, he unknowingly strolled by a
Catholic church without removing his cap and was beaten up by a local
Mexican boy who'd taken offense. Later while taking another walk he was
pushed aside by a man running desperately from a pursuing mob. The man
was caught and dragged screaming to a tall iron gate of a lumberyard. A
rope was thrown over the arch of the gate and he was strung up on the spot,
his legs and arms flailing for several minutes. That night the boy told his
mother that he missed Virginia and wanted to go home.

Sue, the children, and her father were living in two rooms of Andrew
Glassell's house in Los Angeles. (Willie had gone on to Santa Cruz to try
his luck as a rancher.) Andrew was rebuilding his law practice after having
been disbarred during the Civil War for not taking the U.S. oath of
allegiance. With six children of her own and another on the way, Andrew's
wife, Lucy, made clear her dissatisfaction with this housing arrangement.
Sue understood. "I am determined to put my shoulder to the wheel and do
all in my power to avoid being a burden." For the first time in her life she
cleaned rooms ("except slops") and did laundry. She gave weekly sewing
lessons, and three months later, though she'd never had any formal education, she opened a private school for girls, enrolling eleven students for
three dollars each per month. Her daughter Nellie described her as "always
exhausted," but Sue was bent on "living independently if it is possible." By
July the enrollment had grown to eighteen. Within a year she was able to
rent a small adobe house for herself and her children.

Skeptical of the quality of local public schools, she smuggled George
William into her own school by growing his hair long and clothing him in
dresses. His apple cheeks, caused by frequent fevers, promoted the ruse.

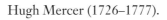

Hugh Mercer (1726–1777).

John Mercer Patton, his wife,
Peggy, and their daughter,
Eliza, circa 1855.

Robert Patton (1745?–1828).

George Smith Patton I, Virginia
Military Institute, class of 1852.

Waller Tazewell Patton
(1835–1863).

William Thornton Glassell
(1832–1876).

Susan Glassell Patton and her son,
George, Los Angeles, 1866.

Virginia Military Institute, class of 1877. George Smith Patton II ("Papa") is at left.

Ruth Wilson, circa 1884.

Anne Wilson ("Nannie"), circa 1884.

George Smith Patton, Jr. ("Georgie"),
San Gabriel, 1886.

Ruth Patton with her children,
Georgie and Anne ("Nita"), 1895.

Georgie and Nita at Lake Vineyard, 1893.

The front parlor at Lake Vineyard.

Georgie in his bedroom, circa 1899.

Georgie, Los Angeles, 1900.

Beatrice Ayer, Boston, 1902.

The Pattons and assorted relatives, Catalina Island, 1902. Georgie is sitting on the grass at far right. The woman farthest to the left is Beatrice Ayer; Nita Patton is sitting next to her. Seated at center are Beatrice's parents, Ellen and Frederick Ayer. Standing at rear center is Nannie Wilson; the white-haired man next to her is Georgie's step-grandfather, Colonel George Hugh Smith, formerly of the Confederate Army. *(Photograph courtesy of the General Phineas Banning Residence Museum)*

The Patton family, West Point, 1906: Ruth, Nita, Papa, and Georgie.

Georgie, at right, the summer after his West Point graduation, 1909.

Beatrice and Georgie at
their wedding, 1910.

Beatrice and Georgie,
Lake Vineyard, 1911.

His persistent ill health gave rise to fears that he'd contracted TB from Willie Glassell. The boy was never diagnosed; wartime glimpses of wounds and amputations had inspired his hysterical dread of doctors. Like leaving his beloved Virginia and being made to wear a dress each schoolday, susceptibility to illness seemed one more trial to endure. By summer, however, he was relieved to be deemed too tall to be disguised as a girl any longer.

Southern California was becoming an increasingly popular destination for former Confederates seeking new lives out west. This was good news to Sue, whose chief complaint was of an "utter lack of society." She brought her isolation on herself, keeping a cool distance not only from the local Mexicans and Indians, but from most of the whites as well. When she said that she longed for "congenial spirits," she meant white Protestant southerners. Sue's snobbery was in compensation for her reduced circumstances; she instilled that snobbery in her children in the form of family pride both overweening and tenuous, blithely arrogant and easily bruised. The best that any Patton could aspire to was embodied in their ancestry, she instructed her children. Its excellence could not be surpassed. It could be matched, perhaps; or it could be disgraced. "Ma is one," George William wrote a cousin, "who never feels satisfied unless her children stand highest."

A few weeks after his eleventh birthday, the boy made a surprising request of his mother. He asked to be allowed to change his name from George William to George *Smith* Patton. Sue hesitated. No one in her universe stood higher than her late husband. Favoring her other son, Glassell, Sue doubted whether George William could live up to his father's name. When at last she consented to rechristen him, he was ecstatic yet apprehensive: "I only hope I may be worthy of it."

Ultimately the name change would have a paradoxical effect on the boy. It confirmed his tendency to overly inflate the images of people he perceived to be his betters, staking out other men's shadows as the place he felt most comfortable in. Yet too, it initiated an adolescent blooming that seemed in no way coincidental. Described in the past as sickly, weepy, insecure, young George grew tall and began to excel in school. He helped his mother run the house and her school, and took a job cleaning their local church. His status as the emergent star of the family was cemented in near-tragedy when Glassell, while flying a kite off the roof of a stable, fell and severely injured his head. It would later be said that the injury stunted Glassell's growth and rendered him haplessly eccentric. Everyone loved

Glassell. "Full of fun and very gentle, he could arrange pillows better than a woman"—and when drunk he would give away all his money to fellow patrons of the bar. Everyone loved him, but no one expected him to amount to anything. That expectation was now on George, the late great colonel's namesake.

"My heart still clings to Virginia and I often long to be back there." But, Sue prophesied, "My destiny is sealed and here I shall live and die." Her health was fragile and she looked much older than her thirty-two years, bone thin, dark circles around her eyes, her unhappiness highlighted by the black dresses she wore each day. Anxious about illness and earthquakes (from which she feared "not so much death, but being mangled"), her constant hope was that her orphaned children might be reared in Virginia. After enduring the shortages of the war years, she had thrilled at California's abundant fruits and vegetables; the thrill had since faded to where she was "so tired of eating oranges that I do not take the trouble to peel one to eat." Though enrollment at her school was growing, she cleared little after expenses. "Hard work and poor pay is my experience in teaching." Her house in Charleston had been sold at a pittance and only half the proceeds forwarded to her. She sent achingly discreet pleas for money to relatives back home, and could not suppress her anger that "my children have never received a cent from their father's mother since his death." She walked the floor of her schoolroom after-hours, "pressing my head between my hands" and praying aloud for "the all important love and peace denied me." And she sank into depression each anniversary of the battle of Winchester. "This is the saddest time of the year to me and I feel like a stricken, broken down woman when I remember the fell blow that came upon me . . . blotting out the light of my life for me, and sending me and mine forth in the world homeless wanderers."

Her interest in church matters revived her spirits for a time. She spoke highly of a new preacher from Kentucky who'd founded a church society for ladies that convened weekly at Sue's school, himself presiding. Before long, however, he "turned out a regular scamp. . . . Among other sins, drunkenness was by no means worst." Sue herself had come to appreciate the medicinal comforts of alcohol, taking "whiskey three times a day, beginning before breakfast." George, whom she now termed "a very uncommon boy . . . he grows astonishingly in mind and body," prepared his mother's morning eggnog. Sheepishly she asked a friend, "Don't you fear I will become intemperate?"

But finally it wasn't liquor or religion or even her son's accomplishments that led Sue to see her new life more positively. Her husband's first cousin George Hugh Smith recently had joined his brother Isaac in California. (Isaac had transcribed Tazewell Patton's deathbed letter, now stored in Sue's tin box.) At the close of the Civil War, Smith had refused to swear allegiance to the restored Union. He and some other unreconstructed Rebels had ridden to Mexico to become cotton planters. Failing at this, Smith wrote his brother to ask about any employment opportunities in California for a former Virginia lawyer. Isaac found him a job in Andrew Glassell's firm, and the connection was made: George Smith, after losing Sue to his friend George Patton seventeen years earlier, was united with her at last. Before long she was again "becoming interested in those around me," and observing happily that the pleasant time she spent in Smith's company "reminds me so of home and dear ones in Virginia."

She noted that Smith, who'd come here broke, was making one hundred dollars a month at her brother's law firm with good prospects for being offered a partnership. The partnership came through, Sue's black attire brightened, and she and Smith were married in 1870. A week after the wedding, Susie Patton, six years old, ran into their bedroom to wish "Cousin George" good night. "He is 'Papa' to you now," her mother corrected. Susie considered. "Good night, Papa," she said after a moment, following her mother's lead in finally putting the past behind them.

The Patton children came to adore George Smith—the only time he punished one of them was for being cruel to a dog. His wartime reputation had blended fury and chivalry; it was said he fed his prisoners before he fed his own men. His stepdaughter Nellie called him "a man of remarkable physique, whose proportions and powers were in correspondence to his mental gifts." But far from replacing Colonel Patton as the honored family patriarch, he went out of his way to keep alive the children's memory of their natural father, to polish Patton's myth with the glow of personal witness. It was through him that the children learned the details of their father's wartime exploits. And it was George Smith, being greatly interested in history and world affairs, who first put Patton's life and death in a context of military tradition. The family had always considered its sons to have taken up arms only in times of their nation's need. Smith cast them as natural-born warriors, as models of military professionalism. Enthralled, his eldest stepson decided that he, like his father, would attend the Virginia Military Institute—but not with the intention, like his father, of returning to civilian life. George would seek an officer's commission and become a career soldier.

*   *   *

At thirteen, George was described in a Los Angeles newspaper as a high school debater "of great force and polish." After returning to Virginia in 1872 to prepare for VMI's entrance examinations, he turned his speaking talent to entertaining his cousins at The Meadows with tales of the exotic West Coast: how violets grew as tall as flagpoles, and how when you chopped down a California pine "the people in China had to be warned . . . to keep clear of the upper branches." George entered the Institute in 1873, gaining one of the state scholarships reserved for sons of killed Confederate officers.

As an underclassman at VMI he often was asked to address local civic groups as a kind of Institute ambassador. Two such speeches were titled "To Memory" and "Auld Lang Syne," topics suited to his sentimental nature. The first speech began, "For some, the past, with all that lulls and soothes the troubled heart, is the theme that most affects." The latter closed by challenging listeners to live life with vigor so that someday, when old, "you may sit and dream of the past, and as you dream, may smile."

George's rhetoric was most flamboyant when conjuring images, still fresh and raw, of Virginia's calamitous "struggle for liberty" in the Civil War of a decade ago. Sometimes those images drew from experience, as when he described a soldier's family joyfully reading news accounts of a victorious battle until "at length the list of killed is reached. One glance and then—Oh! God." His evocations of war scenes he'd never witnessed aimed for similar impact: "See them again! Hear their dear thin singing voices cheering them on to the charge, see their swords flashing through the dust and smoke of battle, see them as they dash like a whirlwind down the valley. Where are they now? Every battlefield from Pennsylvania to the Gulf announces, 'Here!' "

This paean to (as he once termed it) "grand, glorious, yet terrible and gloomy war," was more accurately a paean to his dead father, whose memory haunted George through his college years like a ghost at his shoulder. While fitting George for his cadet uniform, the Institute's old tailor confirmed in his records that the boy's measurements matched his father's exactly. During a summer spent at the White Sulphur Springs resort, which gave cadets free room and board to provide dance partners for local girls, young men being scarce in those parts after the war, George was hailed as "Colonel Patton!" by a retired Confederate general he'd never met before, so striking was the resemblance. White Sulphur Springs was near the site of his father's battle at Dry Creek, and one day an old woman invited George to her house, where his father had breakfasted that morning in 1863, leaping from her window when his aides outside had shouted, "The Yankees are coming!" The colonel had barely escaped the enemy patrol and had to return later to retrieve his saber, "which the lady of the house had secreted under the mattress." She showed young George the mattress, the window, the breakfast table, with the pride of someone who has entertained a hero in her home.

After the war, there had been talk of retrieving his uncle Tazewell Patton's body from its vault in Baltimore, where Isaac Smith had placed it after Gettysburg, and burying it at VMI. The move was delayed, memories faded, and Tazewell remained up north. Here was George's chance to become a kind of hero himself. For years just a bystander to the extraordinary upheaval around him, now he could step up and contribute. With the help of Tazewell's brother John, George arranged to bring the body to Virginia for burial at Winchester's newly dedicated Confederate Cemetery, side by side with George's father.

He went alone by train to Baltimore, wearing his gray cadet uniform, the only formal clothes he owned. On the return trip he sat in the dark of the baggage car on top of his uncle's casket. Rather than pride or even unease, loneliness overwhelmed the young man. He felt as forgotten and lost as his uncle's body had been, lying ten years in a burial vault etched with another man's name. The train was delayed at several stops and was hours late into Winchester. Night had fallen, and George assumed that his Uncle John's arrangements to have him met at the station had fallen through. A steady rain drummed the top of the railcar. Having intended this gesture to help set the past right, George feared it was all turning wrong.

At Winchester, the doors of the baggage car clanged open. A tight huddle of men stood on the train platform, the light of their lanterns rippling on their oilskin ponchos. George became frightened. If his uncle had not properly cleared Tazewell's transfer to Virginia (a delicate matter given the still volatile postwar feeling), then George was at risk of arrest. "Who are you?" he called. "What do you want?" One of the men stepped forward and unbuttoned his poncho. Underneath he was wearing the full dress uniform of a Confederate Army officer, a criminal offense in itself. Wordlessly the other men boarded the train and carried Tazewell's casket to a mule-drawn wagon at the end of the platform. Behind the wagon, at silent attention in the falling rain, was an elderly soldier carrying a muffled drum and a flag bearer holding high the outlawed Stars and Bars.

George and the others walked behind the makeshift cortege to the Confederate Cemetery. A trench already had been dug beside his father's grave. As Tazewell's coffin was lowered inside, it jammed against the dirt walls and was lifted out again. George took a shovel and climbed down into the hole to widen it. Someone held a lantern above him, and it was then that George, glancing up, made out through the flickering light the exposed length of the adjacent buried casket directly in front of his eyes. The wood planks along the side of the casket, ten years in the ground, had rotted away, revealing the face and shoulders of the figure contained inside: his father.

What did you see? What did he look like? For the rest of his life, whenever George recounted this story, these questions would understandably follow. People have recalled George replying variously that his father's beard was long; that his father was in uniform, with gold brocade at his throat; that all he could see in the dimness was his father's "noble brow." But one of his answers seemed to supersede the others. "He looked," George said, "exactly as I remembered him." It is the kind of answer someone might give who'd been too shocked, too taken aback, to really take a good look at his father's ten-year-old corpse. And it is the kind of answer someone might give who in fact had examined the thing quite closely, and now, describing the moment all these years later, saw no need to get specific. "He looked exactly as I remembered him," George would tell his children and grandchildren, who thus did clearly understand that their ancestor must have looked great.

As time went by, the notion arose that George's teenage experience at Winchester was the climactic event of his life, that nothing he might accomplish in the future could equal the wonder of that night. A harsh judgment, George strove for more than fifty years to prove it wrong, though his labors were made more difficult for having passed it on himself.

☆ ☆ **7** ☆ ☆

Playing Tiger

HE eldest of Peggy Patton's eight sons, the no-account Robert, died of drink in 1876. Her five other surviving sons resumed their lives in the transformed world of the postwar South. Isaac Patton became mayor of New Orleans. When President Ulysses Grant later visited the city, Isaac rode beside him in a parade down Bourbon Street. A Rebel diehard stepped from the crowd and hurled a brick at Grant, who, Isaac reported with admiration, did not flinch as it zipped past his head. Brother Hugh became a clerk in the Virginia Senate; it was said that he broke his mother's heart with his intemperance. James became a judge on the West Virginia Supreme Court and died a year later of heart failure. William was a professor of engineering at the Virginia Military Institute and later at Virginia Polytechnic. John Patton lived at The Meadows, practicing law and, as the eldest responsible sibling, caring for the clan's unbowed, unregenerate matriarch.

Peggy Patton died in 1873, not long after her sixteen-year-old grandson George Smith Patton II returned east from California to enter VMI. Though he remembered her from his childhood in wartime Virginia, George's impression of his grandmother had since been negatively colored by his mother, Sue, who believed her own privations as a Civil War widow had been ignored by Peggy Patton out of miserliness and unfeeling.

A well-spoken, outwardly confident young man, George carried a skittish streak left over from his traumatic childhood, a streak that his grandmother, a scary old battle-ax dressed in black, provoked to awe and trembling. Shortly before her death, Peggy and George were seated together in a buggy after Sunday church. A dignified old gentleman—a former Confederate colonel—tipped his hat to Peggy as he rode by on his horse. "Tell me, Colonel," she asked him abruptly, "did you say 'amen' when the minister prayed for 'the president of the United States and all others in authority?'"

The gentleman nodded carefully, knowing she'd lost two sons to the Yankees. "Yes, ma'am, I did. The war is over, after all."

Peggy pursed her lips in silence. Suddenly she seized George's buggy whip and lashed it across the colonel's face. "Drive on," she told her grandson sternly, handing him back his whip. Clearly, the war wasn't over for her. George, amazed by her feisty example, did not wish it to be over for him, either. His grandmother's relentless loathing for Yankees seemed a fit tribute to her martyred sons, George's father and his Uncle Tazewell. George wanted to be as tough as Peggy, as proud. If it wasn't in his nature to be so, then he would *change* his nature and reinvent himself as the kind of stalwart man he admired.

On a July afternoon four years later, George attempted to embody his ideal of such a man in a valedictory speech delivered to VMI's class of 1877. He opened with a gloomy description of the auditorium in which the graduation ceremony was taking place, its walls "still scarred and blackened" from the torches of Union invaders, "continually reminding the sons of the South that their fathers once dared to strike for Liberty." He told his fellow graduates,

We do not look out today on a land flowing with milk and honey, great and prosperous as of yore; we see on the other hand sad and mournful evidence of the terrible war which inflicted such deep and ghastly wounds on the fair bosom of our beloved land. We see a people who manfully adhered to principle ground and oppressed by those who never owned a principle save that of expediency. . . . *Expediency:* that vile goddess of the North!

The anger of George's speech arose from his personal loss in the war and from "the ten years horror of Reconstruction," as he later termed it, which began when the withdrawing Union Army was replaced by "noncombatant scavengers and camp followers," the infamous carpetbaggers who exploited the poverty of the defeated whites and the sudden, unaccustomed freedom of the land's four million former slaves. No doubt these grievances were shared by his audience and instantly understood. He could rage at northern "expediency" throughout the speech without ever defining it. He could vaguely trumpet southern principle as "all that remains of our Old English Conservatism . . . the tradition of a people reaching back to Saxon England . . . who look down on us from heaven and blush for our shame." Stirring words to these downbeaten southern aristocrats, the speech was a great success. George's classmates cheered his exhortation to "imitate the conduct of our heroes of old," which is precisely what he was doing in his speech. He was imitating his father's passionate Virginia patriotism. And he was imitating the grim adherence to "principle" of his grandmother Peggy Patton.

His speech rang truer in its quieter moments. He reflected on his four years at college as "a sweet and long-remembered dream." He paid homage to the ceremony's guest of honor, Virginia Governor James Kemper, who'd been Tazewell Patton's brigade commander at Gettysburg. Most movingly, he expressed his thoughts about leaving "the little college world" for the larger world ahead: "Youth is proverbially the season of intense passions . . . when the heart is most open, the sensibilities most alive to deep and lasting impressions: as we grow older we grow colder, more reserved and more skeptical concerning the virtue of our fellow men. . . . No wonder that we shudder and shrink from uttering the last farewells."

George cherished his youth and hated to see it pass. But in fact it already had passed long before that day. As a boy during the war he'd seen too much death and experienced too much sorrow to preserve uncalloused the optimism of youth. "Somehow," he wrote a few years later, "the spring and elasticity of my nature have been impaired." In the future he would veer uncertainly between the ennui of a prematurely aged young man and the drum-beating passion that he believed an essential trait of a person of backbone and action. Often when he exhibited such passion it was a performance like much of his valedictory speech, hollow at its core and enacted clumsily, like a dancer straining to move with grace to an alien melody.

Becoming a soldier like his father had been an ambition of George in his college years. But after staying on at the Institute for a year to teach French, he returned to California to begin his newly avowed profession as an attorney. His relatives assumed that he'd abandoned his military ambition out of family obligation, with good reason. His mother, Sue, had had two children with her second husband, George Smith, bringing to five the number of children at home. Sue's father had died of old age, but she still was supporting her brother Willie—the former Confederate naval hero now was in full-time treatment for tuberculosis at a California sanatorium. Smith's law firm was struggling, and lately Sue had been weakened by illness. Her eldest son felt compelled to go help them.

Another man might have chosen more selfishly, and in the future George often wondered if perhaps he'd let himself down by not pursuing his ambition no matter the consequences to his loved ones. Had he yielded too easily? Conditioned as a youngster to accept the turns of fate passively, had he secretly welcomed the excuse of family necessity to choose a stable civilian life in Los Angeles rather than brave the upheaval and risk of a military career? His mixed feelings on his decision haunted him, imbuing him with a child's adventure book romanticism that he never outgrew. All that was mundane and dull about his existence was, he imagined, paralleled by a road not taken, an alternate, undoubtedly more exciting life in the profession of arms.

His return to California in 1878 forced his breakup with Maggie French, a distant cousin with whom he was in love; this too weighed on him when he reflected on his past. Even several years after settling down to his job as an attorney in his stepfather's firm, he considered brashly throwing it over, arranging to get an officer's commission in, of all things, the British Army based in Egypt. At that time, northeast Africa was perhaps the world's hottest spot for "grand, glorious" war, with the British occupation under endless attack by Moslem insurgents. He was all set to join the command of England's Colonel William Hicks, to leap headlong into glamorous danger as young men have often done—but at the last minute he again decided to stay home and care for his now severely ill mother. Later, in early 1884, Hicks and his men were slaughtered in the Sudan. George learned too that his former fiancée, Maggie French, had died suddenly in New York. His boyhood sense of fate's dominant hand struck him with new force. Surrendering to circumstance, choosing always for family over private ambition—this, and not some dreamy heroic adventure, seemed George's evident destiny. Though never completely content with his lot, in time he grew into it as into a suit of clothes that, once ill fitting, eventually prove the tailor a seer.

If at heart he was a quiet, rather docile man, his early public reputation tilted so far and so fiercely the other way as to imply he was overcompensating for the lack of fire in his nature. As a lawyer in private practice and later as Los Angeles district attorney, he was a tough courtroom battler and a vehement, some said "incendiary," spokesman for California's Democratic Party. As DA, he fought to limit the power of Collis P. Huntington's Southern Pacific Railroad, which controlled all rail transportation to and from Los Angeles. Much of his passion for this fight derived from its usual wellspring: the past. The railroads were aligned with the Republican Party, predominate in northern California, and which, on a national level, had held the White House since the Civil War, when the largely Democratic southern states had damned themselves (and their political party) by supporting secession and slavery. Though George had publicly repudiated the Confederate cause, his sentimental attachment to its martyrs still smoldered inside him.

The high emotional pitch of his debates with the railroad and with state Republicans suggested he was fighting as much to settle old scores as to make specific policy points. In 1884, he vigorously supported Grover Cleveland for president. Taunted by their Republican opponents as former traitors and slavemasters, Democrats were desperate to put one of their own in the White House and so begin to emerge from twenty years of political probation. For several days after the November election, votes were counted and recounted. Charges of fraud escalated on both sides. George took the podium at a local rally and according to the pro-Republican *Los Angeles Times,* declared that "Cleveland and [vice-president] Hendrick have been elected by five millions of white people in the United States, and we will inaugurate them, or we will make the streets of Washington run knee-deep in blood!"

Newspapers throughout the state condemned "the young Democrat rooster" for "trying to play the played-out role of fire-eater." His uncharacteristically crude rhetoric, issuing less from principle than from callow emotion, seemed obviously forced. On the political stump George was like a would-be seducer who camouflages his insecurity by pouring on the smooth talk and cologne; and like that seducer, he'd fallen on his face. The *Times* noted his retraction a week later, when he said that "some mistaken parties had accused him of being blood-thirsty, but no man felt less so than he. It is time," George had continued, "that the memory of Sumter, Gettysburg, and Appomattox be forgotten." On November 16, Cleveland was finally declared the winner. The Democrats saw it as redemption. George saw it as a duty fulfilled. His father, himself a staunch Democrat and southern partisan who'd lain now two decades in a soldier's grave in Virginia, surely would have been proud.

The widespread reputation George gained during the election was not soon forgotten. It was mentioned in the *Arizona Citizen,* December 27, 1884: "The rash young orator in Los Angeles who proposed making the streets of Washington run deep with blood, if necessary, to inaugurate Grover Cleveland, has been overtaken by a terrible retribution. He has got married."

Benjamin Davis Wilson, a prosperous vintner, cattleman, and state politician, at one time owned nearly 20,000 acres in and around Los Angeles. He sold off much of his land and moved out of the city after the economic boom of the 1849 California gold rush brought an escalation in local crime. Vigilante groups had adopted Wilson's front yard tree as a convenient gallows, and too many mornings he awoke to find a corpse swinging outside his bedroom window.

Recently married to his second wife, the former Margaret Hereford of St. Louis, he desired more peaceful surroundings in which to raise his young daughter and son from his first marriage and to start a new family with Margaret. He built a $20,000 adobe ranch house on 2,000 acres of citrus groves in nearby San Gabriel. The land included a small reservoir, inspiring Wilson to name his estate Lake Vineyard. His daughters Nannie and Ruth were born there. Removed from the hubbub of Los Angeles, the girls became each other's closest companion; and there George Patton would call on them one day with an invitation to dance.

Tutored at home in piano, languages, and literature, the girls had different reactions to their sheltered existence. Ruth accepted it placidly. Her sister was restive. "I know it is wrong to feel this way," Nannie wrote, "no cares, no anxieties in the world, but I want something *more."* Three years older than Ruth, Nannie dominated her in the small decisions of how to occupy their languid days. She was alternately adoring and critical of Lake Vineyard's qualities as an insular paradise. Her ambivalence was reflected in her vision of the future. She couldn't imagine ever leaving the ranch, yet she feared that spending her life there would bring her no joy, turning her instead into "a cross, unloved, unloving old maid. That is the future I see before me."

The sisters' one escape from the lovely but isolated Lake Vineyard was imagination. Both enjoyed the literature of chivalry and make-believe ("trashy," Nannie admitted, though she read it "a great deal"). These sentimental inclinations colored their view of their father, whose business and political ventures paled in their minds beside the tales of his early exploits as a fur trapper, Indian fighter, and as a soldier in California's fight for independence from Mexico. They considered him the romantic embodiment of Horace Greeley's admonition, "Go west, young man, and grow up with the country." In fact, Wilson had migrated west from his birthplace in Mississippi and struggled for wealth for reasons of unremarkable need. Orphaned as a boy, he was sickly, alone, and dirt poor.

Despite his success, Wilson was a melancholy man who increasingly tended to dwell on his troubles as he grew old. His first wife, the daughter of a Mexican land baron, died at twenty-one from complications of her third pregnancy. His son of that marriage, named Johnny, was a hard-drinking ne'er-do-well. His daughter Sue had married an ambitious, flamboyant businessman named James de Barth Shorb; she and her husband were impatient to take over Wilson's wine and citrus businesses. As Wilson neared sixty, he looked to his two young daughters from his second marriage to give him the uncomplicated devotion that his older children did not. And Nannie and Ruth complied. He became their darling "Don Benito," the affectionate title his Mexican friends had bestowed on him in California's frontier days.

Wilson had long wished to see Los Angeles become a world-class seaport. In 1870 he emerged from pastoral retirement at Lake Vineyard to lobby Congress for funds to dredge the harbor; his pride in this effort was forever dampened by the suicide of his son, Johnny, just weeks before the appropriation was approved. On the afternoon of March 9, 1878, he and Nannie stopped their buggy at the home of the district's new state senator, George Hugh Smith, and his wife, Sue, to get the latest news on the harbor development. During the visit Wilson experienced a dizzy spell and asked to lie down. He continued to feel unwell throughout the next day, and that night he suffered a heart attack.

Nannie heard her father climb from his bed and collapse to the floor. She was up and running from her bedroom down the hall when she heard her mother cry out. Wilson lay against his bedroom door and it took all Nannie's strength ("God gave it to me") to force the door open. Her father's hands and feet were ice cold. He couldn't catch his breath. Ruth appeared. Wilson gazed up at his younger daughter and gasped, "Pray for me." More words came in a hoarse whisper. Nannie knelt low to catch them. Wilson called for his mother. Then he called for his dead son. "Where is Johnny? I want Johnny!" Nannie and Ruth listened in anguish until his voice quieted and he fell into a raspy sleep. They lifted him into bed, where he died sometime before dawn. As sunrise swept across Lake Vineyard the first of Wilson's Mexican farmhands came into the bedroom, as Nannie described it, "to say *adios* to his old *Patron.*"

A procession of seventy-five carriages followed Wilson's hearse from Lake Vineyard to the small cemetery adjoining San Gabriel's Church of Our Saviour. Senator Smith was unable to attend the funeral. Standing in for him, recently returned from the Virginia Military Institute, was his stepson George Patton.

"Beautiful dark eyes with long black lashes, a Grecian nose, fine eyebrows . . . dark brown curly hair, a soft mustache of the same color, and a sweet but manly voice." Written by Ruth a month later, the description was not specifically of Patton but rather a model of the man she fantasized marrying someday; yet it rather fit the twenty-two-year-old former cadet. If in her grief Ruth hadn't noticed George at her father's funeral, certainly she did in the days afterward when neighbors and friends called on the Wilsons to offer their condolences.

Nannie noticed him, too. But unlike Ruth, she didn't project him (not consciously anyway) into marriage material. She'd predicted in her diary the year before that she would never marry, for "the kind of man I would marry, and could love, I am afraid would never care for me." She would rather, Nannie wrote, adore "my ideal" from afar, "and never have him care a bit for me," than settle for the love of someone less worthy. And she trusted that if she never wed, then her sister likewise would remain single, would remain Nannie's "ever present cherished companion" so that they might spend the rest of their lives together at Lake Vineyard.

The sisters lived at home with their mother, who grew increasingly distant from them, lost in fitful contemplations of Jesus and in various nervous disorders. The family's finances were managed by Benjamin Wilson's son-in-law, James de Barth Shorb, who'd parlayed his interest in the Wilson enterprises to a $2 million fortune; he, his wife, Sue, and their nine surviving children lived in a Victorian mansion, traveled in a luxurious private railroad car, and threw parties that were the talk of Los Angeles. Nannie was fond of Shorb ("I like to talk to him, he repeats pretty verses of poetry"); Ruth was not. No one, least of all Nannie, imagined that Ruth had any particular opinion about Shorb or much else. Inscrutable and laconic, plumply maternal whereas Nannie was edgy and lithe, Ruth was considered by more than a few people to be on the simple side.

George Patton didn't see it that way. Nannie noted his visits with pleasure, describing him as "a splendid talker, he is so smart and well read."

When he asked Ruth out to dance, Nannie couldn't comprehend the implication. Nannie was nearer his age—and she was prettier and smarter than Ruth, everyone thought so. She rationalized that he was seeking in Ruth "a distraction or something of that sort." Yes, that was it. Ruth's serene, simple nature would be just the antidote for any young man in mourning for his mother.

When Sue Patton Smith died of breast cancer at age forty-eight, she was a far different person from the shallow, pampered plantation belle she'd been twenty years earlier in the antebellum South. In addition to the hardships of the Civil War and its immediate aftermath, she since had lost her young son with George Smith to lockjaw; and her brother Willie Glassell finally had succumbed to tuberculosis in 1879. The former naval officer never shed his bitterness over the war. "Nearly everything I had in the world was lost," he wrote in his last weeks, "even the commission I had received for gallant and meritorious conduct, and I possess not even a token of esteem from those for whom I fought, to leave, when I die, to those I love."

All of these sorrows had conditioned Sue to self-reliance, which even thirteen years into her second marriage she was loath to relinquish. By all accounts she loved George Smith a lot. Still, in April 1883, when her breast was removed under a crude chloroform anesthetic, she asked that he *not* accompany her to San Francisco for the operation. Her doctor broke the news to her husband, softening the blow by explaining that Smith's presence at the mastectomy "can do no good. You will feel so acutely miserable that no words may describe your condition. She wishes to be alone and I think her wishes should be respected."

Sue would not be alone. At her request, her daughter Nellie sat beside her throughout the procedure. Perhaps Nellie offered her a comforting reminder of her first husband, George Patton, as if the memory, or the example, of his suffering in Winchester in 1864 would somehow help her through this moment of her own agony. As the doctor applied his scalpel, she tightly clasped her daughter's hand and said, "Observe how a lady bears pain."

The cancer was not eradicated, and Sue died in Los Angeles the following November. Some years earlier, she'd asked a cousin in Virginia an odd earnest question: "How does the present status of Negroes affect society with you all? Does it make any material change? Write me on this point."

It was a subject that in her youth would never have occurred to Sue, who'd been raised to view blacks as furniture. Evidently her eyes had been opened over the course of her life to a more enlightened, more inquiring view, a possibility enforced by the testimony of her son George.

During her last days alive he was sitting at her bedside when he heard his mother distinctly murmur, "Mary," the name of the woman who had been Sue's property from childhood through the war years. The twisted protocol between slave owner and slave had obscured the closeness of the two women's long companionship. Yet through the smothering press of Sue's fading consciousness Mary's name had ascended like a bubble of air for this last acknowledgment.

The Pattons cherished their death scenes. How an ancestor died, with what words on his lips, what ravings or silence, was, in their view, as pertinent to that ancestor's life as any biographical fact. Those whose passing lacked provocative detail were often diminished in the family memory, as if to make a proper enduring myth a life must supply its own tag line. Sue's murmuring "Mary" provided such a detail. It wasn't necessary to analyze its meaning or even for it to have meaning. It need only possess mystery, an obscurely feasible logic that might imply human existence was somehow fated and so could bolster the Pattons' belief that God cared how they lived and died.

George first began sending notes to "My Dear Miss Wilson" several months after his mother's mastectomy. During the last of Sue's decline he made no efforts to conceal his gloom from Ruth, writing her that "my hope has vanished in the smoke whither so many have preceded it."

After Sue's death he unconvincingly affected an air of jaunty black humor to disguise his sorrow. Six months later he confessed to being "a little inconsistent in failing to live up to the high standard of cynicism which I once tried to set up—yet it is an inconsistency of which I am proud." Ruth was the reason. Her "unruffled temper" and "restful presence" had, he said, inspired "my metamorphosis." And though it took him a full month longer to get her to call him "George" and not "my dear Mister Patton," Ruth accepted his marriage proposal in May 1884. "The world bears a very different look from yesterday," he wrote her from his office the next day. His duties as district attorney forced them to conduct their engagement largely through the mail. But at last he was able to declare, "Only one night more and I can have a kiss from your lips and not the cold paper."

They were married on December 10, 1884. As he and Ruth prepared to board the train for their New Orleans honeymoon, they were confronted by Ruth's sister, Nannie, whose bags were packed and ready to go: Nannie intended to accompany the newlyweds on their honeymoon. The awkward moment was finessed somehow, and Nannie returned to Lake Vineyard with her mother.

That evening, as Nannie sat at her desk to write in her diary, the impact of the day's events struck her full force. She recalled her diary entry of seven years ago, written at an age when brazenly to predict that one will never marry is almost standard behavior for an attractive intelligent woman, but which now, at twenty-seven, rang with the finality of a slamming door: "My youth is slipping by fast and I begin to feel old already. . . . Oh, I wonder if I shall always go on this same way!"

Nannie had faithfully written in her diary every evening since childhood. That night she closed the volume without writing a word, never to resume it again. She walked from her bedroom to the front of the house. Out of a glass decanter she poured some brandy fermented at her father's San Gabriel winery. Drinking alone in the darkened parlor, Nannie was well on her way toward becoming a very strange woman. In time she would play a dominant part in the life of her family. But for now there was just the memory of the afternoon's wedding, her mind's image of George and Ruth Patton riding blissfully together on an eastbound train, and the liquid trickle and crystal clink of minutes and hours crawling by until finally she could sleep.

In July of the next year George was delivering his closing argument in a Los Angeles courtroom when suddenly he lost his air and fainted to the floor. The collapse focused everyone's concern on his health rather than on his wife's—Ruth was five months pregnant and bearing up just fine. On doctor's orders George spent a week at a mountain spa called Bartlett Springs. Ruth left their home in Los Angeles and went to stay with her mother and sister at Lake Vineyard. Her husband wrote her every day from the spa. Ruth, a bit irritated that the thrill and attention of carrying her first child had been undercut by George's dramatic breakdown, wrote him back only once.

George joined Ruth at Lake Vineyard, where he was tended side by side with his wife by his mother-in-law, an Irish nurse named Mary Scally, and above all Nannie, who gloried in her newfound sense of being needed, being necessary. As Ruth's due date approached, Nannie became so obsessive about Ruth resting and eating right as to give the impression that she regarded the baby as much her own as her sister's. During the birth on November 11, 1885, she was there with Ruth in the same bedroom where their father had died eight years before. The baby, a boy, wasn't named for Benjamin Wilson. It had long been decided to name him George Smith Patton, Junior—"Georgie."

Soon after his birth Georgie developed the croup. Fearing he would die unchristened, Georgie's nurse, a devout Irish Catholic, performed an emergency "citizen's baptism" by sprinkling water on the baby's brow when the rest of the family was out of the room. Eventually Georgie was baptized an Episcopalian at San Gabriel's Church of Our Saviour, but (so the story concludes) his nurse's clandestine action accounted for his later rapport with clergymen and especially with Catholic priests, whom he preferred to serve as his military chaplains because he considered them suitably militant.

He grew to be a large "almost painfully beautiful" infant (said Nannie): "curly golden hair, big blue eyes, a lovely nose and a sensitive, tender mouth." From the moment he could raise his head off the blanket he displayed an uncommon restlessness and physical energy, driving, it was said, the entire household to exhaustion. Everyone doted on him. Nannie often monopolized Georgie's care to the exclusion of his nurse and his mother. But no one doted on him more than his father, who cherished the boy as a gift of new life: his own.

Suddenly politics, the law, any obligation that took him away from his family, lost all appeal to George. "I would rather be home than anywhere else." Reveling in the discovery of himself as "a domestic animal," he tussled on the carpet with his baby son, just as many years earlier his Uncle Tazewell had tussled with George in the Patton home in Virginia. Tazewell had called the game "playing tiger," and that's what George now played for hours on end with Georgie—"the big man," "my big boy," "my dear little towhead"—who, incidentally, everyone commented, played tiger as though he were born to it.

Forty-two years later, Georgie Patton would write a lengthy memoir of his father, which by its closing lines had become a posthumous letter of love: "Oh! darling Papa I never called you that in life as both of us were too self-contained but you were and are my darling." Georgie's regret over not having expressed his love was needless. His father had known full well how his son felt and had returned those feelings tenfold. Though he continued as a businessman and as an occasional lawyer and politician;

though all his life he remained the son of a killed Confederate hero and the husband of a rich man's daughter, after 1885 these were eclipsed by the title Georgie conferred on him: "Darling Papa." Nothing else identified him more truly than this. Nothing else made him happier, nothing else more fulfilled him. Such an emotional investment has its price, however, and it was in the understanding that Papa somehow had paid it that Georgie concluded his long loving memoir with an apology.

God grant that you see and appreciate my very piteous attempt to show here your lovely life. I never did much for you and you did all for me. Accept this as a slight offering of what I would have done.

Your devoted son
G S Patton Jr.

2

GEORGIE

To die will be an awfully big adventure.

—J. M. Barrie
Peter Pan

The Happiest Boy in the World

L AKE VINEYARD became the permanent home of the Pattons and Wilsons together, and on its acres of orchards and pasture Georgie grew up a country boy. The family lived comfortably if not lavishly on its share of earnings from the Wilson businesses, still under the management of James de Barth Shorb. Three hundred dollars a month was Georgie's later estimate of household expenses, including the salaries of several Mexican servants.

His Aunt Nannie maintained an appearance of independence by keeping her finances separate from her sister's. Her personal driver and carriage, which she retained on call seven days a week, gave weight to that appearance, as if at any instant she might actually move out—but she wasn't going anywhere. Years earlier she'd tried to imagine in her diary "the kind of man I could care for." It seemed that in her nephew Georgie she'd found her ideal. She wasn't about to miss her chance with him as she'd missed it with his father.

It would later be said that Nannie exerted "a tyranny of weakness" over the Lake Vineyard household. The impression she gave was of shyness and fragility. A cross word never passed her lips. Fainting spells, pouts, sudden fits of depression and mysterious illnesses were her means of influence. Sometimes she stayed in bed all day, had her meals and perhaps a toddy or two brought to her in her room. She demanded that there be two kinds of meat served at each evening meal, as a sign of sophistication. Her brother-in-law dutifully kept a cured Virginia ham on the sideboard at all times.

But Nannie's wishes and whims were more on her nephew's behalf than her own. She'd always dominated her sister, so it isn't surprising that she dominated Ruth in the matter of Georgie's upbringing. In 1887, Ruth bore a daughter, whom she named Anne and called Nita. Nannie's interest in the new baby was minimal: for her, there was only Georgie. As for Papa, he loved his daughter, but without the extreme soul-to-soul tie he felt with his namesake. Papa's favoritism was imperceptible in the children's early years; it grew more evident as he, like Nannie, increasingly invested his own thwarted hopes in Georgie. To right the imbalance, Ruth's attentions tilted toward Nita. Georgie took no notice of this duel of allegiances. He was oblivious to the beneficent spotlight that shone on him from Nannie and Papa. From the day of his birth he'd never been without it and so took it as a God-given blessing, like a sunbeam illuminating a saint.

Nannie insisted that he be tutored at home, by her, rather than attend school with other children. He was delicate, she argued. He might be bullied, might catch disease. She also feared, though it went unspoken, that Georgie might be mocked as stupid by his fellow students. As a baby he'd been early to walk but slow to talk. Nannie noticed that in comparison to her many nieces and nephews by her half-sister, Sue Shorb, Georgie showed no acumen in reading and writing. So she didn't push him. She showered him in praise, forbidding any mention of his possible shortcomings. Georgie's thoughts and opinions were given full credence and encouragement. His announcement that he would be a fireman when he grew up was not accepted winkingly: Georgie would be a great fireman someday.

For the first twelve years of his life, his academic education consisted of being read to three to four hours a day by his aunt and later by his father as well. Nannie and Papa chose literature to suit their own tastes and to nurture their idea of a healthy-minded American boy. Georgie proved their perfect disciple. In the safe cocoon of his aunt's encouragement he was welcome to comment on the books she read, but mostly he just listened in silence. Her interpretation was as integral to his education as the poems and stories themselves, and Georgie's later remarks about the various works give a glimpse into the mind of his tutor.

Nannie's fundamental textbook was the Bible. The Old Testament, she said (and Georgie echoed), was "a manual of survival" chronicling "the folklore and history of a tough and single-minded race who had survived every kind of persecution from gods and men." The New Testament portrayed Roman history and the possibilities of human heroism as exemplified by Jesus. Sitting beside her nephew at church each Sunday, Nannie recited *The Book of Common Prayer* along with the preacher until before long Georgie could recite it too. Nannie was drawn to mysticism (late in life she became a great fan of the Ouija), and on equal terms with Christian texts she read Georgie translations of *The Bhagavad Gita* and portions of the Koran. Combined with such works as *Beowulf*, Thomas Bulfinch's *The Age of Fable*, Tennyson's *The Idylls of the King*, Washington Irving's fanciful collection of Moorish folktales, *The Alhambra*, and John Bunyan's Christian allegory, *The Pilgrim's Progress*, Nannie's religious readings made her nephew's head swirl with alluring myths and legends that coalesced like a planet from a gaseous cloud into a worldview all his own. Except no one knew this—not even Nannie could be sure how much of this stuff Georgie was retaining. Listening, he would idly twirl his blond ringlets, which she'd insisted on letting grow long, between his fingers and purse his "pretty cherub mouth" in an expression of agreeable vacancy. Fearing that he indeed might truly be dim, Nannie inclined her heart to him still more protectively.

G. A. Henty's popular juvenile adventure books, in which young boys participate in pivotal moments of military history, got a more discernible rise out of Georgie. *The Young Buglers, Under Drake's Flag,* and *With Lee in Virginia* captivated Georgie and were absorbed by him as inspiration, not unlike the Bible and *The Bhagavad Gita,* for a good and happy life. But it was after his aunt read him Sir Walter Scott's *Ivanhoe* that he ultimately revealed the great effect her instruction was having. He confided to her that he'd written a poem—in his head, for he still couldn't write. Astonished, she transcribed his recitation with the reverent wonder of a medium receiving an oracle:

> Forward Knight! Forward Knight!
> Go and do your best, Knight,
> In the tournament.

> Forward Knight! Forward Knight!
> Don't lose the prize, Knight,
> On jousting day.

> Forward Knight! Forward Knight!
> Knock down the champion, Knight,
> Of the lot, lot, lot.

Nannie dated the poem November 30, 1892, and placed it with other keepsakes of Georgie in her bedroom bureau. On his recent seventh birthday he'd announced that instead of a fireman, he now would be a soldier when he grew up. Why the change, no one could say. Nannie credited Plato, who wrote, "Let early education be a sort of amusement; you will then be better able to find out the natural bent."

Georgie himself speculated years later, only half jokingly, that perhaps the notion of a military career had occurred to him in answer to unwitting nightly prayers. Before retiring to his room, he always knelt beside his mother's chair to recite with her his bedtime devotions. On the wall behind her hung two small etched portraits he assumed were of God and Jesus, the former a somber gentleman with white hair and beard (as God's surely must be), the latter portrait a younger man whose hair and beard were brown. Georgie beseechingly fixed his upturned eyes on these faces as he prayed. Only later did he realize that these men weren't God and Jesus at all. They were Robert E. Lee and Stonewall Jackson.

Papa was pleased by Georgie's new military ambition. One of his favorite sayings was "Good blood does not lie." Certainly Papa's blood didn't lie; its frequent infusions of melancholy deepened his sense of inadequacy, especially after he'd had a few drinks, which in his usual quiet and dreamy way, he increasingly tended to do. Given the examples in his ancestry, to muddle along as an unwell, underachieving, yet generally contented family man constituted a sort of quiet disgrace. Georgie, however, might make amends for that disgrace, succeeding for himself and his father both.

On reading his son's poem, Papa no doubt was pleased but also a bit intimidated by how, with its blunt challenge to win, the poem seemed to put its finger on Papa's fundamental flaw: a lack of plain old drive. Georgie loved his father, but "Forward Knight" suggests that his affection carried an unconscious hedge and maybe even a rebuke. He loved his father, he liked and appreciated him. But he sure as hell would not live Papa's calm domestic life and end up the same kind of failure.

Shortly after Georgie composed his poem, Nannie fell ill and had to go east with her sister for an operation, leaving Georgie, his father, and five-year-old sister home in California. The women's absence was a pleasant discovery. Papa had his little ones all to himself. They in turn had him.

Papa, thirty-six now, liked ceremony. The three of them would dress for dinner. He'd have whiskey before the meal and wine with it. He'd pour brandy over a lump of sugar, light it afire in his teaspoon, and stir it flaming into his coffee. After dinner, he donned a dressing gown over his collar and tie, his dry gentility turning suddenly warm and beckoning. The gown's pattern was a tattered brown-and-white check. He wore it, Ruth Patton once said, because Georgie as an infant had often been cuddled against it. To this day it carried his baby scent.

Papa took his children on his lap in the big easy chair in the parlor. He read them *The Iliad, The Odyssey*, and the tragedies of Sophocles and Euripides, translating from the original Greek as he read. When Nita fell asleep he eased her into an adjacent chair. The course of each evening seemed aimed at this moment, the household pared down to its core of father and son alone together. Papa would set aside his book and lie back in the easy chair with his arms around Georgie. As the fire burned in the fireplace he spoke to his son, and to himself, too, about the people they came from, the family they were, and what sort of blood ran in their veins.

As a boy, Papa had been a rapt audience for his mother's reminiscences of life in antebellum Virginia. In reminding her children of their southern heritage, Sue had assuaged her own need, in the hard years after the war, to perceive that heritage as lofty and fine and sure to be revived someday. She'd dangled pride in family before her children like a last precious heirloom saved from a burning house—proof, as it were, that they once had been rich. Now Papa dangled it before his son, this dusty tapestry of hubris, but interwoven with the added element of Papa's youthful dream of a great military career. Papa of course had set aside that dream before committing to it. His son by contrast had no such instinct for caution, no experience of disappointment to shy from. When Georgie grabbed the dream at seven years old, he had no intention of letting go.

With Papa contributing more and more to Georgie's home schooling (both in Nannie's absence and after her return), that schooling was matched to the boy's military interest. Papa read Herodotus's history of the Persian Wars to Georgie. He read Plutarch's *Lives;* Caesar's *Commentaries;* biographies of Napoleon and Alexander the Great. He read Georgie Lord Thomas Macaulay's popular, jingoistic ("irredeemably shallow," some critics say) essays on English history. He read him Shakespeare, the poetry of the English Romantics, and, for a kick, the stories and colloquial barrack room ballads of the young British literary sensation, Rudyard Kipling.

Papa often invited his stepfather, George Hugh Smith, to Lake Vine-

yard. Smith's fond recollections of Papa's father were Georgie's first introduction to the late Confederate colonel. All the clichés that to this day
perpetuate the mystique of the Confederacy's martyrs—the men seeming
so young, brave, and somehow innocent—applied to George Patton I and
were made doubly alluring in Georgie's mind. He was Georgie's own
grandfather. He'd actually lived and actually died, leaving behind for his
heirs a legacy of dynamism and early death that was perfect in its way.

Memories of his father were only part of Papa's store of family lore and
legend. Perceiving Georgie's ambition as a spark that might indeed become
fire, he told his son stories linking the family's illustrious past to Georgie's
hoped-for future. When reading the classics, Papa skipped around to the
good parts here and there. Likewise in his fireside stories, he shifted from
era to era, anecdote to anecdote. The effect was to create an array of
ancestral figures gathered into a single immortal gallery: Catherine DuBois,
Robert Patton, Philip Slaughter, George and Tazewell Patton. Papa's voice
was proud as he told his stories, but its wistful undertone implied unmis-
takably that he himself wasn't part of that gallery, wasn't worthy of it—an
admission guaranteed to stoke his loyal son's fire to still higher heat.

What was perhaps Papa's most influential story didn't concern a family
member. One evening Papa was conjuring images of Tazewell Patton at
the battle of Bull Run in 1861 when Georgie fixed on a peripheral anecdote
about Barnard Bee, a Confederate brigadier general of minor significance
in the history of the Civil War. The battle had seemed lost when attacking
Federal troops overran the Rebel line. General Bee's men were in full flight
when he galloped before them and waved his saber at nearby Henry House
Hill, still being defended by a brigade under the command of a little-
known former professor from Papa's alma mater. "There stands Jackson
like a stone wall!" Bee exhorted his men. "Rally behind the Virginians!"
The words were barely out of his mouth when a minié ball struck him
square in the forehead and pitched him dead off his horse. The tide of battle
turned for the Confederacy. Stonewall Jackson had his immortal nickname.
And Georgie had his model, his ideal of a desirable end. Barnard Bee must
have lived an exemplary life to have been blessed with so fine a death, he
thought. Too bad Bee wasn't family. To find a comparable figure among
his own forebears, that would be fine.

One can imagine Papa smiling then as he brought to Georgie's attention
the boy's great-great-great-grandfather. His name was Hugh Mercer, Papa
said. He fought in the American Revolution, was a patriot and honored
soldier, and he died as he had lived. . . .

Nearly forty years later Georgie recorded in his memoir of Papa these traditions of some of my ancestors as nearly as I remember them from what my father told me. It may well be that some of the deeds are applied to wrong names but the fact that they were performed by men of my blood remains and it is these facts which have ever inspired me. . . . Should my own end be fitting, as I pray it may be, it will be to such traditions that I owe what ever valor I may have shown. Should I falter I will have disgraced my blood.

"Forward Knight" indeed. Go and do your best, Knight. Knock down the champion, Knight. Or else.

Devoting less and less time to his law practice, Papa involved himself in the management of the Lake Vineyard ranch, producing grapes for his late father-in-law's San Gabriel Winery and oranges for sale upstate. He was always around for his children, teaching them to ride horses, helping Georgie play with his train set and build a fort out of rocks. Sometimes the children wore blue brass-buttoned jackets and pretended that Nita was a major and Georgie a private (which Georgie thought was superior). "When Papa would drive away in the morning he would salute us and ask how the private and major were." As to the children's habit of sometimes wearing each other's clothes to dinner, Nita in pants and Georgie in a dress, Papa soon put a stop to the game, though without shaming his son with mockery or sharp anger; he casually began talking about Robert E. Lee's great Civil War victories. "I got all excited," Georgie recalled, but his father only shrugged and said "that since I was dressed as a girl I should not get so bloodthirsty." Georgie got the hint. He didn't wear Nita's clothes again.

The toys Papa gave him carried a common theme. One of the first was a wooden doll dressed as a French general. Next came a soldier suit with a black busby for Georgie's head, a bolt-action rifle, "and two empty .22 shells with which I religiously loaded it to shoot at lions and robbers," and then a special homemade toy: "we took a lathe out of the chicken yard fence and he made me a cross handled sword. . . . Some times he would take his father's sword and I my toy one and he would kneel down and we would fight."

Many fathers and sons have played with swords. But in the parrying of these two particular swords, one a toy and the other genuine, a bridge was forged between Georgie and Colonel George Patton, C.S.A., who'd been carrying his saber when a shell fragment fatally penetrated his hip. The colonel was not famous except within his family, where his luster shone like a god's. His saber was not treated as a forbidding museum relic but as a thing to be touched, examined, tried out. The same was true of the colonel's McClellan-style saddle, on which Georgie learned to ride and on which, Georgie knew, "my grandfather had been killed. On the pommel was a stain, which I thought was his blood. Papa had also learned to ride on this saddle."

When Georgie was ten his father, who was rich in assets but somewhat strapped for cash, borrowed $125 from a bank to purchase him a real shotgun. He spent hours making Georgie bamboo fishing rods, and though he fretted inordinately about money and creditors, one summer he bought his son a small sailboat. Papa hated hunting, fishing, and sailing. He arranged such excursions and accompanied Georgie on them because Georgie adored them and because Papa felt they were the proper pastimes of a gentleman-soldier.

While playing with his sister, Nita, one afternoon, Georgie got the idea to enact a scene from *The Iliad* with her. He would play the Greek hero Achilles. Nita would play Hector, the young Trojan prince—the *dead* young Trojan prince, that is, slain by Achilles and then dragged behind his chariot before the walls of Troy. Georgie looped a rope around his sister's waist and knotted it to the saddle of his Shetland pony, Peach Blossom. But Nita, two years younger than Georgie, was not then nor ever would be her brother's fool. She tied a dead rat to the rope and told Georgie to haul *that* around the stableyard instead, while from the hayloft she wailed in anguish as Queen Hecuba had done for Hector her son.

After touring a naval frigate in San Diego harbor, Georgie climbed atop a greenhouse, pretending to be Admiral Horatio Nelson striding across the glass deadlights on the deck of his flagship *Victory* at the battle of Trafalgar. Georgie smashed through the glass and broke his arm in the first of a lifetime of mishaps that he would survive again and again.

Then there was his attempt, without identifiable precedent, to mimic an ancient feat of armored mobile warfare with the help of several young cousins and an abandoned farm wagon. The boys hauled the wagon to the top of a small hill overlooking Lake Vineyard's turkey shed. At Georgie's order, the cousins crouched in the wagon preparing to hurl sticks (as spears and arrows) from behind round wooden wine barrel tops (as shields). Georgie pushed the wagon down the hill. It ripped through the flock of turkeys at peak speed and killed and mangled quite a few. Georgie was triumphant until his mother stormed out of the house and asked what in the world he was doing. He said he was copying the famous war wagons of John the Blind of Bohemia, who won many victories this way in the fifteenth century. And how did the boy know this? "Oh," Georgie shrugged. "I was there."

If Ruth thought her son's answer was flippant, Nannie and Papa did not. Papa had been brought up in the understanding that his great-uncle Will Thornton, his mother, Sue, and possibly his Uncle Tazewell all had been psychic to some degree; the notion of reincarnation, which Georgie's remark alluded to, was not something Papa was inclined to dismiss out of hand. Nannie, of course, was intrigued with spiritualism and Eastern religions. In the future her nephew would often, indeed incessantly, invoke two quotations from the Bible and *The Bhagavad Gita* (from a period translation) which Nannie had explained, during her readings to him, were mutually affirming of the cycles of life in death.

As a man casting off worn out garments taketh new ones, so the dweller in the body, casting off worn out bodies, entereth into ones that are new.

The Bhagavad Gita 2:22

Him that overcometh will I make a pillar in the temple of my God, and he shall go no more out.

Revelations 3:12

Georgie's claim of divine inspiration didn't spare him from punishment for his attack on the turkeys. His subsequent spanking was one of the few times in his childhood that he was disciplined at all. Papa was reluctant to rein in his rambunctious boy, and Nannie always tried to intercede in her nephew's behalf. Ruth was steadfast. Before spanking him, however, she summoned the doctor and turned down Nannie's bed in anticipation of the physical collapse her sister invariably suffered whenever Georgie was punished.

Composed, laconic, sober but not brooding, Ruth would not deign to compete with her husband and sister for her son's affection. Georgie, reared in the expectation of total fealty, was somewhat thrown by his mother's manner. "When I went to tell Papa and Mama good night I used to kiss Papa many times and Mama only once," he recalled, adding contritely, "this was childish and thoughtless." He'd been reacting to what appeared, compared with Papa's and Nannie's demonstrativeness, to be his mother's diffidence toward him. At later times in his life when he found himself tongue-tied in expressing affection, he attributed it to Ruth's influence. He reconsidered this opinion in a letter he wrote to her in 1931, three years after she died—a date not even too late, thanks to Georgie's absolute belief in reincarnation and eternal life, for putting matters right with someone you may have neglected. "I never showed you in life the love I really felt. . . . Children are cruel things. Forgive me. . . . But you know that I still love you and in the presence of your soul I feel very new and very young and helpless even as I must have been 46 years ago. . . . Nothing you ever did to me was anything but loving."

The emotional remove between Georgie and his mother was matched by the remove he maintained from her side of the family in general. For one so fixated on heritage, his indifference to his Wilson ancestry was entirely in keeping with his perception of himself—a perception, it could be said, which in developing so early was like poured concrete that sets too fast, running the risk of turning brittle and eventually cracking.

As a young boy he was quick to appraise his pet horses as thoroughbred or not, his dogs as purebred or mutt. He likewise began to categorize people (with whom, outside of cousins, farmhands, and servants, he had virtually no social contact) on the basis of background and breeding. The maxim that all prejudice is learned behavior held true in Georgie's case. The Pattons' desperate faith in their former glories fostered a sense of themselves as natural-born noblemen. The more uncertain their circumstances, the more the Pattons waved their tattered flag of precious bloodlines. And none was more uncertain of himself and his place in the world than Georgie's father, at whose feet Georgie learned, through observing Papa's genteel expressions of ingrained bigotry, that the Pattons and their Anglo-Saxon Protestant kind were better than other people. Including, curiously, the Wilsons.

Not that the Pattons put down the Wilsons. It was more a matter of omission, an unconscious disregard of, particularly, the person and accomplishments of the late Benjamin Wilson, that characterized Papa and Georgie's attitude. Since it was by Wilson's bequest that they were living as well as they were, there was no small injustice in this. But Wilson seemed dull beside the doomed, forever young Patton brothers of the Civil War. He lacked color and, in a phrase, lacked class. Papa's sisters, Nellie and Susie, both married now, had commissioned a genealogist to trace their lineage back to medieval England. Fulfilling the women's hopes of royal descent, the genealogist had linked the Pattons to sixteen barons who signed the Magna Charta in 1215; to Sir Henry Percy (1364–1403), Hotspur in

Shakespeare's *Henry IV*; and, for good measure, had linked them to America's own George Washington through the president's great-aunt. Benjamin Wilson couldn't match this pedigree. He was a diligent, decent, self-made survivor. But he hadn't been born a gentleman.

Out of necessity and an innate industriousness, Wilson had devoted much of his life to business. This was rather vulgar in his grandson's view. Georgie liked having money, he expected it always to be handy and plentiful, but he was uninterested in (indeed was contemptuous of) a career spent in the accumulation of wealth. Another mark against Wilson was his first marriage to a Mexican girl. Evidently he'd so little valued his Protestant heritage he hadn't cared that his children by her were reared as Spanish-speaking papists. There was even a rumor that Wilson at one time had kept an Indian mistress—a squaw!

It is no wonder, given the impressions of his youth, that Papa extolled the virtues of his forebears and rather downplayed those of his father-in-law. But why did Wilson's own daughter collaborate in the subtle denigration of her father's legacy? Nannie could have instilled in Georgie an awe for the man just as she'd instilled in him an awe for her favorite themes of religion and literature. In complexion Benjamin Wilson was dark and Georgie fair. But they resembled each other in height, build, and visage, a seemingly superficial connection that young Georgie would have considered signified more profound similarities if someone only had pointed it out to him. He might then have realized that his Grandfather Wilson had displayed qualities of determination and grit often lacking in the Pattons, and certainly lacking in Papa. But Georgie's gaze was directed elsewhere. It was fixed on his father and through his father, as through a magnifying lens, on every extant memory of the Patton past. Nannie allowed those memories to eclipse the memory of Benjamin Wilson because her gaze too was fixed on the Pattons. Fixed on Georgie, that is, and on his father, to the exclusion of everything else in her life.

"Papa gave me two horses. First a black named Galahad, then a brown named Marmion. They were both about ¾ bred. . . . I had a dog named Polvo about this time and he slept by Marmion. I remember once going to the stable at night when I was supposed to be studying and laying by Polvo looking at Marmion and thinking that I was the happiest boy in the world. I was probably right."

This sense of his own happiness struck Georgie "when I was ten or eleven." It has been said, however, that when youth begins to savor itself it isn't so young anymore. The moment may have been as touched with uncertainty about the future as it was touched with joy in the present, for Georgie's tenth and eleventh years would prove pivotal. In the future he would accept his own prescience as a fact of life. So perhaps on that evening, basking alone in his father's stable, he'd felt trouble in the air.

Not long before Georgie turned eleven in 1896, his mother's brother-in-law, James de Barth Shorb, died. Shorb had been running the Wilson businesses since Wilson's death eighteen years ago. He and his large family had been living what the Pattons considered a gaudy nouveau riche lifestyle, but as long as the money came in, the Pattons kept their criticisms to themselves. In recent years there were signs that business was suffering. Summer droughts and winter freezes had damaged the citrus crops; disease had destroyed valuable vineyards. After Shorb's death it was discovered that to survive these setbacks, he'd heavily mortgaged the winery and his wife's five-hundred-acre estate, leaving his family destitute and exposing his Wilson in-laws, Ruth, Nannie, and their elderly mother, to huge debt liabilities to the mortgage holder, the Farmers and Merchants Bank of Los Angeles. Lake Vineyard itself—and Georgie's happy life there—was suddenly at risk.

It fell to Georgie's father to salvage the situation. Negotiating with the bank to delay foreclosure proceedings, he took control of the winery and produce businesses in hopes of making them profitable again. After having lived for nearly twelve years as a passive beneficiary of the late Benjamin Wilson, Papa now was supporting not only his wife, sister, and mother-in-law, but also Sue Shorb and her ten orphaned children as well. The zeal with which he undertook the task was both rare for him and logical, for it tapped into his life's one ruling passion: the welfare and social status of his family. The Civil War and its aftermath had beaten into him "an intense aversion to poverty," as Georgie put it. But it had taken a midlife threat of financial ruin to reawaken that aversion and give Papa direction. Only now, at age forty, could he declare with conviction that "his fixed purpose in life was to so arrange his affairs that his wife and children should never know the hardships he had endured." In a sense, then, the collapse of the Wilson businesses was a blessing for Papa. Georgie didn't see it that way, however.

For the rest of his life he bitterly contended that Shorb "was either a fool or a crook" for letting the family finances deteriorate. Georgie had never much liked his uncle. Though of age to fight, the secessionist Shorb had sat out the Civil War, a definite minus in his nephew's opinion. Too, he'd lived to make money, sired a houseful of part-Mexican kids, and was Catholic, conditions that tarnished Georgie's view of all his Wilson-Shorb cousins, and, however indirectly, tarnished his mother and aunt as well. And now Shorb seemed to have disgraced the family by leaving it virtually broke. But even this was not the true source of Georgie's condemnation of his uncle. Georgie had spent his boyhood at Lake Vineyard in a perfect cocoon of encouragement and security; he'd been the center of everyone's life there. But due to Shorb's failure and the need to redress it, Georgie's father no longer was available to shower his son with attention; he had more pressing obligations now. For the first time in Georgie's life the earth shifted under him, unsettling him with intimations of further change to come. He resented it intensely.

He would have felt better had Papa been called to some more elegant purpose, something appealing, at least, to Georgie's idea of worthy aspiration. Two years earlier Papa somewhat reluctantly had run for Congress. George and Nita had openly rooted for him to lose "as we hated the thought of leaving home; so we said that if he was beaten we would celebrate by having a boat race." Papa was defeated, and in defeat he exhibited a quality indicative of his tepid ambition: he was a good and gracious loser. "The day he was beaten he must have felt very badly but he took us to the reservoir and we had a race with two toy boats."

In 1896 Papa ran for Congress again. The race was so close it had to be decided by ballot at the Democratic State Convention. In a remarkable month-long session, 248 ballots were held, each resulting in a tie. Rather than fracture the party, Papa finally conceded victory to his opponent on the condition that the party adopt as part of its platform his position against any control by the Southern Pacific Railroad of the area's "free harbor" at Wilmington on San Pedro Bay. The move was pure Papa. He preferred to go down with dignity rather than fight tooth-and-nail to win. He battled the railroads as his father had battled the North thirty years ago, with pride if not with success. In losing the election, he consoled himself with having blackened the eye of the Republican railroad magnate Collis P. Huntington. He'd lost, yes, but at least he'd lost well.

Georgie again had been ambivalent about his father's 1896 race. But any relief he felt that Papa, in losing, would resume life as usual at Lake Vineyard was shattered by revelations about the family's financial straits, which followed on the heels of the election. A congressional seat looked pretty good next to the unglamorous necessity of Papa's having to work for wages. Five hundred dollars a month was what the Farmers and Merchants Bank paid him to manage the bankrupt Shorb estate. Georgie noted with pride that his father kept only his salary for running his wife's share of the business and none for running her sister-in-law's. "Though really poor at the time he gave it all to Mrs. Shorb and also went on notes for her."

Georgie and his father tried to put a noble face on their diminished circumstances. "Papa used to tell me that he was worried to death trying to keep out of the poor house." Of course Papa always had worried about money; only now his worry carried the weight of actual trouble. "I told him that I was worried too." The sale of housing lots on the Lake Vineyard property eventually put the Pattons back in the black. Papa's very vocal dread of pauperism continued, however. Exaggerating his money woes served to inflate the perception of his efforts to restore the family to wealth. He didn't like wine making, farming, or real estate speculation; they were means to an end that in itself did not thrill him. But to pursue wealth for his family's sake rather than his own? That was a reputation he could live with.

Georgie likewise strove to cast his father's efforts in an heroic light. Of an old man named Mr. McKee who'd lived on the place for many years, Georgie wrote approvingly, "After observing Papa for some time he said: 'God sent that young man to save the widow and orphan [Grandmother Wilson and Aunt Nannie].'" The nurse, Mary Scally, called Papa "a handsome western millionaire" much to the boy's satisfaction (though her definition of a millionaire was, disappointingly, any man who was "a farmer"). And Georgie was proud to note that Papa "never economised so far as his family were concerned but would get nothing for himself," reflecting his father's view that self-sacrifice and not merely success was the ennobling aspect of his business endeavors.

In a few years the family's situation quite comfortably stabilized. Yet Papa went on to develop housing tracts and expand his farm operation. In time Georgie realized that Papa's fear of financial ruin was partly neurotic and partly an excuse to forego his ambitions of public service, ambitions that each considered loftier than business. Georgie poked fun at his father ("I hear you are going to the poor house? On which floor will you have rooms?"), cajoling at first, then later demanding that he resume his political career: *"Remember* this is no practice game but the whole show the *finals*. . . . You must win." But that was far in the future. For now, he applauded his father's vigilant service to the family. Besides, there was something of the bygone southern planter to Papa's new guise as a businessman that had definite appeal to the boy: "I used to accompany Papa almost daily to the San Gabriel Winery of which he was manager and over all the ranches. . . . Often we went in a Concord singleseated wagon without top, called by us The Yellow Wagon. . . . Papa had a very fine driving horse called Pompey. . . . Once in a while we drove the Stallion Brocken which thrilled me as he was a very handsome horse."

Georgie's happy life seemed to have righted itself after the passing squall of uncertainty that had followed his uncle's death. Two months before his twelfth birthday, Georgie's parents announced their decision (pointedly made without Nannie's input) to enroll him in a private academy in Pasadena. Nannie took to her bed in protest while Georgie nodded uncomprehendingly. It was high time for him to begin formal schooling. Still, it marked a crossroads in Georgie's life whose significance was apparent to Papa if not yet to his son. On the first day of school Georgie said good-bye to Mama and Nannie on the Lake Vineyard veranda and rode off in the wagon with his father: "Just after we had turned into Lake Avenue off California Street, Papa turned to me and said very sadly, 'Son hence forth our paths diverge for ever.' I have never forgotten that but though we lived more and more apart our hearts and minds never separated."

☆ ☆ **9** ☆ ☆

Undine and Kuhlborn

IN AUGUST 1902 an elderly Massachusetts industrialist named Frederick Ayer brought his family to California to visit his wife's cousins. His wife, the former Ellen Banning, was distantly related to the husband of Papa's half-sister Annie Ophelia (daughter of George Hugh Smith and the late Sue Patton). The Ayers resided with the Bannings on the resort island of Santa Catalina. The Pattons were summering there as well, and on August 27 Beatrice Ayer and Georgie Patton met.

His expectations were high. Beatrice was the belle of Boston, the Bannings had told him; only sixteen, she'd already had three proposals of marriage. But though she turned out pretty enough—oval face, dimpled chin, and expressive dark eyebrows—she wore her auburn hair in long braids and carried a porcelain doll dressed in the same outfit Beatrice wore. She looked about twelve years old.

Georgie backed away fast. He couldn't escort this child around. His friends would laugh at him. His consciousness of how others judged him, of how he compared to his peers in appearance, achievement, reputation, and popularity, was little different from what most teenage boys feel as they muddle toward manhood—except that in Georgie it often prompted attacks of insecurity unknown in the once blithely self-certain "happiest boy in the world." What had happened? What changed in the five years since his father first drove him to Stephen Clark's Classical School for Boys in Pasadena?

The answer was the truth from which his aunt, his father, and his Lake Vineyard childhood all had conspired to shelter him. Georgie was not perfect, not superior, not bound for glory. Why? His own opinion, as scrawled in a letter several years later, was harsh. "I am stupid there is no use talking I am stupid."

The bitter revelation struck him in his first days at Clark's school. He was alone among other boys his age in his inability to read and write. This was attributed to his home schooling, but even with tutoring improvement came slowly. The boy who'd known nothing but praise and flattery became the butt of classroom snickering as he stammered through his oral readings and froze at the blackboard unable to write the simplest words and sentences. But even as he accepted this verdict of stupidity, Georgie summoned every trick, knack, and instinctive resource he could to succeed in spite of it.

He amazed the class by reciting verbatim long passages of scripture, prose, and poetry recalled from hours of listening to Papa and Nannie. It was said that Papa's father had possessed remarkable powers of concentration and memory. Georgie sharpened this inherited talent through diligent exercise. (He later said that prayer was a little-used muscle that strengthened with use; memory was the same.) Once sufficiently able to read his schoolbooks, he pored over them for hours each night, committing them to memory page by page and word by word. Regurgitating memorized text (albeit shot through with misspellings) got him by in literature and language courses, but was useless in math and science, always his weakest subjects. His best subject was history, military history in particular. He'd long been interested in it, but soon a boyhood hobby became an obsessive, defensive facility. Unable to grasp a wider breadth of the world, he seized on military history as the one area in which he might excel. The narrowness of his focus was quite known to him. He later told his fiancée, "I don't know or care about other things." The admission characteristically blended apology, defiance, and fair warning.

At sixteen, Georgie had a thin fluty voice that he was anxiously (and vainly) waiting to break into a tougher-sounding lower register. He laughed a lot, frequently at himself; thinking his wide smile to be goofy and unmanly, he labored to maintain a dignified frown; the result was a rather comical look of a man with stomach pain. He could be a show-off, a blowhard, then undercut his posturing with self-depreciation almost pathetic in its candor. Among his school essays were fantastic descriptions of his future fame and opulent life-style. But then he wrote a story identifying himself with a football player who admits to his teammates that he "was affraid to charge the line and stumbeled on purpose," costing them the victory. The blend of bravura and insecurity; the distance maintained from classmates; the vividly imagined daydreams and tall tales; the craving for attention and praise, and the subsequent bitter resentment when that attention and praise didn't come—all these traits of his also often occur in children with learning disabilities.

Since he was never diagnosed, there is no way to know whether Georgie suffered from dyslexia. His biographers who have made the claim cite the evidence of his early illiteracy and lifelong poor spelling. "I don't see what makes me spell so badly," was his constant complaint. "I seem to make always the same mistakes." On learning that Napoleon couldn't spell, Georgie quit consulting a dictionary as he wrote (unless the letter or essay had some official purpose) and tried to make a joke of his problem: "Any idiot can spell a word the same way time after time. But it calls for imagination and is much more distinguished to spell it different ways as I do." It was no joke to him during his school years, however. The belief that he was "dum" (as he intentionally misspelled it when mocking himself) deeply troubled the formerly confident youth. It inflamed an insecurity that always would simmer just below his skin, insecurity that Georgie felt driven to conceal behind a mask of bravado unless he was within the safe shelter of family. His great fear was that the mask would slip at some crucial, public moment. To prevent such a humiliation, he was determined to make the mask real.

The favorite of Georgie's many credos was "for as he thinketh in his heart, so *is* he," from Proverbs 23:7. It defined his life's method. In order to become his ideal of greatness, it wasn't enough to disguise the flaws in his nature or even to suppress them. His nature had to be transformed at its core, at its heart; even in his thoughts there could be no room for doubt. Another of his school stories described a swim race where "the one who at first appeared the strongest gave up and the one who at first seemed the weakest got the prize." When Georgie composed "Forward Knight" nine years earlier, "the prize" had seemed virtually in his possession already, because of his fancy pedigree and supportive home life ("Don't lose the prize, Knight"). But as he saw it now, at sixteen, it could only be won by overcoming his own dim-wittedness, just as the swimmer had to overcome weakness in order to prevail. But prevail he did, in Georgie's hopeful, wishful tale.

Dyslexia is a genetic disorder. It has since been diagnosed in at least three of Georgie's descendants—a significant point. There is no known cure for the condition, and despite learning to cope with his problem, reading and writing never came easily to him. Yet during his life he accumulated a vast personal library of military history, its hundreds of volumes annotated with his comments and underlinings. His writing—letters, journals, articles, lectures—eventually filled fifty metal filing cabinets and is housed today at the Library of Congress, an output whose unlikely prodigiousness offers the plainest measure of his will to overcome what, by age sixteen, he'd begun to see as the long odds against his success. Unfortunately, this sense of himself as an underdog would not (in his harsh opinion) relieve him of fault should he fall short of his ambitions, ambitions he later wrote down with the implacable terseness of a directive received from heaven: "Remember you have placed all on war.... Therefore you must never fail.... If you do not die a soldier and having had a chance to be one I pray God to dam you George Patton.... Never Never Never stop being ambitious. You have but one life. Live it to the full of glory and be willing to pay."

Another of his personal dictums was taken from St. Luke: "For unto whomsoever much is given, of him shall be much required." To Georgie, the words constituted a flat-out threat. If he didn't become great, he would have failed not only himself but the inherited gift of his family's proud traditions. Yet even if he succeeded, "It will be to such traditions that I owe what ever valor I have shown." His family would get the credit, in other words. So it was a no-win situation, a maze of ambition guaranteed to disappoint him and maybe drive him crazy. He wanted to be there, in that maze, that trap; his own fantasies of "the prize" had put him there. Still, it isn't surprising that in his teens an alternate fantasy began to attract him. Escape.

First it was The Call. Robbie Patton, a cousin of Papa's from Virginia, had suddenly abandoned his wild ways to become an Episcopalian minister. During a brief visit east in 1898, a wide-eyed Georgie heard Cousin Robbie explain how Jesus himself had inspired this transformation, calling Robbie to the ministry by touching him on the shoulder one night. How did he know it was Jesus? "Georgie," Robbie said serenely, "when Jesus touches you, you know it." Georgie was fascinated. Would he too get The Call? It was the only thing imaginable that might divert him from a military career. Soon he was telling everyone of his dread that Jesus would call him as he'd called Cousin Robbie. Georgie was protesting a bit too much. That glance over his shoulder as he prayed each night was half fearful and half expectant.

On that same trip east he got drunk for the first time. His parents were out for the evening when the hotel bartender brought a complimentary mint julep to the Pattons' cottage. Georgie drank the julep and "had to be put to bed in a hazy condition." It was not his first taste of alcohol. When Georgie was "between eight and ten" years old, his father had poured him a whiskey in his office one night. Pointing to the liquor cabinet, Papa said, " 'Son this is not locked and you can get a drink whenever you want one.' I never took one without him and seldom then. . . . Papa's idea was to make me think drinking common place and so set less store by it."

Papa drank, of course. When tipsy he took on the gentle gloom of a firelit drawing room, murmuring poetry and humming strange lilting snippets of sea chanties and Civil War ballads. He harbored many disappointments but no rage. The sight of him pouring himself another glass caused his wife and children only to blush a little, knowing that soon he would be telling them effusively how dear to him they all were. Nannie, on the other hand, would slowly sink with ladylike sips of brandy into glum silence interrupted only by bursts of petty anger aimed at her sister, Ruth, who drank only wine and rarely even that.

Recalling his father's admonition that "an ambitious man could not afford to drink," Georgie perhaps understood that Papa's and Nannie's drinking willfully dulled the ambitions they'd once had. In the years to come Georgie too would begin to drink, first in occasional collegiate binges, later in the usual social settings for the enhancement of good times, and finally with the blunt purpose of an arsonist splashing flammable liquids. The heavy drinking of Georgie's great-uncles, Robert and Hugh Patton, his uncle Glassell, and later his father, may suggest a genetic disposition toward alcoholism. But Georgie's drinking was more a choice than the result of a family tendency. It facilitated his mask of swaggering confidence. Then it set about destroying that mask and the ambitions underlying it, freeing him to be afraid or enraged or, most corrosive of all, indifferent.

His other means of escape from his own burdensome dreams were the many high-risk entertainments he pursued all his life. Almost comically accident-prone, by the time Georgie was forty his "annual mishaps" had resulted in at least ten broken bones, three concussions, and countless severe lacerations, many of them in the head. Nevertheless, he played polo furiously into his fifties. He fenced, fox hunted, and rode steeplechase, a sport considered among the most dangerous in the world. Often nervous before a race, he bolstered his courage with a bloodcurdling "Rebel yell" at the starting gun. He first flew in an airplane in 1916. "I had always thought it would frighten me but it did not." Later he got his pilot's license. In 1934 he skippered a fifty-foot schooner halfway across the Pacific Ocean with virtually no prior sailing experience, having taught himself navigation by venturing with sextant and manual in hand and taking celestial fixes in the fields around his home.

Napoleon, when advised of a promising young officer, is supposed to have responded, "Yes, but is he lucky?" Georgie put the same question to himself, playing these dangerous games "to test my luck." Each time he survived a brush with death or serious injury it seemed heartening evidence of some benevolent guiding destiny. A maniac behind the wheel, he had three blowouts in his roadster during his honeymoon in Europe in 1910, losing a tire off its axle at sixty miles an hour. "Nothing happened," he said with a shrug to his father, who wasn't surprised. Papa always had said that Georgie's persistent good fortune "was Fate, and that I was being specially prepared for some special work. . . . He was most convincing and I believed him particularly as I have always felt the same thing myself."

As much as this risk taking sought to affirm his destiny, it also was self-destructive. Twice—once while a cadet at the U.S. Military Academy, and once while a cavalry lieutenant at Fort Sheridan, Illinois—he impulsively stepped from behind cover to stand erect by the targets during rifle practice to see how he'd react to bullets whistling by his ear. His fascination with dying young betrayed a gnawing pessimism about his long-term prospects for glory. Better, he said, to "go early" in a blaze of aspiration than to live long years in uneventful ease, for "if I should live that way I would die all through life." The decay of old age scared him. Scarier still was "that slackness at the middle distance which loses the race of life." Complacency was the true enemy. "I may be crazy but if with sanity comes contentment with the middle of life may I never be sane. I don't fear failure I only fear a slowing up of the engine which is pounding on the in side saying up—up—some one must be on top why not you."

The story of Achilles, who according to Greek legend consciously chose glory over long life, was in Georgie's mind when he wrote that he "would be willing to live in torture, die tomorrow if for one day I could be really great." But his more immediate model was his paternal grandfather, Colonel Patton of the Confederate Army. The man had fought for a lost, discredited cause; this didn't diminish the mythic qualities of his death. A life cut short by an honorable death-in-action had the advantage of avoiding midlife complacency and the disappointments of old age. It avoided the suspense of wondering what the future held, whether laurels or disgrace, lasting fame or oblivion, pride of accomplishment or the curdle of regret. And it predetermined posterity's judgment by leaving, as it were, on a positive note.

Georgie's compulsive thrill seeking was as integral to the pursuit of his goals as any steps in a career path. It tested his mettle and his ability to perform under pressure. By fostering a tough image, it helped make his mask real. And it was fun. But in the paradoxical manner of most death-defying hobbies, it was more than a little cowardly, too. Better to burn out than to fade away is a modern expression of an age-old dread. Fading away terrifies some people, not least because it is so common.

Thrown together with Beatrice Ayer on Catalina Island in 1902, Georgie was irritated by the relish with which his family and cousins, obviously expecting an instant love match, observed them. He was standoffish with Beatrice. When the Patton, Ayer, and Banning children decided to put on a play for the grown-ups—Caro Atherton Dugan's *Undine*—he petulantly refused to take the male lead opposite Beatrice in the title role, persuading his sister, Nita, to play the part. Georgie instead played Kuhlborn, a water spirit who retrieves Undine from the mortal world and returns her to the river divinities. Despite his initial reluctance to perform, once onstage Georgie hammed it up "to the huge satisfaction of his admiring audience," according to a Los Angeles newspaper reporter who was covering this "pretty feature of the prettiest society function of the season."

Years later, Georgie apologized to Beatrice for "acting mean" to her when they'd first met. She'd considered him more awkward than mean: her immature appearance masked a certain wise composure. He was the opposite. Over six feet tall, dressed in suits made by his father's tailor, he looked his age; and unless he forgot himself and let slip his giggly laugh, his manner convincingly conveyed the stern ambition and high-minded gravity of a future important person. But there was something else about him, a bumbling innocence confirmed rather than disguised by his outward hauteur, that Beatrice began to recognize during her several weeks in his company. It held the kind of irrational, unreliable, wrongheaded charm she usually alertly resisted—but not always.

Her father, Frederick Ayer, was a vigilant, serious-minded Yankee capitalist known for his dogged labors in the patent medicine business, in lumber, textiles, railroads, and real estate. Yet after his first wife's death in

1878, he'd surprised all who knew him by marrying Ellen Banning, a former diseuse (or parlor actress) thirty-one years his junior. Frederick's four adult children from his first marriage lived in fear of him, referring to him among themselves as "Sir Frederick" or "The Governor." His three children with Ellie, on the other hand, were totally indulged by their father—as was Ellie, whose worshipful adoration no doubt felt pretty gratifying to Frederick, who turned eighty in 1902.

Ellie played the part of an industrialist's wife with a luxuriant air that came off both grand and girlish. Fresh roses pinned in her hair, gold bangles on her arm for each year of her marriage, a low stagy voice that defied interruption, and a penchant for imperious histrionics—these affectations were wearisome to some people, but she lived entirely for her husband and children and hence was blissfully insulated from outside sniping thanks to Frederick Ayer's formidable wealth. Ellie hadn't been born to the rarefied world to which her marriage had elevated her, and later in life she showed a surprising common touch in letting her eldest daughter volunteer at a settlement house for European immigrant children located on the Boston waterfront. The Beacon Hill ladies clucked at this act, but Ellie wanted her daughter to experience life beyond their world of servants and calling cards and sterling tea services. Beatrice could handle it, Ellie knew. At her daughter's birth she'd chosen *Beatrice* for its Italian meaning: "blessed one." Ellie since had found another pet name, this one expressed in French: *Ma fleur qui pense*—my flower who thinks.

Her delicate appearance aside, Beatrice displayed a judicious temperament that contributed to her reputation as the proverbial good daughter, constant and true. Yet like her father, she carried a streak of unpredictability beneath her no-nonsense facade. This streak was exemplified by some escapades she pulled while in Egypt cruising the Nile aboard a yacht with her family when she was eleven years old.

Usually little Beatrice could be counted on to tend to her younger siblings every bit as well as the governesses traveling with the Ayers. Yet on impulse she bribed their Egyptian boatman with ten dollars to bring her to a local tattoo parlor where she hoped to receive a tattoo just like the boatman's: a full-rigged ship across the chest. Thwarted in this quest, she did get a souvenir of Egypt while touring a recently discovered ancient tomb. The guide warned "don't touch" as the Ayers filed behind him through the dark narrow cave. His lamp cast slithery shadows across the open sarcophagus and the discernibly human-shaped thing inside it. Beatrice lingered behind. She took a quick breath, as if leaping through space, and reached her hand into the sarcophagus and took hold of the mummy's linen-wrapped foot. She snapped off its toe like a piece of charred wood and hid it in her pocket.

That night on the boat, she put the mummy's toe, a hard black nugget still wrapped in gray linen, in a jelly jar she'd taken from the galley—so began her lifelong interest in collecting, archaeology, and ancient civilizations. When she unscrewed the lid to give her brother and sister a peek, they recoiled in disgust at the strange scent wafting from the relic. Beatrice breathed it deeply. "Something like tar, and something sweeter and more lonely." The scent was unnameable, but she named it anyway: "The odor of eternity." If her siblings were puzzled by Beatrice's remark, it seems likely that Georgie, with his attention ever fixed on the ages of past and future, would have understood exactly.

It is easy to imagine Beatrice eventually fading from the world in a gray haze of good works and upstanding behavior had she not possessed that quirky streak. More to the point, it is easy to imagine that without it she would not have fallen so quickly and completely in love with the likes of Georgie in Catalina in 1902.

She was clever. After her family left for Massachusetts, her first letter to California wasn't addressed to Georgie or his parents. Nannie Wilson still held great sway with her nephew, so it was to "Dear Aunt Nannie" that Beatrice wrote, signing herself "Your affectionate Niece." Nannie wrote back at once. Ruth Patton followed with a letter of her own, her appreciation of Beatrice as a fine girl for Georgie overcoming her usual reluctance to compete with her sister in managing Georgie's life. In her November reply to Ruth's note, Beatrice said that she too hoped the Ayers would return soon to California. "I know that Georgie's birthday comes some time this month," she added. "When it comes, please spank him seventeen times for me and give him my very best birthday compliments." When at last she wrote Georgie, the groundwork had been laid for their relationship. It would take him years to catch on, however.

She sent him a fox head tie pin for Christmas. In her accompanying note she asked how Kuhlborn was faring. Georgie replied, "As to Kuhlborns self there is little to say except that owing to his immortal nature he lived through foot-ball season and did not even break a bon[e] . . . and that he is now devoting more time than he should to making a polo team; (for above all things he is desirus of an early and glorious death)." The letter's blend of self-mockery and drama greatly accounted for his appeal to Beatrice. Another ingredient of that appeal was captured in his guileless confession to her, in the same letter, of how he'd put on the tie pin, posed before a mirror, and then "involuntarily raised my hat"—saluting himself like a little toy king.

During the Ayer-Patton-Banning sojourn in Catalina that past summer, a photographer took several pictures of the clan, twenty-three cousins ranging in age from over eighty to under ten, languidly posed on the manicured lawn of the Banning family preserve. The women wear bonnets and white linen, the men suits of summer-weight wool. Their obvious monied self-satisfaction is leavened with unpretentiousness. The kids are caught in midfidget. The older folks, gamely smiling to varying degrees, are tiring a bit of the photographer's labored calibrations. And the teenagers, Georgie and Beatrice among them, are aware of nothing so much as themselves and one another.

Beatrice appears in the pictures a little girl no longer. Gone are the doll and the grade school braids; her hair done up, her dress high collared, long sleeved, and down to the ankles, she could easily pass for twenty. Her few weeks on Catalina have effected a change in her whose cause is no mystery. As for Georgie, in one of the posed seating arrangements he is kneeling on an embroidered pillow, as if to protect his trousers from grass stains. His legs are tucked under him gracefully, like a woman riding sidesaddle. He sports a decorative handkerchief in his lapel pocket and his socks are foppishly striped. Yet his suit appears about two sizes too big. His bow tie is cockeyed, and his blond hair tends to unruly ringlets as it spills over his collar and ears: in trying to cut a sharp figure, he hasn't quite pulled it off. Georgie is a boy here. A sun-tanned, happy boy. He has forgotten for the moment to be severe. He has forgotten not to smile.

☆ ☆ **10** ☆ ☆

My Every Slightest Wish

G EORGIE'S sister could never decide what to call herself. Christened Anne Wilson Patton, she was Nita to her family, Anne or Anita to her friends at school. She might sign her letters with any of these, and often instead of her name she substituted some self-description that captured her mood of the moment, "Your own little child" when feeling sentimental in a letter to her parents, "Spinster" when feeling frustrated by the quandaries in her love life. A name she never chose was the one many of her Ayer and Banning cousins called her for several years after their production of *Undine* on Catalina in 1902. Huldbrand was the part Nita had performed after her brother, Georgie, had refused it, and which, wrote the society columnist, "was given a graceful portrayal by Miss Anita Patton, whose tall figure set off to good advantage the rich habiliments of the sir knight." Though meant to be complimentary, the review cut to her deepest insecurity. All the other girls were given flattering female roles. Nita, awkward, big boned, with her mother's wide features and build, was made to play a man. Her cousins never realized that calling Nita Huldbrand did not inspire a fond memory. But she, being one to keep quiet and smile through her pain, never said a word to correct them.

Georgie left home in September 1903 to attend college in the East. The next year, Nita wrote a short story about a sixteen-year-old rich girl from

New York City. Isabelle (nicknamed Belle) is visiting her Aunt Maggie's small California ranch. She mourns for her older brother, recently passed away. "He and she had been all in all to each other, and all Aunt Maggie's love and kindness could not fill that lonely void." During her visit Isabelle meets an attractive young man, but dismisses him as a serious suitor because he is a mere "working man . . . a day labourer." Her aunt chides her for judging him on his clothes and background rather than on his character. The plot turns on Aunt Maggie's efforts to open her niece's mind and heart to the fellow's true qualities. But even as Isabelle begins to understand that her "old ignorant prejudices" are shortsighted and wrong, it is the young man who begins to resist his feelings, considering himself unworthy of such a well-born girl. Finally Aunt Maggie tricks both into believing that Isabelle's father has suddenly met with financial ruin and hence left the lovers on equal terms. At once they embrace, vowing to struggle through life together. "The selfishness of lovers was theirs," Nita wrote, "nothing mattered now, the grief of their elders, the poverty of the future, nothing, for they had love."

Perhaps Nita based Maggie on her own Aunt Nannie Wilson. Certainly Nannie, who as a young girl had written so achingly of her romantic desires, could have been the model for a character who was determined that her niece not let true love slip by. But what is certain about the story is that it reveals much about its author. Like Isabelle, Nita was "on occasion very obstinate." Too, Nita was harshly self-analytical. At one point in the story Isabelle complains, "Money, money, always the man that hasn't it, wants it, and the man who has it, wants more. Oh! why was money ever invented?" Her aunt says don't be a hypocrite. "Money has always given you what you want." It's true. Though Isabelle longs "to do good" with her money to help the less fortunate, "instead of helping them, I buy a pearl necklace and a few Paris gowns." She is "a spoiled child of luxury," she concludes guiltily. Hardly an earthshaking authorial insight, it would never have occurred to Nita's brother, Georgie, for whom inherited wealth was like water to a fish, just part of nature's perfect design.

If not as encouraging of Georgie's self-absorption as others in the family, Nita was amazingly tolerant of it. They attended a weekly dancing school the summer before he left for college. Snappily dressed in their formal evening clothes, they rode to town in a horse-drawn buggy, Georgie at the reins. Whenever they came to the Lake Vineyard gate he would have Nita climb out, open the gate, and then shut it behind them while he staunchly gripped the buggy reins so the horse wouldn't run away. She never let on that she knew this was just a ploy. "Really," Nita acknowledged later, "he did not want to get his pumps dusty."

She accepted as a fact of life their father's favoritism toward Georgie. From the start of Georgie's last year of high school, Papa devoted himself to getting him admitted to the U.S. Military Academy at West Point. For sentimental reasons, Papa would just as soon have seen Georgie attend VMI (from which honor graduates could be commissioned as army officers). He felt that "a better class of men" attended the Institute, namely the scions of old Virginia families. Georgie wanted West Point, alma mater of generals Lee, Jackson, Stuart; also Grant, Sherman, Sheridan, Custer, the list went on and on. But admission there involved an arcane application process that Georgie in no way could have negotiated without his father's step-by-step assistance. A lawyer, Papa understood paperwork, bureaucracy, the fine print of contracts. He knew how to curry favor with politicians to secure Georgie the necessary congressional appointment to the academy.

Two years later, the time came for Nita to leave home for finishing school. She traveled to New York with her mother to inspect Miss Spence's and Dobbs Ferry, two of the fanciest establishments in the country. Papa stayed home, assuring them blithely, "Even if you can't get in Spence's or Dobbs, the others must be nearly as good in all but merely the name." But Ruth had tolerated her daughter's second-class status long enough. She wanted the best for Nita, just once. It made no difference to Papa. Getting his son into West Point had been his all-consuming mission for nearly two years. Nita would do fine wherever.

She attended Miss Spence's but liked neither the place nor its milieu of Manhattan society. She wrote disparagingly of "the little world of the social set" and its "men of fashion and leisure." Like her fictional creation Isabelle, Nita was drawn to men "cast in a different mould from the idle society youths . . . different too from the brother she had loved, yet the difference seemed less here." It was important above all "to be real," Nita wrote, "to know and feel as one is *meant* to know and feel." That was all she wanted in life. Nothing more than that.

In 1898, Papa had told Georgie that he'd been offered a colonelcy in the U.S. Army to go fight in the Spanish-American War. If he accepted the post, Papa promised to take Georgie with him. "I do not know whether he was in earnest," Georgie recalled, "but I was mightily excited and anxious to go." Nothing had come of it, of course. Papa was teasing both of them, throwing fuel on the embers of his old boyhood dream, a dream that was starting to fade inside him and starting to flame inside Georgie.

One summer while hunting wild goats on Catalina, Georgie asked why his father didn't shoot. Papa considered the question as if for the first time, though in all the years they'd hunted and fished together he'd never once carried a gun nor dipped a line in the water. "I am a man of peace," he answered at length. Spoken almost in apology, the truth was out at last. His step visibly lightened as he continued with Georgie up the island slope in search of their quarry, the pair of them, father and son, resembling an unarmed, unhurrying native guide and a would-be great white hunter.

Papa felt a protective concern about his son's military ambitions. He feared the boy might be disappointed someday. He tried to temper Georgie's braggadocio, telling him that it was "more like a gentleman" to keep modestly quiet about how many goats he killed or fish he caught. He urged Georgie "to be more restrained in my conversation which was and is apt to become over emphatic when I am excited by the sound of my own voice." Don't be the club wit, Papa said. Don't be vulgar, smutty, or profane. When he caught Georgie throwing potato bugs in a brush fire, "he told me not to be cruel." Yet these admonishments were undercut by a subtle prodding of his son to aim high in his aspirations.

For a confirmation gift in 1901, Papa gave Georgie his father's leather-bound 1857 edition of *The Book of Common Prayer* that Colonel Patton had carried through the Civil War. Papa's inscription in the book invoked the memory of the late colonel, "who died gloriously at the head of his men, and who in being a soldier did not cease to be also a Christian man." Of course, the colonel had not precisely died at the head of his men—and as for "gloriously," who could say? But this was the Patton ballad as sung by Papa and heard by Georgie, passed along like campfire folklore.

With such an emotional stake in Georgie's future, Papa spared no effort to get him into West Point. He wrote letters soliciting recommendations from relatives and friends. Opening these letters with a disclaimer—"I am actuated by no foolish pride of ancestry"—Papa then would go on to describe Georgie's pedigree, hoping to persuade the reader (as Colonel George Smith concurred) that "if inheritance counts, the young man ought to have all the qualifications required of a soldier."

One thing Papa couldn't do for his son was take the West Point entrance examination. Georgie's academic difficulties had persisted through high school; the prospect of this written test filled father and son with dread.

Then Papa got an idea. West Point sometimes accepted students from other colleges "without the usual mental exam." With his family background, Georgie could easily enter VMI. From there, provided he did well, he could transfer to West Point as a plebe—a freshman. It would mean five years of college, but Georgie didn't mind. The plan was so perfect it seemed almost illegal. He wrote his sister excitedly, "Don't say anything about getting into W.P. without the examination as it is sort of secret."

As Georgie's day of matriculation neared—and with it the first step toward a professional army career—he became gripped with fears of inadequacy and of possibly proving cowardly under fire. "No Patton could be a coward," Uncle Glassell Patton assured him. Georgie recalled later, "I told this to Papa and he said that while ages of gentility might make a man of my breeding reluctant to engage in a fist fight, the same breeding made him perfectly willing to face death from weapons with a smile. I think that this is true." But Papa's confident words didn't reflect his misgivings. He worried for Georgie's future as a soldier and also as a cadet. All through Georgie's college years Papa installed either his wife or sister-in-law in hotels near the school. Ruth or Nannie (sometimes with Nita in tow) were always available to purchase necessities for Georgie, take him to dinner, watch him play sports or march on the parade ground, and generally to prevent any homesickness that might undercut his performance. Ruth took the first shift, as it were, remaining in Lexington outside the VMI campus after she and her husband delivered Georgie there in September 1903. Nannie had remained behind in California, and predictably Papa found on his return to Lake Vineyard that she'd taken to her bed in Georgie's absence. Only Papa's detailed report of how well Georgie was faring "restored her to something like cheerfulness." Nannie had only to be patient, however. Her turn in Lexington would come during Georgie's second term.

Georgie took this support for granted. His letters home or addressed to his mother or aunt in their nearby hotel contained orders so sharp as to seem barked out to buck privates at boot camp. "Do not bring me any blue writing paper. It is not military and I don't like it. I like white." Or: "Send me a cake both for Christmas and my birthday. There is nothing else I want." Orders came for "candied fruit" and "lots of good canday," only to be countermanded in the next mail: "Do *not* bring any more canday because I will eat it." (He had a major sweet tooth and fretted obsessively about his figure. He lifted weights hoping "to have a pair of very pretty arms which to wear in a bathing suit" and worked out at a gym to build up "my confounded legs," which were long and stick thin.) Very fashion conscious, he directed Nita to "save all the old *Vogues* with articles about men's clothes in them and send them when I tell you to." In order to look sharp, with creases creased and shirts unrumpled, Georgie sometimes changed clothes more than ten times a day. He needed extra cadet uniforms, shirt buttons, cuff links, and gloves—size seven; his hands, like his feet, were rather small for a man of his height, another source of chagrin for one who wished to be imposing in every aspect. To stem the alarming retreat of his hairline, hair tonic became a frequent item on Georgie's shopping lists. He applied the stuff to his scalp religiously, though the results were not encouraging. "In spite of my hair tonic all my hair seems coming out. I shall need a wig."

Any delay in response from his family brought a scolding: "I have not had a letter from home for four days. Are you all dead?" He insisted on full reports "not postal cards" about the care of his horses at Lake Vineyard: "I don't want people to get out of good habits while I'm gone." Impatient for compliance in others, he did not trouble himself to respond in kind if it inconvenienced him. Aunt Nannie in particular suffered under his capriciousness. Georgie understood full well her slavish devotion to him. When he needed instant action on some matter or other, needed money to gamble on his college sports teams or someone to send flowers or write thank-you notes on his behalf, it was Nannie he solicited and Nannie who always came through. Yet he could turn around and treat her like a pest, telling his mother, "If Aunt Nannie has any idea of staying here this winter you had better dissuade her . . . she would only be in the way." He forbade his aunt from engaging in embarrassing "scenes of rejoicing" whenever she visited him on campus. And while craving praise from outsiders, he could lash out at her for lovingly offering the same: "Come off telling me I did well. I did not do badly but I did not do *well* either. . . . I make mistakes of which a baby would be ashamed."

Georgie's selfish behavior was in great part the result of his indulgent upbringing. But why did Nannie and the rest of his family tolerate it all through his adulthood? The question applies to Georgie's relations with people throughout his life. Why did they tolerate him? What did he offer in compensation for chewing the scenery, hogging the spotlight, tormenting himself and others with his imagined woes, and for generally sucking the life out of anyone venturing too near, like a black hole inhaling a star? One answer lay in his childlike qualities, qualities that only a forgiving observer could distinguish from child*ish*. But then, any relationship with

Georgie required a certain ongoing forgiveness of his flaws and his excesses. Why did people (some people) do it? Maybe because he was handsome, or amusing. Maybe because he got hay fever and hives when nervous and gushed tears when happy or sad. Maybe to some people his arrogance seemed more a function of naïveté than of self-assurance, a defense measure based on panic, like a blowfish puffing up itself so the sharks cannot swallow it. Maybe they forgave him because he enjoyed debunking his gruff image when in the right company, pleased to play the fool instead, the sweetheart, the regular guy. Or maybe people (some people) forgave him because he asked them to. By Georgie's own admission he was "not normal." Without others' good graces, without their devotion and lenience, he knew he could only fail.

His future wife forgave him because she loved him and because life with him was an exhilarating drama of passionate highs and lows. His future military superiors forgave him because they liked him personally and/or respected him professionally. Some appreciated his birddog loyalty to them. Some, like General Dwight D. Eisenhower in World War II, forgave him time and time again because ultimately he was more useful than troublesome in conducting the business of war. Georgie's family forgave him because counterweighing his neglect and ingratitude were timely expressions of love that rewarded their affection and made it seem worthwhile again, as when he wrote, "Often I wake up at night and think what a wonderful mother and father and aunt and sister I have to have done so much for me and how little I deserve it for I usually succeed in being rude to some of you every time I see you, but it is not through lack of love."

Beatrice Ayer, who had no patience for poseurs, said when she and Georgie were courting that he was "one of the few people in the world who can be courteous without being idiotic." This wasn't to say that he wasn't a poseur—she understood that truth about him better than anyone. But even when he was performing, trying to charm, cajole, compel, or intimidate with whatever mask seemed appropriate to the task, there was something disarmingly sincere about the performance that enabled him to pull it off without sinking into caricature—most of the time. The best salesmen use the product themselves. A good liar subscribes to the lies he tells. A good actor inhabits his role. A leader too must be an actor, Georgie believed: "But with him as with his bewigged counterpart he is unconvincing unless he lives his part." Or to put it another way (recalling his favorite line from Proverbs), "For as he thinketh in his heart, so *is* he."

Throughout his youth ("my days of dreaming") Georgie embraced the challenge of reinventing himself. Using personal experience as a model, he later applied his ideas to converting civilian men into powerful war-making machinery. The process followed two paths. First came impersonation: "A coward dressed as a brave man will change from cowardice." Hence he demanded of his men an unflagging adherence to regulation codes of military dress and comportment—if they looked like soldiers, they would fight like soldiers. Second, he tried to instill in them a sense of themselves as part of an American tradition of manliness, patriotism, competition, and sacrifice. Victory would inevitably result from the "inward and spiritual grace" that this tradition conferred on its defenders. Victory would be assured.

In his own case, however, the "inward and spiritual grace" had nothing to do with America. While still in college he wrote brazenly, "I would just as gladly fight for any country against any country, except this one." His plan for after graduation? "To resign and join the first foreign nation which might have a war. For it is in war alone that I am fitted to do anything of importance." The colors of Georgie's flag were the colors of the sunset over a soldier's grave; he named the flag Red Battle's Sun in a 1919 war poem. The tradition to which he felt he belonged was that of warriors through history. *Felt* he belonged, but wasn't sure. He constantly scanned his psyche for intimations of linkage to that tradition. He looked for signs of fate in all he did. Recalling the cycles of reincarnation he'd learned about from Aunt Nannie, he attuned his internal antennae to hints of déjà vu and to any flashbacks of past lives that might confirm his destiny as an eternal soldier.

The warlike appearance; the diligent training to make the appearance reality; the quasi-mystical underpinnings to lend the effort epic purpose—these were the components of the process by which, in the future, Georgie strove to turn men into fighting soldiers. They were the components of his own transformation as well, of the quest he'd begun in childhood when he realized that despite his apparently conducive ancestry he did not naturally possess the thing he most needed to attain his dream. "That one thing," he wrote at seventeen, "is the undefinable difference which makes a good or a great general." In time he would define it as "the warrior soul." It was the secret of victory, he wrote. And determining himself to be lacking this thing, this warrior soul, he set himself to the dubious goal of acquiring it at all costs.

*   *   *

His reading difficulties cropped up right away at VMI. Without preparation, Georgie had to read aloud the Institute's "no-hazing pledge" to a
crowd of fellow cadets. He froze with nervousness and couldn't make out
the words. But settling down over the course of his first term, he scored
high grades and received no demerits. On Papa's advice, Georgie concentrated on being "military" first and a student second. His uniform was
always impeccable, his comportment ramrod stiff. He felt the same family
ghosts his father had felt as an undergraduate there, but Georgie was not
intimidated. He joked that VMI was so full of his relatives, he was forever
meeting them or walking on them.

He was genial but not close with his classmates. He joined a fraternity
("a lot of foolishness") but was all-business in his relationships with upper-
classmen, lest he incite jealousy in his peers. He liked the military regimen,
though not inordinately, as he explained to his father in one of many fretful
letters about transferring to West Point in 1904: "The only reason I am so
anxious to get in next year [rather than the year after] is that the joys of
cadet life are not so grate as to make me wish to spend six years in the
enjoyment of them. Five years will be bad enough but six o Lord. At the
end of that time I would be so military that it would be impossible for me
to either lounge or sleep. . . . Now to avoid this horrible contingency you
must get me an appointment."

He remained at VMI over Christmas. He spent Christmas Day at the
Institute's memorial cemetery, "eating figs on Stonewall Jackson's grave."
It would become Georgie's lifelong habit to conjure reveries and mystical
moments while wandering cemeteries, old battlefields, and ancient ruins—
preferably at night, alone. It was part of his search for connection to the
past. The romance of death attracted him. It was eerie, magical, dangerous.
It made him feel alive. On one such occasion several years later, he was
visiting the Gettysburg battlefield:

To get in the proper frame of mind I wandered through the cemetary and let
the spirits of the dead thousands laid there in ordered rows sink deep into me.
Then just as the son sank hind South Mountains I walked down to the scene
of Pickett's great charge and seated on a rock just where Olmstead and two of
my great uncles died I watched the wonder of the day go out.

The sunset painted a dull red the fields over which the terrible advance was
made and I could almost see them coming growing fewer and fewer. . . . There
were some quail calling in the trees near by and it seemed strange that they
could do it where man had known his greatest and his last emotions. It was
very wonderful and no one came to bother me. I drank it in till I was quite
happy. A strange pleasure yet a very real one."

Georgie confessed that he felt "a strange fascination" in exploring past scenes of war and destruction. "A fascination and a regret," he clarified. "I would like to have been there too." On May 24, 1904, it appeared that he might get his opportunity to participate in such scenes himself. On that date he was notified of his admittance to West Point, where he was due to report in three weeks. He thanked his father for "the vigerous use of your influence" in securing the appointment. The Virginia Military Institute had been a stepping-stone; the real journey began now. To commemorate the occasion, Georgie got out his dictionary and composed a faultlessly spelled letter to Papa: "I guess the Saturnalian age of childhood has come to an end. But all things must come to an end, and it is indeed well when one ends with as little to mar its quiet beauty as this one has had.... I can wish for no better future than that God shall fulfill my desires for the future as amply as you have satisfied my every slightest wish in the past."

The family came east to see Georgie before he went on to West Point. Mama, Nita, and Nannie took a hotel in New York City to remain near him through the summer. As Papa boarded a train back to California he mailed a letter "to my boy." "I do not feel sad at thus leaving you," it began:

From that day more than eighteen years ago when you first saw the light of this world, you have been a comfort and a joy to me—and now that we have come to a new point of departure I feel neither regret, nor fear, nor doubt. Thus far I have helped you along the road, and to the best of my ability have given you safe conduct. But "Henceforth thy warrant be thy sword."

Success in this world is often the result of prowess in ignoble acts of selfishness and self-seeking. But apart from these is the success of those who have nobly deserved success tho. they may not have achieved it. My hope, and my prayer for you, is that you may be of the latter in preference to the first.

No man may safely venture upon prophecy—but all the signs of the times indicate the approach of a period in which the soldier must play the star part. It is my hope, and my daily prayer, that Providence shall throw upon you the great responsibility by which you may "quit yourself like a man" and act your part in a spirit of responsibility and duty. If you do this, it matters little whether you achieve the fleeting applause of the unthinking multitude or not. You will have fulfilled your destiny—and played nobly your part in the drama of life.

This letter closed a chapter in the relationship of the father and son. Though Papa would remain ready with suggestions, frettings, and praise, no longer would he actively influence Georgie's career. If anything, the two would switch roles in the future, with Georgie pushing and prodding Papa to break out of his semiretirement at Lake Vineyard and enter politics again. But for now Papa was content to dabble in land development and citrus growing and, at last, to spend more time with his wife. In the past Ruth had complained of his "lack of demonstrativeness" with her in comparison with the affection he showered on Georgie. With Nita off at finishing school and Nannie in the East with Georgie, Papa told his wife, "You and I can have our first real honeymoon and be alone together long enough to get thoroughly acquainted. I am anticipating it with delight." In March the next year, he was asked to provide a biographical sketch of himself for the VMI alumni association. In responding, he apologized jovially that his sketch was

bare, as I have not achieved any particular distinction and have reached the age when I do not even regret this fact. . . . From my serene height I contemplate without envy the struggles of those who dream that happiness may be achieved in the acquirement of the wealth and honours of this world. When some years younger, I played a strenuous part in the political fray—I thought differently. Now I am more than content to leave all this to other hands.

Georgie was well launched on his career. And Nita, she was solid—you never had to worry about her. So Papa was satisfied. In that respect, he could not have been a more different kind of man from his son. The promise of repose, "that slackness at the middle distance" which Georgie anticipated with horror, was the answer to a wish Papa had never realized he desired. "I have had a good life," he admitted with a sort of surprised finality. His one hope now was that he and his wife "henceforth stay together, and walk the path of old age side by side." He was forty-eight years old.

☆ ☆ **11** ☆ ☆

A Cure for Brittle Bones

G EORGIE flunked. West Point's term for it was "found," and being found in mathematics meant he would have to repeat his plebe year. The dread he'd expressed to his father while still at VMI of taking six years to graduate had proved prophetic. Six years! Three of them as "a cadet Private." He was stunned and shamed by his failure. It struck at the heart of his insecurity about his intelligence. It marked his lowest point since that insecurity was first awakened at Stephen Clark's school in Pasadena.

Beatrice Ayer, with whom Georgie had continued a friendly correspondence since their meeting in 1902, was quick to bolster him with understanding. "Thanks for what you said about trying my hardest," he wrote her. "I think I did but results do not seem to confirm my opinion so to have you say so is very nice."

But it was his father's sympathy that he most depended on. Upon hearing that Georgie had flunked, Papa wired immediately, "It is all right my boy and all for best God bless you." Papa's advice on how to endure the setback—"in *silence* and without complaint"—derived from his own experience of disappointment: "Come out boldly and frankly and shoulder the whole thing . . . assume a spirit of cheerfulness and good humour." And above all, don't feel guilty. "Never think for a moment that your failure has given me a moment's pain except so far as it has caused my heart to beat in sympathy with you." The man was a good father, it has to be said. So dependent was Georgie on Papa's supportive presence that, Georgie acknowledged with some amazement later, "I could never think that he would die before me."

Papa's legacy to his son was not without blemish, however. He was a snob. He considered himself to be of better stock and therefore of better character than most other men. This became a handy excuse for his reluctance to mix it up in the rough-and-tumble world of politics and business. As Papa rationalized it, his lack of ambition wasn't a flaw but a chosen course, a statement of gentility; he persuaded himself that in prizing dignity over success he was setting himself above his peers. As to African Americans, Roman Catholics, and ethnic minorities, Papa didn't deem it necessary to distinguish himself from them. They were his inferiors, plain and simple. He knew this to be true, he said in a speech delivered to his private men's club in 1904, "by no process of reasoning, no study; but by the thing within me called instinct."

Papa's bigotry was not all-consuming. It crops up only faintly in his many extant letters, a mild, between-the-lines sensibility that is offensive (from today's perspective) not for its virulence but for its casual certitude. His attitude is best exemplified in that 1904 speech to the Sunset Club, the only time (in print anyway) that he expressed it directly. It was a tradition at club dinners that members entertain the company with brief lectures on topics assigned to them by vote. Papa's topic: "Conditions of National Development as Modified by Diversity of Races." He began somewhat sarcastically: "Assuming that my assignment was prompted by the fact of my Southern birth and 'prejudices,' and that I cannot be expected to discuss the Negro in that broad, comprehensive and appreciative manner in which he would be treated by those who know nothing of him, I plunge in."

He gave a brief history of the African slave trade and its part in creating "that society to be scornfully known in latter years as the 'Southern Aristocracy.' " In his view, none profited more from that trade than Puritan New Englanders who built, commissioned, and captained the slave ships. To sustain these profits, the Puritans hypocritically turned a blind eye on the injustice of slavery as long as it suited them—until, that is, Southerners began to migrate into the western territories, taking their slaves with them and thereby gaining a competitive advantage over the North in the development of those territories. Only then, Papa said, did the Puritans' "sleeping conscience" awake. The result was the Civil War.

He disputed the notion that in 1904 Southerners were "lacking in sympathy for the Negro race. . . . They know he has suffered great wrongs. He was wronged when he was snatched by violence from his African home and condemned to the unspeakable horrors of the slave ship. He was wronged every day that he toiled as a slave, though," Papa hastened to add, "the slavery he endured was upon the whole of a mild and benignant character." (Papa once was heard to say that, as a boy, he'd never seen a slave treated as badly as a plow horse in the North, not a particularly comforting comparison.) Finally, he summarized:

As a Southerner I freely admit the wrong of the system of slavery, and I further declare that the Southern people must bear the full brunt of every wrong they inflicted on the Negro, but I strongly resent the common assumption that they were the *only* or even the *chief* wrong-doers.

But the immutable laws of Nature and of God, as well as the monitory finger of history, all forbid any plan of reparation which shall in the slightest degree imperil the continued supremacy of our own race, or threaten the pollution of its Aryan blood.

There it was. Papa could extoll "the good traits of the Negro" and a moment later speak of "the prowling brute of the jungle" and "the spirit of lawlessness . . . among the Negro population, the demon of wild lust let loose." Given his era and background, such thinking is not surprising. A better man might have questioned it, moved forward from it a little. Not Papa. It was a primary part of his fragile contention that the Pattons were the best—a notion, of course, he instilled in his children. Nita reflected her father's influence when she wrote Georgie at VMI, "How do you like all the negras, they must be very funny." Within a year, however, she'd composed the short story about her alter ego, Isabelle, and the need to shed "old ignorant prejudices." In the future Nita would become a Roosevelt liberal active in philanthropy and progressive social causes. Not so her brother.

Despite Georgie's extraordinary devotion to his father, in pursuing a different kind of future he strove to be a different kind of man: ambitious, self-centered, relentless. Only in his social thinking would he always mirror Papa. As descendants of "that Southern white race, the most homogenous British stock in the world today," as Papa described it, both men took comfort and strength from the idea that theirs was superior blood. Should his circumstances ever crumble and leave him standing seemingly alone, Georgie, like his father, would count on family heritage and "Anglo-Saxon principles" to be his last defense.

On first arriving at West Point in 1904, Georgie wrote home that his roommates were "very nice and work hared and try to keep the room and them selves clean but they are not gentlemen in the sense of being refined." He supposed, however, that since they were "respectable middle class fellows" he would continue to room with them unless he found "some other fellows who are gentlemen." This kind of vacillation between his often congenial impressions of the world and his ingrained belief in its social hierarchies figured constantly in Georgie's thinking, especially when he was young; as he aged, the vacillations grew less and the prejudices more brittle and harsh. Throughout his life, however, any desire he showed to accept people on the basis of *who* not *what* they were occurred only in unguarded moments, after which, like a sentry snapping back to attention, he quickly resumed his supercilious pose. In the future, when in doubt about matters of soldiering, he often looked to the past for answers, gleaning from history "all sorts of military possibilities" that would provide "a parallel" to the problem at hand. He applied the same principle to the rest of his life: when in doubt, look to the past. It did not serve him as well.

Georgie's social attitudes were admirable only in their frequent inconsistency. Of a West Point cadet promoted to first captain, Georgie derided his looks and culture ("a German from Chicago") but allowed that he was "a good man at heart." Georgie was appalled, however, when other cadets mocked the fellow. "They sneared in his very face which only made me more noisy in my congratulations."

As a newly commissioned army lieutenant, his first impression of U.S. enlisted soldiers was that they were ignorant rabble. Yet after punctuating one soldier's order with "Damn you!", he called the man up before his unit and publicly begged his pardon. "Damn *it!*" would have been okay. "Damn *you!*" was not. "The soldiers try hard and are very respectful." The apology was warranted, Georgie felt, "but was one of the hardest things I ever did." This was in 1910. Before his career was over, he would offer many more apologies, private, public, voluntary, coerced. He would turn apologizing into an art form, though it would never get any easier.

An inveterate diarist and correspondent, his alert curiosity about the places he saw in his far-ranging travels inspired vivid descriptions of local architecture, topography, history, and archaeology. As to his thoughts on the inhabitants, these were colored by the same haughty provincialism with which he viewed his fellow citizens. Religion wasn't an issue. Georgie wrote of the world's various rituals of worship, "I think [God] is quite impartial to the form in which he is approached." Rather, his reaction to foreigners was based on how they looked, smelled, and behaved according to his patrician sensibilities. Mexico was "a country where neither life nor virtue is respected." The Arabs of North Africa were "bathrobed mendicants. Truly," he wrote, "the costume of the Arab is the index of his inefficiency." There were exceptions: "The high cast whom I know are the most courteous, considerate, and generous gentlemen I have ever met." But overall the typical Arab exhibited "pure dumbness" and was "in his filth and poverty contented." Georgie's observations in North Africa led him additionally to conclude: "Another factor tending to retard racial development is the status of women. To me it seems patent that if the mothers of a race are utterly degraded and utterly uneducated, are treated as chattels, and are deprived even of the debatable attribute of a soul, it must react on the children."

After invading Sicily in 1943, he judged the Sicilian peasants to be "worse" than Arabs and Mexicans, "lower than the bottom." Mainland Italians were a marginal improvement, though their food was "horrid" and the women "ate enough to founder a horse." The brutal execution of Mussolini was "a typical Italian stunt . . . he should have been properly hanged." Russians were "a scurvy race and simply savages." British women were "hideous, with fat ankles." France was quickly moving toward "decadence." As to people of the United States, he supported the internment of Japanese Americans after Japan's attack on Pearl Harbor because they were "my country's enemies." American blacks were "niggers"; as part of the old southern parlance he'd grown up hearing from Papa, the term was so common as scarcely to seem a conscious slur, except that both men were careful not to say it in public. During World War II, Georgie said that the black troops under his command were among the best soldiers he'd ever seen. In his diary, he suggested that they lacked "the reflexes" for modern combat. The first statement resulted from personal observation. It was overruled by that same unreasoned "instinct" Papa had invoked in 1904. It was overruled by the past.

A historian in the 1940s praised Georgie's interest in "ethnology." This is like calling a woodpecker a carpenter. As a young man he'd admitted his ignorance of nonmilitary matters to Beatrice Ayer: "I don't know or care about other things." But his ignorance didn't stop him from expressing opinions anyway. For example, for most of Georgie's life he had almost no personal experience with Jews. Cruising to Europe on an oceanliner in 1913, he wrote that he and his wife were sharing a table with "a Jewish couple, very nice." In 1930 he told his younger daughter about a Jewish West Pointer who'd bravely sacrificed his life in battle during World War

I; Georgie's point was that the Military Academy could instill heroic values even in "a dirty little Jew." He once described the wife of a government official as "a very Jewy Jewess," a designation his biographer Martin Blumenson accurately characterized as intended to be "a double pejorative." These three instances mark the extent of Georgie's recorded comments on the subject before 1945. In that year, however, the greatest and worst of his life, he often would express his thoughts about Jews in his diary and private letters. After that, Arabs, Mexicans, Sicilians, and Russians would seem not to have fared so poorly after all in the estimation of the world-famous general.

After Georgie returned to West Point in September 1905 to repeat his plebe year, his academic performance improved and his military performance, which had always been sharp, aspired to a kind of vengeful perfection. Cadet leaders within each class were designated as "corporals." After three years at the bottom of the totem pole, Georgie thought he might become "the meanest corporal in the world." Eventually many cadets would feel he deserved the title. They dubbed him a "quilloid"—someone who fanatically put underclassmen on report ("skinned" them, in West Point slang) for the slightest lapses in conduct and dress.

Like everyone, he had his complaints about the academy. "The guard here is hell . . . all I live for is sleep . . . this place has more old customs than England and if you run foul of things you are in a bad fix . . . the meat was so tough the more you chewed it the bigger it got . . . if General Sherman's definition of war be right west point *is* war." But he accepted the difficult regimen and soon became one of its severest enforcers. He said of the cadets under him, "It is true that they don't like me but when I get out in front of them the foolishness stops." His zeal isolated him. He developed no close friendships. When in June 1906 he was promoted to second corporal (number two in his class in military comportment), he thought, "perhaps the price was too high." Two months later he was *de*moted. "I was too damed military."

Toning down his intensity brought about his promotion back to second corporal the next year. Georgie was headstrong and iconoclastic, but his later reputation as a rebel is misleading. He always bowed to authority and, though often wont to push the boundaries of convention, he generally conformed to peer pressure whenever it was prudent to do so. Said General Dwight Eisenhower during World War II, "[Patton] is fundamentally so avid for recognition as a great military commander that he will ruthlessly suppress any habit of his that will tend to jeopardize it." The observation went to the heart of Georgie's lifelong effort to become the kind of man he felt he had to be in order to succeed, even if that man was not genuinely him. Playing by rules for which he felt contempt was just another aspect of the inexorable self-suppression begun when the happiest boy in the world had decided that he needed a warrior soul.

His slavish desire to curry favor with his superiors, a trait at odds with his egotism but not with his career plans, earned him the title of "bootlick" in his senior yearbook. He was called "spoony" as well, a reference to his avid interest in women. West Point held frequent dance hops for the cadets and visiting society girls. Georgie was a regular. "I have the hop habit and can't help going." To his embarrassment he gained "a reputation of being easy" for his eager reliability as a blind date for anyone's daughter, sister, or friend of a friend. While marching on the parade ground he would scan the crowd for "pretty girls in white" who came to watch the cadets. He developed "a terrible case" on Misses Harriman, Dunn, Grosvenor, and Hardee, and on a New York heiress named Kate Fowler, "a nice quiet girl and very pretty . . . her complexion is wonderful."

He could be cockily disdainful of conquests. "These Vassar girls are the easiest lot to flirt with I ever met they have no brains at all and will laugh at almost anything." But his infatuations never lasted long, nor, it seems, did they go very far. The West Point social scene was rigidly chaperoned, and Georgie, who sometimes signed himself, "Gee Willikers," was as sexually innocent as he was exuberant. Throughout his college years, his letters home were remarkably candid on all subjects, recounting in detail his every triumph and failure in academics, athletics, military matters, and love. Yet only once, in a letter to his mother written in February 1909, well into his last year at West Point, did he mention kissing a girl or even holding one's hand. At an afternoon luncheon at New York's Plaza Hotel, he and his date had evidently sought privacy where they might express their affection in peace: "I think we shocked Miss Cary [the chaperone] and all the niggers at the hotel for they insist on coming around and naturally see more than they should as it takes a long time to get long hair unfouled from small buttons. I guess I have said a little more than I should but if you have any doubt about my being very devoted get rid of it for I am."

The woman in question was Beatrice Ayer. She and Georgie had corresponded steadily since his days at VMI. "B," "Beat," or "Beaty" to him, she had his standing invitation "to every dance to be given at West Point from now until I graduate." He wasn't lonely at dances she couldn't attend, however, and his delight in other women's company made him resent her a little. "Why did I ever go to Catalina in July 1902 and why did I see a little girl who I thought I did not like and why have I been in a hell of a fix ever since?"

It wasn't that his relationship with Beatrice precluded his outside socializing. "It is perfectly proper for me to tell Vassar girls how much I love them but I don't think she should dance with every man who comes along." Rather, the problem lay in his feelings for her. "I am in love with B. to the point of madness." She was "a wonder . . . a peach . . . the best thing in her line in the world." *But:* "It seems ridiculous that I should have fallen in love with a girl so completely useless as a wife for an army officer and there is no use avoiding that fact she has not one redeeming feature for a wife aside from the fact that I am madly in love with her."

He told himself that she was too rich, too pampered and spoiled for the rigors of army life. Then again she might not be rich enough, "This because money seems an excellent tool, not for my own use, but to buy success." He wondered if a young officer ought not to marry, the better to "pay attention to daughters of prominent people." In confessing these cold calculations to his father, he admitted that "these things are not nice but they are logical. . . . But when I see B. all logic goes to hell."

As Georgie saw it, "A woman to like the army ought to be narrow minded not over bright and half educated," unlike Beatrice, who was none of these things. Perhaps if he gained glory she "will like it and forget the mud of the road. . . . But if I don't get there mud mud mud and finally a six foot hole in the same old mud." But even as he decried her unsuitability, he would forward her letters to his family for deciphering ("What is your translation of that Valentine?") and issue directions to find out through the Banning grapevine how much Beatrice liked him. On that score he'd remained quite thick for several years. She'd called him "an Adonis" in one of her earliest letters to him. Since then, she'd dropped every conceivable discreet hint to convey her feelings, always wearing the corsages he sent her and dresses that were his favorite color, sending him frequent notes of praise just as if she were a family member. But it was this sense of her as family (she was his distant cousin through her Banning mother) that clouded Georgie's view of Beatrice, made him unable to see her in the same dizzy romantic light as he saw other girls. With them he was a "spoon-noid," a charmer, a young man on the rise. With Beatrice he was only himself.

*　　*　　*

In writing to his Aunt Nannie from West Point, Georgie often played on her neurotic attachment to him by lamenting in grim detail his academic difficulties and his many athletic injuries, particularly in football: "I have scratches all over the right side of my face, while there is very little skin on the left side of my chin. I also got kicked in the nose so that there is a black spot on the left side of it, and my right eye is blacked but I don't care if I can only make that team."

He never did make the varsity football team. At polo, track, and fencing he was, shruggingly, "a star." But it was football that he couldn't play well and therefore football to which he devoted maximum hope and effort. After five years of frustration, Georgie finally blamed not his own inability but his coach, who, he told his sister, "don't like me and won't give me a chance. My desire now is to die and get to hell before him . . . I am going to make him walk up and down a red hot side line for all eternity and tell him every day I will put him in tomorrow."

Georgie complained mostly to his father, of course. "I am stupid and worthless" was his constant refrain, prompting as a kind of call-and-response Papa's patient reassurance that Georgie never could fail in his eyes. Georgie kept no secrets from Papa, not needing to maintain the staunch mask of the "quilloid," the fierce cadet corporal who tolerated no foolishness. He could tell him about his fears of cowardice and unintelligence, could admit his small-minded jealousy of men who outperformed him. But even more secret and potentially embarrassing than Georgie's self-doubt were his intimations of glorious destiny that persisted in spite of that doubt. "I don't know whether you knew it or not," he wrote his father at age eighteen, "I have always thought that I was a military genius or that I was or would be a great general." And if this hunch proved a delusion? "I can at least die happy in my own vanity knowing that I stood alone and that alone I fell."

He could admit these secrets to Papa because he knew that Papa once had harbored similar dreams and therefore would never mock him. But admitting the secrets did not relieve his anxiety, as he told both his parents during his last year at West Point: "God knows I am worried to death. I have got to, do you understand got to be great it is no foolish child dream it is me as I ever will be. Perhaps I am crazy," he went on. "Do you think me a unusually brainless fool?" They did not, of course. The curious tenor of their son's ambition had precedent in the family past. Straight-faced talk about destiny, spiritualism, violence, and glory didn't sound odd in the least.

Still, recognizing that others might not be as charitable, in the past Georgie had divulged such thoughts only to members of his immediate family. More recently, almost without realizing, he'd divulged them little by little to Beatrice. Ignoring the complimentary, interested tone of her early letters to him (he was so used to flattery from family that he took it for granted), Georgie initially had replied with perfunctory cousinly niceness because he still thought of her as that immature sixteen-year-old from Catalina in 1902. "Don't get angry," he wrote her, "but you don't seem very old." As their correspondence continued, he let slip certain admissions whose apparent offhandedness belied their deeper significance. "I am either very lazy or very stupid for it is beastly hard for me to learn." Or, "I just hate to grow old and be oppressed with the knowledge of how little I have done; it makes me feel absolutely worthless."

He confessed to his father that he'd faked illness to get out of taking an exam. (Today, such a ruse would be a potential violation of West Point's honor code.) After debating it for a day, he made the same confession to Beatrice. He told Papa and then Beatrice about a nightmare in which "every body was pointing their fingers at me and calling me stupid." In time his letters to each were equally replete with anxieties and flagellations, and in one instance he was more readily candid with Beatrice than with Papa. Georgie was ending his letters with various signatures, seeking a way to sign his name that bespoke gravity and flash. He told Beatrice that he was considering dropping his middle initial and also the "junior." The urge to move beyond the shadow of the two previous George Smith Pattons was strong in him. When at last he consulted his father about it, Papa gave no objection, never letting on how much it hurt him. Ultimately Georgie retained his full name, upholding the old traditions.

Beatrice's response to Georgie's letters took a sharp turn from the response they received from the rest of his family when she criticized him, albeit gently, for talking about himself too much and for always putting himself down. He seemed to be fishing for compliments, she said; he ought to be more self-assured. Her criticism didn't curtail his habitual self-depreciation, but it did make him realize that in addition to having "a good deal of sense," Beatrice was "tuffened." He sent her a poem he'd written (one that had "alarmed" his father): "Oh! here's to the snarl of the striving steel,/ . . . In the days when war was war." And after vowing never to invite her to a football game until he'd made the team, he accepted his failure in that sport and gave up trying to impress her. "I can see no use in cutting off my nose no matter how little I like my face please come."

With continued amazement "that Beatrice likes me for she answers all my letters," he began to show her the other side of his insecurity: the ambitions, the vanity, the sense of himself as special. He was "a boy dreamer," he said, "who has so long lived in a world of imaginary battles that they only seem real and every thing else unreal." He described a childhood fantasy that he'd revealed to no one before: "I used to fancy that I was [King] Arthur . . . I realy used to be quite sure I was. There was an old iron stick or bolt in a wall near the wood house and I used to pull at the thing quite sure it was Excalibur. But it was not. At least it is still there. I have never pulled it out. I had best stop this foolish talk."

From his first day at West Point Georgie had hoped to be the cadet adjutant in his senior year. The appointment was based less on academic than military performance. The adjutant took a visible and vocal role in cadet formations and parades, and therefore was usually a cadet who looked and sounded sharp. Papa had been first captain at VMI, the head of his class, but Georgie never aspired to the same position at West Point, though it was superior to adjutant. Maybe he unconsciously sensed that he was fitted for command but not for *supreme* command. He needed someone above him, someone to steer him, anchor him, hold his reins. He needed this in military life and in his private life also. Papa had been Georgie's guide in the past. Would it be Beatrice in the future?

She was socializing with young men in Boston, but it was for Georgie that she kept her heart "like a cold storage turkey," waiting for him to come warm it. He resisted his attraction to her. Always living, as he said, "in the land of 'tomorrow,' " he couldn't picture her as an army wife. And he couldn't square the sisterly presence to which he addressed his letters with the kind of woman he imagined marrying someday—couldn't square it, that is, until whenever he was with her in person.

"Though she was nice before," he wrote home after a West Point dance, "she is nicer and a lot prettier infact she is the prettiest girl I ever saw." Reconsidering the impression some days later, he called it "puppy love" and continued his wooing elsewhere. After spending a holiday at the Ayers' beachfront estate on Boston's North Shore, he declared himself "hard hit" over Beatrice, "the only girl I ever loved." The sentiment soon was adjusted downward, only to be revived the next time he saw her. If this was puppy love, he wrote his father in puzzlement, "I must be having the mange now."

Late in Georgie's junior year he was named cadet adjutant. The appointment was a huge confidence boost both professionally and personally. He
began to think his military ambitions might indeed come true someday.
And he began to acknowledge in his own mind the depth of his feelings for
Beatrice. Still he needed a last bit of bolstering before he could fully open
his heart to her. It came from the usual source. During a visit to West Point
the following winter, Papa eased his son's fears of rejection and urged him
to propose to Beatrice over the Christmas break, which Georgie was
scheduled to spend in Boston with the Ayers. Alone in still doubting
Beatrice's feelings, before leaving for Boston Georgie prepared an undated
telegram addressed to him at the Ayers' house on Commonwealth Avenue:
the telegram was an urgent summons back to West Point. Kept hidden in
his pocket until such time as he needed it, the telegram would provide an
excuse, should Beatrice turn him down, for Georgie to cut short his visit
with the Ayers and get the hell out of there, minimizing his humiliation.
A year later, he recalled the evening of December 30, 1908, in a letter to
Beatrice:

> The snow in the white light was almost as beautiful as you are Beautiful
> One. I can see your face now as it looked the evening the lamps went out.
> Beaty you were so perfectly lovely that it was sort of sacred. I think that
> that evening and new years were more perfect than hours on this earth
> are. I was so happy that I feared to wake up and when I did it was even
> more wonderful being still true.

So the telegram wasn't necessary. Beatrice said she loved him.

He didn't propose marriage, however. "I told Beatrice that I loved her, but
I asked nothing in return." What's more, "she did not want me to propose."
Their reasons for hesitancy differed. Georgie felt his future was so uncertain, he could not yet ask her to commit to be his bride. Beatrice felt that
after six years in the closed environment of military school, he ought to
graduate and date other girls before leaping into marriage; that way, she
said, she could catch him fairly. He sheepishly agreed this was sensible, for
though he loved her, he confided to his father, "this did not prevent me
from going up to Vassar with Kate and falling in love with her for the entire
afternoon." Kate Fowler still held some allure. "Aunt Nannie said that Kate
was worth forty million in her own name how much is B. worth. That is

asside from the fact that she is priceless in point of self I mean how much in point of pocket." Ultimately, however, he had to admit that given the choice he preferred Beatrice to Kate's millions, "ass that I am, when with the money I could be a general in no time." His naïveté about money made him completely discount Beatrice's wealth. She lived in a Boston mansion and a Gatsbyesque beachfront estate called Avalon. She'd grown up in all possible comfort, but so had everyone else in Georgie's sphere. Not until eight months after graduation did he receive, for the first time, a report from his father about the Patton family finances. Like a child breaking open a piggy bank, Georgie was amazed. "I had no notion I was so wealthy."

But concern about his professional future and about any lingering mixed emotions wasn't the real reason why Georgie was in no rush to propose to Beatrice. He knew her father would forbid the marriage under current circumstances. Frederick Ayer liked Georgie fine. What he didn't like was the military.

Mr. Ayer had more or less retired from business. His wife, Ellie, in Georgie's opinion, "would drive a saint crazy" with her grandiose airs, but for Mr. Ayer Georgie had great respect. A Connecticut Yankee, he was a self-made millionaire and carried himself with the plainspoken assurance of a man with nothing to prove; his only boast was to claim that he'd never made a dollar he was ashamed of. When he built his summer home in 1906, the local bluebloods had turned up their noses at him because he represented vulgar new money. Mr. Ayer, eighty-four and still vigorous, seemed intent on outlasting all dissent.

Georgie had been a frequent houseguest during his West Point years, and Mr. Ayer was neither surprised nor displeased that he and Beatrice had fallen in love. But he expected Georgie to do the right thing and resign his army commission and come work for him. They'd had several "high old discussions" about the military during Georgie's visits, and when Georgie wrote in January 1909 officially to declare his love for Beatrice, Mr. Ayer reiterated his position. Though the military was a respectable profession, he said, "I believe that it is narrowing in tendency." Since Georgie hadn't yet actually proposed marriage to his daughter, Mr. Ayer stopped short of giving him an ultimatum to get out of the army or else get lost. But Georgie had no doubt that such an ultimatum was inevitable. The old man was used to getting his way. In their youth, one of his older sons had wished to be a violinist and another a farmer. Frederick Ayer hadn't worked all his life to see his sons backslide into frivolity. He steered both into proper professions in medicine and business.

During the last months before Georgie's graduation, he and Mr. Ayer exchanged a series of mutually unyielding letters on the subject of Georgie's future. To Ayer's comment that the military was "narrowing," Georgie argued "that a man of only very ordinary capacity in order to succeed against great competition must be narrow." Pressed to explain "Why I want to be a soldier," Georgie attributed it to instinct: "For my own satisfaction I have tried to give my self reasons but have never found any logical ones. I only feel it inside. It is as natural for me to be a soldier as it is to breathe and would be as hard to give up all thought of it as it would be to stop breathing."

His letters to Mr. Ayer were stiffly polite. But he griped to his father that the Ayers "don't understand the army business at all. It is inconceavable to them that a man can have no desire to gain [money] and can wish to kill a fellow being by any such coarse method as shooting."

Even Beatrice had suggested that things might go easier for them if Georgie became a civilian—and honestly, she asked him, how much glory could an army career hold in such an era of world peace? His retort to her was sharp: "I dare say that for every man remembered for acts of peace there are fifteen made immortal by war and since in my mind all life is a struggle to perpetuate your name war is naturally my choice. It is true that there is nothing particularly heroic in drilling a troop yet is there anything very elevating in an office chair?" He didn't want to make money, he said, "and that is all success in business amounts to in the last aspect."

Calling it "too cruel" that destiny would burden him first with dreams and then with a lover incompatible with those dreams, Georgie lost weight and sleep as he wrestled with his decision. Beatrice feared that if he indeed were forced to choose between her and the military, she would lose him. Nevertheless she took the matter of his best interests into her own hands (as she often would in the future) and assured him that she loved him more than her family, than her father, than herself: "So you had best not consider me at all in making your decision. . . . A girl might just ruin a man's life by upsetting it at the beginning. You can decide better if you consider your self as one instead of as two. You must decide alone and then I will go with you *any* where."

As if legally released from liability, Georgie at once declared that it was demeaning "to continually apologize for ones profession when one is proud of it." He wrote Beatrice's father and told him that he would not quit the army. "I regret that my resolution may not in all respects accord with your judgement nor perhaps with that of Beatrice. Yet as I am acting in good faith and to the best of my ability what I do cannot be very wrong."

Mr. Ayer's reply was grudging. "You state very fully and clearly your position and decision, upon which I have very little comment to make." He would bide his time, evidently.

Meanwhile Beatrice continued to turn from her earlier tack of softly nudging Georgie toward her father's point of view. She told Georgie she loved him without condition or expectation. She had previously voiced concern about the roughness and transience of army life. (He'd retorted sharply that a pampered life-style could be limiting: "It is hard for me but vastly harder for you to appreciate this for both of us have had all we want and more than was good for us.") Now, Beatrice praised the adventurousness and the patriotism of army professionals who so selflessly served their nation. Georgie delighted in her words at first. When they'd confessed their love for each other the previous December, he'd been amazed to learn that she "had known it a long long time six years. She said I should have known it too what an ass I have been." But now, like a schoolboy who has bagged his first kiss, he began to strut a bit, crowing that Beatrice loved him even more than he loved her. Or, put another way: "I love her as much only I am not part Banning so don't show it as much."

Before long, however, the depth of her affection began to scare him. He joked that she was "a poor little fool girl" for adoring him so, but inside he questioned whether he deserved it. So he swallowed hard, picked up a pen, and ("to clear up in your mind though it hurt you") tried to pop any illusions she might have about him, beginning with this one: "I am *not* a *patriot*. The only thing I care for are you and my self, my self in that I may be worthy of you. . . . I say this because I am what you should know me. Perhaps I am no worse than others only more honest but if I were worse I could not help it."

He then went on to say something that an egocentric artist might say to a person he cherishes almost as much as his art: "Please love me inspite of my folly but don't love me by reason of ignorance of it. You see the chance of my doing what I wish is so small that I will very likely be dissapointed and being so dissapointed it might revert to others who I love so I must tell them." Written when he was twenty-three, the words captured perfectly Georgie's gift for combining apology with nonapology, entreaty with neglect, invitation with warning. Charm was the salve, the lubricant he depended on to get others to swallow this offering. Charm, and a cards-on-the-table honesty that left the judgment of him entirely up to the beholder. "I am rather strange," he'd told Beatrice last spring. She didn't dispute it.

Last spring, too, he'd described to her a dream in which he'd awakened to see a man with folded arms standing at the foot of his bed. "He seemed to be gray and his head was sort of like the head of an Egyptian mummy." Georgie had sat up in bed as the figure drifted out of the room, leaving the door open behind it. "Perhaps it was me," he mused, "as I was 4,000 years ago."

The story might have reminded Beatrice of the time in 1896 when she'd stolen a mummy's toe; she still had the toe, sealed tight in its jelly jar in the back of her dresser drawer. That childish prank was the most unlikely thing she'd ever done, next to loving Georgie. He, for one, didn't think her love unlikely at all; he thought it destined. Eleven years later he wrote a poem telling how "for ever and forever" he and she had fallen in love through one lifetime after another.

> Yes, forever and as truly
> As the waters changeless are,
> Have I fought for, sought and found thee
> As tonight beneath the star.
>
> Ever fearing, ever hoping,
> Ever winning thee at last,
> But to lose thee to regain thee,
> In the present from the past.

No one understands me, he once complained to Beatrice. "My hopes and views are so insane . . . no one does, not even you, and Lord knows I bother you seven days in the week with them—Poor B." Poor B? She didn't see it that way at all.

"It is certainly a delight to find a girl so utterly independent of superstition and conventions as pretty Beatrice Ayer, who, despite the fact that the month of May has been tabooed by brides from earliest recollection as fatal for weddings, has defied fate by choosing it for her marriage to Lieutenant George S. Patton, Jr." So reported the Boston newspapers at the announcement of Beatrice and Georgie's engagement in April 1910. It had taken several months' worth of stubborn letters from Georgie, and a brief hunger strike by Beatrice (who was supplied food on the sly by her siblings and mother), to get Beatrice's father to consent to the marriage. But Frederick

Ayer bowed out gracefully in the end, telling his prospective son-in-law that each man should do what he did best: Mr. Ayer to earn the money, Georgie to earn the glory. He asked only that Georgie "keep ever in mind" the Ayers' wish to see Beatrice as often as possible. As a last tip of the hat in his letter of consent to Georgie, the old man allowed that "I admire your firmness of purpose in sticking to the army," and signed himself "sincerely your friend, F. Ayer."

Georgie had been assigned to the Fifteenth Cavalry at Fort Sheridan, Illinois, after graduating from West Point. In addition to his military duties, he'd pursued an active social life in nearby Chicago ("More than Beat. would care to hear about," he confided to his father). One possible fruit of these new big city experiences was the more forwardly sensual tone in his love letters to Beatrice. In one he groused, "This is a ____ ____ foolish letter [censoring himself uncharacteristically] but it is the result of an honest effort keep off a certain subject." He gave a clue about that subject when he teased her that she must be careful not to catch cold, lest she transmit that cold to him, "because when you come to Chicago you will ___ me." In the space he drew what would become characteristic "kiss marks" in his letters to her throughout their marriage: tiny drawn circles with crosses inside them like the crosshairs of a telescope sight. "Can you understand that sentence," he wrote. "I could demonstrate it so beautifully if you would but give me the chance."

He'd proposed to Beatrice by mail in February 1910. Her hunger strike began when the letter arrived, and a week later she wired him, "Rejoice." To his parents she wrote, "The Ideal has become the Real, and is still Ideal." Their wedding took place on May 26 at St. John's Episcopal Church in Beverly Farms, near the Ayers' summer home. Beatrice wore her mother's embroidered cream-colored wedding gown and carried a prayer book instead of a bouquet. Her brother Fred was best man. The ushers, military officers in dress uniforms, formed an arch of drawn sabers as the newlyweds departed the church.

No one was happier that day than Georgie's Aunt Nannie. His mother, Ruth, had taken ill and couldn't attend the ceremony. Nannie took her place in all the proceedings. In a fantasy come true, she held Papa's arm at the reception, sat at the head table, received toasts in her honor with a modest blush. She danced with Georgie and kissed him good-bye as he left with his new bride. This fleeting moment of recognition as Georgie's true mentor, true mother, and as Papa's should-have-been wife, was the greatest day of her life.

Georgie and Beatrice spent their wedding night at Boston's Hotel Touraine. Years later he apologized to her for hurting her that night. If his roughness with her was the result of inexperience or passion, or was a show of masculine dominance that he might have thought befitted a young warrior, during the long cruise to Europe for their honeymoon they got things agreeably worked out. Beatrice wrote her mother of happily spending most of their time in their stateroom bed. From Europe she wrote Georgie's mother that his hay fever had kicked up. While on the matter of his health, Beatrice wondered if, Georgie being so accident prone, she ought to feed him "powdered china. I think it might make his bones less brittle." Then again, never mind: "Don't worry about Georgie, he is all right—and I have such fun curing him."

Georgie's honeymoon letters were less chatty. "I am well. So is B. We have not fought yet." A married man now, he would share his inner thoughts mostly with Beatrice rather than, as he had in the past, with other family members. "A soldier's heart," said Robert E. Lee, "is divided between love and glory." Georgie believed that in Beatrice he'd found the means to have love and glory both. "May our love be never less than now. And our ambition as fortunate and great as our love."

So had closed his final letter to her written before they were married. In the future it truly would be "our love" and "our ambition" they shared. This was their prayer, and like a prayer, Georgie ended his letter, "Amen."

☆ ☆ **12** ☆ ☆

We Are Living So Intensely Lately

BEATRICE got pregnant on the honeymoon. When she began show-ing that winter at Fort Sheridan, Georgie sullenly teased her for "living the life of a turnip" by eating and sleeping so much. She thought he was anxious that she wouldn't bear him a son, an heir to carry forward his name. Would he be upset if she had a girl? Of course not, he said. "I married one, didn't I?" What Georgie resented was the prospect of losing his new bride's attention to a howling infant. He consid-ered it rotten luck to have conceived on his honeymoon, an opinion he didn't hesitate to share with his wife or anyone else who asked.

Family members from both coasts convened at the Pattons' small Fort Sheridan quarters as Beatrice's due date neared. She wanted Georgie to witness the joyful event, so insisted he stay in the bedroom with her for the birth. What he saw during her long and difficult labor horrified him. The sight of blood always had sickened him—and this was Beaty's blood, Beaty's cries of pain in his ears. He fought to hold down his nausea, but when the nurse presented his newborn daughter to him, he rushed from the room, ran downstairs, and vomited in the kitchen sink.

The infant initially was called "Smith," then "Little Bee," and finally just "Bee." When Georgie wrote his mother about the birth (Ruth and Nannie had remained in California), he described Bee as "brownish blue . . . a hideous specimen, though physically perfect." To Aunt Nannie he wrote, "The accursed infant is very ugly and is said by some dastardly people to resemble me, which it does not." In both letters he went on to celebrate his recent acquisition of a Chalmers automobile, "a very handsome machine indeed." Since leasing a car on his honeymoon, he'd developed a keen interest in driving and auto mechanics. The hobbies later would help draw his professional interest from horse cavalry to tanks. In so doing, they would deepen his future conviction that every event and interest in his life had in some way contributed to his destiny as a tank commander. Everything except fatherhood, that is. Like counting birthdays and watching his hair thin, fatherhood was simply an annoyance.

He had no desire for more children. Beatrice wanted to give him a son, however, and in February 1915 their second child was born at Lake Vineyard: another girl. Georgie remained at his new cavalry station at Fort Riley, Kansas ("so far from every thing, you can not even go to hell"). He'd notified Beatrice's doctor beforehand "that if there is the least question between her life and that of the child the child must go." She again had a hard labor. Papa paced the hallway outside her room for hours. Disappointed at not having a son, Beatrice sighed to her mother-in-law afterward, "Better luck next time." Ruth quickly shushed her: "Please don't mention next time. My husband has had a very hard day."

By letter Georgie proposed "Beatrice Second" for the new baby's name, "like a race horse." His wife's choice of "Ruth Ellen" was a tactful nod to her mother and mother-in-law. Beatrice had a knack for social diplomacy, a knack that already had won Georgie points with his superiors and their wives.

She was not especially maternal. Though nowhere near as aloof from her kids as Georgie was, she didn't hesitate to leave them for months at a time with her parents or in-laws if it freed her to spend time with Georgie. Her desire to be with him at even his farthest-flung postings conflicted with the obligation she felt to attend her elderly parents. The Ayers had relatives around them, plenty of money and plenty of help. Still, Beatrice felt guilty for being distant from them, and her parents played on this guilt by frequently calling her home. In the future she would scold herself for letting "divided loyalty" intrude in her marriage. Georgie's career caused enough unavoidable separations without adding to them by choice. "What a stupid fool I was," she wrote.

At Georgie's insistence, the Pattons always dressed for dinner, Georgie in a tuxedo, Beatrice in a floor-length gown, no matter the shabbiness of their army quarters. They employed multiple servants wherever they lived. A core group of three (maid, handyman, nanny) was sometimes augmented with a nurse for the girls, a cook, chauffeur, laundress, and later an enlisted orderly (or two), which in those days the army assigned to all officers above the rank of captain. As a young wife, Beatrice managed her household with an air of burdened exasperation. "When I get home, I may have to get a new nurse and certainly a new man, so my work is cut out for me. They do not grow on every bush!" Because Georgie considered it humiliating to be bumped from larger to smaller quarters by a higher ranking officer, he took the smallest quarters to start with, then expanded the place to accommodate the live-in help. He depended on a large monthly allowance from his father-in-law to support this life-style, which far exceeded a lieutenant's salary. One consequence of Mr. Ayer's generosity was that Georgie became known as the richest officer in the army and also the most ostentatious, the latter impression a result of his unapologetic fondness for throwing parties, buying thoroughbred horses, and driving ever new and faster automobiles. People knew the money was his wife's. This bothered him, increasing the pressure he felt to prove himself worthy, to succeed not just for himself but for Beatrice.

In September 1915 Georgie joined the Eighth Cavalry Regiment at Fort Bliss, just outside El Paso, Texas. The post was commanded by Brigadier General John J. Pershing, whose brigade had been moved from California to West Texas as a security measure against the political unrest across the border. Mexico had fallen into chaos when its dictator, Porfirio Diaz, was overthrown in 1910. Two presidents had since come and gone, and now armed factions under Pascual Orozco, Venustiano Carranza, and Francisco "Pancho" Villa were competing for the control of Mexico.

Beatrice and the children stayed behind in Massachusetts, awaiting word from Georgie that suitable quarters were available and that life on the post was not too dangerous. If rumors were to be believed, the United States might at any time be drawn into the Mexican conflict. The rumors increased in October when President Woodrow Wilson threw his support to Carranza, infuriating the volatile Villa, who threatened retaliation from his base of operations just south of Texas and New Mexico. This was real Wild West country, with sprawling cattle ranches and gritty ramshackle towns full of gun-toting cattlemen, assorted frontier ladies ranging from painted to rough to, in Georgie's words, "dashing," also Indians, Texas Rangers, and Mexican outlaws. "I would not miss this for the world," he wrote his wife. "I guess there are few places like it left."

When not drilling troops at Fort Bliss, Georgie inspected army outposts along the Rio Grande. Spending as much as eleven hours a day in the saddle, he rode for hundreds of miles through "the most desolate country you ever saw. Rocks and these thorny bushes." For diversion he hunted the plentiful game, engaged in shooting matches with local cowboys, and listened eagerly to their tales of adventure. Georgie wrote Aunt Nannie about a "panther hunter" he met. "He was very dark and commented on it. Saying 'Dam it a fellow took me for a Mex and I had to shoot him three times before he believed I was white.' This impressed me very much and I assured him that he was the whitest man I ever had seen."

Georgie got on well with the Texans. "I usually do with that sort of people." For his prowess as a pistol shot, he won the admiration of a Colonel Sterling of the Texas Rangers, who gave him the classic frontier six-shooter that would be one of several sidearms Georgie carried all his life: a .45-caliber Colt single-action revolver, model 1873. Sterling was a brute who dressed as a kind of rodeo peacock in tassels and spurs and silver shirt studs. To the question of how many men he'd killed, he once was heard to reply, "Thirty-five, not counting niggers and Mexicans." Georgie already had begun tentatively copying one old rancher's ear-popping use of gutter profanity ("I have never heard one say a thing with so much emphasis"), testing it out for effect on his troops. Colonel Sterling's sartorial vividness seemed something else worth copying. So Georgie had the walnut grips of the Colt .45 replaced with ivory—on one side a carved eagle, on the other his initials set in black enamel. In recent years he'd been riding in public horse shows as often as possible. "It is the best sort of advertising. It makes people talk and that is a sign that they are noticing." Ivory grips on his pistol served the same purpose. "The notice of others has been the start of many successful men."

The threat of Mexican attack kept the Americans in a high state of alert. On Thanksgiving Eve, Georgie heard that El Paso might be raided the next day. To his disappointment, it proved a false alarm. Two days later, he was ordered to move out with his cavalry troop and attack a band of eighty Mexicans who were camped along the Rio Grande. Though his previous "eve of battle" had seemed "not at all interesting nor so exciting as a polo game," on this night Georgie couldn't sleep for excitement. He intended to lead a saber charge on the enemy. "I thought I had my medal of honor sewed up and laid awake planning my report." But by dawn the Mexicans had slipped over the river and fled.

Worried that Georgie would be killed before she could see him again,

Beatrice left the girls with her parents and traveled to Fort Bliss in December. As always when they were united after a period of separation, there was an initial awkwardness between them as they reaccustomed themselves to each other, an unease in expressing emotions in person that flowed so easily in their letters. During a summer-long separation several years earlier, Beatrice had angered Georgie by suggesting in a letter that his favorite pastime was reading history. "What in H do you mean," he wrote back furiously. "I would rather a damned sight look at some thing else than a book and you know what it is too. It looks like a skunk." He did not want her to forget his sexual interest in her: it hurt his image to be perceived as a bookworm rather than a hot-blooded lover. Georgie's conception of a proper warrior had certain specific attributes. As he told his wife's nephew many years later, "A man who won't fuck, won't fight."

He once observed that a husband "must be just as careful to keep his wifes love as he was to get it. That is he should always be spoony and make love to her so she will continue to like him." Behaving this way toward Beatrice was not a chore. "In fact," he wrote her eight years after their marriage, "my attitude towards you is more that of a lover uncertain of his chances than of a husband." His uncertainty arose soon after Beatrice's arrival in Texas. She and Georgie attended a dinner party of local ranchers and their wives at a hotel near Sierra Blanca. During coffee, a gun went off in the room. Everyone dove to the floor. Though no more shots sounded, the party nervously broke up. Georgie and Beatrice climbed out from under a table, said their good-byes, and left in his automobile. He drove in silence through the moonlit night until he crashed headlong into a cattle gate without making any effort to brake. Beatrice, shaken by the collision, was more shaken by the sight of tears rolling down Georgie's face. "You don't give a damn about me!" he cried. "That was *my* pistol that went off. I might have been killed, and you didn't even ask if I was okay!" He'd been trying to mimic the local men by carrying a pistol in his waistband. Somehow the gun had gone off, blowing a hole in his trousers and the hotel floor. Calming him down, she assured him that her love hadn't diminished during their recent separation. Yet a part of him was never completely convinced. He often felt, sometimes with reason, that he was on the verge of losing Beatrice and had to win her affection anew. "Still it is a good way to be," he decided.

In addition to Georgie's insecurity, Beatrice in time came to accept his amazing penchant for mishap. In the 1930s she was hosting a quiet tea party while he was cleaning his many firearms upstairs. Suddenly a shot rang out,

a bullet exploded through the ceiling and embedded in the floor at Beatrice's feet. The women at the party froze in shock. Beatrice sighed, "I wish
he'd be more careful." Such reserve in the face of her husband's erratic
behavior was hard won. Through the first ten years of her marriage she was
constantly nervous about the welfare of Georgie, her kids, her parents. Her
heart would race with tachycardia, she often suffered insomnia, and she
could explode in fits of temper that surprised her and frightened Georgie.
As gray streaks appeared in her hair, he pestered her to dye it. "I always
think of you as Undine so I don't want you to look 33," he wrote her in
1918, "even if I do." In fact, he always looked much younger than she did.
Beatrice neither dyed her hair nor wore makeup nor fretted about her
thickened figure after bearing two babies—her anxieties were not about
herself. But in trying to mother Georgie, her parents, her kids, she imagined she was failing at all three.

She usually put on a calm front for her husband, but on a stormy night
soon after her arrival at Fort Bliss she broke down weeping and begged him
to quit the army. It was out of the question. So she returned to Boston,
collected her children and servants, and came back to Texas to resume this
strange ride with Georgie. He'd prevailed on her as he prevailed on
everyone close to him, getting his way with a spoiled child's irresistible
blend of sweetness and stubborn presumption.

In February 1916, Nita Patton left California on the Southern Pacific
Railroad to visit her brother and sister-in-law at Fort Bliss. She hadn't
wanted to go, but then in recent years she hadn't wanted to do much of
anything.

In what she later would term "my savage period," Nita had grown sour
and depressed living at Lake Vineyard with her parents. She'd got heavy,
too, a condition not helped by her brother's fretful letters about striving to
maintain his college weight of 165 pounds and his twenty-eight-inch waist.
The source of Nita's blues was simple: no man. At age twenty-eight she
seemed well on the way toward seeing her dream of finding love fall to
dust. She was turning into Aunt Nannie.

During Nita's first social season after making her formal debut ten years
ago, she'd written her brother expressing mild worry over her "lack of
conquests." Georgie had tried to dispel her fears, joking that if he were
"half as much of a heller with girls [as she was with boys] my future as a
spoon-noid would rest assured." But privately he shared Nita's worry. He

wanted to find a beau for her but knew of no one suitable, that is, one who met Georgie's standards. "I hope she does not marry a soldier, a sailor, a doctor, a lawyer, or a parvenu. In fact I can't thing of any one good enough for her, so she had best not get married." Papa, too, had high demands about the kind of man acceptable for Nita, so much so that even Georgie, who shared his father's snobbery, chided him for his inhospitable chilliness toward the suitors Nita brought home. But ultimately it was Nita herself who posed the main obstacle. The few men that had expressed interest in her had fallen short of "ideals" she couldn't define but was determined not to forego. She would have perfection or she would have nothing. Before Nita left for Texas, her mother threw her a small party. It only depressed Nita. Her friends looked "quite middle-aged," she wrote. "I wonder if I match them?"

Apart from a general downhearted inertia, another reason Nita was not looking forward to visiting Fort Bliss was that she didn't particularly get along with Georgie's wife. In 1912, Nita had spent a month in Europe with Papa, Georgie, and Beatrice. She'd envied the easy rapport Beatrice developed with Papa, and had felt slightly patronized by Beatrice as the unwed, unconsummated little sister not quite worldly enough to share the gaiety of beer halls, nightclubs, and four-star restaurants. An unkind word was never spoken; Beatrice's manner toward Nita was impeccably sweet. Still, Nita confided to her mother (who was her confidante as Papa had been Georgie's), "I guess she thinks I am awfully slow and have no music in my soul."

The Pattons had been assigned "a good house" by the parade ground opposite the enlisted men's barracks. It was Nita's first experience of life on an army post, and the active social scene, particularly among the many bachelor officers who were thrilled to have a new young woman to escort to the dances and dinners, was a pleasant surprise to Nita. "Everyone is gay and fun down here in spite of wars and rumours of war," she wrote her mother. "We are surely leading the wild life, and the worst of it is I like it!" A country girl used to roughing it, Nita took secret satisfaction in Beatrice's quite different reaction to life on the border. "Poor B. is not fitted for the strenuous life, she gets too excited over mishaps. . . . She is like Papa and gazes on the dark side. I'd hate to live my life expecting the worst—or being insanely happy."

Nita rejoiced over having "beaus galore," though she remained cautiously aware of her vulnerability to the young officers' "fatal charm." Soon she met the post commander, General Pershing. "He is awfully good-looking and entertaining—and is sort of historical too." Pershing, then fifty-five, was one of the most renowned military officers of the period, having campaigned with distinction in the Indian Wars and the Spanish-American War. Nita was probably the only person at Fort Bliss who considered him "such fun," for he was a rigidly formal man with fierce eyes, thick steel gray hair, and a clipped mustache. His mania for discipline had earned him the nickname "Black Jack."

A few months earlier, Pershing's wife and three daughters had died in a fire in California; only his adolescent son, Warren, had survived. Nita noted wryly after first meeting the general, "He is not exactly dying of grief." Soon it became apparent that Pershing was attracted to her. "What can a mere woman do," she wrote her mother, "when a general looks her in the eye and says 'Now promise me you won't go.' " For the first time in her life she preened in the attentions of a singular man. Georgie told Beatrice with some ambivalence, "Nita may rank us yet."

On March 9, Pancho Villa fulfilled his threat to strike the United States, attacking Columbus, New Mexico, and killing seventeen Americans. Georgie had been praying for such a provocation, and the next night, Nita reported, "he got out every kind of gun" in preparation to move out with his unit in pursuit of the raiders. Nita described Beatrice as "white and little looking," weeping at the thought of his leaving: "She isn't built for worry." Nita's own feelings were mixed. "I am all chills one minute thinking Geo. is going and all anxiety the next for fear he won't." She knew how desperately he wanted to get into battle. Hence she told only her mother, "I may not be a good American, but I don't want war." To Georgie that would have been sacrilege.

He was horrified to learn that his unit was to remain behind at Fort Bliss while other forces under Pershing's command would pursue the Mexicans. Certain that his regimental commander had been deemed too overweight for field duty ("there should be a law killing fat colonels on sight"), Georgie decided to transfer out of the Eighth Cavalry at once. He asked General Pershing to take him along as his aide-de-camp. In getting the assignment, Georgie was lucky on three counts. Pershing's usual aide was temporarily absent; as a young officer, the general had finagled his way out of a staff job to get into combat in Cuba, so he identified with Georgie's frantic request; and finally, Pershing's fondness for Nita disposed him favorably toward her brother. This last bit of luck occurred to Georgie, but he downplayed its significance. He didn't like to think that he'd gained an advantage through his sister. Neither did Beatrice. Having now committed herself fully to supporting her husband's career, she wanted nothing to taint his eventual triumph. If there was to be any behind-the-scenes help, it must come only from her, and no one must ever know about it. Her farewell to Georgie when he rode out on March 16 revealed her newly hardened conviction. At previous partings she always had wept profusely. This time, he noted with some surprise, "B acted fine and did not cry or anything."

Nita was unaware of her part in helping Georgie to join the expedition. "Golly life was never so exciting before" summed up her thoughts of the moment. She decided to stay on in Texas. Devoted to her nieces, she called Little Bee "a great kid," delicately pretty and ever eager to please the grown-ups. The baby, Ruth Ellen, had a fierce pug face and a character to match: "She is a perfect ring-tailed heller." Nita drove her brother's "machine" in his absence, often with a pistol in the car seat beside her. Since Villa's raid on Columbus, the fear was that he might now attack the undermanned post. "We are living so intensely lately," Nita wrote her mother. "I think I will be nicer, and younger, if I ever do come home again."

She began to establish a better relationship with Beatrice. On nights when Beatrice couldn't sleep, Nita would slip into bed with her. Beatrice was worried about Georgie, of course—Nita was rather less worried. She'd grown up hearing him obsess about his ambitions. "His dearest wish is realized," she knew. "He has gone to war."

It has been said that one trait of genius is the ability to concentrate with extraordinary intensity on the particular matter at hand. Though George S. Patton has often been called a military genius, the merits of that judgment are for others to debate. He careened all his life between manic self-assurance and almost incapacitating despondence. His own estimation of his military capabilities was similarly erratic, ranging from "I am a genius" to "I am not such a great commander . . . just a fighting animal"; from "I am a profound military student and the thoughts I express . . . are the result of years of thought and study" to "the funny thing is that I don't know how I do it." On the basis of concentration alone, however, Patton clearly was gifted.

From the age of seven until his death, his focus never wavered. The romance of war, which first had attracted him, was supplemented but never displaced by his study of war's technical aspects and his experience of war's actuality. As an unblooded twenty-two-year-old, he wrote that war was "an art . . . a very beautiful intellectual contest." As a veteran general of nearly sixty, the dazzlement still held: "I guess that I am the only one who sees glory in war." By fortunate coincidence, his dreams and talent were well matched. Patton sensed this affinity early on, and that awareness, without promising fulfillment, gave him the confidence of knowing that he was suited to no other path. Later he theorized, "You can have doubts about your good looks, about your intelligence, or about your self-control, but to win in a war, you must have no doubt about your ability as a soldier." For proof of this theory, he looked inside himself. He carried exactly those doubts and others. He was confident *only* in his ability as a soldier, and even there his confidence sometimes faltered, as in Sicily in 1943 when generals Omar Bradley and Lucien Truscott criticized his battle plan as too risky: "Last night I remembered Frederick [the Great]'s 'l'audace . . .' and Nelson putting the glass to his blind eye and saying, 'Mark well, gentlemen. I have searched diligently and see no signal to withdraw.' . . . those historic memories cheered me no end."

Patton stressed the importance of "book knowledge" of war while he was still at West Point. He often bid Aunt Nannie to send him volumes of military history for extracurricular reading. Throughout his adult life he stayed up past midnight reading everything from junky popular biographies of famous war heroes to obscure European treatises on tactics, logistics, and armaments. Patton learned much about his craft from these books. Apart from seeking to learn *from* them, however, he was seeking to confirm *in* them certain conclusions about warfare and leadership that he'd already arrived at on his own, long before he had the education or experience on which to base those conclusions. Where, then, did those conclusions come from?

His early writings were full of the uncertainty we might expect of any teenager—except in the area of military matters. There young Patton pontificated with the assurance of a field marshal. "I have a sixth sense about war," was his explanation many years later, but he seemed to have always possessed it. At sixteen, he cited the ancient Greek general Epaminondas (410–362 B.C.) as his favorite commander. Alexander the Great would seem the more obvious choice, having most famously met Patton's main requirement of a great general ("not to be beaten"). But fifteen years before Alexander's birth, Epaminondas of Thebes conceived the battle formation known as the oblique order, which Alexander later refined and deployed in a twelve-year stretch of unbroken Macedonian victories. The convention of the period was for armies to line up in opposing fronts of uniform depth and then trudge forward and start hacking; victory usually went to the stronger, larger, more disciplined army, which in Epaminondas's day was the Spartans. The oblique order, by contrast, presented an unbalanced line, stacked on one end with a heavily manned striking force. The more thinly manned parts of the line held the enemy at bay while this striking force crushed the opposing flank and swept around it, slaughtering the enemy and, more importantly, causing it to panic and run. One of the most significant innovations in the history of warfare, the formation has appealed to commanders through history because it brings to bear an overwhelming force against one critical point of the enemy line while limiting the commitment of other forces elsewhere in the attack—two essential principles of modern war known as mass and economy of force.

The oblique order enabled Epaminondas to whip the Spartans at Leuctra in 371 B.C., securing nine years of peace for Thebes. Frederick the Great used it to defeat the Austrians at Leuthen in the Seven Years' War (1756–1763). And it was the forerunner of the wide-sweeping ground attack used by the coalition forces against Iraq in the Gulf War of 1991 (a type of maneuver Patton famously characterized as grabbing the enemy by the nose and kicking him in the ass). Patton admired Epaminondas because his tactics were offensive-minded and seized the initiative from the enemy. But his boyhood appreciation was sparked by something else as well. In confronting the powerful Spartan Army, Epaminondas was an underdog, outnumbered two to one. At sixteen, Patton felt like an underdog. His dreams seemed too big, his capacities too small—it was only natural that he admire a commander who through inspiration and daring so resoundingly beat the odds.

Patton often quoted Robert E. Lee's reason for mounting counterattacks against the larger Union forces moving against him. Said Lee, "I was too weakened to defend." It is well known that Patton's professional style was basically "in case of doubt, attack!" Or, as went one of his orders: "Go until the last shot is fired and the last drop of gasoline is gone. Then go forward on foot." This was his personal style as well. "Fame never yet found a man who waited to be found." He always was aggressive as a commander and in his private life. "Bumptious" was how he saw himself; "boisterous." He feared to be otherwise. "As long as you attack them," he believed, "they cannot find the time to attack you." That is, the best defense is a good offense, especially if you secretly suspect yourself to be "too weakened to defend."

Patton's will to strike preemptively enabled the happy circumstance of notifying his wife from Mexico on May 14, 1916, "I have at last succeeded in getting into a fight." In miniature, his action exemplified what Patton later called the golden rule of war, "Speed-Simplicity-Boldness," a rule as useful to him in dominating a battlefield as in dominating a drawing room.

On May 2, twelve days before Georgie wrote Beatrice about "getting into a fight," he and a small number of soldiers entered an adobe ranch house called San Miguelito just west of Rubio, Mexico, in search of one of Pancho Villa's raiders, a colonel named Julio Cardenas. Cardenas had fled the ranch house, leaving behind his wife, baby, and uncle. "Tried to get information out of uncle," Georgie noted tersely in his diary: "Failed." In a letter to his father about the event, his description echoed the prose of Ernest Hemingway in the brutality it implied but did not detail: "The uncle was a very brave man and nearly died before he would tell me anything."

Georgie originally had joined the cavalry branch of the army because he felt artillery operated too far from the front and infantry lacked panache. ("Infantry and artillery win battles," he later quoted British Field Marshal Douglas Haig, "but only cavalry makes them worth winning!") Whenever fighting imaginary battles in his head, he pictured himself leading cavalry charges like Jeb Stuart or Napoleon's Marshal Ney, "the bravest of the brave." However, he was not on horseback when he and his men returned to Rubio on May 14. They rolled into battle in three rickety Dodge touring cars doing twenty down a Mexican mule path: it wasn't tanks or half-tracks, but it was motorized warfare all the same, the first instance of it in U.S. Army history, a fact Georgie later was pleased to point out as one more indication of the hand of fate guiding his life.

Earlier that day, May 14, General Pershing ordered Georgie to take the vehicles and fourteen men to Rubio to purchase corn for the U.S. soldiers. Georgie bristled at the sight of fifty or sixty Mexican men idling suspiciously in the center of town. The corn bought and loaded, he decided to pay an extracurricular visit back to San Miguelito, where he'd nearly captured Julio Cardenas twelve days before. On the way, he stopped at the nearby Saltillo ranch, which also belonged to the Cardenas family. Georgie found the uncle he'd interrogated earlier. Evidently recovered now, the uncle sold him some corn, but as before would reveal nothing of his nephew's whereabouts. Georgie didn't press the issue. His sixth sense was aroused. He proceeded on to San Miguelito, certain it would pay off.

The three touring cars arrived at noon. The San Miguelito ranch house was a large adobe hacienda with a flat dirt roof and a courtyard whose arched gateway faced east. Georgie knew the layout and planned his approach accordingly. Coming up from the south, his lead car drove to the north end of the house where Georgie and a civilian interpreter got out and headed around the corner toward the courtyard gate. He carried a rifle in his left hand. His Colt revolver was holstered on his right hip. Out in front of the gate three old men and a boy were skinning a cow in the dirt. They paid Georgie no mind, and in fact never ceased their work through all that happened next.

The other two cars halted at the southern end of the house, cutting off the exit road. Four soldiers stayed in place, six rushed toward the corner of the house to hook up with Georgie coming around from the other direction. Before the men got there, three Mexican riders carrying rifles and pistols galloped out of the gate fifteen yards in front of Georgie. Georgie drew his pistol but did not shoot—because of the difficulty of discerning Mexican friend from foe, Pershing had ordered his soldiers not to fire unless fired upon. The three riders wheeled away from Georgie only to run headlong into the six soldiers coming up the other way. The riders turned back and bore down again on Georgie, who stood, he recalled, "waiting to see what would happen . . . all three shot at me, one bullet threw gravel on me. I fired back with my new pistol, five times." He hit one rider in the arm, breaking the bone, and shot the man's horse through the gut.

The other soldiers began shooting at the Mexicans. Georgie retreated from their line of fire and crouched against the house's adobe wall. "Three bullets hit it about seven feet from the ground and put adobe [dust] all over me." Reloading his pistol, Georgie did not see the rider he'd hit spur his injured mount back into the courtyard and into the front door of the house. Looking up after reloading, "I saw [another] man on a horse come right in front of me." As the man made to escape Georgie recalled what one of the Texas lawmen had advised him about stopping a fleeing rider: aim at the horse, not the man. Georgie did so, "and broke the horses hip, he fell on his rider."

Then Georgie did an odd thing. "Impelled by misplaced notions of chivalry," he waited for the man to extricate himself from his floundering horse. He and his soldiers surrounded the Mexican, their weapons leveled at him as he struggled to stand. The *Villistas* had a mixed reputation. To their supporters they were like Robin Hood's Merry Men, stealing from the rich to give to the poor. To their enemies they were plain killers; one of Villa's lieutenants was nicknamed the Butcherer for the pleasure he took in personally executing prisoners. So probably the Americans were not chivalrous for long. They fired together. "It was only ten yards, we all hit him, he crumpled up."

They shot at another rider a hundred yards off. He went down. The man Georgie had wounded in the arm in the first exchange appeared running on foot along a wall about three hundred yards away. He had ditched his horse inside the house and jumped out a back window. After he too "was dropped," one of the Americans approached him where he slumped on the ground. The man raised a hand in surrender, then quickly raised his pistol with the other hand and tried to kill the soldier. He missed. The soldier "blew out his brains."

Up to this moment, Georgie had been too busy to be scared. Only vaguely during the shootout had he "kept wondering why they did not hit me. The guns seemed pointed right at me." But now, in the quiet aftermath, he began to picture all the bad possibilities that somehow he'd dodged in this really quite amazing event. His sudden dread posed a problem, because for all he knew, there were more *Villistas* inside the house—in which case it was crucial that a soldier immediately secure the roof lest the enemy get there first and start shooting down on the Americans. Georgie made himself go. "I hated to climb up but hated worse not to." There, his old clumsiness struck. At his first step onto the roof he plunged through it up to his armpits. The idea of his legs and torso dangling in a roomful of vengeful *Villistas* shot Georgie out of that hole like a rocket.

The absence of response encouraged him to search the house. He climbed off the roof and summoned two soldiers and the three Mexican men who were still skinning the cow out front. "We each got behind a Mex and went in . . . and following a blood trail, we found a horse in one of the rooms with a silver saddle and saber." They found some huddled old men, old women, and a young woman holding her baby. She was Julio Cardenas's wife. The baby was his child. Colonel Cardenas, one of the old men said, was lying out by the stone wall. He was the one shot in the arm at the start of the fight and shot in the head at the end.

Georgie left the house with Cardenas's saber and silver-studded saddle, as trophies. The saddle, he thought, "will look well in Pa's office." Set in the pommel was a tiny hand-painted cameo of Cardenas's wife. The colonel evidently had liked to look at her as he rode. Over the coming years the cameo faded, leaving barely a silhouette.

The two dead Mexicans lying nearest the house were tied to the hoods of the cars like deer, their weapons loaded in back. As the soldiers went to fetch Cardenas's body, a distant drumming of hooves quickened everyone's pulse. Forty riders galloped over the ridge a thousand yards away. Having come here on a whim, Georgie could expect no reinforcements; and the cars were vulnerable to shots in the gas tank. As gunfire cracked in the distance, he made his decision. "We withdrew gracefully," leaving Cardenas behind.

On the way back to Rubio, he remembered the "bad lot" of Mexicans he'd seen there earlier that day. He halted the car. "I had a man cut the telephone wires so they could not be warned and lay for us." His soldiers liked that. When it came to war, Lieutenant Patton never stopped thinking.

The U.S. Punitive Expedition had been a bore till then, with hardly a single violent exchange between the Americans and the elusive Mexicans. General Pershing, at first furious at Georgie's maverick move, brightened when he saw the corpses and captured weapons. He told his other officers that Lieutenant Patton had done more in half a day than the Thirteenth Cavalry had done in a week. He nicknamed Georgie "Bandit." The reporters covering the expedition had been scrounging for stories, so when Georgie appeared with an adventurous tale and two bodies to prove it, they flocked around him almost thankfully. "Cardenas had nerve," he told them, "even if he was a Mexican." They gave the story extravagant play, short on facts but long on color. Nine days later the *The New York Times* headlined: "Cardenas' Family Saw Him Die at Bay—Shot Four Times, Villa Captain—Dramatic Fight at Ranch—Lieut. Patton and Ten Men Killed Three Bandits—Peons Kept on Skinning a Beef."

Georgie was most pleased with his good fortune. Whenever something positive happened to him, he interpreted it as a sign that even better things lay ahead. If this reduced his pleasure in the present, it made his hopes for the future shimmer, hopes that through his early career seemed to grow more possible as he pursued them. He never dwelled on the past. He told Beatrice, "You are probably wondering if my conscience hurts me for killing a man. It does not. I feel about it just as I did when I got my first sword fish, surprised at my luck." To drive the point home, he cut two notches in the grip of his ivory-handled revolver. That warrior's mask of steely bravado, he would make it genuine yet.

Beatrice was overjoyed. "I am so proud of him I am nearly dead." Her father read about the Rubio scrap and wrote Georgie ("my dear son") that he lacked words to express his admiration and relief over Georgie's survival, but truly, Frederick Ayer exclaimed, "It is good to be alive." Only

Nita Patton expressed mixed feelings. "As to this fight," she wrote her mother from Fort Bliss,

> I am sick at the thought that he killed somebody. I wish he hadn't. It isn't noble in my eyes to shoot a poor ignorant creature that does not even know why he is fighting. Of course Georgie was brave, and the man shot first, but I should think it was a disagreeable duty, well performed, not an act of wonderful courage.
>
> But O! Ma isn't it great that the man missed!! I am so glad of that I like to forget the other. Everyone at the post is ringing up and all are thrilled over it. Don't think that I am not proud of your son, I am; only I can't rejoice over a thing like that.

Nita's ambivalence was not limited to her brother's exploit. Her social life had continued with various cavalry officers not involved in the Punitive Expedition, whipsawing her emotions between euphoria and disgust. The problem? She had the naïveté of an inexperienced girl, falling hard for successive "delightful" men without safeguarding her heart with reserve; and yet she also had the intelligence to observe her behavior, mock it, decry it—but not change it. At times her sojourn at Fort Bliss seemed the happiest period of her life. She'd lost ten pounds and bought some new linen outfits. Some young captain would call on her and her spirits would soar through "my latest crush." Then a lull in invitations would set her to thinking it was time to go. "I have an awful case on Miss Taylor's beau," she wrote her mother that summer. Of course it was hopeless, still the letdown hit hard a few weeks later. "Things are pretty bleak just now . . . Miss Taylor's wedding was very pretty."

She met a civilian man she liked a lot. But in mentioning this Mr. Solomon in a letter to her father, she incurred Papa's instant displeasure. He expressed it mildly, never said why—but the understanding was that Mr. Solomon was possibly Jewish and therefore not an acceptable date. But what brought Nita to new lows was the arrival at Fort Bliss of Beatrice's younger sister. Kay Ayer was everything Nita was not: slim, pretty, coquettish. And she was competition, a situation Beatrice seemed to promote. "Bea is always saying how these suitors would be nice for K. and how *she* could amuse them." Of a Captain Stuart whom Nita had her eye on: "He seems to have been as nice to K. as he was to me. Bea of course thinks he was rushing K. not ever me." These tensions wore Nita down, even after Kay returned to Massachusetts. She talked of heading home "still unattached." But she stayed at Fort Bliss through the summer, telling herself that Beatrice and the girls needed her as long as the Punitive Expedition dragged on, keeping Georgie off somewhere in Mexico.

Late one August night after drinking so much tea that she couldn't sleep, Nita could contain her feelings no longer. "So here goes," she wrote her mother:

> I wonder why I am different from other girls, and no one ever thinks it is necessary to amuse me. Is it a compliment or an insult? I have never been able to decide. I do not count except when people want things done. Then I am useful.
>
> Don't think me unhappy, because I am not. I am glad I stayed here and I regret nothing, but it is unwise to stay too long.
>
> > Your devoted daughter,
> > Anne W. Patton
> > *Spinster*

Her mood brightened a few weeks later. "Someone was glad to see me—John J. Pershing." The general had returned from Mexico with Georgie and others of his staff for a brief leave. Beatrice had gone to meet them at Columbus, New Mexico. Nita, arriving at Columbus a day later, realized at once that her brother "wasn't a bit glad to see me, and Bea was sorry I came." They were uneasy with the association of her and General Pershing. It might cause resentment in Georgie's peers, might bring mutters of favoritism. Nita didn't care. "I have seen him and he is looking splendidly. That is why I came."

So long the second fiddle in her family, Nita took sly pleasure in her sudden eminence. Chatting with Pershing, she got a kick out of her brother fidgeting nervously nearby, "so afraid I will say the wrong thing." When Pershing invited Nita into his office, she could not help but exalt to her mother afterward, "There was Georgie on the outskirts, being military, and Bea with him, your younger one in the inner shrine." She savored another small victory when the general's entourage climbed into waiting automobiles for a drive. "Bea is quite peevish because she had to ride behind with mere colonels, and the dust gave her hay fever. It is too bad." But Nita's ultimate satisfaction came after she mentioned that she must soon return to California. Pershing said nothing, but later Georgie got her in private and rather stiffly asked her to stay a while longer. She had an inkling why but wanted to hear it from Georgie. "Because the general expects it," he mumbled. Nita rejoiced to her mother, "Are you glad that I am having such a grand time? I am ashamed but unregenerate."

The general took her along on an inspection of the post. When their car passed a truck overturned in a collapsed culvert, he observed that the army engineers had no regard for government property. Nita retorted, "I wonder if the poor man in the truck felt that way? He might have had a regard for his life." Pershing gave no reaction. They passed a barracks where some soldiers were arguing out front. "The enlisted men fuss sometimes," the general explained, to which Nita added, "They would fuss in heaven." For a moment his face was stony. Then to her pleasure "he smiled and showed his dimples."

When they parted, Pershing to return to Mexico, she to California, each looked forward to continuing the relationship once the Punitive Expedition was over. Nita's mother was thrilled for her daughter; her heart had risen and fallen all summer with each of Nita's letters. Strangely, Papa seemed cool to the idea of Nita and Pershing in love. After years of semiretirement he recently had recharged his political career and now was seeking a U.S. Senate seat in the November 1916 election. Nita assumed that he was too busy campaigning to rejoice in her romance. She was wrong. Her father shared Georgie and Beatrice's concern about appearances of nepotism tainting Georgie's career. And there was another reason for his reservation. He'd checked out Pershing's background. It turned out the general was the son of a railroad brakeman. Not exactly the Pattons' kind of people.

Two months before election day, Papa bolted upright from a fitful sleep in his hotel on the campaign trail. He'd heard his wife cry "George!" in distress. He looked around for her in panic before realizing she was miles away at Lake Vineyard. He couldn't sleep after the nightmare. "With my psychic superstitions, I was done for," he wrote her later that day. "I saw you in a train wreck and imagined all sorts of things." Ruth was perfectly fine. It would be fifteen years before she died, on a train.

Papa's nightmare was a symptom of the misery he felt in his run for the Senate. Elated after winning the Democratic Party nomination, his first weeks on the campaign had been heady. "I am told I am an excellent campaigner. I am really beginning to believe I will be elected." But soon it became an ordeal for him. He wrote Ruth, "I do not sleep much and am even thinner than when I started. The atmosphere of politics with its suspicions and meanness never appeared more distasteful." He was sure he was going to lose; in his heart he welcomed the prospect. He'd never wanted to run in the first place. He'd done it for his son. Georgie had been pestering him to get back into politics for years. Papa had been content to dabble in land development and to live the quiet life of a country squire. Though Georgie was too loyal to condemn his father's withdrawal outright, beginning in 1910 his letters to Papa sounded the same cry over and over: "For heavens sake do some thing in politics and *DO IT NOW!!*"

Always active in the Democratic Party, Papa first put out feelers about gaining the party's Senate nomination in 1912. He failed in this bid, but his contacts in the new administration of Woodrow Wilson encouraged him to seek a government position in Washington, possibly in the War Department. He was hesitant; he had grown accustomed to playing it safe. Georgie wouldn't hear of it. He harangued his father in the same lacerating way that he drove himself in his own career. Papa *must* go to Washington and lobby for a job, "otherwise all you have done will be utterly wasted and you will get nothing and have only regret that you slumped at the last minute." Georgie harangued his mother as well: "He is a fool if he does not take the chance, and you are one if you do not urge him to do so." At last agreeing to seek some job interviews, Papa insisted on a post "that I can accept with dignity." Even Assistant Secretary of War, he groused, "seems really rather small." He wrote his wife from the capital, "If disappointed, I will believe that my good angel was wiser than I." Unsurprisingly, he got no offers.

His son kept after him. Run for governor, seek an ambassadorship—the specific job didn't matter as long as it carried prestige. Georgie's politics were a sort of reactionary royalism. Fancying himself an American nobleman, he liked to spout off about the nation's ignorant masses, its "Bolshevik" labor unions, its "grafting politicians." As a young man he joked that he would like to be dictator. "The few must run the many for the latters good," he huffed. "To Hell with the people!" He later put such pronouncements into perspective: "I have no more gift for politics than a cow has for fox hunting. . . . I am sure that it is very bad for a man's military reputation to be confounded with it. Personally, I have never voted and do not intend to." He once told his father, "Vote for the Army appropriation bill. I don't know what it is, but it sounds very military." That about summarized his political acumen. He wanted only two things from government: "Consistent military preperation"—and someday, please, a declaration of war.

Frustration in this latter wish was the root of Georgie's disdain for "that creature" Woodrow Wilson. "He has not the soul of a louse nor the mind of a worm. Or the backbone of a jellyfish." Since the outbreak of World War I in Europe in 1914, Georgie had been anxious to get into it, even to the point of brazenly (for a second lieutenant) soliciting the highest echelons of U.S. Army command to let him have "a years leave on some pretext and go to France and take part in this war"—in the French Army, at his own expense. "Please do not think this plan a spontaneous folly. I have contemplated it for years." His request was denied, but his hopes lifted when the British ship *Lusitania* was sunk by a German submarine in 1915, killing 128 Americans. When President Wilson didn't immediately declare war on Germany, Georgie was apoplectic. Wilson said a nation could be too proud to fight. Georgie sneered, "In another country or age that pride has always been called another name." He wrote a long derisive poem "To Wilson" whose last stanza condemned the president

> For making soldiers play the part
> Of dogs who will not fight;
> Of Dogs, who fearful not to growl
> Fear far too much to bite.

To Georgie's dismay, his father, a loyal Democrat, supported Wilson's position of neutrality. They debated it back and forth, Papa standing on tenets of international law and diplomacy while his son held the view that "there is but one International Law—the best army." But Georgie knew that his father might be carried into the Senate on the wave of Wilson's reelection, so he swallowed his dislike of Wilson for his father's sake. His advice to Papa on how to beat his opponent was a political version of total war. "Go after his private life," Georgie said. "Also don't hesitate at rough stuff. . . . He will probably sling mud. If he does you sling rocks. In fact I would start it as you have more on him than he can have on you. . . . You must win."

Nita left Fort Bliss in September to help in the last weeks of Papa's campaign. Beatrice followed with the girls. In October, Georgie returned to his tent one night and fired up his gasoline lantern so he could so some paperwork. In this year's mishap, he overpumped the fuel tank and the flame flashed into his face. He was sent home to Lake Vineyard to recuperate from his burns, and so was with his father on election night in November. The results were the worst of both worlds for Georgie: President Wilson was reelected, and Papa was soundly defeated.

As the returns came in, his father "never flinched and took it with a smile." Georgie consoled himself with the mistaken belief that his father had been instrumental in carrying the state for Wilson; the president now would reward Papa with a prestigious government appointment. It never happened. Papa retired to Lake Vineyard with a secret relief that he was finished with politics, finished with vain aspiration. Such a reaction to defeat was so foreign to Georgie that he couldn't comprehend it. He felt Papa had been treated unfairly by Wilson and was merely too "high souled" to complain.

Georgie perceived the world in strict terms of triumph and failure. In most cases he could briskly appraise all he saw as falling into one of these categories. But he could not consider his beloved father a failure, so he had to imagine that Papa had been undone by powers beyond his control—by Wilson or perhaps by fate. The dilemma would arise again in Georgie's life. There would come a time when he himself felt not quite a failure and not quite triumphant. Extremes he could cope with; he'd careened between them since childhood. But the middle ground, the gray area, the world-ending whimper—to be confronted with *this* after all he'd worked for, it seemed surely the result of betrayal.

☆ ☆ **13** ☆ ☆

Talking Blood

I T ALL spells advancement for Georgie." So Beatrice told herself each time she went "pioneering off" to her husband's next station. And through his twenties and early thirties, it did indeed spell advancement. Though promotion came slowly in a peacetime army, Georgie rose rapidly in reputation if not in rank, gaining notoriety and praise even before his gunfight in Mexico.

Five years earlier, the Pattons had done a brief stint at Fort Myer, Virginia. Located outside Washington, D.C., Fort Myer was home to the highest military brass; its troops' main mission was ceremonial, parading on holidays and at state functions, staging fancy military funerals at Arlington Cemetery. Officers there socialized with the Washington elite, and in this capacity Beatrice's independent means offered a huge advantage, which her husband exploited to the maximum. Georgie bought polo ponies and thoroughbreds to race and show. He joined the best clubs and ate at the best restaurants. When his father-in-law questioned this glittery social schedule, Georgie was defensive. "What I am doing looks like play to you but in my business it is the best sort of advertising." Washington, he said, was "nearer God than else where," the only place to make connections with "all the big men." Beatrice was convinced if her father was not. "G. has said so much about his charmed life that I half believe it sometimes."

The connections he made while at Fort Myer had helped Georgie win a place on the U.S. Olympic team in the summer of 1912. The modern pentathlon consisted of five events originally conceived as tests of a young military officer carrying a message through hostile territory. That officer must race on horseback, shoot a pistol, fence with a sword, swim, and run cross-country. Georgie was capable in all these events; too, he struck his commanders at Fort Myer as a fine representative of the army. The Olympics were held in Stockholm, Sweden. Georgie went with Beatrice, Papa, and Nita, and placed fifth.

He'd been especially impressive in fencing, having excelled at swordsmanship at West Point. Returning to Fort Myer, he wrote (with Beatrice's help as an editor) several articles for military publications on the history and proper use of the cavalry saber. (Though the notion of fighting on horseback with saber and lance seems hopelessly archaic today, in 1913 it was still common military practice.) Georgie argued that the army's then standard-issue saber was useless and antiquated. Its curved blade inclined soldiers to flail with it as though in "a carpet beating contest" rather than to thrust with the point. "In the charge the point will always beat the edge. It gets there first." On the basis of these articles, the army commissioned him to design a new saber. The resulting "Patton sword" would later be likened to his whole command style: light and maneuverable, straight and sharp—purely an offensive weapon.

At his own expense he'd attended the Cavalry School at Saumur, France, where he studied swordsmanship under the French fencing champion. Beatrice had accompanied Georgie, and during their three months in France they drove around the surrounding countryside paying particular attention to the supply routes, campsites, and battlefields of the Roman legions that had conquered these lands 2,000 years ago. Georgie told her that he'd fought here before, in an earlier life, and that he would fight here in the future. She realized he was serious. As it turned out, this was the infamous hedgerow country south of Normandy where so many Americans would fight and die after the Allied invasion of France in 1944.

Graduating from Saumur as a Master of the Sword, Georgie had attended the Mounted Service School at Fort Riley, Kansas. By the end of the two-year course of instruction he'd emerged as one of the cavalry's most promising second lieutenants. His performance report lauded his initiative, energy, and devotion to duty; the one negative was his occasional "impulsive intolerance of restraint by superiors." While at Fort Riley he helped stop the lynching of a Negro soldier believed by the townspeople to have raped a white girl, an incident he later recorded as one of his career highlights: "I informed the leading citizens that if any such attempt were made, it would be over my dead body. As a result of my stand, the man was not lynched, and, later, was proven not guilty."

Georgie's confidence boomed in the early years of his career. The many opinions he cockily expressed favored snappy phrases over sense. Woodrow Wilson, said Georgie, was foolishly "doing just what one would expect of a creature who represents an ideal rather than a personality." He dismissively called his step-grandfather, George Hugh Smith, when the former Confederate colonel died in 1915, "a great mind wasted. . . . He did not have the military mind in its highest development because he was swayed by ideas of right and wrong rather than those of policy." Georgie got snippy with Papa about events unfolding in Europe ("as to your notion that I am probably less informed on the war than you are I doubt it"), and he even stood up, in a backhanded way, to his imperious in-laws.

Irritated that Frederick and Ellie were always summoning Beatrice back to Massachusetts, he quietly taught his daughters a nursery rhyme that he told them to recite one evening when all the Ayers were gathered at supper. This the girls did, treating the elegant crowd to "There was a goddamn spider/Lived up a goddamn spout/There came a hell of a thunderstorm/And washed the bastard out." Frederick Ayer got the hint. He told Beatrice the next day, "I feel I have had a communication from George that he wants his family around him. I have taken the liberty of purchasing train tickets for your return on the first of the week."

Just before he left for Mexico from Fort Bliss, Georgie watched a parade where all the mounted cavalrymen were carrying the newly issued Patton sword. "My eyes filled with tears. . . . The nearest similar feeling I can remember is on the occasion of certain very noisy Opera music." He talked incessantly about his saber design, so much so that on the Punitive Expedition his men teased him for killing a rattlesnake outside his tent with a pistol instead of a sword. He saw no reason to laugh. Of course he'd used a pistol—he was on foot at the time, and a saber was to be used strictly on horseback. On the wave of confidence after his gunfight at San Miguelito, he engaged the formidable General Pershing in a spat about his cherished saber, pushing Pershing against his wishes to specify in a written article that the saber was an essential part of the cavalry arsenal. The general finally acquiesced. Georgie told Beatrice triumphantly, "The more I see of the man the better my opinion of his brains becomes."

Beatrice was feeling as confident about her husband's prospects as he was. When the Punitive Expedition returned from Mexico in February 1917, she urged Georgie, a first lieutenant now, to leave Pershing's staff and take a position with the Seventh Cavalry in El Paso. She'd got used to the idea of Pershing and Nita Patton marrying, and had even helped lay the groundwork for the general's entrance into the family by having Little Bee and Ruth Ellen send him a Christmas card. On reading the card, Georgie reported of Pershing, "He seemed to think of his dead children and his eyes filled with tears." But with such personal ties taking shape, Beatrice considered it urgent that Georgie break out on his own. He didn't need Pershing's favor anymore. He only needed her.

For a while Pershing delayed Georgie's transfer to the Seventh Cavalry, apparently intending to keep him on his staff. Beatrice was alarmed. Taking matters into her own hands, she determined to find out exactly what Pershing's intentions were concerning Nita. She had to get him alone, away even from Georgie, because in her previous attempts to question Pershing, "every time the General would be at all jovial or confidential and I would feel like loosening up a bit, G. would give him one of those sickening 'aide' looks and it would be all off." When finally she cornered him, Pershing admitted that he was "crazy about Nita." He then asked Beatrice, "Now frankly, what would you think of it?"

She was ambivalent on the matter, but not destructive. "I think you'd be the luckiest man on earth—if she took you."

"No, what do you think of me?"

"Georgie thinks you are fine, but I don't know you very well. What do you think of yourself?" The general blinked in the face of this interrogation. Nita once had observed that a lot of officers at Fort Bliss were afraid of Beatrice. Her social polish and delicate features camouflaged a nononsense character. She still got anxious over her parents, her kids, and Georgie most of all. She still could cry herself to sleep believing that she was "not thorough" in managing her life. But she was toughening. With intelligence, wealth, and a rising star husband, she increasingly was emboldened to cut to the heart of issues she deemed important to Georgie's future. She pressed the general, "Do you think it would be a good thing for Nita if she married you?"

"Yes." Pershing did not express such feelings easily, especially to a lieutenant's wife. "I do." The only possible problem, he said, was his adolescent son, Warren. Since the deaths of Pershing's wife and daughters eighteen months ago, Warren had been in the care of the general's sister. Becoming a stepmother to the boy might be difficult for Nita, Pershing said, "and I want her to marry me with her eyes wide open." Beatrice, in later reporting all this to Nita's very interested mother, noted that "there was much more on this line" but she did not elaborate. She did say that her impression of the often taciturn Pershing had improved as a result of this conversation. "I like to hear a man stand right up and throw out his chest and say 'I am committed.' "

Ruth was pleased by the general's mention of marriage (her daughter was almost thirty now). She invited Pershing to visit the Pattons at Lake Vineyard. It was hardly necessary of Georgie to remind her to be nice to the general, though his emphatic "And Pa too!" was perhaps more called for. Papa had been depressed and moody since his election defeat the previous November, and already he'd grumbled a bit about Pershing's common background. It was sadly predictable that Papa's snobbery soared as his self-esteem sank. Sadder still, of all the traits that Georgie might have absorbed from his father, this flaw was the most enduring.

As ordered, Papa kept his qualms to himself and rolled out the red carpet when Pershing visited in March 1917. The general got Papa's clearance to propose to Nita during his stay, and she accepted. In his thank-you note to Nita's parents after leaving Lake Vineyard, the general acknowledged, "It is going to be very hard for you both to give her up. I cannot tell you how fully I recognize the responsibilities I assume in taking her. She is a woman of rare qualities of soul. I shall be all to her that I can be always." Pershing, who at fifty-six was only four years younger than Papa, signed himself, "Your Devoted Son."

Ruth was thrilled. Papa grudgingly got used to the idea. No one was happier than Nannie Wilson, who told Pershing, "Nita and Georgie always have been my whole world, and my whole interest in life. So whatever happiness comes to them comes to 'Aunt Nannie' too." Then on April 6 the United States declared war on Germany. Pershing was summoned to Washington, where he received orders to organize a division of troops and take it to Europe to join the Allies. A newspaper reported a rumor that Miss Anita Patton of Los Angeles was to marry the commander in chief of the American Expeditionary Force—after the war. It was true. The wedding was postponed indefinitely. Nita had not wanted to wait, but these were demanding times for her fiancé, now at the peak of his career. And being Georgie's younger sister, she'd learned how and when to get out of the way.

Georgie meanwhile had joined the Seventh Cavalry to get out of Pershing's shadow. Upon the declaration of war, he immediately went on leave to begin casting about for an assignment that would get him into action in Europe. In May he was promoted to captain. Three days later he received a wire at the Ayers' house in Massachusetts ordering him to report at once to Pershing in Washington. The general was assembling a headquarters staff to precede the main body of troops overseas. Georgie's job on the staff wouldn't be glamorous—he would oversee the enlisted orderlies serving the officers—but he didn't care. On June 8, after a parting of "much tears" from his wife and family, he boarded H.M.S *Baltic* at New York harbor with 188 officers, soldiers, and civilians comprising the initial AEF contingent. He was going to Europe, to a theater of colossal war. General Pershing had wanted him because of his fine performance in Mexico. The Nita connection didn't hurt, a circumstance Georgie wasn't about to question now.

Nita and Beatrice desperately wanted to travel abroad to be with their men, who were at AEF headquarters in Paris, far from the dangers of the front. It was almost impossible for Nita. Pershing had issued an order forbidding spouses to follow the troops; it would look bad if he made an exception for his fiancée. He confided to Georgie that he was thinking of sending for her anyway. "I told him not to try," Georgie wrote Beatrice. "It would ruin him and as I am one of [Pershing's staff members] it would ruin me too." In frustration, Nita threw herself into Red Cross work in California, trying to help in any small way to end the war and bring the troops, namely Pershing, home.

Beatrice stood a better chance of getting around the no-spouse rule because Georgie was not as visible as Pershing. To go abroad legally, she considered joining the International Red Cross or becoming a European buyer for a Boston dress shop. Georgie, who calculated that in their seven-year marriage they'd been separated more than two years, told her to damn the rules and come immediately. Bored in his staff job, he didn't care if he got in trouble.

Papa was furious on hearing of their plans. How could Beatrice jeopardize her husband's career like that? How could Georgie risk Pershing's wrath after all the general had done for him? Georgie wasn't worried. He told Beatrice that if Pershing (referred to now as "John" or "J." in their letters) found out that she was in Paris, "he will be awfully angry but it will wear off in time. I have as you know a rather unfair advantage over J. which I have never used but I could in that particular case." His uneasiness with his status as Pershing's future brother-in-law had evidently worn off. He would play it for all it was worth.

Beatrice decided to travel to London on the pretext of visiting her sister Kay, whose new husband was a diplomat there; from London she would cross the channel to France. Georgie rented a flat in Paris and bought a car in anticipation of her arrival. But Papa, directed by Georgie to use his connections to get Beatrice a passport, dragged his feet until this last travel loophole closed. Georgie was irritated but revealed it only to Beatrice. "If I had been in Pa's place I could have made it. His legal training gives him a too great respect for the law. The real thing about law is knowing when to break it." And more cuttingly: "I suppose the idea of taking the bull by the horns scared Pa to death."

More and more Americans were arriving in France. Pershing's task was to prepare these raw troops for the harrowing experience of trench warfare. A few American units joined Allied forces at the front soon after arriving. (Among the first were several black units, which were accepted by European troops more readily than by their white American compatriots.) But it would be a year before most of the AEF saw action. Against French and British wishes, Pershing demanded that the Americans fight as a separate army rather than be used piecemeal to replenish Allied armies under Allied command. His insistence on this point would later be credited with having helped create the modern American Army, but it caused great friction at the time. Georgie, for one, cheered him. Without Pershing, he wrote, American manpower "would have been bled white to fill the depleted ranks of allied units, where their valor would have been unmarked and their achievements unheralded."

In September, AEF headquarters moved to Chaumont, southeast of Paris. Georgie was busy, managing some 250 orderlies, clerks, drivers, medical personnel, and military police, but he hated the work. For diversion he wrote love poems to his wife and war poems to himself, that is, poems depicting World War I battle scenes that as yet he could only imagine. Georgie had written about two dozen poems to date. He denigrated them sheepishly whenever he showed them to anyone, and once rhymingly described himself as having "never as yet done a useful thing" except "write bum verse for which he will swing." Even so, he'd tried unsuccessfully to get his poems published.

Though he could compose a striking phrase now and then, Georgie's poetry was simplistic and frequently awful. He took it seriously, however, experimenting with different rhyme schemes and subject matter. He got angry when his father took the liberty of editing out his poems' black-humored vernacular. He defended his profane and scatological mimicry of the speech of frontline soldiers: "The fact that it is the common parlance of heroes in no way detracts from the splendor of their deeds." He wrote many slangy, Kiplingesque ballads, including one in early 1918 in which he imagined a soldier, while counting down the minutes before an attack, asking himself if he has any regrets in life. Yes, the soldier decides. He regrets "The drinks I failed to guzzle/The pay I never blew." In a more contemplative poem called "Soldier's Religion," a soldier pities a "Luckless God" in whose image, so the chaplains say, the soldier was made. "I have no virtues such as He." God doesn't kill people, drink whiskey, or chew tobacco, "nor go into the 'Cat Houses'/To do the things I do." To the man's wonder, however, in the anxious lull before battle "I sort of felt God near me/And it eased a heap my fright." No less welcome is the comfort of God's presence *after* the battle, when in the pitted mud of No Man's Land the body of a German he killed moments before seems to move in the night. Shockingly, the German too seems made in God's image.

> Yet that damn Boche looked just like Him
> Leastwise he looked like me
> So why God should be partial
> I don't just rightly see.
>
> This damned God business may be bunk
> I don't just rightly know
> Still, when the corpses walk at night
> I'd rather believe it's so.

Georgie's war poems affected the hardened outlook of a frontline veteran. But his skirmish in Mexico remained his only combat experience, an incident trivial compared to the mammoth battles and incomprehensible slaughter of the war going on just a few dozen miles from his billet at Chaumont, the war from which, he wrote his wife, "I am disgustingly safe."

He consoled himself with the conceit that his combat experience, if small in life, was boundless in what he called the "far memory" of his soul. His ancestry; his interest in military history; his fantasies about heroic, violent death—for a long time he'd almost playfully added to this mixture a mystical ingredient of reincarnation to give his lifelong fascination with war the logic of destiny. It comforted him to think that he'd fought wars repeatedly in the distant past, dying horribly but bravely each time: having done it before, he could surely do it again. "I was there," he might jokingly say about this or that famous battle. But in late 1917 he first put down on paper, in a poem called "Memories Roused by a Roman Theater," the real yearning with which he postulated these previous warrior incarnations. As he later explained it, the poem was inspired by an experience of déjà vu. Entering the town of Chamlieu after dark one night, he asked his driver if the base camp was over that hill. "Our camp is farther ahead," the driver said. "But there is an old Roman camp there." Georgie asked if there was a theater nearby. He was told there was no theater in Chamlieu. But the next day, he walked outside to find the ruins of a Roman amphitheater three hundred yards away, and "knew that despite the dimming years/This place had once been home."

> Yes, more than once have I seen these walls
> Rise sharp on the brow of the hill;
> And more than once have I trod that road
> That winds like a snake from the rill.
> . . . .
> And now again I am here for war
> Where as Roman and knight I have been;
> Again I practice to fight the Hun
> And attack him by machine.

"Attack him by machine"—this was the reason why Georgie suddenly was so anxious to steady his nerves with intimations of guiding fate. He'd quit his job on Pershing's staff to bet his future on a bold and possibly foolish venture. The machine referred to in his poem was warfare's latest newfangled development: the tank.

Conceived as armored "land ships," tanks were invented by the British in 1914. The thirty-ton Mark I was first used on the Somme in September 1916. A lighter, more nimble French version, the Renault, was first deployed in April 1917. In July a French tank officer regaled Georgie "with lurid tales of the value of his pet hobby as a certain means of winning the war." Georgie was skeptical. "The Frenchman was crazy and the Tank not worth a damn."

But as he learned more about tanks—and saw less and less future in his present job—he considered applying to join the fledgling U.S. Tank Corps. It might help him distinguish himself. Tanks were new; the press would cover them for their curiosity value alone. There were hundreds of young officers in the infantry and artillery, and none as yet in the Tank Corps—advancement should come quickly as a result. And commanding tanks might get him into combat sooner. Recently, the more removed he felt from the fighting, the tougher he talked about it, as in a letter to his wife's cousin in the States: "The more one sees of war the better it is. Of course there are a few deaths but all of us must 'pay the piper' sooner or later and the party is worth the cost of admission"—this from a guy who had yet to visit the front. His bravado began to ring hollow to him, however. "I have always talked blood and murder and am looked on as an advocate of close up fighting. I could never look myself in the face if I was a staff officer and comparatively safe."

Beatrice had mixed feelings about the Tank Corps. To ease her fears for his safety, her husband explained that it would be months before the unit was even supplied with tanks; and once in battle, he assured her, casualties among tank crewmen were fewer than among the doughboys. (To his father he was more candid on one point: "In tanks you are not apt to be wounded. You either get blown to bitts or you are not touched.") Georgie didn't ask Beatrice's consent, but he solicited her support by linking his ambition to his devotion to her: "I love you too much to try to get killed but also too much to sit on my tail and do nothing." To her mind, one good thing about his joining the Tank Corps was that it would remove him from General Pershing's orbit. Georgie agreed. "I think you are right about my pull with John and it is for that reason that I am going to get away from him and stand on my own feet."

In October he formally applied to join the Tank Corps. He cited his experience with automatic weapons, auto mechanics, and his own quick judgment and willingness to take chances. In the weeks of waiting for approval, he had second thoughts and slept fitfully at night. He leaned on fate to ease his mind. "I have a hunch that my Mexican Auto Battle was the fore runner of this. Who can say?" In November the order came for Georgie to travel to Chamlieu to study French tank installations located there. Then he was to proceed to Langres and open an AEF Light Tank Center and School based on what he had learned at Chamlieu. It would be his show from start to finish. He would teach tank operations to American troops, and then he would lead them into battle. "I feel unusually small in self esteem," he wrote Beatrice on the eve of his departure. "I am sure I will do it but just at this moment I don't see how. I will have to grow and grow a lot. If I fail it will be only my fault," he said, adding a joke that carried real truth: "I won't even have you to pick on."

*   *   *

In the weeks after leaving Pershing's staff, Georgie wrote many letters of appreciation to friends and superiors who'd helped his career so far. He told his father-in-law that a letter from Mr. Ayer had arrived during Georgie's deliberations about joining the Tank Corps. In it, Frederick Ayer had observed that war was so wasteful of life that surely there must be some way of reducing the casualties. "Your letter decided me," Georgie wrote back, "and the next morning I asked for the Tanks. They save life as two men in a tank are as good as ten men out of one." Mr. Ayer was touched. He put Georgie's note in his wallet.

The Ayers had rented an estate at Thomasville, Georgia, to get away from the New England winter. Beatrice and her daughters were there also, and in March 1918 Georgie wrote to her: "There is a strange thing that happened on the seventeenth. I was most restless and all the people at the mess noticed it. I thought of you every moment and longed to be with you more than usual which is always a lot." As on earlier occasions when he'd dreamed about her or felt strangely uneasy, Georgie, like his father, was led by "psychic superstitions" to think something bad had happened. On March 21 he received a cable from his mother-in-law that Frederick Ayer had died the previous week. Mr. Ayer had lived a full and successful life; he'd enjoyed fine health for all but the very last of his ninety-five years, and had contracted the bronchitis that led to his death only after riding his horse in the rain. (In fact his wife, Ellie, though she was thirty-one years younger, had seemed the more frail, for like Beatrice she had a shaky heart.) Still, the family was taking his death hard—except for three-year-old Ruth Ellen Patton, who took the opportunity of her grandfather's absence to balance herself on his clanky bathroom scale, a pleasure hitherto forbidden her.

Beatrice had been away for a few days when her father died. Returning to Thomasville, she discovered that a Boston funeral parlor had, weeks before, shipped a matched pair of expensive bronze caskets to Georgia, fully expecting that neither Frederick nor Ellie, who both had been ailing, would return to New England alive. Beatrice, who never forgave a slight nor forgot a grudge, henceforth would view all undertakers with undisguised loathing. No funeral for her when she died, she declared. Just scatter her ashes somewhere and be done with it.

The management of that Boston funeral parlor evidently knew its business. Ellie Ayer died at Thomasville three weeks after her husband. She hadn't attended Frederick's funeral up north but had helped lay out his body before loading it on the train, dressing him in a tuxedo, folding his fingers around a handwritten note from her. Recalled Beatrice, "Everyone thought that Ma would die when he did—of a broken heart. She lived just long enough to demonstrate she could do it." Beatrice and her brother Fred were with their mother as she slept in her bedroom. Suddenly Ellie cried out, "Oh, darling!" Fred took her in his arms. Beatrice spoke into her ear to revive her. Fred shook his head. This was the first time that he and Beatrice had seen someone die. As Beatrice called to her mother to wake up, to breathe, the very strangeness of the moment prompted Fred to speak in French. *"Elle ne pourrait pas t'entendre."* She cannot hear you.

Beatrice slumped on Ellie's bed. "I watched the column of blood slowly sink in the vein in her temple. With each heart beat it lowered, then drained out and back to the heart." She was in charge of the family now. With Georgie overseas and both parents dead, she was overwhelmed with anxiety. She punished herself with accusations of having been an inattentive daughter and wife. In the past Beatrice often had joked about an older half-sister who hired mediums to contact the dead—now she got the name of a medium from that sister in hopes of contacting her parents to apologize to them. Maybe it was the Pattons' influence on her; Ouija boards, ghosts, and premonitions were common topics of conversation with them. Maybe it was that incongruous streak of irrationality that Beatrice had carried all her life. She went alone to the medium's apartment. Middle-aged and quite unprepossessing, he spoke with Beatrice for a while, then he closed his eyes and began to hum. She recognized the tune of an obscure ballad her mother used to sing: "Come rest in my bosom, my own stricken dear." Then he picked up a pencil and inscribed "Fredk Ayer" on a piece of paper. As much as seeing her father's name, it was the writing itself that shocked Beatrice and sent her running out of there. Her father had suffered from palsy in his last years. A mild case, it was noticeable mostly in his handwriting, a distinctive, painstaking print of wobbly block letters that she saw again in "Fredk Ayer."

To ease her mind about Georgie, Beatrice extolled his virtues to her daughters to the point where Little Bee and Ruth Ellen grew sick of hearing how handsome he was, how noble, how perfect. Beatrice often spoke of her last conversation with her father, in which he'd instructed her to be sure her husband's finances were well managed. "George is bringing us all much glory and we must help him all we can," Mr. Ayer had said, echoing her sentiments. And last, Beatrice renewed her efforts to visit Georgie in Europe.

He'd written her tenderly on the deaths of her parents. He'd sent his mother and sister to help Beatrice manage ("they are so solid and natural that I feel sure that they would have been a great comfort"). He told her how much he missed her—her company, her advice, her body. But in a change from just a few months ago, he also told her that under no circumstances should she try to come to Europe. Before, he hadn't cared if Beatrice's arrival got him in trouble with his superiors. Now it mattered to him a lot; he loved his new job in the Tank Corps and didn't want to risk losing it. Soon after receiving his instructions on this point, Beatrice hit her daughter Ruth Ellen for the first time, slapping her in the face for breaking a toy doll. Ruth Ellen and Beatrice wept together, each more angry than hurt, more bewildered than in pain.

If all was not well on the homefront, things were just great with Georgie. "I am a wonder to behold," he wrote his wife in the summer of 1918. "I wear silk khaki shirts made to order, Khaki socks also made to order. I change my boots at least once during the day and my belts are wonders to see they are so shiney and polished. I have the leather on my knees [buffed] every time I ride and my spurs polished with silver polish." With promotions accelerated in wartime, he was a lieutenant colonel now. "How do you feel being a Mrs. Colonel. We never thought to reach it so soon did we." His connection to Pershing had again been helpful: "Gen P. had a hell of a time getting me promoted as they said I was too young but he finally put it over." As commander of the nine-hundred-member 304th Light Tank Brigade, Georgie carried a decorative walking stick wherever he went. He wore four rings on his fingers: a coiled gold snake with ruby eyes; his West Point class ring; a wedding band; a diamond pinky ring. He was keeping young, he said—horseback riding, drinking barely at all, applying hair tonic every day. His grandfather had designed a flashy uniform for his militia company before the Civil War, and Georgie did the same for his brigade, purchasing colorful shoulder patches at his own expense and requisitioning new belts and trimmer overcoats. "We were different all right," recalled one of his lieutenants. "If there was anything he wanted it was to make the Tank Corps tougher than the Marines and more spectacular than the Matterhorn."

The best thing about Georgie's job was its independence. Because tanks were new and separate from other AEF units, "No one watches you and you can go to hell or heaven in your own way as long as you get results." A terror in discipline, he upbraided his men on everything from their dress to their hygiene to the offhand way they saluted. The brigade was still undersupplied with the little two-man Renault tanks. While awaiting more to be delivered, he kept his men sharp with nonstop drilling and field exercises. "A pint of sweat saves a gallon of blood." In the evenings he taught engine maintenance, mapping, communications, and principles of tank warfare as he conceived them—conceived from scratch, since as yet no such principles existed.

He'd discovered his knack for public speaking on a Christmas holiday at the Ayers' house during his undergraduate years at West Point. Feeling compelled to toast his hosts after dinner, he was so nervous as he raised his glass that afterward he had no idea what he'd said, though the Ayers seemed to like it. Since then, he'd come thoroughly to enjoy the attention offered by a dais, a lectern, a journalist's notepad, or the expectant stares of soldiers waiting for him to address them. In his application to join the Tank Corps, Georgie had observed that tanks were analogous to horse cavalry in earlier wars. (The relationship was by no means obvious at the time; it was thought that tanks would be strictly an adjunct to infantry.) From that initial observation flowed all his theories about tank warfare, theories that he drove into his men through the spring and summer of 1918.

To an audience of officers from other service branches who were suspicious of any intrusion on their turf, he diplomatically downplayed the tank's role in battle, saying it was "but a means of aiding infantry." But he was excited about the possibilities of tanks in their own right. All his favorite precepts applied: speed, mobility, shock effect, and that all-important element of glamour that tanks possessed by virtue of their novelty. They were far from foolproof. They broke down frequently, ran out of gas, got stuck in the mud, sometimes fell into trenches and couldn't climb out. But he loved them just the same. He compared tanks to small children, "feeble, clumsy, nearsighted," and wrote an ode to them called "The Precious Babies," a term of endearment he'd never applied to his daughters.

One day a tank crew was firing a cannon when a defective round exploded in the muzzle, injuring several men. The next round exploded in the breech and blew the head off the gunner. "The men were reluctant to fire the next round," so to restore their confidence Georgie shot the cannon three times. "I have never in my life been more reluctant to pull a trigger." He felt sometimes that his men hated him, and he joked that he should eat only fresh eggs to avoid being poisoned. He considered it unavoidable that as brigade commander he should have no friends, still the absence of familiar company became a strain. He had no sense that his soldiers might appreciate him for sharing their dangers, or for looking after their welfare as vigorously as he scolded their shortcomings. Though he lectured on morals and venereal disease, he had no real complaint about fraternization, "as men who are about to be killed are entitled to what pleasures they can get." (He took the same position in World War II, though he believed that rape should be punished by death.) After emceeing an amateur night for his men, Georgie was serenaded with a song that went, "We will follow the Colonel through hell and out the other side." He was touched and surprised. "I don't see why they like me as I curse them freely on all occasions."

Increasingly, other AEF units began to see action. Georgie feared the war would end before his unit was called up. He lost sleep at night, thinking he'd been wrong to join the Tank Corps. On August 16 he attended an officers' banquet. Some officers were scheduled to advance to the front soon, and he envied them. "Of course not many will be killed but if they do their duty some are bound to. Still that rather adds zest to the entertainment as each hopes it will be the other and none are sure." Four days later he was ordered to report "equipped for field service" to his commanding general, Samuel Rockenbach ("a good-hearted wind bag"). No specifics were given, but Georgie was certain his moment had come. He was going to "the party" at last.

Faces in the Clouds

ORE than half a million Americans would enter their first major battle against German entrenchments around St. Mihiel, located on the Meuse River about twenty miles south of Verdun. Only Georgie's excitement prevented him from collapsing with exhaustion in the weeks leading up to the engagement. Every other day, he drove four hours from the tank center outside Langres to St. Mihiel, where he made on-site preparations for his brigade's role in the attack. He set up command links with the infantry units his tanks would be supporting, established depots for gasoline and other supplies, and arranged where he would detrain his 150 new tanks before moving them into action.

He apologized to his wife for not writing daily. His diary entries were rushed and terse, often mere blasts of frustration at people and problems obstructing him. Superiors who ignored his fanatical pestering were asses and SOB's. High praise was for anyone interested in his concerns. Like an irate parent defending his child, Georgie was damned if his tanks, a small part of the overall operation, were going to be treated as insignificant.

He worried about the terrain over which the tanks would advance. Soft ground could mean disaster, for the Renaults were designed to make up in mobility what they lacked in armor; mire them in No Man's Land between Allied and enemy lines and they would be quickly destroyed. The only way to make an accurate judgment was personally to inspect the attack route. He arranged to accompany a French night reconnaissance patrol into No Man's Land. Crawling on the ground across two lines of barbed wire, he was a hundred meters from German trenches when he heard the enemy whistle. The French patrol leader explained that it was a warning. If the patrol continued farther, the Germans would reluctantly open fire. This was trench warfare in its fourth exhausting year. "Both sides were anxious not to disturb the other." Before crawling back to friendly territory, Georgie picked a daisy blooming in the barbed wire to mail home to Beatrice.

The ground was firm enough for tanks—but suddenly the attack was postponed and all the plans changed. The 304th would operate on a different part of the battlefield in support of a different infantry corps. The whole process of preparation was repeated. On September 11, the day before the battle, Georgie reconnoitered the new site. German shelling was intense. He told Beatrice that he got used to it after a while—in truth he never did, and even as a general in World War II he fought to suppress the reflex to flinch at the impact of incoming artillery. But the worst part was leaving No Man's Land for home. "I hated the idea of being shot at from behind." A bullet wound in the back would be humiliating.

He wrote last letters to his wife and father. If he was killed, Beatrice could have his sword—he urged her to marry again if she fell in love. To Papa he bequeathed what little money he had; his horse was for General Pershing. The night before the attack "was awfull." It rained hard. He got his last tanks detrained at 3 A.M., with "H Hour" scheduled for 5 A.M. He issued final instructions to his officers: "No tank is to be surrendered or abandoned to the enemy. If you are left alone in the midst of the enemy keep shooting. If your gun is disabled use your pistols and squash the enemy with your tracks. . . . This is OUR BIG CHANCE; WHAT WE HAVE WORKED FOR . . . MAKE IT WORTH WHILE." He wanted to sleep at his forward command post. As he made his way there, enemy artillery began to rain down. Bright plumes of fire burst around him and he hid in a deep crater. "It was very lonely in the wet dark being shelled and all."

Before dawn, French and American artillery opened up with 2,800 guns in a thunderous barrage. German artillery had begun to reply when Georgie climbed on a parapet to observe through the heavy rain and fog his precious babies moving out. His brigade's two battalions were split to his right and left. Their mission was to flatten barbed wire and eliminate

German machine gun nests for American infantry following several hundred yards behind. Georgie was irritated to see some of his tanks slow down as they crossed enemy trenches. He followed on foot as far as his telephone wire extended, then continued with four runners in tow to relay messages back to corps headquarters. Small-arms fire cracked in the distance. He passed some dead and wounded troops. One doughboy crouched in a shell crater. Georgie was about to cuss him for cowardice when he saw the bullet hole above his right eye.

Even as the dawn brightened, the air remained thick with a smoke screen laid down by the artillery. A battalion messenger told Georgie that the tanks spearheading the advance were bogging down in the mud—at least five were disabled. Georgie and his men ran through several demolished French hamlets on their way to catch up with the tanks. He ducked a few times under showers of dirt from nearby shell bursts, "but soon saw the futility of dodging fate." He wore the bright shoulder straps designating his rank whereas many officers left theirs off the uniform lest snipers pick them out in a crowd. "I had to live up to them . . . and the feeling, foolish probably, of being admired by the men lying down is a great stimulus."

A French tank unit was supporting his brigade, and he paused to speak with its major, who was extricating a stuck tank with the help of some of his soldiers. As Georgie turned to continue on, a German cannon scored a direct hit on the tank and killed fifteen Frenchmen instantly. He stared back at the carnage in amazement. Then he took a briar pipe from his haversack and lit it up. He once had read a Kipling story where a commander calmed his men by idly puffing away through the fiercest fighting. Georgie worked that pipe like a furnace.

He reached the forward line of American infantry outside the village of Essey. The men lay prone in a long line and poured rifle fire across a narrow river into the town. Georgie gauged the enemy's return fire to be aimed too high, and so confidently walked along the American line swinging his walking stick and puffing his pipe. Thinking that he was truly getting the hang of gallantry, he noticed a figure standing atop a little hill even more exposed than Georgie was. It was Douglas MacArthur, a thirty-eight-year-old brigadier general known throughout the army for his fierce intelligence and imperious command presence.

Georgie joined MacArthur on the hilltop as a creeping barrage of German artillery slowly blanketed the ground before them. In a comic game of chicken, these two Arthurian throwbacks, MacArthur and Patton, chatted blithely in stiff-necked disregard of the shells exploding nearer and nearer, neither man hearing nor caring what the other said, yet damned if he would admit distraction. "I think each one wanted to leave," Georgie recalled, "but each hated to say so, so we let it come over us." It was he who flinched first at a nearby shell burst. MacArthur was there with a zinger. "Relax, Colonel. You never hear the one that gets you."

Some of the 304th's tanks had delayed on the near side of the bridge into Essey. When Georgie got there, he was told that the bridge had been mined by the retreating enemy. The only way to convince his men otherwise was to walk the bridge himself "in a catlike manner, expecting to be blown to heaven any moment." He felt disembodied as he moved across, saw himself from above like a strange small figure to whom he had no connection. When he learned later that his men had been impressed with his action, he was surprised. "Soldiers are funny," he said.

By now, German resistance was strictly a rearguard action, covering a headlong retreat. They'd withdrawn through Pannes, two miles away, Allied artillery pummeling them as they went. Americans in pursuit found the road between Essey and Pannes strewn with equipment, dead men, and dead horses. All but one of Georgie's tanks had run out of gas. He ordered the remaining tank to continue the attack. The sergeant inside grumbled about going on alone, so Georgie and two soldiers climbed atop the Renault. As it motored through the village, Georgie scanning one side of the street and his companions the other, thirty Germans stepped into the open with their hands raised in surrender. Georgie's companions stayed to guard them while he and the tank headed out of Pannes toward the next village up the road, Beney.

He was exhausted, having covered nearly ten miles on foot, and it was restful riding on the tank with his legs dangling down and the engine rumbling under him. In this languid moment he was slow to realize that the paint chips that began to leap like crickets off the side of the tank were caused by enemy bullets striking the armor. He jumped off and dove into a shallow shell crater. With his head pressed to the ground, he watched the lip of the crater a few inches above him being pecked away by bullets, sending tiny cascades of dirt down into his eyes.

"Here I was nearvous." Oblivious, the sergeant in the tank bobbed along, leaving him stranded behind like a man overboard. "I was on the point of getting scared as I was about a hundred yards ahead of the infantry and all alone in the field. If I went back the infantry would think I was running and there was no reason to go forward alone"—no reason, because it would only mean suicide. He decided to retreat in long diagonals, traverse back and forth across the field rather than make a straight dash for safety. Running, hitting the dirt at each burst of gunfire, he reached the infantry positions only to have his order to pursue the tank refused by the major in charge. "Then send a runner after it," Georgie said. "Hell no," said the major. "It ain't my tank."

Georgie drew a long breath and took off after the tank four hundred yards away. He did not feel afraid as he ran, "though I could see the guns spitting at me"—he simply wanted to catch that tank. He pounded on its rear door with his walking stick. The sergeant peered out. "What do you want now, Colonel?" Georgie told him to turn around and head back. The sergeant seemed disappointed. "I walked just ahead of him on the return trip and was quite safe."

The Germans continued to withdraw, leaving Beney to the Americans. It was late afternoon. Georgie halted the advance and walked seven miles back to the gasoline dump to arrange to refuel his tanks. "It was most interesting over the battlefield. Like the books but more dramatic. The dead were about mostly hit in the head. There were a lot of men stripping off buttons and other things but they always covered the face of the dead in a nice way." The roads congested toward the rear with soldiers and traffic. An officer gave him a lift in his car. A moment later, two soldiers Georgie had been walking with were killed by a bomb dropped from a German biplane. Fate again. "If they are going to get you they will." His experiences had confirmed one other thing: "I at least proved to my own satisfaction that I have nerve."

He sent Beatrice his field map and some cap ornaments taken off a dead German, as souvenirs. "Personally, I never fired a shot except to kill two poor horses with broken legs." General Rockenbach reprimanded him for going too far forward during the battle and losing communication with headquarters. Georgie was unrepentant. "I will not sit in a dug out and have my men out in the fighting."

Newspapers in Chicago and Los Angeles ran the headline "Californian Perched on Tank During Battle" over an account of the American victory at St. Mihiel. But that victory had come against light resistance. The American Army was already moving north to attack the Germans through a narrow gap between the Meuse River and the Argonne Forest west of Verdun. "I fancy our next show will be less easy than the first," Georgie wrote.

As he moved his brigade into position before the Meuse-Argonne offensive two weeks later, enemy shelling was more intense than he'd ever seen.

He wondered if he would survive this fight. "It is a big if. Hellish big." But then, he wrote Beatrice just before the dawn attack on September 26, "I am always nearvous about this time just as at Polo or at Foot ball before the game starts but so far I have been all right after that. I hope I keep on that way it is more plesant." He told her he loved her, signed and sealed the letter, then went to eat a last meal before the five-thirty kickoff.

As at St. Mihiel, the air was thick with fog and smoke. Georgie lost sight of his advancing tanks almost immediately. Following Rockenbach's orders, he remained at his command post for as long as he could stand it. But after an hour of knowing and seeing nothing of the action at the front, he and twelve runners plunged into the morning mist and followed the sounds of gunfire. Small pods of American tanks and infantry crisscrossed the area in confusion, looking for their commanders, one another, the enemy. Nearing the village of Cheppy, Georgie did not know how close the enemy was until "all at once we got shot at from all sides." Bullets churned the ground. Several soldiers fell hit. He and his runners ducked into a railroad cut and were soon joined by a hundred infantrymen from various scattered units.

The Americans fell back behind a small hill, where they lay flat against its reverse slope as machine-gun fire skimmed above their heads. Several tanks were visible at the bottom of the hill. Georgie dispatched a captain to bring them up fast. When neither the tanks nor the captain returned, he sent a lieutenant and then a sergeant to get those tanks moving. The wait was agonizing for him. The fog had lifted, giving the enemy a clear view of the pinned-down Americans. Some soldiers started to run. Georgie cursed them "and called them all sorts of names" to make them stay. "Some put on gas masks, some covered their face with their hands but none did a damed thing to kill Bosch. There were no officers there but me. So I decided to do some business."

He ran down the hill to see what was the delay. One tank had bogged down while crossing a wide German trench, blocking the others behind it. The crewmen had tried to dig the first one free but were forced to take cover as enemy machine guns raked them. Georgie flew into a rage. He and the commander of the tank group, Captain Mathew English, removed the picks and shovels strapped to the tanks and handed them out to the men hiding in the trench. Georgie told them to ignore the bullets and start digging. A German spotter plane circled overhead directing enemy gunners to zero in. As the fire intensified the soldiers leaped in the trench again, calling the colonel and captain to follow. "To hell with them!" Georgie shouted. "They can't hit me."

He got the men digging again. Bullets chewed paint off the tanks and smacked the wet ground at their feet. Several soldiers were hit as they dug. Others took their place. "I think I killed one man here," Georgie later recalled—an American soldier. "He would not work so I hit him over the head with a shovel." Was it true? Did he kill one of his own men in fury? He never elaborated on the matter later, and it was never described or documented by others. So the only answer remains Georgie's own: maybe.

Chaining five tanks together for better traction, he got them over the trench and in position to attack the enemy. He ran up the hill and waved his walking stick at the soldiers lying there. "Let's go get them, who's with me!" They all jumped up hollering, but fifty yards past the crest of the hill they faltered before a concentrated onslaught of gunfire. Dozens fell killed or wounded. The rest hugged the bare ground for protection.

Georgie, too, hugged the ground. Through the chaos and roar he felt silence envelop him like a bubble. He began to shake with terror. He wanted to run. All the parts of the veneer he'd so carefully appropriated— the profanity, the tough talk, the pipe, the walking stick—were suddenly stripped away.

He lifted his face off the dirt and gazed out over the German line. Autumn clouds billowed in the sky overhead. He stared into the clouds and saw faces. He blinked and squinted and the faces remained. Georgie saw his ancestors watching him in wait. They looked just like the old portraits and daguerreotypes on Lake Vineyard's walls and mantels. Hugh Mercer, Robert Patton, the Slaughters and Williamses; Benjamin Wilson; George and Tazewell Patton and their mother, Peggy; and Sue Patton, Willie Glassell, Will Thornton—all those dead cousins whose examples showed not how to live but how to die. "Always willing and wishing to obtain the desirable end," was how poor Nelly Davenport's father had described Nelly's last thoughts as she lay dying on Antigua in 1790. No wonder the Pattons had kept Davenport's letters, even though Nelly wasn't a relative. That wish to obtain "the desirable end" was something they understood.

Georgie understood it, too. Aloud he said, "It is time for another Patton to die." He grabbed his walking stick and stood, called behind him, "Who is with me?" and headed across the open plain through the sweeping enemy gunfire. Six men joined him, including his orderly, Private Joseph Angelo. Soon only he and Angelo were still standing. The others lay dead or wounded on the ground behind them. "We could see the machine guns right ahead so we yelled to keep up our courage and went on."

There was nothing impulsive about it. During the battle of St. Mihiel two weeks earlier, he'd been similarly stranded under fire after jumping off the tank outside Beney; at that time, realizing that to go forward alone was both suicidal and useless, he'd retreated to get reinforcements. Here at Cheppy no such prudence applied. It didn't matter that Georgie's action was foolhardy. It mattered only that he was going to die in this field to appease the clouds in the sky.

He received a bullet through the groin. It felt like a slap on the thigh, he said later. He walked several paces before realizing he'd been hit, then collapsed weakly on the ground.

"Our education is at fault in picturing death as such a terrible thing," he wrote several weeks later. "It is nothing and very easy to get." Eventually Georgie would rewrite scripture to explain his motivation that day. According to St. Paul, "The last enemy that shall be destroyed is death." (I. Corinthians 15:26) Georgie amended the line: "The last enemy that shall be destroyed is *fear of* death." In September 1918 he conquered that fear and made his bid to go out a winner at age thirty-two, one year older than his grandfather had been at his death at Winchester in 1864. Thirty-two was as good an age to die as any. After all, as Frederick the Great once famously challenged his wavering troops, "Dogs! Would you live forever?"

Joe Angelo saved his life. He dragged Georgie to a shallow crater that offered scant protection for one man, much less two. He knelt over Georgie and cut open his trousers as bullets sang about his head. The entry wound was clean and small; the mess was in Georgie's buttock where the bullet had exited. Angelo mopped away the pool of blood Georgie was sitting in, then bandaged the wound with a field dressing. Between gun bursts both men could hear the Germans talking in their emplacements forty yards away. Enemy fire diminished as the tanks appeared. Georgie sent Angelo to instruct the tanks where the machine gun nests were located. In an hour the area was secured. Giving his billfold and pistol to Angelo for safekeeping, Georgie was carried on a litter to the medical station three kilometers away. He wrote Beatrice two days later, "It has hurt very little and I have slept fine. I will be out in ten days."

He was still in the hospital more than a month later, his wound infected and leaking pus. The Meuse-Argonne offensive had continued without letup; in seven weeks 26,000 Americans died and 95,000 were wounded. His anxiety about missing the action was somewhat mollified by his promotion to full colonel on October 17. General Rockenbach had recommended him for the Distinguished Service Cross. Georgie in turn recommended Captain English for the DSC and Private Angelo for the Medal of Honor.

While laid up in the hospital, he caught up with his mail from home. He wrote his wife as often as twice a day; with time to reflect, he was feeling especially lonesome for her. He told her to keep young, buy low-cut dresses, exchange their double bed for a single, "it is more sociable." He wanted to take a second honeymoon when the war was over. "We will have to get used to each other." Beatrice joyfully wrote back of herself and the girls. She wanted another child. Forget it, he said. Little Bee and Ruth Ellen "do not interest me at all. I love you too much and am jealous or something of children." And no, he replied to her decorous inquiry about the state of his reproductive ability, "I was not altered by the gas as I was not gased." Even so, as far as he was concerned, she could expect to get pregnant again only by "accident or emaculate conception."

On November 11, two weeks after Georgie's release from the hospital, Armistice was declared. The streets of Langres erupted in celebration. He sat inside and gloomily composed two poems. The first was an elegy to Mathew English, the captain who'd braved enemy fire with Georgie at Cheppy, and who'd been killed in action a week later. Its last lines, "The grave promoted him to be/A hero for all time," echoed Georgie's wish for himself. The second poem, called "Peace," postulated a day when he and the Germans might someday "clasp our gory hands as friends / In high Valhalla's hall." In his own future he foresaw "sleek virtues soft and cheap" and none of war's "bold and blatant sin," which he believed brought maximum heat to the experience of being alive.

Georgie turned thirty-three on Armistice Day, so it was a scary occasion all around. His fear of aging went hand in hand with his fear of an America at peace. He knew that he needed high-pressure action to ward off the discontent that stirred in him like a parasite that feeds when its host rests. He wasn't concerned only for himself. His disappointment, he'd warned Beatrice before their marriage, "might revert to others who I love." It wasn't a hollow threat.

He stayed on in Europe for five more months. The letdown after the excitement of war left him moody and sluggish. "Life has lost its zest," he said. In his increasing spare time from commanding his brigade, he busied himself writing melancholy verse, essays on tank tactics, and with lobbying his superiors to confirm his DSC. He desperately wanted that medal. "It is the whole war to me." He prayed for it. When at last he received it he felt very fine and proudly wore it everywhere. But less than a month later he wrote, "I must come back [to war] to get the Medal of Honor which I missed getting this time on account of all the witnesses getting killed or being Bosch."

After his promotion to colonel in October, Georgie detected that many of his peers weren't happy for him; in fact they were "soar as hell," he wrote, "and probably lay it to Nita or some other hellish plot." But the continued whispers about his inside pull with General Pershing bothered Georgie much less than in the past. Of those officers spreading the rumor, he retorted angrily, "If they had wanted to risk their skins in fighting instead of looking for staff jobs they might have been promoted too." He'd proved himself, he believed, and feeling now removed from any fallout of Nita and Pershing's engagement, he supported it wholeheartedly.

The engagement had continued somewhat bumpily in the nearly two years since the AEF had departed the United States for Europe. During those years, Nita and Pershing (like Georgie and Beatrice) hadn't seen each other and had communicated only by letter and telegram. Reserved in person, Pershing was even more reserved in his writing. Nita scrutinized his letters for expressions of affection or, so she feared, for hints that his ardor had cooled. Between 1917 and 1918 she grew increasingly impatient with his diffidence, yet reluctant to impose on him (he was running a war, after all), she sought Georgie's advice on how to proceed.

He promptly stirred up a mess by telling Nita not to write Pershing directly but to write him care of Georgie. Furious, she accused him and General Pershing of "subterfuge," of conspiring to let her down easy and end the engagement. She was calmed by quick apologizes from both men. Pershing wrote Georgie afterward, "I am getting sane letters from Anne again and suppose she is over her rage—poor girl, it is hard for her to be anything but open and frank." Georgie contritely told Beatrice that the whole silly episode "shows that with out your advice I am apt to make mistakes of judgment."

The episode did move Pershing to express his emotions more openly. He said he wished that he and Nita had married before the war. He considered defying his own order and bringing her to Europe to visit him. The man truly was love struck, reported Georgie, who once had suggested that so great were Pershing's military responsibilities, "it would never do for him to admit so human a feeling as love." But to Nita's joy, Georgie said the general often expressed his affection for her these days. "It is the most intense case I have ever seen."

Beatrice, for one, had doubts. Her feelings about Nita and Pershing's eventual marriage had changed from displeasure to high hopes—apparently. Yet her continued suspicion about Pershing's degree of commitment to Nita was somewhat self-serving. As ever, her main concern was her husband. Should Nita's engagement fall through, all traces of nepotism would be dispelled from Georgie's career. Beatrice would feel badly for her sister-in-law, but her own heart would not be broken.

Adamant that Nita should not seek to visit Pershing during the war, Beatrice presented her with several arguments. It was better, in catching a man, to answer diffidence with diffidence, not to appear too eager. If the war continued a long time, "he will surely condescend to let you visit." Lastly, Nita should consider what was right for the U.S. war effort. "J's got to run this marriage business as well as the war," Beatrice said, "and if he were stupid enough to deviate the *least* bit from what he thinks is just the right thing to do, neither of you would ever forgive yourselves as long as you live." In the end, Nita took her advice and stayed home for the duration, even though she worried that she was imperiling her romance with Pershing.

If Beatrice had ulterior motives in dampening Nita's excitement, these were diminished by the closeness that developed between the two women when Nita stayed with Beatrice for several weeks after Beatrice's parents died; and were further diminished after Georgie's exploits in battle and his promotion to colonel. Georgie had distinguished himself in his own right. Pershing's past nepotism didn't matter any longer. Beatrice finally accepted Nita's engagement completely, writing her joyfully after Armistice was declared, "You had better get busy in earnest on your hope chest!" Then came a shocker from Georgie: "As to J. and Nita. It is possible that the game is up."

Pershing was awash in acclaim and flattery as commander of the victorious American Army. As Georgie explained it, "Ambition is a great thing"—but it is heartless; "without soul." The war had catapulted Pershing to world fame; Nita's luster had dimmed proportionately. And there were rumors that Pershing had taken a French mistress. Beatrice told Nita to break off the relationship at once, but Nita gave it one more chance with a letter to Pershing in which she asked his consent to visit him in Europe and, more to the point, asked whether or not they were still engaged. His reply came in April. In the past, thinking "that we could talk better than write," he'd wanted her to come. "But after all it would be best for you not to come." As to their status, "Our understanding should be kept entirely to ourselves. I have always denied any engagement and shall continue to do so. Possibly this is not fully understood on your side."

This seemed to seal it. Papa now joined with Beatrice in urging Nita to withdraw. Yet Georgie took it on himself to meet with Pershing to settle the matter. Immediately after the meeting he sent Beatrice instructions to tell Nita that she should forget her hurt pride and travel to Europe at once—Pershing had expressly asked for her. "You may not like it but here it is," Georgie wrote. "Nita loves him and he her. One more year of separation might ruin two lives and loves." Knowing his wife's stubbornness, he admonished her to "consider what I have said from your *head* not from *sentiment*."

Nita decided to travel to England with the Red Cross. She was nervous but willing. "Once in a while it is good to go alone with your own soul. I never tried it before, and it is rather interesting." But when she notified Pershing in France of her arrival, he professed total surprise that she'd come to Europe. "How long are you staying?" he asked. "And what are you going to do over here?"

Pershing had had second thoughts about continuing with Nita. He'd mailed her a letter explaining his misgivings—mailed it to her in the United States. Now she had to wait for it to be forwarded to her in London. It arrived on June 11. "You can never guess what is all the excitement," she reported to her mother after reading it. "I am a villain on three counts." Pershing, Nita said, "wants to see me and he loves me, but these terrible things have come between us." He'd begun to worry about their twenty-seven-year age difference. Second, he still had feelings for his late wife. "She comes to him in dreams," Nita said, almost amused. "Did you ever hear such a silly letter?"

Pershing's third reservation was that he feared she would be unkind to his son from his first marriage. "If John sat up nights thinking he could not further miss the mark with me." She was devoted to her nieces and they were devoted to her; if there was anything she was cut out for, it was mothering. "The whole idea is so grotesque I don't even feel mad or sad. I just find myself grinning at the picture of the *c-cruel* step-mamma." Evidently he'd gotten this idea "when nearly two years ago he read a letter by me *not* meant for him" in which Nita complained that Pershing's sister was needlessly keeping Pershing's memories of his perished wife and daughters raw and painful by always sending him pictures and keepsakes of them.

"How he got [Nita's letter] he does not say." This was the question which most irked her: "Who in H— gave him this morbid poison. I would bet he never thought of those things alone. It would take the female of the species." Perhaps it was Pershing's sister, she thought. But the incriminating letter, as best Nita could recall, "must have been to Geo." Had her brother showed the letter to Pershing, or told him about it? Had Beatrice? Two years ago Beatrice had been very ambivalent about Pershing and Nita's relationship. Was Pershing, in order to torpedo his engagement and put the blame on Nita, dredging up something Beatrice had confided to him long ago when her feelings were different? The truth would never be known.

Nita thought the relationship was still salvable. Pershing was coming to London from France for an international Peace Parade in July—they would talk then, "and he'll change his tune." In the meantime, she went to work as a Red Cross volunteer. One day she walked out of her London office on the way to lunch when a convoy of military vehicles drove by. Pershing and two British generals stood in one of the vehicles waving to the crowd. Nita waved back and caught Pershing's eye, "but he gave no reaction and his face never changed." One of her Red Cross friends said, "Did you hear he is engaged to a California girl? I don't believe it." Nita was too stunned to reply. That evening she tried to bury her hurt in contempt. "He is not great as real men are great," she wrote her mother. "I pray that I may never be guilty of believing myself a little tin god on wheels."

She continued to pursue him, however. After waiting two days for him to phone and tell her he was in London, Nita phoned Pershing. He was too busy to see her. "If he cares that little for me, I am well rid of him." On July 19 she attended the Peace Parade, a grand procession of Allied forces marching through the city with their commanders and various international dignitaries. Nita was pleased to report that Pershing's ovation from the crowd as he rode by was less than the cheers for the French and British commanders. In fact Americans in general were not all that popular in Europe. "I do not wonder," Nita wrote. "There were long hard years when others died, and suffered, and we lay back at ease. Now we say we *won* the war. Alas, we are a very holy, and a boastful lot. The Puritan taint goes a long, long way."

To her surprise, Pershing contacted her the day after the parade and asked to see her. They had "one hell of an evening" discussing all the "bugaboos" haunting him. "Men are just little boys," she observed afterward. "He is like one who has played too long with the street gang and wants to be cuddled by his mother." The upshot of their meeting? "We are going to be married before he goes home."

To cement his proposal he sent her flowers the next day, with a note suggesting they marry at the U.S. embassy. Nita was overjoyed. "I prefer a church to the embassy but I will not kick even if he decides on the zoo." He never did decide, however. He wrote her once more to say his old doubts had returned. "Chasing shadows," she sighed, but her opinion was irrelevant. He thought it best that they not see each other for a while. "He must have a low opinion of women," Nita wrote. "If his love is so unforgiving that it asks perfection of me, it is as well to know it in time."

Weeks of silence went by. She could not bring herself to formally terminate the engagement. "Why did it all occur? Just to torture me it would seem. I had been too jolly, life was too easy—still I had tried to do right, hadn't I, Mother?" At last she accepted the inevitable, composing her own epitaph on the aborted romance: "She played the game, and she followed her ideals, even though being human, she stumbled." She wrote Pershing a last note, sent telegrams to her brother and parents, and boarded a ship for America. On receiving Nita's wire, Beatrice wired Papa and Ruth: "She is wonderful. We also approve her action."

Nita looked forward to returning home "and being again me, though never the same me as before I fancy." She wanted to see Lake Vineyard again, also Catalina Island. "We were young there together once," she wrote her parents. "I suppose all this boom has spoiled it a little, as fame and prosperity spoils us all." She told them that henceforth she would devote her life to their happiness. She asked one favor in return. Of her engagement to General Pershing, "Let us *never never* speak of it again." And they never did.

Georgie still had hopes for his sister. He'd disembarked with his brigade at New York harbor in March 1919. In September, while stationed at Camp Meade, Maryland, he wrote his mother on the subject of Pershing: "My own opinion is that he being purely selfish wanted to let the affair rest for a while to see if his feelings revived. It is perfectly possible that his mind, driven as it has been for three years, is incapable of emotion. Or it may be that the war has aged his mind so that like a very old man he can only live in the past." He thought the general might "renew his suit" with Nita. But as far as Nita was concerned, she was relieved to be done with him. "Anything is better than the H— of wishing longing and futile hoping that I have been through," she wrote.

Georgie was speaking from new experience in regard to the war's effect on Pershing's character. Though thrilled to be home with Beatrice, Georgie's adjustment was difficult. He was jumpy around the house and uncomfortable with his daughters. Bee remembered him a little from before the war, Ruth Ellen not at all. They looked on their father as an intimidating intruder who fell far short of the knight their mother had led them to expect.

It was several days after his return from France before Georgie even spoke to Ruth Ellen directly. She burst into the parlor where he had dismantled all his firearms and was cleaning them on the floor. Georgie looked at her and tried to launch a fatherly smile. "Hello, little girl." Ruth Ellen let out a howl and began bawling hysterically. Georgie howled, too. "Goddamn it, Beaty! Come take this kid out of here. She's making a goddamn awful noise, and I didn't do a thing to her." Beatrice took her daughter into her arms. Georgie watched sullenly as she cuddled Ruth Ellen and calmed her. His foreboding had proved valid. Peace was going to be painful.

The Eighth Cavalry on parade in El Paso, 1915.

Georgie in Mexico, 1916.

Papa Patton, during his run for the
U.S. Senate, 1916.

The Patton family, 1917: Beatrice, Ruth Ellen, Georgie, and Bee.

Georgie, in front of one of his brigade's Renault tanks, France, 1918.

Beatrice and Nita, Thomasville, Georgia, 1918.

Papa, Georgie, and George S. Patton IV, 1926.

Papa and Georgie at the grave of George and Tazewell Patton, Winchester, Virginia, 1920.

The Patton family, 1931: George IV,
Beatrice, Ruth Ellen, Bee, and Georgie.

Ruth Ellen Patton, 1931.

Georgie, 1932.

Georgie's polo team, Hawaii, 1927.

Georgie and Bee at Bee's wedding, 1934.

Georgie and Ruth Ellen at Ruth Ellen's wedding, 1940.

Georgie and Beatrice, Fort Benning, Georgia, 1940.

The Patton family at home, 1945, from left: Bee, George Patton Waters, Beatrice, Michael Totten, Ruth Ellen, Beatrice Totten, John K. Waters, Jr., George S. Patton IV.

Beatrice with Kate Smith, 1945.

Georgie, Third Army com-
mander, Germany, 1945.

Beatrice and Georgie, their
post-war reunion, June 1945.

Georgie's welcome-home parade, Boston, June 1945.

Georgie's funeral,
December 1945.
Sergeant George
Meeks is the leading
pallbearer.

Beatrice and George IV,
West Point, 1946.

The Patton family,
West Point, 1949.

KEEPING FAITH

There is a glory of the Sun
('Pity it passeth soon!),
But those whose work is nearer done
Look, rather, towards the Moon.

—Rudyard Kipling
The Glories

☆ ☆ **15** ☆ ☆

Au Revoir, Son

JUST before Christmas, 1918, Little Bee Patton was told by a school-friend that there was no Santa Claus. Bee confronted her mother with this heresy, and Beatrice explained that Santa was a saint in heaven rather than a fat man at the North Pole, and that parents were his earthly agents, distributing gifts and filling Christmas stockings according to his direction. "Who fills your stocking?" Bee asked.

"Well, no one. My parents died last spring."

The seven-year-old considered a moment. "From now on, one day a year, *I* will be your mother and prepare your stocking." Bee made good on her promise every Christmas until she left home to marry in 1934. Her father, after he returned from Europe in 1919, enjoyed giving flowers and surprise presents that appealed to his own taste, such as dogs, horses, and equestrian gear. Whenever he bought a toy for his children (he liked contraptions: ship models, building kits, train sets) he was always the first to open the package and begin playing with the toy on the living room floor. But he could not be relied on to provide such a quaint remembrance as stocking knickknacks. The girls and their mother accepted his self-centeredness as a fact of life. Anticipating his lapses, they looked out for one another protectively.

Beatrice once pasted little hand-lettered signs across the dining table from her daughters, one reminding Bee to "Swallow" and the other reminding Ruth Ellen to "Chew." The eating habits the signs addressed corresponded to the girls' personalities in general. Bee reacted to the world as rigidly and tentatively as she did to a morsel of food, while Ruth Ellen absorbed experience in incautious gulps. Bee was pretty, retiring, and shared her mother's serious demeanor. Ruth Ellen, four years younger, was a garrulous tomboy. She sensed her parents' unspoken disappointment that she hadn't been born a son; and since her sister was the prettier and more feminine girl, it seemed better to take an opposite path than palely to imitate Bee. In moments alone, however, Ruth Ellen wove flowers in her reddish-blond hair and swayed before a mirror dreaming of gallant knights and magical kingdoms. Beatrice recognized this dual impulse in her younger daughter. "She comes home from school usually having been in a fight or with a present from some small boy—sometimes both." Ruth Ellen had been unpleasantly jolted by her father's return. He was a strange and overwhelming presence, a mad genie sprung from a bottle. Three years later she was rebuked by her first-grade teacher for cursing in class. "My father does," was her blithe excuse. Though often at loggerheads with Georgie, circling him as warily as he circled her, she began to mimic him like a devoted disciple.

The key element of Georgie's leadership style was something he called "visible personality." Creating it required a conscious performance that, in his heady years as a brigade commander in France, he was able to refine, rehearse, and finally unleash in actual battle. But the preparation had been too prolonged, the experience too intense and too abruptly concluded, for him to quit easily the performance once he returned to his family. So it continued unabated like an actor's big-moment soliloquy that even a dropped curtain can't stop. On the tank training ground outside Langres, on a hill under fire at Cheppy, on a polo field, at a cocktail party, around the dinner table at home, Georgie was compulsively driven to emote, dazzle, dominate—in short, to exhibit visible personality in everything he did. For his daughters and even his wife, this took some getting used to.

Bee and Ruth Ellen observed their father with bemusement, following after him like a pair of pint-size scientists seeking to study the beast in its natural habitat. They commonly saw him on his knees praying before horse shows and steeplechases. Asked if he was praying to win, Georgie seemed offended. "That would be insulting to God. I just pray to do my best." During a polo match the girls watched a veterinarian (the only doctor present) stitch up a cut in Georgie's head as Georgie, leaning over, bled into a bucket to keep from staining his clothes. One morning they spied him primping at his bathroom mirror before leaving for work. His sparse blond hair had begun to go gray. Dabbing his scalp with a toothbrush, he applied a homemade medication of castor oil, rum, and cologne mixed with lemon juice and iodine to thicken his hair and color it yellow. His silent concentration on these fussy exertions was shattered when he stepped back and recited, with gathering volume, King Henry's prebattle exhortation from Shakespeare's *Henry V*:

> "In peace there's nothing so becomes a man
> as modest stillness and humility.
> But when the blast of war blows in our ears,
> Then imitate the action of the tiger:
> Stiffen the sinews, conjure up the blood,
> Disguise fair nature with hard-favored rage."

He wound up with a bellowed crescendo: "On, on, you noblest English!" He threw down his toothbrush like a knight's gauntlet and pivoted to leave the bathroom, his features screwed into a florid war face instead of that "damned mild expression" he usually felt cursed with. The sight of his daughters' gaping upturned faces brought him up short. He forced a saccharine smile to hide his embarrassment—his "sissy baby smile," Bee and Ruth Ellen instantly dubbed it. In the future they were amazed that strangers their father was trying to charm never seemed to realize how phony that smile was, "because even the dogs did."

Claiming "a hell of a memory for poetry and war," Georgie was intent on passing his talent to his daughters. He required them to memorize one poem a week. He made them read a verse of the Bible each night and report to him at breakfast with their interpretation of it, not least for the opportunity it gave him to express his own opinion about it. Though uncomfortable in his role as a family man, when at home he didn't like to be alone. In the library after dinner he preferred his wife to read aloud to his daughters while he sat nearby in his tuxedo or dress uniform and quietly perused volumes of history and poetry. The girls knew that sometimes he feigned absorption in his book while secretly listening to their mother read *The Secret Garden* or *Little Women*, possibly recalling his hours of being read to by his father and aunt when he was a boy.

Georgie often burst out with snippets of verse that sometimes related to the matter at hand and sometimes seemed non sequiturs. He would then proceed to analyze the verse just as, in France, he'd analyzed the fine points of tank warfare in lecture after lecture to an audience of troops no less captive than his three-member audience at home. Far from being bored by these literary excursions, Bee and Ruth Ellen were enthralled. He previously had tried to ingratiate himself with them by giving them a pet puppy. The gesture had been well meaning but clumsily done—the dog's name, Tank, was more Georgie's choice than theirs. Yet in such moments of listening wide-eyed to his pronouncements, they began to understand that "Daddy" was as uneasy with them as they were with him, but that if given the opportunity to perform, he could be kind of fun, kind of funny, kind of neat. Other fathers were sheep compared to him. Other men were dull and forgettable.

At dinner, say, after grandly intoning Rupert Brooke's "The Soldier" ("If I should die, think only this of me/There is some corner in a foreign field/That is forever England"), Georgie might offer his fond prediction that he would die in a foreign land, since, as Napoleon said, the boundaries of an empire are marked by the graves of her soldiers. Beatrice would nod, the fire in the fireplace would crackle significantly, and the meal would resume as the girls furtively eyed their father in expectation of his next trick.

If discussing reincarnation (one of his favorite topics), he would offer up as evidence pertinent bits of *The Bhagavad Gita* ("For sure is the death of him that is born, and sure the birth of him that is dead"), and his old standby, Revelations 3:12: "Him that overcometh will I make a pillar in the temple of my God, and he shall go no more out." To these he added the fifth stanza of Papa's favorite poem, Wordsworth's "Intimations" ode: "Our birth is but a sleep and a forgetting,/The soul that rises with us, our life's Star,/Hath had elsewhere its setting/And cometh from afar." Clearly, Georgie said, Wordsworth shared his belief in reincarnation.

Still riding the momentum of wartime excitement, he wrote many poems in the first years after Armistice. Most reflected nostalgically on his recent battle experiences; some cast back to scenes of bloody conflict from prehistoric times forward, scenes in which he imagined he had lived and died in countless previous incarnations:

> Through the travail of the ages
> Midst the pomp and toil of war
> Have I fought and strove and perished
> Countless times upon this star.

. . . .

> I have sinned and I have suffered
> Played the hero and the knave
> Fought for belly, shame or country
> And for each have found a grave.
>
> . . . .
>
> So as through a glass and darkly
> The age long strife I see
> Where I fought in many guises,
> Many names—but always me.

He also wrote poems expressing his dissatisfaction with the present and his pessimism about the future. The national euphoria of the postwar Jazz Age left him cold; in the name of progress, peace, and prosperity the nation was sinking into sloth and decadence. Typically, however, his indignation was more self-concerned than self-righteous. Even as he lamented having to "curb the promptings of my warrior soul," he was attracted to the opulent pleasures that his wife's wealth afforded him. A man could try to maintain his discipline amid such temptation, "but soon or late," Georgie feared, "his tainted spirit wearies of the fray/His ideals languish and his virtues yield."

He liked a good time, that was the problem. "I believe in enjoying my self between wars" had been his excuse for buying an expensive Pierce-Arrow automobile after returning to the States in 1919. Reassigned to Fort Myer in 1920, he again plunged into the capital high life—banquets, country clubs, White House invitations. Fox hunting from fall to spring, horse shows in summer, polo year-round—his stable of thoroughbreds and polo ponies was considered one of the finest in America. But good times were one thing, complacency was another. Complacency was the enemy, and his poetry was intended to fight it.

As part of the army's peacetime downsizing, Georgie was reduced in rank from colonel to major—standard procedure, still it stung a little. The National Defense Act of 1920 reorganized the military's service branches, with the dissolution of the Tank Corps as one result. On learning that tanks and tankers were to be assigned to the infantry, he rejoined the cavalry. His enjoyment of equestrian sports and his familiarity with cavalry posts and cavalry soldiers had decided him against remaining with his precious babies.

For the next twenty years, a bitter debate raged within the army about the role of tanks and horses in future wars. Senior cavalry officers realized that tanks were in competition with horses, that the tide of mechanization threatened to do away with their branch of service entirely. Georgie straddled the issue. He appreciated better than most the combat potential of tanks. But he was sentimental about horses (he wrote more endearingly of his favorite thoroughbreds than of his children), and he was as loyal to his cavalry superiors as he was to his father, who, flawed and recalcitrant, likewise represented an inevitably waning past.

Through these years of debate Georgie published articles about tanks in military journals, kept up with developments in tank design, stayed in touch with former Tank Corps colleagues who'd followed tanks into the infantry. But whenever pressed on the question of tanks versus horses, he dutifully voiced the cavalry line that under certain adverse conditions of terrain, weather, and scanty supplies, nothing could outperform a horse. His doubts troubled him, however, and undercut the confidence of his war years in the Tank Corps. Then he'd known exactly where he stood on conducting modern warfare. Now he wasn't so sure.

Just before Georgie was reduced in rank in 1920, he and his father drove to Winchester, Virginia, to visit the grave of the Confederate brothers George and Tazewell Patton. Papa hadn't been there since the rainy night forty years earlier when he'd brought Uncle Tazewell's body down from Baltimore to be buried beside Papa's father. A single headstone marked the spot. Someone snapped a picture of Georgie and Papa standing beside it. In the picture, Papa, shrouded in shadow, looks dapper and frail. Georgie wears his uniform and a colonel's eagle on his overseas cap. His gloved hand rests on the stone in a gesture of fraternity: like the soldiers lying here, he too is a colonel and a combat veteran. How often in his youth had he dreamed of standing shoulder to shoulder with these two men? Their faces had been foremost in the ghostly company he'd seen in the clouds over Cheppy. Yet in the moment of claiming position alongside them, Georgie's expression shows little satisfaction and certainly no joy, as if somehow the moment has not carried the savor he expected. Rather, he has donned his fiercest war face. Tazewell Patton's last words, "In Christ alone, perfectly resigned," are carved on top of the stone. Perfectly resigned? Not Georgie. Not now, and, so he prayed, not ever.

Some veterans return home from war desiring only repose in their lives. Some cannot shed their taste for war's tension and exhilaration, and continue to whet it through blood sport, aggression, and coarseness. Georgie was the latter type. At social gatherings with friends and colleagues, he maintained a courtliness just rakish enough to be warm but never vulgar. In private moments with his family, however, he exhibited a savage streak that his combat experience evidently had aroused in him. He wasn't violent at home. He'd never struck his wife or children, and rarely even raised his voice. He didn't have to; when angry, a steely edge came to his voice and a coldness to his eye that were plenty intimidating. Rather, his savage streak showed up in the stories he told and in his excited reaction to particular events that somehow seemed to recall for him intense times on the Western Front.

In January 1922, the roof of Washington's Knickerbocker Theater collapsed under a heavy snowfall, killing nearly a hundred people. Georgie's unit was detailed from Fort Myer to clear the wreckage and remove the bodies. Returning home from these labors, he was pale and nauseated. "It was horrible," he told Beatrice. Yet, like cauterizing a wound with fire, he then turned to Bee and Ruth Ellen, ages ten and six, and described with grim relish how, when he pulled out a woman by her legs from under a fallen roof beam, her head had come off. Beatrice was furious at him for telling them this gruesome story. Georgie dismissed her sharply. "They can't go through life with blinders on. They should know that these things happen."

After seeing a Hollywood war movie he declared that the shell bursts and gunfire had made him "homesick." During a steeplechase, the fatal fall of a jockey appalled the crowd and prompted calls to abolish the sport. "We are loosing all hardihood!" Georgie scoffed. "Such squeamishness is fatal to any race." He wanted to incorporate polo into cavalry training. "A few cuts and broken bones on the polo fields [are] not a drawback but a decided advantage." The risk of injury prepared a man, he wrote with mordant lyricism, to confront "the insinuating whisper of bullets about his sacred person."

And then there was the bedtime story he began telling his daughters at night. Making it up as he went along, Georgie's story evolved into a long, graphic, blackly comic Rabelaisian fantasy about a tenth-century nobleman in Anjou, France (near Saumur, where Georgie and Beatrice had briefly lived in 1912). Count Reginald Fulk the Black was nicknamed "Shark" (by Georgie) for his three rows of sharp teeth, with which as an infant he bit off the nipples of his wet nurses; with which, as a boy, he bit off the testicles of certain unfortunate knights; and with which, as an amorous adult, he bit off women's breasts in the middle of lovemaking, an outrage they were happy to endure because the third hand projecting from Reginald's lower back offered them unique if unspecified sexual pleasures that apparently more than compensated for the loss of a breast or two.

Georgie's tale featured cannibalism, patri-, matri-, and infanticide. It had witches, devils, and mermaids. One anecdote focused on doings in the royal outhouse, the other on a hapless priest left to dangle in an iron cage until he turned to bones. The priest's crime? His homilies and penances were tedious beyond words. The other priest of the castle was reluctant to continue the count's religious instruction. Reginald himself acknowledged that he was a hard case. "I have many grievous sins," he told the priest, "but how dull would be thy confessional were it not for me. Admit that my transgressions titillate thee more than the breviary thou carriest where thy manhood ought to be."

Well, this was terrific stuff as far as Bee and Ruth Ellen were concerned. Their mother was far from pleased that they were receiving all this "raw history," as Beatrice called it, at such tender ages. But Georgie's mind was steeped in raw history these days. "Do you want them to grow up ignorant?" he snapped. It was a rhetorical question. He enjoyed telling the stories, therefore the stories got told.

Even his lighthearted moods could seem manic and aggressive. Wrote a family friend after hosting a dinner party soon after the war, "George was the cutup of the evening. He had an abundance of new stories which kept everybody killing themselves with laughter." Such performances gave outsiders the impression that he was a perpetual fountain of boyish exuberance. But Beatrice knew he was troubled. "He has been so changed since the war," she wrote in 1923, "so serious and restless." And she knew that more than career worries were haunting him. With Prohibition in force since 1919, Georgie had begun brewing beer at home. He stored it in a shed outside the kitchen, and one day in the summer heat the sealed beer bottles began suddenly exploding. Inside the house, he hit the floor at this apparent sound of gunshots. Beatrice smiled and ribbingly called him her hero, but her smile fell away at the sight of Georgie's blushing face. She realized he'd been terrified—terrified at the explosions just now, terrified in France—and his terror was still with him.

Bee and Ruth Ellen knew that something was unsettling their father, but they couldn't fathom what it might be. Bee kept her head down around him, heard his tales, observed his performance with a mixture of fascination and fright. Just after her eleventh birthday, a Washington newspaper carried a photograph of her on horseback in a children's horse show. Georgie's mixed reaction when he saw the picture took Bee aback; the pleasure and pride she'd felt in herself were undercut by the understanding, later made explicit by their mother, that photos and press clippings were Georgie's domain. His wife and children were to stay in the background, a directive Bee followed all too willingly.

Ruth Ellen, though four years younger than her sister, didn't accept their father's domination as passively. On even trivial matters of household life Ruth Ellen took stands against Georgie that irritated and rather unnerved him. They argued all the time, this blustery cavalryman and his stubborn, pug-nosed daughter. "Why don't Daddy and I get along?" Ruth Ellen asked her mother. "Because you two are alike," Beatrice said. Despite the friction between them, Ruth Ellen felt closer to her father than to her mother. She liked the way he, for better or worse, carried his passions upfront and uncut; her mother was more cloaked in her feelings, and therefore seemed more distant and, oddly, more formidable than Georgie. After Ruth Ellen learned to write, she often recorded the stories he told, the latest nugget of visible personality he dropped at dinner or when the family was gathered in the library. "I can't put all the glory into it that Daddy did," she noted after making one such entry, "but I think it is worth remembering."

Georgie began to emerge from his postwar moodiness in the summer of 1923. He'd just completed the five-month field officers' course at Fort Riley. His high standing in the class had earned him an assignment to Fort Leavenworth, Kansas, where he was to report in September to begin the year-long course at the Command and General Staff College. His self-confidence, which had waned since his return to the cavalry, was bolstered by his fine performance at Fort Riley. And though the prospect of academic work always made him, in Beatrice's words, "irritable and desperate," he knew that Fort Leavenworth was an essential next step to career advancement. He was back on track, he felt.

Between the assignments he took three months' leave with his family at the Ayers' beachfront estate in Massachusetts. "Such a summer!" Beatrice recalled afterward. "It couldn't have been more perfect." The Pattons brought seven horses north with them. Georgie played polo, Beatrice swam and sailed, Bee rode, and Ruth Ellen played on the beach. The event of the summer was Georgie's rescue of three small boys whose boat had overturned off Salem harbor. Georgie and Beatrice were sailing in a two-person runabout when they heard cries for help and then saw the boys in the water waving their arms. Georgie, at the tiller, tacked toward them and hauled them aboard. Under the weight of five passengers the tiny sailboat hung dangerously low in the water. Beatrice thought it would be safer to drop the sail and row home. Georgie felt the boys would catch pneumonia if they didn't get to shore soon. "We must sail!" he declared, his voice fierce with the old adrenaline. "I've done all I can, and if there is anyone in this boat worth saving, the Lord will have to help us now."

On reaching shore, all were thrilled and grateful—but Beatrice wasn't about to leave it at that. She had each of the boys give sworn affidavits attesting to Georgie's courage. She wrote up a narrative of the episode and transmitted the documents to the Massachusetts Humane Society and the Treasury Department, which awarded life-saving medals. She totally downplayed her own part in the rescue. She knew her husband loved medals and that they would improve his morale. When both departments eventually recognized Georgie with silver medals, no one was happier than Beatrice. "I have never been prouder of him in my life."

Believing they sensed what their father needed to lift his spirits, the girls, too, had been doing their part to help him, praying together every night for heaven to send down a little brother. In July their mother pressed their hands to her belly, and they felt the baby move. Georgie seemed pleased enough to be having another child. This vacation, Beatrice noted, marked "the first time he has ever chummed with his children." He left for Fort Leavenworth in August "looking as if something had wiped every line off his face. This happy summer has brought him back."

Her extraordinary solicitousness of Georgie's welfare was never more apparent than when Beatrice gave birth in December. Remaining in Massachusetts for her health, she didn't see her husband again until December 23, when he returned on Christmas leave from Fort Leavenworth. She'd wanted to deliver the baby before Georgie arrived so that she could be "slim and lively, handsomer and thin," knowing his distaste for overweight women. At Bee's suggestion, she'd gone for a bumpy trot on a pony to try to break her water and induce labor. "But no use," Beatrice lamented.

Her contractions began the night Georgie arrived and quickly became intense. At the hospital ten hours later, the baby hadn't yet appeared. The doctor decided to take it. He was about to inform Georgie outside the delivery room when Beatrice stopped him. "No!" She was remembering his queasiness over her previous births. "Wait till after you've done it." Even now, as she lay exhausted and sweat-soaked in her eleventh hour of labor, she was thinking of her husband first.

She was etherized. The baby was born in a breech position. "When I came to and saw that dear little round red face beside me, I could have shouted for joy." It was a boy. "Ruth Ellen," wrote Beatrice, "has prayed for him *by name* for two years." And of course there was no debate about what the name would be. George Smith Patton IV.

Papa, Ruth, Nita, and Nannie had come east for the birth. Papa was thrilled that the Patton name would be carried on in George IV. As if to certify the line of succession, he insisted on baptizing the child as soon as possible. Papa's joy was mixed with morbid relief. His grandson's birth seemed to signify that his work was done, his patriarchal duties fulfilled. "After this time," Georgie wrote later, "he never really was well, took less interest in life and no exercise."

Georgie's feelings about his son's birth were harder to gauge. When his daughters were born, his reaction was candidly negative. He was jealous of the time they took from his wife; he wasn't pleased to share the spotlight. But to his son's birth he reacted barely at all. Given Georgie's egotism, it would seem that having a blond, blue-eyed namesake might have filled him with a sort of pride of ownership. But his egotism was more surpassing than that. Georgie considered his family heritage to have, like numbers building to a perfect sum, added up to him. Over preceding generations the family bloodlines had converged like so many tributaries and ultimately come to confluence at his birth thirty-eight years ago. He hoped that future generations—of his family, of the world—would remember him well. But other questions about the future, such as whether his surname survived or not, didn't concern him in the least.

His daughters were integrated into his life whether he liked it or not. Their characters had formed while he was *re*forming in those troubled first years after the war; consequently Bee and Ruth Ellen were bound to their father in an intimate way that their brother was not. By the time George IV was born, Georgie had shaken his postwar blues and thrown himself into his career. He was feeling confident again; his outward mask of toughness, high spirits, and grandeur was securely back in place. Four years later the mask would falter once more, but at that time his son would still be too young to realize that the mask and the man, the performance and performer, as yet were not the same.

"I am fated to be free," Nita wrote Aunt Nannie in June 1922. Vacationing in England for the first time since breaking off with John Pershing three years earlier, Nita had renewed an acquaintance with a young man named

Harry Brain whom she'd first met in 1919. The previous night, Harry had proposed marriage to her. "He is so good true and tender that I'd nearly said 'yes' but my guardian angel came to me and showed me in a vision of the night that unless I could mate with a master, I'd better steer clear of the shoals. And the worst of it is I'm glad. Love is not for such as I."

In the past, Nita's brother had urged her to go into business ("You have shown that you possess ability"), but Nita instead had devoted herself to taking care of her parents and aunt. They were increasingly unwell, a development unknown to Georgie, who had little time to visit California and anyway was lost in his own worries. Ruth Patton had severe arthritis. In a natural remedy believed to ease the condition, she would direct Lake Vineyard's gardener to collect a bagful of honeybees and then open the bag around her stiff knees, letting the insects sting her until they died.

Papa and Nannie were pushing seventy and beginning to decline. They weren't helping themselves with their drinking. Both had become apparent alcoholics, tippling quietly and steadily through each day and evening. Georgie had an inkling of the problem (during his father's 1916 Senate campaign, he'd advised Papa to keep up his stamina by drinking lots of water "and nothing else"), but it was never discussed openly. Georgie was fortunate to have Nita at Lake Vineyard to watch over his parents and aunt. She understood the unspoken rule: nothing must distract Georgie from his all-important career.

He graduated with honors from the Command and General Staff College in June 1924. For the next eight months he held a staff job in Boston. He disliked the work but enjoyed the pastimes of riding, sailing, picnicking, and entertaining. In 1925 he moved his family to Schofield Barracks outside Honolulu, Hawaii, where he began a three-year assignment on the headquarters staff of the Hawaiian Division. Again the work was dull, but the low intensity of an office job in a demobilized army left him plenty of time for sports, partying, and his private military studies.

In November 1926 Papa wrote his son asking that the Pattons visit Lake Vineyard next month, "so that we could have one more Christmas together." Georgie found his father ailing and somewhat dotty. Papa muttered elegiacally over everything he did, as if each meal, each drink, each evening sunset, would be his last. His lifelong neuroses about money and health had become still more pronounced. Trivial problems of daily life became insurmountable obstacles. Yet it was Papa's resignation before these problems that worried his son most.

One continuing source of joy was Papa's grandchildren. He read *The*

Odyssey aloud to Bee and Ruth Ellen as he had when they were younger, and as he had to Georgie years ago; the girls loved the sound of his lilting southern drawl. With a frisky glee that was most unlike him, he taught them his favorite sea chanties and an old Confederate drinking song remembered from his youth:

> "I'm a good ol' Rebel,
> Yes that's what I am—
> And for the land of freedom,
> I do not give a damn."

Beatrice had purchased a 16-millimeter movie camera. Her film taken during that Christmas visit captured her dapper white-haired father-in-law nuzzling and playing with George IV in an echo of the easy and enduring intimacy Papa had established with Georgie forty years earlier. Later Georgie would recall with pleasure the fun his father and son had shared, and how they walked the grounds of Lake Vineyard, young George with a popgun, pretending to kill lions "as I had once done."

Beatrice's film also captured Georgie in the background watching his father and son play. He wears a three-piece banker's suit cut tight to his slender frame. He looks mildly interested, mildly contented, and not at all inclined to join in the fun. He had no knack for parenting. Too, he may have had other things on his mind, for during that vacation Papa took Georgie aside and confided that he'd been diagnosed with tuberculosis of the kidney and cirrhosis of the liver. Terrified of doctors ever since his experiences in the Civil War, he had no intention of checking into a hospital, he said. His implication was that his life could end at any moment and it would be no tragedy. "He felt that death was the only adventure left for him," Georgie wrote, "and yearned for it with out fear and with great curiosity."

Papa's anticipation of death had awakened his interest in mysticism. He was studying C.A.L. Totten's books of prophecy based on measurements of the Egyptian pyramids. In the Patton house such investigations seemed completely plausible. Georgie, worried "that wars were getting scarce" (thus denying him the opportunity to make his mark as a great warrior), was gratified to hear his father's prediction that Georgie "would yet be in the biggest war in history." Papa even supplied the date the war would begin: April 30, 1928.

Georgie asked Papa to dictate his memories of the Civil War. The moment marked a conscious summing up. Papa had changed his name from George William to George *Smith* Patton fifty-eight years ago. As he spoke and Georgie transcribed, it was George William's memories they recorded, the passive, wistful, slightly shell-shocked boy still starstruck by his illustrious father. It wasn't a sad moment. In fact, said Georgie, "He was as cheerful and animated as I ever saw him though I think that he knew he was not long for this life."

Afterward, Papa remarked without bitterness, "Son, you had more experiences and saw more of life in two years in France than I have in all my seventy years." Georgie agreed in his heart; he'd long believed that Papa had played his life too safe. But in writing of that evening he excused his father understandingly. "He had a romantic and venturesome spirit which had ever been curbed by circumstances and a sense of duty to those he loved." It was an excuse that Georgie would have been ashamed to accept for himself.

He returned to Hawaii after Christmas but sailed back from Honolulu in February when advised that Papa's condition had deteriorated and he would need an operation.

I was in the room with him when the attendants came to wheel him into the operating room. I kissed him and as he went out the door he waved his thin brown hand at me and smiling said "Au Revoir, Son." The courage of that act would have won the Medal of Honor on any field of battle. He was seventy, had never been operated on, so dreaded it, and he was very weak; yet going to what he thought was death he tried to cheer me with out thought of self.

Papa survived the operation. Georgie remained with him for two weeks, then shipped out again for Hawaii. On June 10, 1927, he received word that his father was dead. Georgie wept bitterly through the days of waiting for a ship to take him to California. Then one evening he came dry-eyed to Ruth Ellen and George IV and handed them a book of poems opened to Edwin Arnold's translation from the Arabic of "After Death." In the poem, the soul of "he who died at Azan" tries to comfort his friends who mourn over his lifeless body as it is being prepared for burial:

> Sweet friends! what the woman lave
> For its last bed of the grave
> Is a tent which I am quitting,
> Is a garment no more fitting,

Is a cage, from which at last
Like a hawk, my soul hath passed.
Love the inmate, not the room;
The wearer, not the garb; the plume
Of the falcon, not the bars
That kept him from the splendid stars.

Georgie told his children to memorize the poem. "So you'll never forget it," he said.

Bee Patton had never much liked the constant change of army life, and on Hawaii that change had felt doubly drastic. Schofield Barracks was the raw frontier compared to Fort Myer and especially to Boston, where the Pattons had leased a servant-filled mansion called Sunset Hill during Georgie's recent assignment there. At Bee's request, her mother had enrolled her at Foxcroft, a posh girls' school in Middleburg, Virginia. Sixteen now, Bee was traveling by train to California for summer vacation when her grandfather died. Georgie arrived from Hawaii too late to attend Papa's funeral. Bee made it, however, and what she saw during the ceremony puzzled and frightened her.

She arrived at Lake Vineyard in the middle of a three-day wake. The scene seemed nightmarish to the sensitive young woman. Papa's body lay in an open coffin before the living room fireplace, candles burning at his head and feet. The downstairs was crowded with mourners, but two groups had separately gathered in the pantry and kitchen. In one room, Lake Vineyard's Mexican farmhands prayed and sang in Spanish. In the other, the friends of Georgie's childhood nurse, Mary Scally, were shrilly keening Irish dirges for the dead, the lamentations in both rooms fueled not a little by strong San Gabriel wine.

Overwhelming all the cries was a drunken wail coming from the bedroom at the top of the stairs. It was Nannie Wilson, who after all these years was finally venting her frustrated love for Papa. "Wait for me, George! Wait for me!" she howled. "He should have been our child! Georgie should have been ours!" If Nannie's alcoholism had been hushed up all these years, her passion for Papa was even more of a graveyard secret. But most astonishing to Bee was the revelation that the secret was no surprise to her grandmother and aunt. Ruth and Nita sat in the living room with Papa's body as Nannie's cries cascaded around them. Ruth knitted quietly in her black gown. Nita gazed straight ahead. Their stony expressions conveyed neither disavowal nor acknowledgment of Nannie's crazed passion. They were merely ignoring it, as they had done for years.

When Georgie arrived at Lake Vineyard several days later, the house had been cleared, peace restored, and Papa laid in the ground. Nannie was already making preparations to move out of Lake Vineyard and into a house of her own across town. The man she loved was dead. There was no reason to stay.

Georgie went alone in his uniform to his father's grave at San Gabriel's Church of Our Saviour. For an hour he stood there weeping. Then in the corner of his eye, as he described it later, he saw his father's ghost strolling along the path beside the cemetery. Ever the dandy, Papa wore his fedora and houndstooth overcoat and carried his walking stick, in Georgie's words, "the way a knight would carry a sword." As in life, Papa was whacking the buds off wildflowers with his stick—until he paused, "waved at me as he used to do when he was impatient and wanted to go somewhere," and strolled on down the path.

A few nights later, Georgie was in Papa's basement office at Lake Vineyard, going through some of his father's effects. The office was walled with books and photographs. Most of the photos were of Georgie. In the hall outside the office were the shell of a sea turtle Georgie had harpooned as a boy; his first swordfish; the tasseled saddle of Julio Cardenas, the *Villista* colonel he'd shot in Mexico; a German helmet from a trench in France— all mementos of Georgie, all part of Papa's shrine to him.

He opened a tin strongbox and laid its contents out on Papa's desk. It was the box that his grandmother Sue Glassell Patton had brought west from Virginia in 1866. He examined Tazewell Patton's deathbed letter from Gettysburg, and the love letters from George Patton I to Sue. He held in his hand the ten-dollar gold piece that had saved his grandfather's life at Giles Court House, held the fatal shell fragment and bloodstained strip of undershirt that the colonel's slave Peter had smuggled back through Union lines. Georgie shuddered. These treasured relics of lives long past made his love for his father seem ill-expressed and inadequate. Georgie knew he was selfish. He was just better at regret than reform, and in his regret he wept like a baby.

In that moment his father appeared to him again, standing in the office doorway. Papa frowned and shook his head. The message was clear. "All was well; I was not to mourn." Georgie nodded in understanding. Papa smiled, turned, and walked to the stairs leading up to the front hall. As the apparition ascended the stairs, it faded into thin air, leaving Georgie gazing down the empty corridor as he blinked away the last of his tears.

Sixteen months later Ruth Patton died of a heart attack while on a train heading east to visit the Pattons. She was buried beside her husband. Georgie wrote of his feelings on the loss of his mother only three years after that, when his Aunt Nannie died at seventy-three. As usual, he expressed his love in apology when he wrote Ruth a posthumous letter: "When we meet again I hope you will be lenient for my frailties. In most things I have been worthy. Perhaps this is foolish but I think you understand. I loved and love you very much."

When Nannie's effects were removed from her home, it was found that like Papa she'd kept a shrine to Georgie. There in her bureau was every letter he'd written her, every report card and school composition; also his boyhood toothbrushes, snippets of hair, and iodine-stained cotton swabs from when he'd scraped his knees. A strange collection, but no shock to Georgie—it was the kind of devotion he'd been brought up to expect. He returned the favor with loyalty, declaring after Nannie's wake, "I never knew, until I saw her in the majesty of death, what a noble face she had." His family had felt little on the strange old woman's passing, and so looked at him as if he were crazy.

Papa's death had renewed Georgie's dread of aging and mortality. The deaths of his mother and aunt made that dread still more acute. "All the three who I loved and who loved me so much are now gone. It is so sad that we must grow old and separate." He liked thinking of himself as a son, a nephew, a youthful flame burning with hope and potential—after forty-six years that image was doused. "I had always prayed to show my love by doing something famous for you," he wrote his dead mother. "Perhaps I still may, but time grows short." Papa's predicted date of the next war's start, April 30, 1928, had come and gone, and still Georgie saw no war in his future.

He'd been stationed in Washington, D.C., since May 1928, assigned first to the office of the chief of cavalry and then to the Army War College. Nannie died in November 1931. The following July, Georgie reported back to Fort Myer as second in command of the Third Cavalry Regiment. Less than three weeks after he assumed the post, his prayers for armed conflict were answered, though far from the way he'd hoped.

An order from President Herbert Hoover came down through Army

Chief of Staff Douglas MacArthur for the Third Cavalry to drive the so-called Bonus Marchers out of Washington. The Bonus Marchers were a band of 20,000 veterans driven to poverty and unemployment by the Depression. They'd marched on Washington demanding a government bonus promised to them for service in World War I. When Congress adjourned without voting the money, half the veterans remained in the city to protest, disrupting traffic, scuffling with police, living in a makeshift encampment just across the Potomac River in Virginia. The Third Cavalry's mission was, in Georgie's words, "a most distasteful form of service": to move against fellow soldiers.

There was an unpleasant sidelight to the Bonus March episode. One of the protesters was Joe Angelo, the private who'd saved Georgie's life at the Meuse-Argonne battle, bandaging his bullet wound and summoning help under intense enemy fire. Georgie had recommended him for the Medal of Honor (though the army had awarded him the Distinguished Service Cross instead), and after the war he gave Angelo an engraved watch "in grateful memory of the Argonne." Georgie had sent him money several times over the years, receiving gracious letters of thanks from "Your friend always Joe."

The previous year, Angelo had been one of several men to testify before Congress about the plight of veterans. The Associated Press ran the headline, "Veteran, Wearing Medals, Jobless, Stirs Committee." Asked about the ribbons dangling on his chest, Angelo told the congressmen about fighting at Cheppy in 1918. He displayed the watch from Georgie and swore that, though the army owed him $1,400 and he was jobless and broke, he would never pawn the watch. He said he could always get money from Patton but would rather earn it with an honest job. Georgie saw the newspaper story and showed it to Beatrice, who reacted strongly. This wasn't the sort of publicity she had in mind for her husband.

Still, she wanted the children to see the man who'd saved their father. They attended the hearings continuing in the Senate the next day. As at the House of Representatives earlier, Angelo was asked about his exploits in the war. Beatrice squirmed in annoyance: "I hated to see little Angelo all covered with medals and enlarging on the truth. His Veterans of Foreign Wars [medal] looked as silly beside his D.S.C. as some of his statements looked beside what he really did. He is a catspaw—a pathetic type. Too bad." Afterward, she took Bee, Ruth Ellen, and George IV to meet Private Angelo in a senator's office. Angelo shook the boy's hand. "George, if you're as good an officer as your Daddy, the men will follow you anywhere." At Beatrice's urging he told the story of Georgie's wounding at the Argonne. The children had heard it often before. Now their father's dramatic renditions were confirmed in Angelo's shrugging simplicity: "I drug him into a shell hole . . . turned him over and he was spouting blood." Beatrice was pleased. Her opinion of Angelo improved. He was much nicer than she'd expected, she wrote in her journal that night.

Now, a year later, the association of Georgie and Angelo made for unpleasantness again. In reporting the expulsion of the marchers from the city, the *Washington Star* did a sidebar on the shabby conflict between the former comrades-in-arms. "Routs Man Who Saved Him" ran the headline over photos of Angelo and "Maj. George O. Patton." Georgie's discomfort was evident in his snippy reference to Angelo in the story. "Undoubtedly the man saved my life, but his several accounts of the incident vary from the true facts." It was an unfair dismissal. In past interviews Angelo had done nothing but extol Georgie's bravery at the Argonne—Georgie had responded with financial help the few times Angelo had asked it. But because Angelo unwittingly brought embarrassment on him, Georgie cut the friendly ties between them after the Bonus March. Georgie did send him twenty-five dollars in 1939 after hearing through a colleague that Angelo was hard up. Angelo responded with a telegram of sunny gratitude.

"It was more of a war than was publicly admitted," Georgie wrote of the confrontation with the Bonus Marchers. This may have been wishful thinking on his part. Bricks flew, tear gas was used, Georgie and his cavalrymen smacked many backsides with the flats of their sabers to herd the marchers out of town—but the mission went more or less smoothly, with no casualties. Yet with his usual industry, Georgie analyzed the event for its military lessons in a paper on "Federal Troops in Domestic Disturbances." His biographer Martin Blumenson has called it "a savage document," and truly it is. Among Georgie's recommendations: "Designate in advance certain sharpshooters to kill individual rioters . . . Gas is paramount . . . If they resist they must be killed . . . If you must fire do a good job—a few casualties become martyrs, a large number an object lesson."

As second in command of the regiment, Georgie hadn't been obligated to lead the front rank in confronting the marchers. He did it because he wanted to, needed to. It was indeed distasteful service. Yet as he wrote in his afteraction report, "War is war after all." And after fourteen impatient years, he would take it wherever he found it.

*   *   *

His bearings as a professional soldier were shaken by his experience in the Bonus March. His bearings as a Patton were shaken when, two months after the episode, his sister, Nita, announced that she was adopting a baby boy. An inheritance from her parents and aunt had left Nita an income and half-interest in Lake Vineyard with her brother. She became involved with several local charities, and it was through the manager of a Los Angeles orphanage that she learned of a child named Peter currently in the care of his elderly grandparents. It was rare in those days for a single woman to adopt a child, but Nita was independent in means and spirit. With the grandparents' consent, she became the mother of Peter Wilson Patton in September 1932.

Georgie was furious. The boy wasn't really a Patton, he complained. He didn't have the lineage, the bloodlines. How could Nita commit the travesty of giving Peter the Patton name? Nita told her brother flat out that she was just as much a Patton as he was, and she would do as she pleased. No one talked to him that way, and he sulked when Nita issued her ultimatum: accept her son wholeheartedly or lose her as a sister.

Georgie lately had been irritated by Nita's fierce support of Franklin Roosevelt in the 1932 presidential campaign. ("Nita's boy friend," was his private term for FDR, whose proposed New Deal reformations had him fearing for his wife's bank account.) Her adoption of a child was one more betrayal of her lineage and social class as far as Georgie was concerned, and for weeks the tension burned between them as neither budged. Then word came that the adoption was all but finalized. Georgie backed down. "You must be all excited about Peter Wilson," he wrote Nita. "I hope and expect he will turn out satisfactorily." His tone softening, he said that he'd consulted an expert on child rearing who assured him "it was all a question of invironment and training and not at all a question of blood lines. If that is true Peter should be especially fine for I know no one who has higher ideals than you. *Cheers* for Peter!" Chastened, he always made sure to remember Peter "with love" in future letters to Nita—and to remember David Patton as well, after she adopted a second son a year later. Nita knew the adoptions remained hard for Georgie to understand. She accepted his good wishes and left it at that, no doubt amused to have cowed the enfant terrible himself.

"P.S.," Georgie ended a letter to a cousin early in June 1934. "How do you advise birth control for grandchildren—they would cramp my style." His joke concealed real distress. What should have been a proud time for him (he recently had been promoted to lieutenant colonel after fourteen years as a major) was undercut by the impending marriage of his daughter Bee to a cavalry lieutenant named John K. Waters. The marriage alone was an unwelcome enough reminder of Georgie's advancing years. To become a grandfather would be almost intolerable.

More revealing of his anxiety than anything Georgie said, however, was his wife's first reaction to Bee's engagement. As Beatrice recorded it in her journal, her daughter, twenty-three, first asked Georgie's permission (he said yes), then afterward she approached Beatrice. "Of course I said yes—and all is well." But in fact Beatrice did not say yes. When her daughter told her she'd received Georgie's consent to marry, Beatrice burst into tears, slapped Bee's face, and said, "You can't. You're much too young." Ruth Ellen, in the room with them, was stunned. The last time her mother had struck any of her children was in 1918, when she'd slapped Ruth Ellen for breaking a toy doll. At that time, Georgie was away at war and Beatrice's parents had just died within three weeks of each other. Beatrice had been crumbling under the pressure then; now it seemed she was crumbling once again. On reflection years later, Ruth Ellen concluded that in 1934 the pressure her mother felt could only have come from Georgie. The girls always had laughed at their father's ceaseless pestering of their mother to wear makeup, dye her hair, to stay eternally young as he was determined to do. But clearly that pestering was no joke. Georgie was afraid of aging, and such a blatant milestone as his daughter's wedding could only have deepened his fear and, as well, encouraged his attempts to somehow dispel it.

Bee was an enigma to her parents. Fair and pretty with a lithe slim figure, she was shy to the point of awkwardness, with little of her father's flair or her mother's gritty conviction. She was an excellent horsewoman and taught riding to Girl Scouts, but by and large her life was sheltered and dependent. Like many, she found her father both irritating and magnetic. He intimidated her without trying to; when grumpy, Georgie liked to prickle and browbeat people—haze them, in West Point parlance—but Bee was so mild and eager to please he found no sport in it with her.

Bee felt comfortable neither in the earthy, insular world of army posts nor among the society starlets at Foxcroft, where she made few friends. As a girl she'd had no intention of marrying a military man and was quite surprised with herself when she fell in love with a West Pointer. But any similarity between Georgie and her fiancé ended at the uniform. Johnny Waters was modest, soft-spoken, composed. In the future he would become a four-star general, but when he and Bee fell in love he was a second-year cadet whose family had gone broke in the Depression. He decided to wait until well embarked on his career before proposing to her, while in the meantime she lived at home with her parents in Washington.

Bee was shocked when her mother slapped her on hearing of the engagement. But hurt feelings were soothed, the incident glossed over, and wedding plans begun. The marriage took place at St. John's Church in Beverly Farms, Massachusetts, where Georgie and Beatrice had wed. The reception was at nearby Green Meadows, a country estate the Pattons had purchased in 1928. Georgie roared through the reception, generating erratic waves of high spirits and gloom that had some of the guests marveling at his incredible gusto and others wondering if he was feeling unwell.

Now forty-eight, any remotely commemorative occasion turned Georgie's thoughts to the past. His eyes would tear and his jaw tremble as he remembered his mother, his aunt, and especially his father. He most savored Papa's cheery wave to him as he was being wheeled into the operating room on a hospital gurney a few months before he died. "Au revoir, son." Those words may have echoed in Georgie's head. That would explain why, when he and Bee walked arm in arm up the church aisle, his expression was more fitting of a man approaching a gallows than an altar.

☆ ☆ **16** ☆ ☆

Hawaiian Legends

HE PATTONS twice were stationed in Hawaii—from 1925 to 1928, and again from 1935 to 1937. As events in the life of the family, the two tours were essentially one. The Pattons resumed the first tour's friendships, pastimes, and fascination with the islands' exotic allure as if uninterrupted. The difference was that in the interim Georgie's psyche had been battered by the deaths of loved ones, by the Bonus March, and by his daughter's marriage. Under the pressure of these blows, cracks in his facade of self-assurance that had been barely perceptible in 1925 burst open a decade later.

No one was more sensitive to the turmoil in him—and by extension, in the family—than his younger daughter, Ruth Ellen. Aged ten to thirteen during the first tour in Hawaii, and twenty to twenty-two during the second, her contradictory feelings toward her father were an ideal lens through which to observe his contradictory feelings toward himself. She was dazzled by Georgie. She thrilled to his poetry, his own and also the heroic ballads of Macaulay, Kipling, and Tennyson, which she could recite by memory almost as completely as he. She kept faithful record of his stories in her journal ("Daddy was telling of bravery and heredity tonight . . ."), and, parroting her father, she claimed to love war, thinking it "horrible, but grand." When he took her to see Robert E. Lee's grave at

Washington and Lee University, the statue of the sleeping general moved Ruth Ellen to tears. Her father bought her a small Confederate flag at the souvenir shop because, he told her proudly, "You're so unreconstructed."

As devoted as she was to Georgie, however, beginning in adolescence she started to dislike him. He intimidated her on purpose. Since early childhood she'd answered back his bossiness and sharp temper; this rankled but also intrigued him, for not even his wife spoke to him as bluntly as Ruth Ellen. Like a schoolboy unsure of how to express his affection, Georgie would alternately put down, tease, and lovingly embrace her. She grew increasingly uneasy with him as a result, unsure where she stood and what he expected of her.

To teach her how to swim, Georgie had thrown her off a pier into the ocean at three years old; for years he complained of ruining a new pair of white flannel trousers when he'd had to dive in and save her. After the war he got a pilot's license and took her up for a flight one day. Switching off the motor, he screamed that the engine had died and the plane was going to crash. It was a stunt he would never have pulled on Bee; but to see tough little Ruth Ellen melt in terror, *that* was satisfying.

Such treatment led Ruth Ellen to keep a distance from him as she matured—judging by his actions, she thought that was what he preferred. But then Georgie would complain to his wife that he didn't know his daughter and that she ignored him. Warming up to him again, Ruth Ellen's overtures might be as quickly rebuffed in an unprovoked insult. "Beatrice Ayer Patton!" Georgie broke the lunchtime silence one day in Hawaii. "How in hell did a pretty woman like you have two such ugly daughters?" The remark arose, Ruth Ellen wrote at seventeen, out of his compulsive craving for conflict. If bored or depressed, he created tension for the sake of diversion. It amused him. It didn't amuse her.

From 1925 to 1928 Georgie served on the headquarters staff of the Hawaiian Division at Schofield Barracks outside Honolulu. He and Beatrice had brought a live-in English nanny from the States to attend to George IV. Alice Holmes cared for the toddler through each day, took her meals separately with him, and over the first years of his life was his closest companion. Neither Georgie nor Beatrice spent much time with their son. Georgie had his work and his ongoing private studies. He had polo, which was high caliber on Hawaii, as teams from the service branches and various civilian country clubs competed year-round in the tropical climate. And he had the pleasures of socializing with the local white gentry. Fortunes originally made in sugar, pineapple, and Far East trade now supported a leisure class whose "worldly sophistication" mainly meant that the rollicking good times were costumed in elegance. "It is hard to be moral in such a climate," Beatrice wrote of the native Hawaiians' historically sensual ways, their penchant for, as she referred to it, "naughty Polynesian fun." Her observation applied no less to Hawaii's hard-drinking professional sportsmen and their suntanned, linen-clad, amused and amusing wives.

Hawaii was a U.S. territory at the time, not a state. Its isolation in the Pacific Ocean seemed to impart a license for insouciance and eccentricity that appealed to Georgie much more than the straightlaced world of blueblooded Boston. He knew that some of his wife's relatives murmured to themselves that she'd married beneath her. Hawaii's free-spending, freewheeling social set was more to his taste: an ideal audience for his performance as a dashing man. He considered buying a horse ranch and making Hawaii his permanent home. Ultimately, however, he bought Green Meadows in Massachusetts so his wife could be near her relatives in the event that Georgie (he yet hoped) would be sent overseas to war.

Beatrice, too, fell in love with the islands, but for a different reason. They offered fertile territory to indulge her burgeoning interest in archaeology and anthropology. Her childhood visit to Egypt had originally sparked that interest. Her stint with Georgie at Fort Riley had reawakened it in 1914, when she'd been amazed to discover fossilized seashells embedded in the rimrock of the Kansas prairie. Schooling herself in the history of wherever she traveled, she'd come to Hawaii expecting to study the Protestant missionaries to whom she had distant family ties. But quickly she soured on the missionaries, concluding that the introduction of western Christian culture had done more harm than good to the Hawaiian natives. The change of view endeared her to the descendants of those natives, who appreciated her interest in them and their primitive culture as one of benevolent curiosity.

Beatrice was introduced to a Hawaiian fisherman named Kalili who had caught a huge shark on his *ulua* lines. When he gutted the shark he found "jellied" human bones inside, along with swim trunks bearing the laundry mark of an American soldier who recently had disappeared off Haleiwa beach. As local Chinese and Japanese took the shark meat to eat, and as Kalili posed beside the shark's three-foot-wide jaw, several older Hawaiian women begin to chant obscurely while swaying in an understated Hawaiian hula. Kalili explained to Beatrice that the women were mothers of fishermen who feared the shark's kin would seek revenge on their sons. They were conducting a ceremony of propitiation which, she was told, would culminate with throwing a live dog into the blue waters beyond the reef.

Kalili said that in Polynesian mythology sharks were ancestors to man. Beatrice was fascinated, and through him was introduced to many of the older Hawaiians who kept up some of the ancient religious customs even as they followed the Christian teachings their more recent forebears had learned from the missionaries. These introductions blossomed to personal friendships. Soon she was attending luaus and interviewing native faith healers and herbalists, exploring burial caves with local anthropologists, picking through artifacts with museum curators. "To a remarkable degree," wrote one Hawaiian historian several years later, Beatrice possessed a "rare quality of sympathy . . . with native life. She loves the Hawaiians, and the Hawaiians with whom she comes in contact realize it. Her Hawaiian friends have therefore told her things not usually told to people of another race because they knew that such inner thoughts and ideas would meet with a sympathetic reception."

Beneath her proper Yankee exterior she'd always carried a streak of unpredictability. At a cocktail party just after World War I, she'd overheard a man mocking Georgie's colonel's eagle, calling her husband a chicken wearing chicken wings: she'd floored the man with a punch in the mouth. Never one to swear, she once stunned Georgie with the comment that the Irish had no peer in "the three F's: fighting, funerals, and fucking." While living in Washington, she regularly took the children to a black Baptist church "because it had the best choir." She could laugh at an off-color joke and, though fiercely protective of her daughters' virtue, wasn't prudish in discussing with them the facts of life or the pleasures of conjugal love.

Despite such unexpected turns in the past, Beatrice's sudden passion for Hawaiian folklore surprised her family and especially her husband. Forgetting that without a slightly eccentric bent she probably would never have married someone like him, Georgie was skeptical of her new interests and Hawaiian friends, who, as far as he was concerned, were brown-skinned inferiors there to serve drinks and mow the polo field. But he indulged her at first, writing a poem in 1927, "The Sword of Lono," based on a Hawaiian warrior-deity she'd told him about. Thought to have been a shipwrecked sailor whom the Hawaiians received as divine, Lono was "white and fair/While as a god he ruled a savage race." The poem is told by a once-powerful sword now broken, "a shapeless wreck . . . cast to earth in miserable disgrace." Only Lono's sword recalls the heroic age when Lono wielded it; no one else cares. "Glory passes," Georgie lamented. It would be his last poetic verse until World War II.

Though Beatrice continued to socialize with Georgie's friends, increasingly she pursued her own interests. She and Georgie had been separated so often in the past by his army duties, they scarcely noticed their divergence now, and perhaps unconsciously welcomed the independence it offered them. George IV had his nanny for company—but Ruth Ellen, so long used to having her sister as her best friend, lost that friend when Bee went away with their mother to enroll in boarding school. During the two months before Beatrice returned to Hawaii, Ruth Ellen spent a lot of time alone with her father. It made her aware of conflicts inside him that, at twelve years old, she could instinctively feel if not entirely comprehend.

Georgie's swings between embracing her and intimidating her became more pronounced. He could return home from work and almost without realizing it, like a champion boxer unable to temper his blows against a hapless sparring partner, dress her down for her school grades or her messy room with such swift ferocity it left her cowering in the corner; a moment later he might look up from his mail with the sweetest smile and say, "What's wrong, Ruthie? Did I say something?" He might take her sailing in Pearl Harbor, doffing his shirt like a kid on the beach and suggesting, to her embarrassment, "Let's pretend we're pirates!" The next day he might insinuatingly quiz her like a Puritan schoolmaster about talking to island boys. Georgie's inability to strike a balance between being his daughter's chum and being her guardian seemed to exasperate him and make him resentful of Ruth Ellen. Certainly it made her resentful—and afraid—of him.

She fought back. At one lunch she declared that she would not eat her breadfruit. He shrugged into his newspaper, "Eat it or take a licking." She would take a licking, she said. Her words didn't sink in right away. Then he realized he had a challenge on his hands and would have to see it through. She later recalled,

He told me to go out in the lanai and pick out the whip he was going to hit me with. Scared to death, and mad as hell, I picked out what I thought was the worst whip on the rack. It was a hunting whip with a long thong with a red cracker on the end of it. . . . I took the hunting whip back to the dining room, and nonplussed, he cracked it and then laid it along my legs four times. When he had finished, I said as haughtily as I could, "THAT didn't hurt!"

Georgie kept the bargain and let her skip the breadfruit. (He disliked it, too.) That night he wrote Beatrice in the States about the incident "and offered to let her divorce him for maltreating her child."

If Ruth Ellen thought she would gain an ally when her mother returned, that hope ended when, for the second (and last) time ever, she again was hit by her father—and her mother did nothing about it. Ruth Ellen had skipped a grade in school only to crash into mathematics. Georgie was helping her prepare for a test, and to her chagrin, "I was beginning to understand it. I at once closed my mind, realizing that if I understood it, I would have to do it." As midnight passed, Georgie, who'd had his own difficulties with math in school, was pacing, swearing, sweating, and shouting. Ruth Ellen, exhausted and frustrated, became hysterical. "I began to enjoy it. I was standing away from myself watching a poor fat little girl sobbing and crying while her cruel father, nine feet tall, strode up and down the room, cursing and slapping his hands together. All at once he slapped me so hard that I fell right off my chair. I stopped having hysterics."

Georgie stomped out of the room. Ruth Ellen got in bed. Her door squeaked open and her mother asked if she was all right. She was not all right—she'd never felt worse in her life. But she nodded toughly and her mother accepted this and shut the door and went back to Georgie. It became instantly clear to Ruth Ellen that in family rifts her mother always would favor Georgie, always would trust and defer to him. With Bee away at school and her brother too young, Ruth Ellen had no companion, no ally, of her own. Even the family dog preferred her sister to her.

As a child Ruth Ellen often had toyed with the idea that she was adopted. Her parents' focus had seemed so elsewhere directed—Georgie's on his career, and Beatrice's on Georgie—that it made sense to wonder if she was truly their flesh and blood. She'd consoled herself with believing that instead of a Patton she was a long-lost Irish princess. But that night the idea didn't bring the solace it once had. So she decided to kill herself. She got as far as a reservoir not far from her house. A military policeman came by and asked what she doing. She said she was planning to drown herself. "He got a terribly worried look on his face. . . . There seemed to be nothing in the regulations that covered this situation. . . . Because he seemed so genuinely distressed (he told me it was his first time on sentry duty) I told him I wouldn't do it that night and that I would go home and maybe try another day. This suited us both."

When Ruth Ellen left Hawaii with her family a year later, she still didn't fully understand her father's erratic behavior and her mother's seeming obliviousness to it. But the past three years had at least awakened her to a tension building in Georgie that would seem, as she looked back on that period, an indelible part of her growing up. Recognizing that tension and learning to cope with it was the easy part of living with her father. Much harder was reconciling the conflicting emotions he evoked, the distaste and wonder, the fury and love. You had to reconcile them because he did not. He never had, and never would.

Georgie never stopped developing as a soldier. He was always studying, questioning, innovating, and experimenting to find the best means of winning wars. As a person, however, he scarcely seemed to develop at all after the age of twelve, when the dream of military greatness he'd so confidently adopted received the soul-shaking jolt of insecurity about his intellect. That insecurity would fuel his ambition and inform his character every bit as strongly as his original boyhood hubris; it would become, with his hubris, like one of two magnetic poles in an electric motor inside him, a motor that began to spin vigorously when he was twelve and didn't stop until he was sixty.

Georgie's unceasing, lifelong professional development was therefore combined with personal immaturity, even stuntedness. Yet this immaturity, for all its negative manifestations, was a hugely positive factor in his appeal as a man and his success as a battlefield leader. He had the qualities of a child—the point has been made countless times by people who knew him. Throughout his life he displayed the exuberance and energy of a child; also the optimism and daring, the sentimentality, the fragile, extreme emotionalism, the wide-eyed curiosity, the spiritual credulity, the puppy-like loyalty to certain people and principles—in short, the ingenuous spontaneity of unscarred and unchastened youth.

Yet, too, like a child, he was willful and selfish, small-minded, narcissistic, and spiteful. He had to have the last word in every argument, had to be the most captivating guy at the party and the toughest guy in the locker room. He had little ability or inclination to modulate his persona to fit others' sensibilities. He was often tactless though rarely vulgar, coarse but not smutty. The prejudices he carried all his life were learned in childhood and not one bit modified, much less outgrown, in his sixty years of world experience. His ignorance on such matters as politics and racial diversity was such that he could freely admit to knowing nothing about a subject while at the same time issuing fierce opinions about it. "Patton is a problem child," Dwight Eisenhower observed in 1945. But like many who knew Georgie, the supreme commander was willing to take the bad with the good, acknowledging in the same sentence, "but he is a great fighting leader in pursuit and exploitation."

Georgie's immaturity enhanced his ability to play the part he'd set for himself. In a sense, his life had always been a dress-up game. Whether practicing his war face in the bathroom mirror, strutting as King Arthur through a Halloween ball or as "Old Blood and Guts" through a theater of war, his love of costume was lifelong and thoroughly unself-conscious. Like an actor who first gets the look of his role with a false nose or accent and then creates the character to fit it, Georgie donned heroic accoutrements—the pistols, the profanity, the boots and spurs—hoping to fill them out from within, like molten lead hardening in the toy soldier molds he'd played with as a boy. A more mature, more discerning personality might not have been able to sustain the artifice, nor cared to, knowing with a wisdom Georgie didn't possess that masks so diligently applied tend in time to stick.

Beatrice, by contrast, seemed to grow steadily as a person over the course of their marriage. An important part of this growth was her mere "tuffening." As a teenager she'd confessed to Georgie her fear that "the world is so big that [I] will get lost." She'd had some brief experience working in a dress shop and in a settlement house for orphans, but having been schooled by governesses and attended by servants and insulated by her parents' benevolent domination, she was unprepared for the transience of military life and the turmoil of life with Georgie. In the early part of her marriage she strove simply to hang on, to cope.

She learned not to break down when she and Georgie parted and not to kill herself with worry when he was away. She began joining whenever possible in his professional and private pursuits. She edited his lectures and articles, translated French military books into English so that he could study them. She took up fox hunting and show jumping even though the sports frightened her, especially after a bad fall off a horse in 1926 knocked her unconscious for several hours. While stationed at Fort Myer between the tours in Hawaii she overcame her fear ("a great moral victory") and served with her husband as comaster of Virginia's Cobbler Hunt. Very nearsighted, she locked her eyes on Georgie's red blazer and followed it over the fences and fields, her beacon in the haze.

When Georgie received orders back to Hawaii in the spring of 1935, he purchased a fifty-two-foot schooner, intending to skipper it from San Pedro to Honolulu. On the surface it looked like another instance of his perpetual quest for adventure. But shaken by the personal blows of recent years, and by the sense that his career was languishing, he confided to Beatrice that he was sailing the Pacific "to test my luck." As usual when he was feeling anxious, he needed some sign that fate still retained some challenge for him, some mission in his future; and if it did not, then he preferred to drown now and get it over with. Beatrice recognized what was in his mind and told him flatly that she would not let him go off and die without her, and therefore she would join his crew as the galley cook.

His wife's new assertiveness irked Georgie. As his own self-esteem was beginning to erode, hers was beginning to blossom. She'd just published a book, a collection of ancient Hawaiian myths culled from her interviews of island natives and retold as short stories. Privately published in a limited run of three hundred copies and written in French, *Legendes Hawaiienne* was no candidate for the best-seller lists. Rather, it was the sort of discreet parlor indulgence that in past times provided wealthy women with intellectual diversion, while in no way upstaging their husbands—which was why Georgie supported Beatrice when she was writing it. But now, back on Hawaii for a second tour, she was pressing ahead with a novel, a historical romance, with the galling intention of publishing it commercially. Georgie was not pleased.

He was assigned to the Hawaiian department at Fort Shafter. As the department intelligence officer, he was directed to draw up contingency plans for monitoring Hawaii's Japanese population in the event of war with Japan, which had conquered Manchuria and was threatening to expand into China and the Pacific islands. Under War Plan Orange, as it was called, and with the same grim zeal he'd brought to bear against the Bonus Marchers, Georgie proposed to "arrest and intern certain persons of the Orange race who are inimical to American interests." His callous pragmatism was matched with a certain prescience as he harangued his superiors about "the necessity of establishing certain precautionary measures against surprise attack."

Italy had invaded Ethiopia. Civil War had broken out in Spain. Germany, rebuilding its military under Adolph Hitler, also had caught Georgie's attention. In November he wrote a cousin in California, "I am still hopeful that the situation in Europe is simply the lull before the storm. Certainly in less than ten years we will be mixing it with Japan. I will then still have at least four years in which to enjoy my self with a little realy high-powered killing." Such bluster was ringing more and more hollow, however. Other officers in the Hawaiian department paid little attention to his frantic predictions. Soon his intelligence duties seemed no less of a career dead end than any other staff job.

Georgie was so frustrated that he actually began to cultivate an interest in finance. He once had observed uncomplainingly, "I guess that no one ever had so much money and knew so little about it as I do." But in these Depression years his wife's wealth had diminished; often they paid income taxes only on Georgie's army pay. Still, she had more than enough money left to support their life-style, so his burgeoning interest came more of boredom than need. A cousin, Arvin Brown, was managing Georgie's inheritance from Papa. Georgie, perhaps hoping to shed the stigma of living off his wife's money, urged Brown to buy him stock in industries that might benefit from a future war, "particularly aviation and tanks," Georgie wrote, adding with an evil wink, "blessed are the pure in heart." He tried vainly to educate himself ("I have read three books on money lately with the result that I now know less about it than I did before"), and with confusion came irritation: "I just read a book called Inflation Ahead according to this book bank deposits are not so hot but stocks and bonds of the PROPER SORT (God knows what sort that is) will be useful in other words one should become either a creditor or a debtor I forget which—it is a Damned Poor book any how."

Ultimately Georgie discarded his interest as abruptly as he'd adopted it, calling his financial opinions "the vaporing of a rank AMATEUR . . . God alone knows how dumb I am in many walks of life and in all business." The only directions he continued to give Brown were to use some of Georgie's inheritance to provide anonymous monthly support to several California relatives whom the Depression truly had hurt. But lest Brown think Georgie was turning tenderhearted, "Please do not imagine that I am lead to this act by the custimary emotions of decency, loyalty, family feeling etc—I scorn such marks of weakness. I am only actuated by fear of HELL. (Do I hear you say too late??)"

So it was back to staff work, and to his increasingly labored attempts to burn off his frustration through sport and play. "My whole life now is spent in a futile attempt to keep my belly with in bounds." In fact, Georgie was still quite lean and youthful-looking, despite his sparse hair, which he'd allowed to turn its natural white. But no longer feeling young, he was more determined than ever to *be* young. Ruth Ellen had graduated from high school and, having always hated academics, had declined to attend college. She was living at Fort Shafter with her parents and working as an occupational therapist in Honolulu. Older now, and beginning to lead her own life, she kept a polite distance from her father. She was taken aback when he began hanging around with her and her friends among the young officers and ladies of Fort Shafter. Her mother, involved with her Hawaiian research and with writing her novel, took enough stern notice of Georgie's apparent midlife crisis to purchase him a self-help book called *Change of Life in Men*. In a pointed ritual of rebuttal, he burned the book to ashes in the alley behind their house.

Beatrice's niece and nephew visited the Pattons in Hawaii in 1935. Her brother's son Fred Ayer was twenty at the time. Thirty years later he recalled that Georgie's house "was not a happy place, nor were the lives of his wife and children easy." He analyzed the problem this way: "A racehorse in top condition, especially if a stallion, behaves very badly when pent up day after day in a narrow corral. It is not pleasant, not even safe, to be closed in with him, particularly if there are young mares in close vicinity. Also, horses do not drink hard liquor. There were, therefore, quite a few fence rails kicked to pieces during those years on Hawaii."

Ruth Ellen, too, was aware of the "young mares." In the past—at her high school graduation, at her sister's wedding—she'd observed with mystification how her girlfriends flocked around Georgie without seeming to appreciate that he was more than twice their age and, despite, as she put it, "some obvious eye and ear appeal," frequently a pain in the neck. Ten years earlier, Ruth Ellen, Bee, and their mother had recognized that the girls' young governess, Miss Dennett, had developed a crush on Georgie, following him from room to room like a puppy begging a biscuit. And when, during the family's first tour in Hawaii, Beatrice had asked the wives of two of Georgie's colleagues to look in on Ruth Ellen while Beatrice was away depositing Bee at boarding school, it had seemed merely strange to Ruth Ellen that the women paid far more attention to her father than to her when they dropped by the house. In hindsight she realized they'd been flirting with him.

Since in none of these instances had Georgie seemed to reciprocate, Ruth Ellen had reacted only with dry amusement. But she was not amused by his behavior during the second tour in Hawaii. No matter how entertaining he'd been in the past, Georgie always had kept a certain aloofness from people and especially from junior officers. Now he acted like one of the boys, breezy, familiar, telling jokes and slapping backs in a way Ruth Ellen thought unbecoming of a forty-nine-year-old lieutenant colonel. That Georgie made no effort to hide his interest in people younger than himself and his wife seemed somehow to enlist his daughter in his silent war with Beatrice, a tactic that struck Ruth Ellen as doubly cruel.

Ever accident prone, Georgie's annual mishaps had included many head injuries over the years, 126 stitches' worth by one estimation. But a fall in September 1935 while playing polo was especially serious. Knocked unconscious when he hit the ground, he came to and groggily finished the match, which was followed by a rousing cocktail party and a weekend cruise aboard his schooner under the hot Hawaiian sun. Sailing back to Pearl Harbor he quizzically looked at his wife and daughter and asked them where he was. The last thing he remembered was spurring his polo pony, and then—nothing. The next day he was told by his doctor that he'd suffered a severe concussion and that he must avoid alcohol for a while and of course stay out of the sun, a prescription too late on both counts.

Georgie always had held his liquor in the past. But after suffering that concussion, he got tipsy under the influence of even small amounts of alcohol. All the familiar elements of his performance seemed to fray and thicken and lose their polish. His poetry slurred as he recited it, his stories rambled. He turned giddy, mean, or maudlin in a flash. Beatrice criticized his behavior with unaccustomed directness. He'd pour another scotch while confronting her reproval with a glare of punkish rebellion; their arguments lasted into the night. "There is a Mr. Hyde in all of us," Beatrice philosophized years later. "Drink is the door through which he slips in easiest. To see Mr. Hyde take possession of a loved one is one of the most terrifying and disgusting things that can ever happen to me."

Ruth Ellen, too, was angered by Georgie's behavior. She grew protective of her mother in the face of his boozy digs at Beatrice's novel, her Hawaiian research, her Polynesian "nigger" friends. But worst of all was Georgie's apparent loss of pride. Several times he'd gotten falling down drunk in the company of Ruth Ellen's young officer friends. They would steady him as he walked, Georgie giggling self-mockingly or sniffling with self-pity. Her friends thought he was funny. "For this, I could not forgive them. My father, whatever he was, was NOT FUNNY."

Sometimes his antics *were* funny, however—in an unhinged sort of way. While Beatrice sportingly tried any exotic Hawaiian food delicacy at least once, Georgie's taste ran to New England pot roast and the Mexican food of his Southern California youth. When Beatrice became ill after eating dog's liver, a local specialty, he was not sympathetic: "Anybody who would eat dog's liver would eat their own children!" Though he loathed seafood, he was served a tuna dish at a luau and devoured it with relish; when told afterward what it was, he politely excused himself to go vomit. A neighbor asked him to look after her twenty-four pet cats while she was away on vacation. He agreed with a smile, and for the next three weeks enjoyed shooting the cats from his back porch in the evenings, donating the cases of canned milk meant to feed them to a Honolulu orphanage.

George IV was in grade school at the time. One of his most memorable sights of his father occurred at a public beach where they'd been swimming. His father went into the bathhouse to shower off the salt. A moment later he dashed out stark naked and screaming. A large tropical spider had leapt from the bathhouse shadows into his pubic hair, where it clung for dear life as Georgie lit out across the sand. Then there was the night George IV and his mother found Georgie weeping over J. F. C. Fuller's, *Generalship: Its Diseases and Their Cure.* The book lay open to an appendix listing a hundred of history's greatest generals and their ages at the peaks of their careers. Georgie, forty-nine, was older than almost all of them.

On the morning of his fiftieth birthday on November 11, he turned his face to the wall and refused to get out of bed. He was finished, he said; over the hill. Beatrice impatiently explained that today's birthday meant he'd just completed his fiftieth year and was beginning his fifty-first, so it was a little too late to complain. Evidently this logic sank in, for he climbed out of bed and plodded to breakfast. Such behavior seemed funny to his family, and then again not. "It is always horrible," Ruth Ellen wrote, "to see feet of clay where winged heels once were."

Georgie was aware of his slide. "I have too much time on my hands," he wrote his sister. "Too much alcohol and too little persperation." To bestir himself, in September 1936 he resolved to sail his schooner with his wife and son and several friends to Palmyra and Fanning islands, 1,200 miles south of Hawaii. He was not a greatly experienced sailor; and as a self-taught navigator with little aptitude for mathematical calculations and no benefit of modern electronic navigation aids, there was risk in such an undertaking. But danger brought pressure, and pressure, if handled, if bested, offered the confirmation of destiny that was all he was living for now.

Just before embarking, he wrote Arvin Brown of his worry about locating the tiny islands in the middle of the ocean. "It would be most imbarrising if I did not and went sailing around the Pacific like a modern example of the flying dutchman." Then again, with liberal Democrats in power, the international scene cloudy, and his career foundering, "Possibly being lost at sea would be a rather convenient way out."

Beatrice's home movies taken during the sail show her husband in improved spirits. The trip's planning and outfitting, the snap of the trade-winds, the schooner's forward glide through the ocean swells, helped Georgie move out of the doldrums. In the film he sits at the wheel bare chested and grinning. He wears a Panama hat and chews a soggy cigar like an admiral AWOL in the tropics. He takes celestial fixes with a sextant and, leaning naked over the bowsprit, saltwater showers in the warm seaspray. A gnarled dark divot is visible in his rump, the bullet wound scar from 1918, now an artifact of half-forgotten origin, like an old sailor's forearm tattoo.

But Georgie's rejuvenation after the Palmyra cruise was short-lived. He turned fifty-one soon after returning; birthdays always were blue occasions for him. Beatrice meanwhile plunged back into her novel, which was in its last stages of preparation for publication.

A local publisher, Paradise of the Pacific, planned to market *Blood of the Shark* as both a violent and sensual page-turning romance and, citing "the accuracy of the book's historical, ethnological, and anthropological background," as a scholarly study of old Hawaii. Opening in 1793, fifteen years after James Cook planted the English flag on the Sandwich Islands, later named Hawaii, the novel's plot concerns the marriage of a young officer in the Royal Navy to the daughter of a Hawaiian chief; its theme is the violent and ultimately tragic clash between a modern and an ancient culture. Beatrice's sentiments about that clash are made clear in her prologue, in which she accuses the English of "robbing the islands and sowing the seeds of death among their primitive people." In her novel, however, the primitive values prevail, if only temporarily.

The Englishman, Adam Gordon, is driven to madness over his wife Kilohana's persistent adherence to her native customs and especially her totemism: Kilohana claims descent from sharks, and worse (for her husband's state of mind), has appeared to support that claim with eerie displays of psychic connection with the maneaters swimming in Hawaiian waters. On seeing his daughter by Kilohana embrace the island ways, Adam Gordon kills a shark in the water with a knife in a symbolic gesture of loathing. But he himself bleeds to death when his leg is shredded by the shark's teeth.

It is tempting to think that Beatrice might have had her own marriage in mind in conceiving the marriage between the civilized Englishman and the savage, superstitious, unregenerate Hawaiian princess: switch the genders of the novel's protagonists, and a parallel between their relationship and that of Beatrice and Georgie seems clear. But unlike her (possible) surrogate, Adam Gordon, Beatrice would not sacrifice herself to her spouse's idiosyncrasies. Georgie's criticism of her writing, his scowls and pointed disinterest, intensified as *Blood of the Shark* neared publication. His drinking continued also, and the unpleasantness that accompanied it. Beatrice pressed on. After twenty-six years of marriage, this was her moment.

She wasn't one to reveal inner feelings. In the last years of her life, however, she composed a "thought book" in which she obliquely reflected on past hardships. One thought she recorded would seem to refer to Georgie's dramatic decline on Hawaii, for it conveys the pity she felt for him, the helplessness, and, most painful of all to feel for one's lover, the contempt. "I don't know how long it takes for a man to spiritually gut himself," she wrote. "Probably depends on how much guts he had to start with."

Beatrice became so immersed in Hawaiian culture that she gave herself to some of the customs with extraordinary sympathy. One elderly *wahine* taught her a prayer to chant if Beatrice ever fell overboard at sea. "Oh, look to me, *e Kokua mai!* Look to your offspring!" The prayer was to persuade any sharks nearby not to attack; after learning it, Beatrice swam without fear in the open ocean while Georgie nervously scanned the water from the deck of his schooner with a loaded rifle in hand.

When stricken with bronchitis in 1936, she submitted to the cure of an old Hawaiian herbalist. The woman, a Catholic, laid warm *noni* leaves on Beatrice's back, gave her strange jungle potions to sip, kneaded *kukui* nut oil into her skin, all the while reciting "formal prayers" to Jesus and Mary, and "real prayers" to *Ku* and *Hina,* two deities in the Hawaiian pantheon.

Later some of Beatrice's native friends gave her a Hawaiian name, an honor she took most seriously. "This name is a sacred thing," she wrote in her thought book, "to be treasured in love and reverence—a secret not to be shared." She added in the next sentence, "That is my love life to me."

Her husband's love life was scarcely less private, though not for want of inquiry by reporters and historians in the years after his death. In the biographies and published reminiscences about him, for every voice insisting that he wasn't a faithful husband there is a voice insisting he was. During World War II, Lieutenant General Everett Hughes, a classmate of Georgie's and one of Eisenhower's logistics experts, suggested in his diary that Georgie definitely was a womanizer. After one of Georgie's trips to London during the war, for example, Hughes apparently asked, was told, and subsequently recorded the number of condoms Georgie used while away. On the other side of it, the researcher who decoded Hughes's illegibly written diary called him "an old gossip who recorded anything Patton told him, true or fictional." Of Georgie's private life in general through the war years, his aide, Lieutenant Colonel Charles Codman, wrote that "any serious interest on the General's part in any woman other than members of his own family would be news to me."

There were rumors of an affair between Georgie and Marlene Dietrich, who entertained troops of Patton's Third Army over the winter of 1944 to 1945. Some biographers of the actress have made the claim absolutely; others have noted the rumors and the lack of hard evidence to confirm or refute them. Certainly Dietrich and Georgie shared a mutual regard. She called him "a great man" in her autobiography, described him as looking "like a tank too big for the village square." Georgie told his family after the war that he'd found her terrifically charming, and that she'd done him a favor by warning him that the press, always in search of good copy on Patton, was looking to catch the pair in compromising circumstances. Hence, he said, he and Dietrich had kept their friendship public and proper. His only written comment about her was a diary critique of her show for the troops: "Very low comedy, almost an insult to human intelligence."

That Georgie liked women is not in doubt. His cadet reputation as a "spoon-noid" was confirmed by the frequent mention in his private letters, to friends and also to Beatrice, of the looks, dress, and behavior of women he met at social functions over the years. Even a negative impression ("she is chiefly noted for having worn dinner dresses which would have permitted her to nurse a baby at any time with out unbuttoning any thing") betrayed an attentive eye. He was candid with his wife about his tolerance of the fraternization of soldiers with local girls, assuring her at the same time that he wasn't one to indulge himself.

When he was invited at a 1924 West Point banquet to toast the ladies of the army, his winking profession of inexperience with women amused the audience and also his wife, who transcribed Georgie's words in her thought book: "Had I been called upon to toast horseflesh, or profanity, or some other subject on which I may possess erudition, I had been less abashed. As it is, the timorous modesty of my nature and my well-known celibate instincts are confounded. I am at a loss." Continuing, he considered praising the "señoritas" of Mexico, "but refuse to, on the grounds of self-incrimination." He then considered raising his glass "to those generous and spirited ladies of the Paris boulevards, but abstain out of regard for the feelings of some, and from the knowledge that there are others here more qualified to sing their praises than I." At length his toast turned serious, honoring army wives, and Beatrice foremost, for their patient support of their men. "May we live to make them happy," he said, "or, on the great day come, so die as to make them proud."

Georgie and Beatrice were apart for almost five of their first twenty-six years of marriage. Any understanding, spoken or unspoken, they may have had regarding those separations remains as private as Beatrice's Hawaiian name. What is certain is that Beatrice's faith in her husband was founded on such sentiments as he expressed in a letter written to her from France just after World War I: "It is a good thing you and I are safely married??— Other wise I would have to have proposed to you all over again for having seen the world I have yet to see your equal. I love you."

When Beatrice concluded late in the second tour in Hawaii that Georgie was having an affair with a young woman named Jean Gordon, it was the manner as much as the fact of his infidelity that devastated her. She knew he liked the attention of women, and she knew that many women found him attractive. She'd laughed when he was pursued by a naked and none-too-alluring lady through the surf during a late-night beach party. She'd overlooked his clumsy flirtations with Hawaii's younger social set perhaps out of exhausted resignation, perhaps because Beatrice was, for once, putting her own life and interests first. But Georgie's romance with Jean Gordon was an altogether different and deeper affront.

Jean was family. The daughter of Beatrice's half-sister Louise, she'd stopped in Hawaii to visit the Pattons on her way to tour the Far East. Later described by a friend as "a lovely young woman of great charm, intelligence, and sensitivity," at twenty-one Jean was exactly Ruth Ellen's age and one of her best friends—so Georgie's interest in her was a blow to his daughter as well as his wife.

Sensing the current between her father and Jean, Ruth Ellen tried to fix Jean up with several young men she knew. But Jean seemed interested in being only with Georgie, and he only in being with her. In hindsight the affair would seem to Ruth Ellen to have been inevitable, its logic coldly clear. "Georgie was mad at Ma for ceasing to be his adoring public . . . he was scared of getting old; dissatisfied with his static career; and to have an unusually attractive girl his own daughter's age make a play for him, was just what his starved ego needed."

Beatrice seemed oblivious to the flirtation of Georgie and her half-niece, though they made little effort to conceal it. When Beatrice became ill just before they were all to take an excursion of several days to another

Hawaiian island to purchase horses, her decision to remain behind, keep Ruth Ellen with her, and let her husband go on alone with Jean, seemed to invite disaster. What was in Beatrice's mind at the time is a mystery, but years later she wrote in her thought book, "Some of our loved ones we can save from their mistakes by our own experience, but some must make their own. This is hardest to bear—to watch them suffer and do nothing but be ready to help if the time comes." To such people, she observed, "every experience is their own private possession to be lived thru as if it had never happened before. They do not connect themselves with anything else in books or human experience." They are as egocentric as children, she seemed to be saying; as innocent and as hurtful.

After Georgie and Jean returned from their trip together, neither Beatrice nor Ruth Ellen doubted that they'd become intimate. A powerful tension settled over the family just as Beatrice's long-labored novel appeared in the bookstores. A banquet was held in Beatrice's honor on the eve of the book's publication. Jean attended with all the Pattons. One of Beatrice's native friends offered an ancient prayer for the book's success. Within weeks its first run sold out; eventually *Blood of the Shark* went through four printings. But Beatrice's pride of accomplishment was forever undercut by the memory of her marriage's simultaneous fracture. Georgie's action had stolen her moment. This was the cruelest blow.

"Never brood," she wrote. "Be natural, do not regret, fill up life, go forward." She kept her hurt to herself, revealing it only once, hence all the more memorably, to Ruth Ellen on the day Jean Gordon left Hawaii to continue her tour abroad. Georgie had draped the young woman in leis of orchid and jasmine. As Jean's ship pulled away, he waved frantically after her at the end of the pier, "making a damned fool of himself," thought Ruth Ellen, who stood apart with her mother observing him. Suddenly Beatrice turned to her daughter. "You know," she began matter-of-factly, "it's lucky for us that I don't have a mother, because if I did, I'd pack up and go to her now; and your father needs me. He doesn't know it, but he needs me. In fact"—she hesitated over the revelation—"right now he needs me more than I need him."

Ruth Ellen never would forget the contrast of her mother's flatspoken tone and her tearful eyes. "I want you to remember that I didn't leave your father," Beatrice said. "I stuck with him because I am all that he really has." In silence the two women, closer now than they'd ever been, watched Georgie waving after the ship that slowly steamed out of Pearl Harbor.

*   *   *

This difficult time in her marriage sparked Beatrice's growing penchant for pensive philosophical musings. From being wounded, she proposed in her thought book, "you learn where you stand, how much you can take." Or, "I would rather feel love than be the beloved, unless it is mutual. It may mean more suffering, but it is more quickening." Always musical, when now she played piano or strummed guitar a quiet melancholy seemed to inform the melodies more strongly than in the past. She spoke obliquely of marriage, likening it to a tree that endures through harsh and favorable seasons, sometimes in bud, sometimes barren, "but if you keep on cultivating the roots, always cultivating the roots, it will come alive again."

Precisely how she and Georgie came to terms with their difficulties is known only to them. In the years since their deaths, a golden chalice in their home has acquired a legend as a reconciliation gift from Georgie to Beatrice; the facts behind the legend are lost. Whatever peace offerings he brought her in apology, it was through Beatrice's will to forgive that the marriage endured. Her thought book again is revealing: "It is often wise to close our eyes to the peccadilloes in others; but when we pander to ourselves *in any way* we are going downhill." Forgive, in other words; but do not forget.

Like her mother, Ruth Ellen grew reflective after the upheaval at home. Having long sensed the unrest brewing in her father, Ruth Ellen put her impressions to paper in January 1937, just days after Jean Gordon left Hawaii. "Ma has been so happy here," she wrote, "because she has created her book and given herself to it unsparingly. Daddy has been unhappy because he has lost energy, and where before he gave himself unsparingly, now he has no extra to give and misses it without knowing why." Ruth Ellen continued, "But men who live on action seldom stop to realize why they do things... they are trapped by a lack of understanding of themselves which causes fear. No man will be happy if his wife does all the giving. It makes him crave opposition so he can live, and when he doesn't get it—he merely thinks his wife is spineless and seeks further afield for spirit and opposition."

Unfortunately, but perhaps predictably, Georgie didn't submit himself to the same introspection as did his wife and daughter. His moods remained ever dependent on his volatile and never-satisfied sense of his career prospects. Those prospects improved in the spring of 1937 when he received orders back to Fort Riley. But during an interim vacation at his Green Meadows estate, he was kicked in the leg by Beatrice's horse and suffered a compound fracture and then phlebitis, a blood clot condition, for which he was hospitalized for almost four months. The army investigated the accident to determine if it had occurred under the influence of alcohol. The routine inquiry turned up nothing incriminating, still Georgie was humiliated.

When he returned home from the hospital in November, the first thing he did was limp out to his stables and begin beating Beatrice's horse with one of his wood crutches. Beatrice exploded. She told him to quit being dramatic, quit acting like a child, it was his own fault he'd been kicked. Georgie relented grudgingly, accusing her, Ruth Ellen remembered, "of denying him one of the few pleasures he had left, killing the horse that had ruined his career."

During three months' recuperation at home, Georgie became, in his family's view, "suicidally depressed." But that was only part of his performance. For the many relatives Beatrice invited to the house to improve her husband's morale ("that dirty French word," he called it), he put on the devil-may-care facade of a man happy, as he once joked in Hawaii, "to get drunk daily at 10 A.M. and so slosh quickly into the sunset."

Young people of the family were especially drawn to Georgie. Ever since he'd begun vacationing on Boston's North Shore, he'd stood out from their other elders with his love of fast cars, his poetry, his profanity, and for such antics as charging his horses into people's front halls and igniting fireworks in their courtyards for a holiday morning laugh. Beatrice's many nieces and nephews were captivated by Uncle Georgie's seeming high spirits through his long convalescence. He'd gained a wild reputation even while hospitalized. Young Fred Ayer recalled that Georgie kept the hospital "in uproar. Friends decorated his room with festoons of varicolored toilet paper and provided a seemingly inexhaustible liquor supply." When at last able to walk around, Georgie "roamed the corridor visiting other patients and dispensing ribaldry and cheer."

Beatrice and Ruth Ellen observed it all dubiously, fearing his performance was a fragile sham. Everyone else was thoroughly charmed. Somebody tacked up a hand-lettered sign in his hospital room recalling his recent years in Hawaii. "Hula-Hula Night Club: G.S. Patton, Prop."

Torch

IN THE 1930s U.S. Army troop strength dipped below 140,000 men. While Japan and Germany built modern armies many times that size, American isolationism dictated that military appropriations be held to a bare minimum. The little money available was spent primarily on salaries, which were paltry enough; training and new equipment were all but ignored. By the army's own assessment, its troops' main diversions from inactivity were drinking, gambling, and whoring.

Career officers were especially frustrated. Promotion was based on seniority; a general had to retire or die for those under him to advance in rank. The scarcity of command positions and the lack of field maneuvers meant that officers had to learn their profession in the classroom at branch schools and staff colleges. Yet amazingly, many did learn their profession—largely on their own initiative, exchanging ideas and information through letters, articles, lectures, and at informal social gatherings, refighting the last war and imagining the next over cigarettes and coffee.

Army morale had begun to decline during John Pershing's tenure as chief of staff in the early 1920s. Nita's former fiancé had been bored in the job and took long vacations in Europe where his reputation as one of World War I's great generals endured undiminished. A benefit of Pershing's frequent absence, however, was the elevation of his gifted deputy, George

C. Marshall, to de facto chief of staff. After Pershing retired and Marshall was transferred to China and later to Fort Benning, Georgia, Douglas MacArthur became army chief of staff in 1930. He grappled with Congress for the next five years to gain support and money for the military, eventually leaving Washington for the Philippines, where he'd served in the past as department commander and where again he could freely exercise his autocratic leadership style.

Marshall and MacArthur became beacons around which many future generals of World War II gathered to learn their craft. From 1927 to 1932, while serving as assistant commandant of the infantry school at Fort Benning, Marshall presided over an after-hours salon at his home where ambitious young officers such as Omar Bradley, Courtney Hodges, Matthew Ridgway, Joseph Stilwell, and Bedell Smith shared ideas about modern warfare. Robert Eichelberger and Dwight Eisenhower likewise benefited from their association with MacArthur in the Pacific.

Georgie wasn't part of this tight-knit group of emerging army talent. Though he knew many of these men in passing, he progressed alone through his career despite a superficial gregariousness. When Georgie went off to college, his father advised him to keep apart from his peers, advice Georgie had followed ever since. The standoffishness was mutual. Many people resented Georgie's conspicuous wealth. They winced at his snobbery and braggadocio, unaware of the insecurity these pretenses disguised. And as a cavalryman, he was not in the forefront of military progress. Officers in other service branches viewed the cavalry as passé and its advocates, Georgie included, as stubborn fossils from a bygone era.

During the 1920s, he'd prudently maintained a dual allegiance to horses and mechanization. He'd often invited a New Jersey inventor named Walter Christie to his Washington home to build models of Christie's tank designs in the basement, exclaiming enthusiastically, "This is the future!" But as Georgie slipped in his personal life, he slipped professionally as well. His performance ratings remained excellent. However, in contrast to past study habits, he no longer could summon the discipline to absorb, night after night, all the latest technical and tactical developments in warfare. Keeping current wasn't worth the effort anymore, since it seemed he would never get the chance to put his knowledge to use.

He regularly amazed his family, after an exhausting day of work or play, by selecting a title from his traveling library of more than three hundred volumes and reading until early dawn. But the nature of his reading material began to change. Earlier in his career he'd studied logistics, fortifications, tactics, staff structure, annotating the book margins with terse exclamations of agreement or argument, keeping extensive files of typed note cards for reference when he prepared his military lectures. But now, his career faltering, he focused less on war's practical aspects and more on the intangibles that originally had attracted him, what have been called (in *Battle Leadership* by Captain Adolph von Schell, a book Georgie read in the mid-1930s) "the eternal verities of leadership, morale, psychological effects, and the difficulty and confusion which battle entails," verities that, in Georgie's mind, accounted for the romance of war. In this period of his life he needed not technical insight but spiritual revival. "Volumes are devoted to armaments," he complained, "and only pages to inspiration." He found those precious inspiring pages not in books about modern warfare but in books about ancient Greece and Rome, about Napoleon and the American Civil War, the kind of books he'd read as a boy when he was just beginning to dream.

Georgie used to write violent, mystical, chest-pounding poetry whenever he felt himself losing direction or drive. But he'd fallen out of the habit, as if, like his technical studies, it no longer seemed worth the effort. So it isn't surprising that as his personal decline accelerated in the 1930s, he experienced two self-described "flashbacks" of former incarnations of what he'd long believed, and now dearly hoped, was his eternal warrior soul. Whatever the nature of those flashbacks, for Georgie they served, as his poetry once had, to boost his spirit and recharge his sense of destiny.

The first occurred on a frigid winter morning in the Virginia countryside in 1934. The start of the fox hunt had been delayed. Georgie and Beatrice shivered in their saddles, their horses exhaling steam. Georgie had never taken cold weather well; since scorching his face with a fuel lamp in 1916, his ears and cheeks turned tomato red whenever the temperature approached freezing. In his discomfort he became quiet. His eyes were closed. His shoulders and chin were folded into his chest for warmth. With a sudden jolt he sat straight, startling Beatrice beside him. He said to her, "The dead were in carts." There was puzzlement in his voice as much as wonder. "We carried the dead in carts so the Russians wouldn't know how many of us they'd killed. It was so cold the blood was brown on the snow."

Beatrice, who'd come to know military history through him, and come to know his odd turns of mind through outbursts such as this, made an instant, indulgent connection: "Was it the retreat from Moscow, Georgie?"

"I think it was." Later he filled in the memory with more detail for his children. His hat had kept falling over his eyes as he trudged along with the haggard column of the retreating Grande Armée in November 1812. One arm had ached with cold inside his coat. He couldn't feel his other arm, apparently having lost it. He told Beatrice that morning of the fox hunt, "I saw a small man on a horse riding ahead. He didn't care what happened to us."

She understood. "Napoleon."

Georgie experienced a second flashback in 1937 after being kicked in the leg by Beatrice's horse. Passing out from the pain, he awoke in the hospital with an image fixed in his mind of lying bleeding on a round shield of animal hide. As two armored Vikings lifted the shield to bear him away with the other dead, Georgie glimpsed "their hairy asses" under their chain mail skirts. The Vikings, realizing he wasn't dead, shook their heads and left him among the living. Georgie's descriptions of his past lives were always dreadful. (He later had a flashback in Tunisia in which, as a besieged Carthaginian dying of thirst in the second century B.C., he drank urine out of his helmet "because the Romans had ruined the aqueduct.") Georgie suggested that memories of horror survive the trauma of physical death and rebirth. "They scar your soul," he said.

Bitter over his leg injury and long convalescence, he was somewhat heartened by the Viking flashback. "I guess they're not ready to take me yet. I still have a job to do." And to have died from a horse kick would have been shameful. "By the last bullet in the last battle of his final war" was how a soldier should die—or he should die, Georgie asserted, like General Bee at the battle of Bull Run, speaking heroic words ("Rally behind the Virginians!") before receiving a bullet through the head. But such a blessing still seemed remote.

George IV's first memory of his father was of flying a toy airplane with him at Schofield Barracks in 1927. Later on in Hawaii he watched his father swim far off a beach after a man who, just moments before, had screamed that a shark was attacking him. The man had vanished under the water. On the beach panicked onlookers saw imaginary sharks under every ripple. Georgie kept diving in a vain search for the man's body, making his son feel very proud.

While living in Washington between tours in Hawaii, George IV and his father built ship models together—scale replicas of Spanish galleons and British frigates, the rigging and armaments always exact because Georgie was a demon for authenticity. Later they built a twenty-two-foot motorboat in their garage, adding woodworking to Georgie's fatherly lessons in sailing, navigation, the use of firearms, and the handling of horses. Georgie taught his son military history and poetry, taught him to carve a game bird and mix a cocktail. He introduced him to such men as John Pershing and former Secretary of War Henry L. Stimson, who'd grown fond of Georgie and Beatrice on the capital social circuit. And Georgie sometimes let his son listen in when his cronies from World War I dropped by to reminisce. Except during George IV's occasional school vacations at home, such activities ended when the boy went to boarding school in the eighth grade. He and his father had shared hobbies in the past; one day they would share a profession. But their separation in 1937 inhibited the formation of an intimate bond between them. Eventually Georgie would best know his son by his scholastic report cards and athletic awards. George IV, in turn, would know his father primarily by his military accomplishments and public fame.

Like his sisters, young George was conscious of his father as a headline performer playing to an audience that included his wife and children. Often the show was comic. Georgie could devour entire boxes of candy at one sitting. Chocolate samplers were a favorite prey, the few candies he left behind invariably bitten underneath where he'd tasted the filling before replacing the candy in its wrapper for someone else to enjoy. Georgie's sweet tooth extended also to brandied fruitcake—at Christmas he would eat a whole cake himself, and then, fearing weight gain, leave at once for the hospital to have his stomach pumped. And he was tone deaf. He could distinguish bugle calls only by tapping out the time with his fingers, and he once caused an uproar by hollering at a military band during a solemn ceremony, "Quit playing that goddamn music!" unaware that the song was the national anthem.

George saw the unstable side of his father as well, the tears at each passing birthday, the drinking, the time Georgie, meaning to honor a horse that had gone lame, decided to shoot the animal himself rather than allow some stranger—a veterinarian—to put it down with a needle. But the horse flinched as Georgie pulled the trigger. His son remembered, "I saw the poor horse struggling in the driveway with its eye hanging out, and my dad standing there crying, weeping, and trying to hold the horse so he could shoot him again." A groom ran out and finished the job. Georgie was devastated with guilt. He shut himself in his room and didn't emerge for a day.

George was conscious of his father's self-centeredness but wasn't inclined to contest it. He enjoyed riding, though not to the degree Georgie did; still, he dutifully helped exercise Georgie's twenty-six horses, often spending four or five hours a day in the saddle when he was home on school vacation. Any awareness of the strain in his parents' marriage was manifested only in George's ever-growing admiration for his mother. As a child he'd felt closer to his English nanny; his mother was an elegant, stable, rather distant presence whose maternal attentions seemed all the more precious for their intermittence. In the late 1930s he saw that his father had grown "real snappy. He could take your head off in a minute." But it wasn't George or even Ruth Ellen who caught hell from Georgie. It was Beatrice; and her son admired her for enduring it.

Ruth Ellen, nine years older than George and still living at home, was acutely sensitive to the tension in the house and the causes underlying it. Continuing to work as an occupational therapist and nursery school teacher, she traveled to Fort Riley in early 1938 after Georgie recovered from his leg fracture and the complications of phlebitis. Then she went on to Fort Clark, Texas, where Georgie took command of the Fifth Cavalry as, at last, a full colonel. She lived at home in deference to her parents' social customs regarding the living arrangements of unwed twenty-three-year-old women; plus Ruth Ellen loved army life, wanted to marry an officer, and, despite much ambivalence about her father, had never shed that childhood sense that the action was where Georgie was, that life elsewhere just wasn't as vivid. Another reason she stayed with her parents would occur to her only years later. She stayed out of concern for her mother, who no longer had her writing and her Hawaiian friends to insulate her from the storms of Georgie's moods and his witheringly harsh tongue. Ruth Ellen felt Beatrice needed her.

It seemed her concern was misplaced at first. Her father enjoyed his brief assignment teaching at the cavalry school at Fort Riley. At Fort Clark he was back with a combat unit, no longer in a staff job. His division commander, Brigadier General Kenyon Joyce, wrote of him, "Because of his innate dash and great physical courage and endurance he is a cavalry officer from whom extraordinary feats might be expected in war." Not surprisingly, Georgie's spirits improved. He and Beatrice enjoyed each other again.

So confident did Georgie become about his career, he anticipated becoming a brigadier general within two years. To improve his chances, he decided to cultivate some friends in Congress, which ultimately would vote on his promotion. He sent instructions to his cousin Arvin Brown in

California: "Find some deserving democrat who is probably going to win any how and slip him up to $500 (the less the better and still hold face) as a campaign contribution from a devoted admirer. For obvious reasons my name should not appear on any list of contributions . . . but be damn sure he personally knows of my warm interest in his election." Georgie hoped to make a similar contribution to a Massachusetts Republican, "and so emulating the Rothschild family will have friends in both houses." Persuaded by Brown to do neither, he pressed his cousin to at least mention Georgie to his Democrat friends as a newly converted Roosevelt supporter. He winked away his hypocrisy by quoting *Henry IV:* "Paris is worth a Mass."

But only six months after he arrived in Texas, "the blow fell," as Ruth Ellen put it. Georgie was recalled to Fort Myer to command the Third Cavalry. His wife and daughter watched his face fall as the chief of cavalry conveyed the news over the telephone. Georgie hung up and tearfully confronted Beatrice: "You and your money have ruined my career!" Her eyes widened in shock. He'd spent her money freely throughout their marriage, and now he was stooping to this. "A lot of fancy language got thrown around," her daughter recalled, adding in understatement, "and Ma got her feelings hurt." Finally Beatrice threw up her hands and went to bed, exhausted.

Georgie's problem with reassignment to Fort Myer was that the Third Cavalry's mission was largely ceremonial. Parading for visiting dignitaries, providing color guards for state funerals and national holidays, the regiment represented the military to the public as an artifact of cozy grandeur instead of as a combat force. Once it had been exciting for Georgie to serve there, but the Fort Myer of 1939, placid, glitzy, and safe, seemed far out of step with the rumbles of war in Europe and Asia to which he was avidly attuned. "I guessed it right all the way," Georgie had written a week after the Munich Pact surrendering Czechoslovakia to Nazi Germany was signed last September. "Rumania is next." And the French and British who'd signed the pact with Adolph Hitler? "Yellow Dogs," he wrote.

As regimental commander at Fort Myer, Georgie was expected constantly to entertain congressmen in order to lobby on behalf of the military. An outside income was virtually essential to the job, hence his comment about his wife's wealth having led to his assignment there. His years of flaunting it now jeopardized his future—naturally he blamed Beatrice. "Georgie was impossible," Ruth Ellen recalled of his behavior around the house. She asked her mother "why he was always yelling at her and being so disagreeable and feisty." Beatrice offered the rationale that men, when unhappy, "always struck out at the thing they loved best." Her daughter observed, "Mighty cold comfort, that."

Georgie's initial pessimism notwithstanding, his transfer back to Fort Myer was one of the luckiest events in his career. Fort Clark was a remote cavalry outpost where the military future of horses seemed secure. The division commander, General Joyce, was a passionate advocate of horses in combat, a view Georgie, eager to please his boss, had adopted wholeheartedly.

At Fort Myer, however, Georgie's proximity to the army's brain center soon apprised him of how advanced was the push for total mechanization among the young stars of the officer corps now emerging from their tutelage under generals MacArthur and Marshall. Had he remained at Fort Clark, Georgie might not have realized until too late that he and his service branch were on the verge of being phased out.

After General Marshall became acting chief of staff in the spring of 1939, Georgie had reason to panic. Marshall ended the army's seniority system of promotion. Many officers Georgie's age were forced to step aside in favor of younger, progressive types; his lifelong fear of aging seemed a premonition of his downfall. Congratulating former subordinates as they won colonel's eagles and general's stars "really strained his 'mirthless smile,'" his daughter recalled. Feeling unappreciated and unnoticed, Georgie considered soliciting recommendations from John Pershing, now retired, and Henry Stimson. Then in July, despairing that he was not one of Marshall's anointed up-and-comers, Georgie learned that the general needed a place to stay at Fort Myer while his new quarters were being prepared.

He wrote Marshall at once, offering to put him up at his house (empty for now, with Beatrice and Ruth Ellen away). "I can give you a room and bath and meals," he proposed nonchalantly. "I shall not treat you as a guest and shall not cramp your style in any way." When Marshall accepted, Georgie exalted like a beggar over a sackful of cash. "I have just consumated a pretty snappy move," he wrote Beatrice. "Gen George C Marshall is going to live at our house!!!!" Composing himself, he tried to sound slick: "Of course it may cramp my style but there are compensations." Then he got practical, concluding his letter to her, "You had better send me a check for $5,000 as I am getting pretty low."

He'd known George Marshall in the twenties when both had served in Washington. His invitation meant to reestablish their acquaintance rather than bootlick him outright (though certainly Georgie didn't rule that out). He mainly wished to convince the general, by riding with him and taking him boating on the Potomac River, that Georgie was a vigorous fifty-three with many years of good service to offer.

Marshall's visit went well enough, though with no tangible benefit to his host. Later that summer, Georgie led his regiment in field exercises in Virginia, winning praise for his "tireless energy" and "prompt decision." In the exercise, he stressed the combined role "for horse and mechanized cavalry," clearly seeing the new realities of war. On September 1, the world was stunned by the German blitzkrieg into Poland, an overwhelming onslaught of combined air, infantry, and armored forces that conquered that country in days. Also on September 1, George Marshall officially assumed the position of army chief of staff. Georgie immediately sent him a set of sterling silver stars.

The success of the blitzkrieg further dimmed the future of horse cavalry—German tanks had easily cut the Polish cavalry to pieces. Still Georgie walked a middle line, keeping close contact with General Joyce at Fort Clark while renewing a correspondence with Brigadier General Adna Chaffee, the army's leading advocate of mechanization, who eventually would be heralded as the father of the Armored Force.

Georgie finally was forced to choose between them in the spring of 1940 when he umpired war maneuvers at which Joyce and Chaffee competed to determine the supremacy of horse cavalry versus mechanized forces. The cavalry got crushed—in making this judgment, Georgie lost General Joyce as a friend and supporter. The break was liberating for Georgie; his loyalty to such mentors as his father, John Pershing, and recently Kenyon Joyce, tended to blind him to their shortcomings.

The war maneuvers completed, Georgie sent Chaffee a congratulatory letter in which he couched a discreet request that Chaffee keep him in mind for a job in the soon-to-be-organized Armored Force. In response, Chaffee put him on his preferred list of potential armored brigade commanders. "With two light armored regiments and a regiment of light tanks employed in a mobile way, I think you could go to town," Chaffee wrote. No doubt bearing in mind that Germany had conquered Norway, Denmark, and just six days ago, on June 22, accepted the surrender of France, Chaffee concluded his letter to Georgie, "I shall always be happy to know that you are around in any capacity when there is fighting to be done."

Georgie had another psychic experience during those pivotal months. He was touring the Civil War's Wilderness battlefield south of Fort Myer with his family and the German military attaché, General Friedrich von Boetticher, who was a Civil War buff. As usual on such jaunts, Georgie led the group across the terrain explaining troop deployments and the violent ebb and flow of the bloody 1863 battle. He positioned Ruth Ellen and George IV as Confederate units and placed his wife, a Yankee, on the Union line. He ascended a nearby rise where he said General Jubal Early had directed the battle. Von Boetticher, consulting a guidebook, disagreed about Early's location. They argued loudly. Georgie was adamant, if lacking in proof, while von Boetticher thumped his book with Teutonic certitude. Just then an old man hobbled over from a group of tourists passing by. "The other gentleman is right," he told von Boetticher. "General Early was on that rise. I was at this battle as a boy." Georgie was pleased. He'd had a feeling he'd been there before; now it was confirmed. "Of course Early stood there," he declared in triumph. "I saw him myself!"

Georgie and von Boetticher were friends; they viewed their nations' political differences as irrelevant, for the moment, to their shared bond as military professionals. But not long after the incident at the Wilderness battlefield, von Boetticher communicated privately with Beatrice at Fort Myer. At a recent party at the Patton home, the German general had been fiercely accosted by some Jewish guests protesting Hitler's anti-Semitic depredations. Consequently, von Boetticher asked Beatrice not to invite him to her home again: he felt his presence would hurt Georgie's career. Withholding his own opinion about Hitler, von Boetticher offered only that he was a loyal German officer. "No matter what happens, the fatherland is still our fatherland."

General von Boetticher's chivalrous gesture reveals why Georgie's avowal of a previous existence at the battle of the Wilderness had seemed more artful than his other "far memories" as a Napoleonic soldier and a stricken Norseman; why it seemed more a conceit of destiny than a spontaneous, needy wish. Georgie was slowly, like a frozen lake thawing, beginning to feel cocky again. War was coming. He'd been growing increasingly sure of the fact; now von Boetticher's gesture confirmed it. Georgie's role in it was still far from clear, far from assured. But where there was war, there was hope.

When Ruth Ellen came to her father in early 1940 and told him she wished to marry Lieutenant Jim Totten, Georgie's answer was predictably negative. "You can't marry Totten. He's short, he's an artilleryman, and he's a

Catholic." But perhaps because Georgie's overall mood was improving, or perhaps because he bore a respect for his daughter that their earlier years of friction had only enhanced, he almost immediately dropped his opposition and gave Ruth Ellen his blessing.

In something of a role reversal, it was Beatrice who put up the stronger resistance. Despite the broadmindedness she'd shown in her relationships with the Hawaiians and with people of other minority groups she'd encountered over the years, she fell back on the anti-Catholic prejudices of her Yankee Puritan background when it came to her daughter's marriage. She decided to persuade Lieutenant Totten to become a Protestant. Georgie was horrified; religion, anyone's, was no casual calling to him. He threatened to leave Beatrice if she tried to convert Totten. She went ahead, Totten refused ("What do you think of turncoats?" he asked her), while Georgie, in a gesture of protest on Ruth Ellen's behalf, spent most of that night at the post theater, watching a movie three times.

Seeking another ally, Ruth Ellen went to California to see her aunt, Nita Patton. Georgie had officially changed his state of residence to Massachusetts in 1939; that same year he signed away his half-claim to Papa's money and property in favor of his sister. Financially well-fixed, Nita, fifty-two, was raising her adopted sons, Peter and David, while continuing to work with local charities and the state Democratic Party.

Ruth Ellen was stunned when her aunt insisted that under no circumstances should Ruth Ellen marry a Catholic. Nita's cousins through her mother's half-sister, the Shorbs, were Catholic; in recent years they'd sued Nita for parcels of Lake Vineyard land, and Nita was still resentful. Ruth Ellen felt beaten. "I guess that I will never marry," she sighed. "I'll stay home and take care of Ma." These words, and the future they promised, brought forth in a sudden eruption Nita's long-buried sorrow over her aborted romances of years ago. She rose from her chair, her face florid. "What!" Nita shouted. "And be like me? One sacrifice on the altar of family is enough. Go home and marry your young man. I'll attend your wedding if no one else will!"

The wedding took place on July 6, 1940, in the same church where Ruth Ellen's parents had wed. Her mother had come around soon after Nita, and a few days before the wedding Beatrice gave Ruth Ellen a handwritten collection of motherly advice. One tip resonated with the understanding she and her daughter shared of Georgie. "To wish to reform a man is to set yourself above God. Live the best you know, and perhaps one unhappy seeker will see in your behavior the key to his own freedom."

Ruth Ellen and Georgie rode to the church in a limousine. For a long time they didn't speak. He broke the silence. "I guess you know your mother and I will miss you. I hope we gave you a happy childhood." She nodded and started to cry. Then he started crying, too. As the limousine pulled up to the church, he said to her, "If you treat Jim the way your mother has treated me, you'll be all right."

Nine days later, Georgie read in a morning newspaper that he'd been given command of a brigade in the Second Armored Division at Fort Benning, Georgia. It took him several hours to calm down before beginning joyful letters of thanks to the generals whose influence, he knew, had brought him this plum assignment. One of them, George Marshall, responded with a detectable dry amusement: "I am glad this arrangement is pleasing to you."

Georgie received his general's star in October 1940. He giddily wrote a colleague that, in promoting him, "the morals of the army may have shrunk, but the morale would be way up." A month later he assumed command of the 15,000-member Second Armored Division. "All that is now needed is a nice juicy war."

He swiftly rose to national attention. In July 1941, after months of routing all opposition in war maneuvers and of leading the division over hundreds of miles of southern countryside in publicity-heavy simulations of mass advances through unfamiliar territory, Georgie appeared on the cover of *Life* magazine wearing a tank helmet and a killer frown—the war face he'd practiced since childhood. The singular élan with which he captivated journalists and inspired new draftees of the army's now 1.5 million men was only his long-standing code of "visible personality" performed on a larger stage, a dynamic explosion where once had been sparks, flare-ups, and intimidating slow burns of a man waiting all his life for this chance.

The family was scattered. George IV was at boarding school. Bee was in Georgia with two sons. Ruth Ellen, her husband away on extended field maneuvers, was in Massachusetts awaiting the birth of her first child. When the Patton children read in a newspaper of their father declaring, say, "War means fighting and fighting means killing," they recognized that he was talking blood and murder with the help of a favorite quote from the Confederacy's Nathan Bedford Forrest. When they read that Georgie was gaining a reputation for displaying manic nonstop energy; for sharing his troops' physical burdens and challenges; for praising, cursing, bawling, and rejoicing over them; for unleashing volleys of shocking profanity to express anger, pleasure, and sometimes just to turn heads; for bending rules, cutting red tape, blowing through obstacles between him and his objective like a child who simply must have that toy—they recognized Daddy at once. When they saw photographs of him posing with utter seriousness in a ridiculous self-designed tank uniform of green gabardine, brass buttons, and a gold football helmet—it was nothing new. And of the suggestion that Georgie's men swore *at* him but also swore *by* him, well, his children knew that feeling exactly.

Georgie received a second star in April 1941. In December the Japanese attacked Pearl Harbor, bringing America actively into the war against Japan and its Axis ally, Germany. A month later he took command of First Armored Corps with orders to train a tank force capable of battling General Erwin Rommel's famed Afrika Korps in North Africa. He selected a barren desert of twenty million acres in California's Mojave Desert as his training area. Within days, troops, tanks, and supplies were pouring in. "I believe the only way to start things is to start," he wrote.

He learned that his son had been admitted to West Point. He'd never pushed George IV toward a military career; in fact he'd insisted that George attend a civilian preparatory school rather than a military one (his son's preference) "to see how the other half live." Immersed in larger concerns, he dashed off a note of congratulation to his son that was surprisingly chilly considering their amiable if distant relationship. "Well we are real proud of you for the first time in your life. See to it that we stay that way." Georgie's father never would have addressed Georgie so carelessly. But Papa was a great father. Georgie, his son was beginning to think— Georgie was a great man.

Georgie briefly visited his son at West Point in early autumn, 1942. George IV had seen his father only periodically over the last two years, and he sensed that today's visit had some special significance. Georgie, however, remained deliberately vague about his present duties or his plans for the future. As he shook his son's hand good-bye, he seemed to strain for significant words. He opted for one of his favorite maxims: "Be yourself. People who aren't themselves are nobody."

Six months earlier Georgie had said good-bye to his daughters at Fort Benning before heading to the Desert Training Center in California. He'd thought he would see them within a few months; in fact he wouldn't see them, or his son, for three years. Later that autumn, George IV got an inkling why. On a bus returning to West Point after an away football game, he gazed offshore from the coastal highway and saw dozens of anchored navy transport ships. He wondered if the ships were gathering as part of a task force, some secret mission across the sea. He wondered if his father was involved.

Georgie had been planning Operation Torch since July. A joint British-American amphibious invasion of French Morocco, the operation had been conceived by Franklin Roosevelt and Winston Churchill to introduce American forces into combat against Vichy French forces in Morocco rather than against Rommel's battle-hardened German army. The French will to fight was in question. Should they put up a spirited defense, Operation Torch stood less than a 50 percent chance of success in the view of Torch's overall commander, Dwight Eisenhower.

Georgie, who would command the invasion's ground force of 24,000 Americans, also had doubts. "The operation is bad and is mostly political." Yet unlike most other officers involved, he was undaunted: "We must do something now. I feel that I am the only true gambler in the whole outfit." Meetings with Eisenhower prompted an ambivalence in Georgie about his superior that would last throughout the coming war: "Ike is not as rugged mentally as I thought; he vacillates and is not a realist." The ambivalence was mutual. After Torch's initial planning sessions, Eisenhower's report to Chief of Staff Marshall indicated they both appreciated that Patton was a wild card. "Very businesslike," Eisenhower said of Georgie with a trace of surprise. "Sane and enthusiastic."

Beatrice was the only member of Georgie's family aware of the impending invasion. During the last weeks before the task force's departure in late October, she observed her husband with admiration and wonder. The past two years had been somewhat strange for her. Since 1940, she'd spent her summers in Massachusetts while Georgie conducted maneuvers in the South. Even after joining him at Fort Benning, she didn't see him much, for his time at home was taken up with private study. Though he'd never left off his military reading, since his career rebirth in the Armored Force it had grown still more intense; he read everything he could find on mechanized warfare, especially books written by his future adversaries, the Germans. To support Georgie's efforts, to participate in them somehow, Beatrice had dusted off her musical talents and composed an Armored Force march to be played when his tanks paraded.

By the time they relocated to the Desert Training Center in April 1942, she seemed to have accepted that her husband's pinnacle moment was at hand, and that it must be his alone. After helping him toward it, supporting, coddling, loving, and enduring him through his years of near crack-up between the wars, Beatrice now had only to observe and applaud as, in effect, he stepped out of the house and into the sweep of world events.

Perhaps with an eye on posterity, she began a journal to record his thoughts during the preparation of Operation Torch—his debates and dissatisfactions with his colleagues, his private swings between confidence in the operation and utter dread, his startling ability to fire the enthusiasm of everyone from his commander in chief ("A total joy," was Roosevelt's impression of him) to the secretaries in his office, who tearfully bid Georgie good-bye with a farewell gift of smoking tobacco. "The brand?" they wrote in an accompanying poem. "We were quite scared to ask it./But we found a Brigg's can in your wastepaper basket." None of it surprised Beatrice. "What a man," she wrote of her husband. "He is *very great*—has all the flash, and drama, and personality, and everything to back it up with."

Drama: In the last days before leaving for Africa, Georgie displayed it in every gesture. He assured Roosevelt that he would return "a conqueror or a corpse." He visited his former commander John Pershing, kneeling and kissing Pershing's hand, asking his prayers for Georgie's victory. He wrote a long memo to his troops, which ended, "The eyes of the world are watching us. The heart of America beats for us. God is with us. On our victory depends the freedom or slavery of the human race. We shall surely win."

Georgie wrote dozens of letters to former colleagues and superiors, crediting each with contributing to his success so far. To a friend in Hawaii he recalled an instance when Georgie had cursed his teammates for playing poorly in a polo match: "After the game you took me up to the house, soothed my spirit with a long drink and told me what an ass I had been. . . . You simply suggested that when men were doing their best it was foolish and useless to cuss them. I have never forgotten nor repeated my error. As a result I am eledged to have trained the best division in the army and as a result of that I have my present job."

He wrote letters to his children and to his brother-in-law, Fred Ayer: "All my life I have wanted to lead a lot of men in a desperate battle; I am going to do it; and at fifty-six, one can go with equanimity—there is nothing much one has not done. Thanks to you and B., I have had an exceptionally happy life."

He enclosed a sealed letter ("from the other side") to be given to his wife should Georgie be killed. "Darling Beatrice," she read when she opened it years later:

When Fred gives you this I will be definitely dead. Yet even from that position I find it impossible to tell you how much you have meant to me.

Since we were 16 we have been as one most of the time. When we were not it was my fault.

In the past few weeks before I sailed for Africa only you understood the strain I was under. Your confidence in me was the only sure thing in a world of dreadful uncertainty. With your help I have convinced thousands of success when in my own mind I cannot see how it will be accomplished. If we landed safely, yours was the victory.

I love you with all my heart and hope.

George
for ever

The armada of a hundred ships sailed from Norfolk, Virginia, on October 24. Beatrice flew there with Georgie the day before. "He was so excited that he jumped off the plane and I had to call him back to tell him good-bye; but I was glad—the great strain was over for him at last. Proud to tell, I did not cry for once."

Once aboard and sailing, Georgie's excitement settled down. He reflected in his diary, "Inspite of my over developed personal ambition, all I want to do right now is my full duty."

The invasion force landed in Morocco on November 8. Beatrice was dining with Henry Stimson and his wife in Washington. Finding no news on the radio, the secretary of war telephoned his office and relayed to Beatrice the spotty reports of the invasion that were just coming in. She left the Stimsons late and drove across town to her house.

In her journal of Georgie's last weeks in America, she'd noted that his soldiers' password to each other, the challenge and response between units in the dark, was "George" to be followed by "Patton." "This was not his idea," Beatrice wrote, "and it pleased him immensely."

Having mentioned the password twice in her thought book, it perhaps occurred to her as she drove alone through the darkened city. The image fits: A small gray-haired woman stopped at an intersection with her hands on the steering wheel and a faraway look in her eyes. She is hearing hushed voices on an African beach. The voices call "George" and then answer "Patton." Far up on shore comes the sound of gunfire. The voices whisper in her head. "George . . . Patton."

☆ ☆ **18** ☆ ☆

The Fair-Haired Boy

WHEN next Beatrice saw her husband, two years and eight months later, Georgie was famous. He arrived at Bedford Airport outside Boston on June 7, 1945, a month after Germany surrendered to the Allies. Beatrice met him on the tarmac as he disembarked from the plane wearing four stars on his shoulders and helmet. He removed his helmet and kissed her. Reporters crowded around them, cameras flashing. "Oh, I'm so glad to have you back," she said. Georgie was in the States for a brief speaking tour to boost bond sales to support the continuing war in the Pacific. In the days since learning of his return, Beatrice had exclaimed to her children over and over in disbelief, "I really thought I would never see him again!"

His children waited behind her. Georgie kissed his daughters and shook his son's hand. He'd boarded a plane in Bavaria three days ago with a strep throat, deciding only at the last moment to depart as planned. He looked tired, Ruth Ellen thought. He looked old. As the Pattons walked to waiting vehicles, onlookers around them applauded. Georgie climbed into the open lead car and stood in the back as it started the twenty-five-mile journey to Boston. Throngs of people lined the route of the motorcade. The last few miles into the city were a solid wall of cheers on both sides of the road; later estimates put the crowd at one million. "A regular Roman triumph," Ruth Ellen wrote, "lacking only noble conquered chieftains in chains."

An audience of twenty thousand awaited Georgie at the Hatch Shell on the Charles River. There was a special section of four hundred wounded veterans of the U.S. Third Army, a force that at its peak in 1945 was the largest field army in the history of the United States, comprised of some thirty divisions and more than half a million men. Under Georgie's command it had spearheaded the Allied sweep across France in 1944 and launched the decisive counterattack against Germany's last-ditch offensive in the Battle of the Bulge. Speaking off the cuff as he had so often in recent years to striking effect, Georgie praised these wounded veterans as fighters and survivors. "It is a popular idea that a man is a hero just because he was killed in action. Rather, I think a man is frequently a fool when he gets killed." Pointing to them, he declared, "These men are the heroes."

The offensiveness of this remark seemed to pass unnoticed as he continued. Certainly it contradicted his often-expressed reverence for America's war dead ("I can not see the reason why such fine young men get killed") among whom he wished to be buried someday. Yet revealingly, it echoed a consistent theme of Georgie's wartime thinking: the necessity of a hard heart.

He considered it potentially calamitous for a general to "develop personal feelings about sending men to battle." While claiming that "I always try to fight without getting our people killed," and later writing a report on "how to reduce the human expense of war," he still insisted that a combat commander could become paralyzed if he dwelled too much on the duty "to send to certain death, nearly every day, by his own orders, a certain number of men." In Georgie's view of war—and in his speech to the veterans in Boston—the living mattered most.

In addition to hardening himself to death, he'd sought during the war to harden his soldiers. Many *do* die foolishly, he warned them, because of lack of discipline, initiative, vigilance—and, he stressed, due to lack of savagery. "They are too damned complacent," he wrote Beatrice in 1944. "It is fine to be willing to die for their country but a damned sight better to make the German die for his. No one has ever told them that."

Georgie's speech to the audience at the Hatch Shell reiterated his message delivered to troops before the battle of El Guettar in Tunisia two years earlier: "Our bravery is too negative. We talk too much of sacrifice, of the glory of dying. . . . If we die killing, well and good, but if we fight hard enough, viciously enough, we will kill and live." During the war, his men no doubt appreciated his emphasis of life over death—their own, if not the enemy's. There would be time to mourn and exalt their killed comrades later. Thus Georgie's faux pas in Boston: "Later" had arrived. The Nazis had been defeated, the crusade in Europe won. Yet Georgie, to judge by his jarring remark about America's unheroic dead, had not accepted the fact.

The welcome-home celebration continued that evening with a banquet hosted by the mayor of Boston. Photos of the event show Georgie laughing in one instant, weeping the next. Familiar as these mood swings were, he seemed changed to his son, different somehow. Through letters, George IV and his father had become more personally close in this long period apart. George, like his father, had been turned back after his first year at West Point. While nervously preparing for the reentrance exam, George got a note from his father telling him (as Georgie informed Beatrice) "that I was very proud of him what ever happened and that I too would have to take an exam and might fail but not for lack of trying." Georgie's exam? The invasion of Sicily in 1943.

When George passed his exam and thereafter improved his academic performance, his father expressed pride in him without any of the offhand chilliness apparent in his letters before the war. George in turn was proud of his father, quoting favorable news reports to him, writing him that he was a hero. But at the mayor's banquet he sensed a strange remoteness in his father. "I got the feeling that night," he later wrote, "that he belonged to history more than he belonged to us."

The next morning Georgie and Beatrice departed for Denver and Los Angeles, where he addressed huge crowds at the Rose Bowl and the Coliseum. With minimal editing for a civilian audience, he described the torched wastelands of southern Germany left in the wake of his Third Army, and he roared for the defeat of the Japanese, whom he hoped to fight personally, he said. He visited his parents' graves at San Gabriel and had a brief reunion with Nita.

Despite their differences in years past, Nita had cheered Georgie wholeheartedly through the war, assuring him that Papa was proudly observing from heaven "and yearning over his fair-haired boy." Georgie's career overseas had been rocky at times; twice he was nearly shipped home in disgrace for various indiscretions and outrages, of which the most infamous was his slapping of two shellshocked soldiers in 1943. His sister had ached over these woes, ultimately rejoicing that he'd prevailed, in her words, over "all the slimy jealous toads who tried to do you harm. . . . You are a modern knight in shining armour."

But the shine was rapidly tarnishing. Georgie's published remarks in

Boston had brought a storm of protest from America's gold star parents, who felt he'd insulted the memory of their dead sons. A columnist termed Georgie's speeches "atrocities of the mind . . . and atrocious as reflections of what war-making has done to the personality of Patton himself." It was an apt perception. Georgie still had the capacity to laugh, to doubt, to feel; many colleagues, many of his soldiers, and virtually all in his headquarters and personal staff regarded him with affection only such humane traits inspire. Yet those traits now seemed the exception in him, bare flickers of the engaging, insecure boy of many years, and three wars, ago. "War," he observed in 1943, "is very simple, direct, and ruthless. It takes a simple, direct, and ruthless man to wage war." Georgie, it appeared, had become that man at last.

His official duties while in the States were to end with a news conference in Washington, D.C., after which he would have two weeks' leave in Massachusetts before returning to Europe. The furor over his Boston remarks had quieted. Yet Chief of Staff George Marshall was worried that Georgie might again "go off the rocker," as he put it, this time before the lights and cameras of a national news conference. Eisenhower had once described Patton to Marshall as "this mentally unbalanced officer." Ultimately in the past, both generals had attributed Georgie's erratic behavior to eccentricity whose occasional inconvenience was far outweighed by his combat capabilities. But as the dust of war settled, his instability stood exposed, now seeming truly deep-rooted and worrisome.

In the future the possibility would be raised that Georgie's long history of concussions and head wounds had, in accumulation, caused physiological damage to his brain, thus accounting for his mood swings that even more than in the past were jarring in their extremes and volatility. It was possible, too, that he'd simply burned out. As a baby he drove his family to exhaustion with his wakefulness and high energy; his energy was cited in performance ratings throughout his career. During the war he estimated that 80 percent of his job was to inspire his troops through sheer force of personality. Confronted with the harrowing consequences, risks, and demands of leadership in battle, "Any man with a heart would like to sit down and bawl like a baby, but he can't. So he sticks out his jaw, and swaggers and swears." And once having done this, Georgie wrote, the leader can't stop: "Now, no matter how tired, or discouraged, or really even ill I may be, if I don't live up to that picture, my men are going to say, 'The old man's sick, the old son of a bitch has had it.' Then their own confidence, their own morale will take a big drop."

Personal dynamism, wrote Georgie's aide-de-camp Charles Codman, was behind "his uncanny gift for sweeping men into doing things which they do not believe they are capable of doing." The captain of the female Red Cross crew attached to Third Army headquarters toward the end of the war perceived this quality in Georgie: "The tremendous surge of vitality and life that came from him exhilarated everyone present." She also recognized what may be the inevitable cost of such dynamism, glimpsing beneath his surface vitality "a tired, aging man, a sorrowful, solitary man. . . . That General Patton battled with many different conceptions of himself I was sure."

Whatever the causes underlying Georgie's increasingly apparent instability, General Marshall was sufficiently concerned about it to direct a military psychiatrist to observe Georgie secretly during the Washington news conference. The plan was vetoed by Henry Stimson, Georgie's old friend. The secretary of war sat at the microphone during the conference and carefully controlled the proceedings. Georgie performed fine. Typically shunning euphemism, he did say a few things that generals perhaps aren't supposed to say, as when explaining his combat style: "I prefer to hit hard, even if I lose ten thousand men in one day, instead of daudling along and lose five hundred a day for twenty days." But by and large he was amusing, contained, humble. The reason for his military success? "It was simple," he said. "I just had the honor and happiness of commanding some very great men."

That afternoon, Georgie visited the amputation ward at Walter Reed Hospital. He dreaded going. Hospitals made him feel sick, a sensation he'd experienced too often when visiting field hospitals overseas. But daughter Ruth Ellen had worked there for the past two years, and she convinced him that the patients would appreciate it. "He was dressed to the nines," she recalled of her father's arrival. "All his medals, boots aglow, his swagger stick in his gloved left hand—the whole picture." Georgie was nervous, entering the ward. Outside the door, he snapped at the reporters following him, "I'll bet you goddamn buzzards are just following me to see if I'll slap another soldier, aren't you? You're all hoping I will!"

Inside, he walked slowly down the long aisle between the white hospital beds. Ruth Ellen recalled, "All the patients were looking at him with their hearts in their eyes." Returning to the center of the room, Georgie wiped his eyes with a handkerchief. At length he said to the men, "If I had been

a better general, most of you would not be here." With that, he strode out
of the ward, and out of the hospital, to begin his vacation at home.

While attending a society party in Massachusetts with his wife (just the
sort of soiree he'd once delighted in contrarily dominating), Georgie began
telling a story about his recent experiences overseas. He was cut off in
midsentence by one of Beatrice's relatives. "Oh, George," the man said,
"we're all tired of the war. Let's talk about something else." Georgie
blushed and went silent—no outrage, no profanity, no cutting remark
about the man's safe tenure on the home front.

Later, a family friend asked him to pose for a snapshot wearing all his
medals, that is, not only the regulation ribbons of the U.S. military but the
multicolored sashes and silver sunbursts awarded him by governments
throughout North Africa and Europe. The Knight of the British Empire,
the Grand Cross of the Ouissam Alaouite, the French Legion of Honor, the
Luxembourg Croix de Guerre—Georgie had had the ribbons specially
tailored in London so that he might display them to full triumphant effect
during his speaking tour. An unusual self-consciousness at the last minute
persuaded him to appear without them. And after being rebuked at the
party the other evening, he was reluctant to pose in them now. When at
last he relented, the resulting photo caught him with a strangely sheepish
smile. The smile conveyed a certain weariness of the role, of the costume.
In this period when public acclaim most entitled him to preen, Georgie
seemed to have lost the heart for it.

At age twenty-three, on the threshold of his career, he'd declared to
Beatrice, "I am *not* a *patriot*"; he would fight for any country against any
country (except his own), for his goal was glory, not national service. His
attitude changed, however. "I discovered something about myself," he told
his wife during his vacation at home in 1945. "I discovered that I am a
patriot." In less than ten months of combat his Third Army had suffered
a quarter-million casualties (battle and nonbattle), including 21,000 killed
in action, soldiers whose sacrifice he'd demanded and commended in
America's name. Georgie's revelation of his own patriotism, however
belated, clearly had dispelled much of his earlier haughtiness. If it seemed
somewhat improvised, an after-the-fact ennobling of his ambitions and
achievements, it was perhaps more valid for having arisen out of persuasive
experience rather than out of dutiful homage to vague inherited history.
Yet discovering patriotic feeling within himself seemed to bring him no

satisfaction. Perhaps it was too obviously momentous, a lesson of humility he'd needed to learn, after which learning he was, as it were, free to go.

Except he didn't want to go. He didn't want to stop fighting. He'd written Beatrice in May that peace would be "a tremendous letdown." For months he'd been seeking reassignment to the Pacific once hostilities ended in Europe. He was prepared even to command a single division after having commanded more than thirty. MacArthur rejected the idea, unwilling to make room in his theater of operations for a general whose celebrity rivaled his own.

Denied the opportunity to take Berlin or Prague in favor of the Soviet Army approaching from the east, Georgie lamented that the war had "petered out" instead of climaxing in some final epic conquest. On May 9, the day peace terms went into effect, he'd begged the visiting U.S. Under Secretary of War not to transfer frontline units home. America's mission of liberation, he said, was incomplete as long as forces of the Soviet Union occupied Eastern Europe. Georgie's recommendation?

Tell the [Soviets] where their border is, and give them a limited time to get back across. Warn them that if they fail to do so, we will push them back across it.

We did not come over here to acquire jurisdiction over either the people or their countries. We came to give them back the right to govern themselves. We must either finish the job—while we are here and ready—or later under less favorable circumstances.

His vociferous mistrust of Soviet postwar intentions would seem prescient in the light of future events. In violation of agreements made at the Potsdam Conference in July 1945, the Soviet Union did not later withdraw its army and restore the nations of Eastern Europe to self-rule. Its thwarted attempt in 1948 to isolate and annex West Berlin led to the creation of the North Atlantic Treaty Organization to contain further Soviet territorial expansion. The subsequent forty-year Cold War between the Soviet Union and the West disrupted millions of lives and cost untold trillions of dollars.

But to credit political insight as the entire basis of Georgie's largely accurate reading of Soviet intentions ignores the intrinsic link of his political views with his personal prejudices and predilections. Russians were nothing but "recently civilized Mongolian savages" with "devious Oriental minds." As for their massive army, he'd long maintained that the Soviet Union "can't piss a drop in the military sense." He told the under secretary that "in the type of fighting I could give them," the Soviet Army would survive maybe five days. "After that it would make no difference how many million men they have, and if you wanted Moscow, I could give it to you." The statement was an honest if hyperbolic assessment of the Third Army's combat capability at war's end, which many historians have rated as second to none. Beneath its boastfulness, however, the statement reflected Georgie's anxiety about his future should his fighting days truly be over. The under secretary was not encouraging. "You have lost sight of the big picture," he said.

The pessimism that subsequently settled on Georgie colored his interpretation of portents and omens to which he always was attuned. During the war, close encounters with death signified to him that his good fortune was holding, that his life was still charmed. "I have no premonitions and hope to live for ever," he'd proclaimed buoyantly before the Sicily invasion. Likewise, after four German artillery shells exploded near him during one of his periods in Eisenhower's disfavor, he rejoiced to his wife, "The Lord had a perfect cut for me and pulled his punch. . . . You have no idea how much that near miss cheered me up. I know I am needed!"

But as the war drew to a close, he interpreted similar episodes to mean his store of luck, like sands in an hourglass, was dwindling to its last grains. In April 1945 his passenger plane was mistakenly shot at by a British Spitfire. A few weeks later, he barely avoided an ox cart careening down a side street. Rather than revive his sense of destiny, these incidents seemed to foreshadow his downfall, contributing to his depression. "Some times," he wrote, "I feel that I may be nearing the end of this life."

Beatrice, remembering her husband's changed behavior after World War I, anticipated a recurrence after this war. As early as November 1944, he'd written her that Germany was beaten, that if given enough fuel and free rein he could end the war within weeks. However, to her letter savoring their eventual reunion, Georgie's response was cautionary: "I too hope we can have fun together again hunting and sailing but I guess I will be hard to live with. I have been a sort of demi god too long."

The couple sometimes had felt awkward together following long separations. Georgie's new fame threatened to widen the distance between them. Yet Beatrice, in her way, had participated as never before in his combat efforts and his subsequent popular rise, preparing her to meet him on more equal footing than had she stood in quiet support in the background.

As the commanding officer's wife, she was interviewed by the *Washington Post* the day after the successful Torch landings in Morocco in 1942. She told the newspaper she would have liked to be there "shooting at somebody." Of her husband she said proudly (if unrealistically, considering his rank), "I know he landed with the first of them and went on into the fight."

Other newspaper interviews followed. Soon Beatrice was invited to address organizations of the wives of officers and enlisted men. With the experience of one who'd packed her husband for three wars ("I took the other two pretty hard"), she gave advice on how best to endure their spouses' absence and support their efforts overseas: "keep healthy . . . get a regular job of war work . . . when the fighting man is home on leave make a holiday of it, not a family problem study . . . keep your family intact."

Taking her own advice on this last point, Beatrice spent time with her daughter Bee, whose husband, John Waters, was missing in action after the American defeat at Kasserine Pass in Tunisia in 1943. Georgie, who hadn't been involved in the battle, visited the site in search of Waters's remains. Finding nothing, he picked up a spent ammunition clip and sent it to Bee's sons as a memento of their father. Several weeks later he learned that Waters had been captured by the Germans. Georgie's aide summed up Georgie's feelings in a letter to Beatrice: "It certainly lifts a dark feeling we all had. . . . Next job on the calendar is to get him back." Two years later, in an episode of great controversy, Georgie would indeed try to get his son-in-law back.

Waters was transferred to a prison camp in Germany. Bee, living in Washington, went to work for the International Red Cross on behalf of prisoners of war. An enigma to her family, she'd seen little of her parents after her marriage in 1934. Always serious and contained, she'd never been comfortable around Georgie, as if fearing to make a wrong step; his wartime letters to Bee, especially after her husband's capture, were more tenderly expressive than he'd ever been with her in person. Beatrice, aware that Bee lacked the survivor's toughness of Ruth Ellen, described her in her thought book as "slender, straight, and swayed by passing breezes but strong in the time of storm." She was thankful that Bee was holding up reasonably well under the strain of Johnnie's imprisonment, an impression she gathered from an optimistic poem her daughter wrote "To a Prisoner of War":

> For you will return, my darling,
> As sure as the sun will rise,

> To a world that is waiting to greet you
> And kindle the light in your eyes.
>
> This is the prize you'll be given
> When you return to us here:
> The little, safe things of our daily life
> Will be waiting for you, my dear.

Ruth Ellen's husband shipped out for Europe with his artillery battalion in July 1943. She and her (now) two children joined Beatrice at Green Meadows. Together the women ran the estate, dashed for each day's mail and newspapers, and listened to the radio news at night. Beatrice's speaking engagements grew more frequent as Georgie's popularity soared after his successful campaigns in Tunisia and Sicily. She recorded pro-America radio messages for broadcast around the world. She drove to church in a mule cart to set an example of gas rationing and made scrapbooks of newspaper articles about her husband collected by a national clipping service and sent to her each week. "I am so full of his triumph," she wrote, "that I just glow with pride."

Georgie wrote her that on Sicily he'd fought a perfect campaign. He'd been awarded a second Distinguished Service Cross for personally conducting the defense of the town of Gela when it was besieged by enemy counterattack. He'd secured the American Army (and himself) great prestige by audaciously occupying the port city of Messina just hours ahead of British forces under General Bernard Montgomery. Yet a vague tone of foreboding crept into his letters in the weeks following the campaign, leaving Beatrice, despite his triumphs, to puzzle over his "criptic" complaints of anxiety about his professional future.

The fighting continued on the Italian mainland while Georgie languished in Sicily "still unemployed." He sent Beatrice a poem he'd written. Perhaps recognizing it to be, like much of his verse in years past, a symptom of some struggle with doubt on his part, Beatrice set about finding a publisher, knowing it would cheer him. When "God of Battles" appeared in October in *Woman's Home Companion* ("Make strong our souls to conquer,/Give us the victory, Lord"), Georgie brightened a little, calling the poem "pretty good," high praise from him.

A few days after the poem appeared, the radio journalist Drew Pearson reported that during the fighting in Sicily three months earlier, General Patton had slapped two enlisted men suffering from battle fatigue. Patton had been furious to find them in field hospitals being treated alongside wounded troops. He'd called the men cowards and threatened personally to shoot them. Furthermore, Pearson said, the incidents had been covered up by General Eisenhower, who had yet to decide whether Patton should receive a new combat command or be relegated to a stateside assignment. At last Beatrice understood the source of her husband's anxiety.

War correspondents on the scene had known of the slapping incidents since August but had granted Eisenhower's request to bury the scandal in the interest of the war effort. On orders of the supreme commander, Georgie immediately had apologized to the men he'd struck, to the medical personnel who'd witnessed the incidents, and to each division under his command. Since the story had been kept quiet, however, the nation was shocked when Pearson took it public.

Georgie was denounced on the floor of Congress. Newspapers editorialized for his dismissal. Patton, wrote one angry citizen, "has the same heart in him as Adolph Hitler." The image of him wearing a pair of ivory-handled pistols—based on a photograph taken during the Moroccan landings; since then, he'd never worn two pistols at once—was recast from dashing and colorful to cockeyed and fatuous. Journalists who once noted his popularity with his troops now reported that many detested him as a selfish glory hunter. It was a charge he never denied entirely. Glory hunters attack, he said; patriots defend. As for his men's regard for him, Georgie knew it was ultimately based on results alone. "People like to play on a winning team."

He was directed by Eisenhower not to respond publicly to Pearson's report. Beatrice was under no such restriction. "I'm sure Georgie is sorrier and has punished himself more than anyone could realize," she told the *Washington Post*. "But don't you go writing mush about it. I won't have it." Of Pearson himself, she wrote a friend privately, "I am convinced that he is a traitor to America."

At the time of the incidents, Georgie considered the soldiers he struck to be cowards. He said of the second man after ordering him back to the front, "I may have saved his soul if he had one." Any tolerance of malingerers was ruinous to a combat unit, he believed. The sight of casualties in the field hospitals always upset him. To find men without physical wounds being treated beside the severely injured triggered his violent outrage. If there was any excusable rationale for his action, it was, remarkably, the first man he struck who provided it. Said the young private of Georgie, "I think he was suffering a little battle fatigue himself." Georgie himself delivered the final verdict in a letter to Secretary of War Stimson: "There is no possible doubt that my methods were too forthright and very ill chosen. They will not be repeated."

The furor passed. Georgie was not sent home. "That was a near thing, but I feel much better." Then in January 1944, Omar Bradley, his former subordinate, was given command of American ground forces stationed in England preparing for the Normandy invasion. It was a position Georgie had hoped for. Stung, he held tight to his sense of destiny. He told Beatrice later, "I simply did the ostrich act and would neither see nor hear any evil though I did a hell of a lot of thinking." She, on the other hand, raged at this slight against him, *"The only successful U.S. General!"*

But soon Georgie was given Third Army, newly arrived in England. His reaction was measured ("not such a good job, but better than nothing") and determined: "As far as I can remember, this is my twenty-seventh start from zero since entering the U.S. Army. Each time I have made a success of it, and this one must be the biggest."

After Drew Pearson's report, Beatrice even more than Georgie viewed journalists as contemptible adversaries. Recalled Ruth Ellen, "She really began to hate the press the same way she hated undertakers." Forced to defend her husband rather than celebrate him, she curtailed her public appearances. Reporters appeared at her door with combative questions; two of them tried to hire on undercover as laborers at Green Meadows. Crank calls and hate letters replaced the previous fan mail. Newspaper articles about the slapping incidents nauseated her. Turning the scrapbooks over to Ruth Ellen to complete, Beatrice sighed, "Maybe in the light of history we will see how unimportant this is."

While still in North Africa Georgie had predicted that his then favorable press "will turn" one day. Now, training his army in England, he kept his comments to reporters to a terse minimum. Not so with his troops. Since most were inexperienced recruits, Georgie sought to toughen them, to blood them, with language. His speeches were blunt and candid. "You are not all going to die," he often began, addressing every soldier's major concern. "Only two percent of you right here today would die in a major battle." They would likely be frightened in their first battle, "but the real hero is the man who fights even though he is scared." The quickest way to win the war and go home? "Use the means at hand to inflict the maximum amount of wounds, death, and destruction on the enemy in the minimum time," went his written instructions to his officers. Or, as spoken extemporaneously to his enlisted men:

We're not just going to shoot the sons-of-bitches, we're going to murder those lousy Hun bastards by the bushel fucking basket! We are advancing constant-ly and we are not interested in holding on to anything except the enemy's balls. We are going to twist his balls and kick the living shit out of him all the time. We are going to go through him like crap through a goose, like shit through a tinhorn!

No recordings exist of his many Third Army speeches. The various ver-sions as recalled by witnesses agree in tone if not in every word. Most conclude with Georgie's promise that each of his soldiers could look forward someday to relating his exploits to his grandson on his knee. "You can look him straight in the eye and say, 'Son, your granddaddy rode with the great Third Army and a son of a bitch named Georgie Patton!' "

A young officer in attendance at one of these speeches recalled him "literally hypnotizing us with his incomparable, if profane eloquence. When he had finished, you felt as if you had been given a supercharge from some divine source." Eisenhower observed that Georgie's appearances were met "with thunderous applause" from his troops. But according to the historian Martin Blumenson, at least one officer present at a speech deliv-ered in April 1944 felt that Georgie came close to advocating the killing of enemy prisoners. The comment was striking because at the time Geor-gie was under investigation for doing just that in Sicily.

On trial for summarily executing seventy-nine captured German sol-diers, a captain and sergeant had claimed in their defense that Georgie, in addressing their division prior to the Sicily landings, had declared that "if the enemy resisted until we got to within two hundred yards, he had forfeited his right to live." Though admitting to military investigators that his speeches "could be pretty bloody," Georgie insisted—and colleagues corroborated—that he'd never condoned the killing of prisoners, espe-cially since his son-in-law was a prisoner of war. He was exonerated. The accused men were convicted, given suspended sentences, and returned to their units. Both were killed in action later.

As the matter subsided, Georgie dashed off an irritated note to Beatrice: "Some fair-haired boys are trying to say that I killed too many prisoners. Yet the same people cheer at the far greater killing of Japs. Well, the more I killed, the fewer men I lost, but they dont think of that. Sometimes I think that I will quit and join a monestary." The note compares with his statement, written in 1918, that in the heat of the Meuse-Argonne battle he may have killed an American soldier with a shovel. Without further explanation or documentation, Georgie's recollections of the incident at the Meuse-Argonne and, years later, of the murdering of prisoners in Sicily, inject ugly mystery into his story. Perhaps ultimately both episodes, together with his slapping of the shellshocked soldiers, say as much about war as they do about Georgie. "Wars are not won by apparent virtue," he wrote in 1943, "else I would be in a hell of a fix."

The potentially dire charge of condoning the killing of prisoners was dropped without consequence to him. But a seemingly trivial three-minute speech to some British clubwomen came near to ending his career. He suggested to the women that it was "the evident destiny of the British and Americans, and of course the Russians, to rule the world"—or so he recalled the next day. But coverage of the speech in America claimed that he'd neglected to mention the Russians and hence jeopardized the fragile alliance among the three nations. The floor of Congress rang with accusations that he was irresponsible and mischievous. Newspaper editors and columnists again called for his dismissal.

Stunned that his comments had created such a furor, Georgie waited in vain for his superiors on the general staff to speak in his defense. "None of those at Ike's headquarters ever go to bat for juniors. Benedict Arnold is a piker compared with them." It seemed that Eisenhower, fed up with "the immature character of [Patton's] public actions," and under pressure of planning the Normandy invasion, might actually fire him as a result of what Georgie firmly believed was "a frame-up" by the American press. "It is a horrid thought that one may be deprived of doing the only job one is good at," he wrote Ruth Ellen fearfully: "I have never asked a favor or shunned a detail or spared my neck, the soldiers think I am wonderful, but the Press??? Bah! Jesus only suffered one night but I have had months and months of it, and the cross is not yet in sight, though probably just around the corner." If only given the chance to perform in battle, "all will be well," he wrote. He wouldn't hesitate to risk his life in order to succeed. "A nice clean grave would be better than surviving another victory." Ruth Ellen wrote her Aunt Nita, "Gosh, I wish they would invade before something worse happens to him."

Summoned to a meeting with Eisenhower, he offered to step down as Third Army commander. If reduced in rank as punishment for his impolitic remarks to the clubwomen, Georgie demanded to command an assault regiment in the upcoming invasion. He also, rather amazingly under the circumstances, took the opportunity to criticize the supreme commander's invasion plan. Georgie left the meeting with his future still uncertain. "I don't think anyone could tell that I had just been killed. All the way home, 5 hours, I recited poetry to myself."

He waited two days for the verdict. He felt like a Thanksgiving turkey, he said, and broke out "in a cold sweat" each time the telephone rang. Eisenhower's telegram came on May 3: "I have decided to keep you." Georgie wrote his wife in elation, "Well the Lord came through again but I was really badly frightened. I have youthed thirty years since my last letter."

As a result of Patton's latest indiscretion, the Senate delayed its confirmation of his promotion to permanent major general. Beatrice followed the committee hearings closely. She projected each senator beforehand as favorable or unfavorable to her husband's promotion. Senator Downey of California was "apparently favorable." Senator Truman of Missouri: "Professes to be a great admirer." Senator Wallgren of Washington: "Loud-mouthed ignoramus." Which was to say, unfavorable.

Georgie and some advance elements of his army arrived in France on July 6, 1944, a month after the Normandy invasion. On August 1, Third Army became operational in France and began its plunge south and west from Normandy into the Brittany peninsula, then east on its fabled drive across the German Army's southern flank toward Luxembourg and eventually Germany.

Georgie's public image swiftly improved. "A fiction writer couldn't create him," one newsman trilled. "He's dynamite. On a battlefield, he's a warring, roaring comet." The Senate moved to reconsider his promotion to permanent major general. Georgie was thrilled to be back in action. His only complaints were about his superiors, Eisenhower, Bradley, and Montgomery, slowing him down because of "imaginary dangers." He wrote Beatrice, "God deliver us from our friends. We can handle the enemy."

Dozens of books would eventually be written about Third Army operations in 1944 to 1945. Broadly speaking, these operations consisted of four campaigns. The first was the August breakout from Normandy, which generated splashy headlines and set Georgie to wondering if the war might be won in ten days. The second campaign began in September when Third Army encountered intensified resistance along the French-German border near Luxembourg. That autumn, as his cross-country dash slowed to a town by town, village by village, grinding war of attrition, Georgie frequently "earned my pay" by "convincing people who think they are beaten that they are not beaten." Sometimes he accomplished this with rage, as when he scolded three generals for not gaining their objectives. "To make up for their shortcomings," he directed them to lead the next attack personally and victoriously, "or not come back."

Yet Georgie was freer with praise than with fury. He took pains to soothe the bruised egos and reward the successes of his junior officers. He was renowned for giving succinct orders, defining the objective but leaving the tactical planning to commanders in the field—simple instructions, along with a decentralized command structure, promoted individual initiative, he believed. Realizing that his dominating presence could make his officers self-conscious and jittery, he limited his visits to the front "except when things are tight, in which case I go up every day." He particularly avoided areas where the fighting was proceeding well, lest he appear to be meddling or taking the credit. And noting that "it is loyalty from the top to the bottom which binds juniors to their seniors," Georgie was steadfastly loyal to his subordinates, berating many but relieving very few for lapses in performance. Believing that his own superiors had sometimes undermined his self-confidence with their lack of support for him, Georgie was careful not to inhibit his men with undue fear of losing their jobs. He wanted them to take chances. He wanted them to have faith in themselves.

By November, his army had dislodged most of the enemy from the fortified cities east of the Meuse River in France's Lorraine province. The effort had been protracted and difficult, at times forcing Georgie to curb his vaunted aggressiveness. (He delayed one attack on a German fort outside the city of Metz because "the glory of taking the fort is not worth the sacrifices in men which it would demand.") But now the way seemed clear to cross the Saar River into Germany.

On December 9, while battling winter weather and the entrenched enemy, Georgie noted in his diary that he suspected the German Army was "building up east" of the U.S. First Army eighty miles to Georgie's north. Having then prepared his units to "be in position to meet whatever happens," Georgie was able to react with extraordinary swiftness to news, on December 16, of a massive enemy push through the heart of the advancing Allied front. Historians have called the Battle of the Bulge Georgie's finest hour as a commander. He'd gained fame as a master of offensive exploitation. Yet he most clearly displayed his military virtuosity in what was, initially at least, a defensive maneuver. In just a few days and nights, he shifted his huge army from an eastward advance and wheeled it 90 degrees for a thrust due north to relieve American troops besieged in the town of Bastogne.

PATTON OF COURSE, headlined a *Washington Post* editorial on December 30: "It has become a sort of unwritten rule in this war that when there is a fire to be put out, it is Patton who jumps into his boots, slides down the pole, and starts rolling." The enormity of his success was not lost on Georgie. "Perhaps God saved me for this effort," he wrote Beatrice.

The repulse of the German attack in the Battle of the Bulge signaled the Allies' eventual victory. "Remember," Georgie asked Beatrice, "how a tarpon always makes one big flop just before he dies?" In February 1945, Third Army turned east and commenced its fourth and final campaign of the war, driving across central Germany into Czechoslovakia, where in April Georgie was ordered to cease his advance fifty miles west of Prague.

His public image, though still lofty, took a significant drop in March. During Third Army's fourth campaign of the war, the eastward drive across central Germany, Georgie sent a small task force forty miles behind German lines to liberate a prisoner-of-war camp in Hammelburg. Most of the three hundred Americans in the task force were wounded or captured. Nine were killed. All of its tanks and equipment were destroyed. The press reported that the force was wiped out and suggested that its mission had been whimsical and self-serving: to liberate the Hammelburg camp because Georgie's son-in-law John Waters was rumored to be imprisoned there. Though Georgie couldn't know for certain whether Waters was there, he'd optimistically referred to the camp as "John's place" in a letter to Beatrice several days before dispatching the task force. When questioned afterward about his reasons for conceiving the ill-fated raid, he was deliberately vague about his suspicions of his son-in-law's presence at Hammelburg. The camp was liberated by Seventh Army a week later. Waters was found severely wounded but alive after more than two years of imprisonment.

Interestingly, the task force, though failing in its mission, was a tactical success precisely because it was so risky and illogical. German commanders thought the raid heralded a sudden Third Army thrust toward Hammelburg. They diverted three divisions to meet the thrust, opening the way, quite accidentally, for the Third Army's Fourth Armored Division to proceed unopposed through nearly a hundred miles of territory vacated by the three enemy divisions. German commanders reacted as they did because they'd come to expect the unexpected from Georgie. He never moved his army en masse along a single front. He used maneuver and surprise to get units behind enemy positions. "Fire from the rear is more deadly and three times more effective than fire from the front." Enveloping actions cut off the enemy's retreat; perhaps the greatest testament to Georgie's tactical success was the 300,000 prisoners captured by Third Army in eight months of combat, more than were captured by any other Allied army. The Hammelburg raid seemed to the Germans to be another of his unpredictable sweeps behind their lines that since August 1944 had so confounded them.

Its unforeseen benefits notwithstanding, Georgie regarded the Hammelburg raid as his biggest mistake of the war: he should have sent a larger force, he believed. As to his idea for the raid itself, his military position as "sort of a demi god," a position giving him the power to make such life and death decisions each day, no doubt had made the rescue of the American prisoners, his son-in-law included, too tempting to resist. The subsequent scandal quickly vanished in the general euphoria over the approaching end of the war. But it recalled Georgie's earlier troubles with inquiring reporters and presaged more troubles to come. "How I hate the press," he wrote Beatrice wearily.

She didn't note the Hammelburg raid in her thought book. She'd written very little of Georgie since her husband's heady days during the Bulge. Possibly her reticence was due to the reappearance in Georgie's life of Jean Gordon, her half-niece with whom Beatrice suspected Georgie of having an affair more than eight years ago in Hawaii.

To maintain appearances of family propriety, Beatrice had stonily endured Jean's presence as a bridesmaid at Ruth Ellen's wedding in 1940. Trusting that Jean would keep her distance from Georgie thereafter, Beatrice had been alarmed to learn in August 1944 that Jean had volunteered as a Red Cross clubmobile worker attached to Third Army. She wrote Georgie of her concern about the arrangement. He replied that the first he'd heard of it was from Beatrice's letter. With a trace of sarcasm he said he was "in the middle of a battle so don't meet people. So don't worry."

According to Everett Hughes, Georgie's West Point classmate now on Eisenhower's staff, Jean contacted Georgie when he was still in England a month earlier and Georgie then visited her in London. "She's been mine for twelve years," Hughes recorded Georgie telling him later. Jean's clubmobile unit remained with Third Army through the end of the war. At home with their mother, Ruth Ellen and George sensed but didn't inquire into Beatrice's tight-lipped consternation. Rarely expressive of her inner feelings, Beatrice can only have felt helpless and perhaps even foolish to complain about a matter that seemed trivial in comparison to her husband's headline-making exploits in Europe. She loved him, was his most ardent and patient advocate. To think he'd had an affair with Jean in 1936 hurt Beatrice terribly. For Jean now to be with him in his moment of triumph mixed that pain with fury.

When Beatrice again raised the matter in a letter to her husband in March 1945, he was in no mind to discuss Jean. "I have seen her in the company of other Red Cross [girls], but I am not a fool, so quit worrying." Not a fool, he meant, for his often adversarial relationship with journalists made Georgie wary of putting himself into any compromising personal position that, if publicized, might ruin his career.

It isn't known whether Georgie and Beatrice, when they were reunited in June 1945, resolved or even discussed the matter of Jean's role in his life overseas; or if, as might be supposed, it caused some tension between them. What is known is that he was glad to leave the States and return to Europe—as indicated by a comment made by Georgie's personal orderly Sergeant George Meeks, who accompanied him on his 1945 trip home.

Meeks, a black man, had served with Georgie since 1938. In keeping with the old adage that no man is a hero to his valet, Meeks had a relationship with Georgie unlike anyone else. "Sure he takes it from me," Meeks once told a reporter. "I just tell him to sit and be quiet for a while. He never raises his voice at me. He's soft-spoken and a great gentleman." On the plane back to Europe, the sergeant seemed to detect his boss's dissatisfaction with their just-concluded vacation. "General," he said, "we have sure done our thirty days!"—in jail, he meant. Georgie nodded. "I had a similar feeling," he wrote later.

For Georgie, the shock of peacetime that many veterans experience was intensified because he was happy in war, his happiness a sort of steady state in which his swings between feeling good and feeling bad were only incidental anomalies in a prevailing condition of total engagement in life. Between the wars, those mood swings had virtually defined Georgie's existence to deleterious effect. Without a world war to give them a vast and appropriately awesome arena in which to play out, he could not expect to survive very contentedly or very long. He'd already expressed doubt that "hunting and sailing" could sufficiently absorb and satisfy him after World

War II. Perhaps—and perhaps out of honest concern for them—he had similar doubts about his wife and family.

One evening shortly before he returned to Europe, Georgie waited until Beatrice was out of the room, then addressed Bee and Ruth Ellen privately. "I'm not going to see you again," he told them. "I'll be seeing your mother, but I won't be seeing you."

They said he was being silly. "The war is over! You'll be home in a few months for good."

He shook his head. "I've been very lucky, but I've used it all up. It's too damn bad I wasn't killed when the fighting stopped, but I wasn't." He shrugged. "So be it."

Knowing their father's taste for drama, they tried to laugh off this dire parting. Ruth Ellen, recalling his favorite verse from Revelations ("Him that overcometh will I make a pillar in the temple of my God, and he shall go no more out"), playfully asked her father, "Are you ready to become a pillar?"

He was not. "I need a few more times around the wheel."

The exchange left his daughters confused. "I don't think either of us quite believed him," Ruth Ellen wrote later. But Georgie was serious. "Take care of your little brother," he said to them. "And tell John and Jim to take care of you."

An Ironical Thing

ENIED a transfer to the Pacific, Georgie had hoped for an assignment training troops in the States or teaching at the Army War College. The one assignment he didn't want was to be military governor of Third Army's sector of occupation in southeastern Germany.

The military governor was charged with seeking out and removing all former Nazis from their wartime positions as party officials, businessmen, and civil servants until each could be investigated and possibly prosecuted for his part in Hitler's regime. At the same time, the governor was to manage the welfare of the rest of the population under his jurisdiction, which in Third Army's sector included more than 7 million civilians and 1.5 million German Army prisoners, and to restore their shattered society to the beginnings of self-sustenance before the onset of winter. Finally, he was to provide shelter, food, and care to thousands of traumatized refugees liberated from Bavaria's concentration camps. Though these duties were not necessarily in contradiction with one another, to perform them successfully would require a politically deft, discerning, and sensitive administrator. Eisenhower gave Georgie the job.

"I am still confused as to just what to do," Georgie wrote his wife after returning to Germany in July. By late September his confusion had not diminished. He expected to be fired soon, and he considered the prospect "perhaps fortunate." She shouldn't bother mailing him Christmas presents. "If I am not relieved by that time, I shall try and get a leave."

Sparking his pessimism about keeping his job was a report two days earlier in *The New York Times* quoting him as suggesting that it was "silly" to rid the German bureaucracy of "the most intelligent people" in Germany. The statement supported a growing suspicion, particularly in America's liberal press, that Georgie was being lax in his duty to ferret out former Nazis because of some secret sympathy for them. He denied the charge. No one was responsible for killing more Nazis than he, he said. Yet his denials remained unconvincing for the simple reason that there was some truth to the charge. He was indeed opposed to entirely dismantling the German military and the Nazi government structure.

With some justification, Georgie believed that to arrest every Nazi Party member would decimate the civil bureaucracy and leave it unable to provide even minimal services of utilities and transportation to the German people. He'd suggested the previous May that most Nazis had wielded no more real power than Democrats and Republicans in America. Reconsidering his remark, he'd asked reporters present not to print it.

His interest in preserving the German society's ability to function was in part humanitarian. Yet it stemmed as well from his anticipation of a coming war with the Soviet Union, for he expected that war to be waged with a rebuilt Germany as America's ally. During his recent visit to America he'd seen how war weary his countrymen were; his colleagues in the War Department had depressed him with their focus on demobilization instead of on maintaining combat readiness. In the face of these "horrors of peace," he clung to the fighting-and-killing values that had served him so well against the German Army and would do so against the Soviets. His premonitions of downfall and death reflected his understanding that those values were out of step with the times. Yet he kept on behaving as if war were not only inevitable but welcome. His opinions and indeed his whole violent persona struck many observers as alarmingly reactionary, and others as merely pathetic.

His soldiers, more of them leaving for home each day, no longer listened transfixed to his fiery orations. It didn't matter that once he'd impressed them as a consistent battlefield winner. As one man in attendance recalled, "They had come to a parting of the ways with Patton and all that he stood for." His "sulphurous son-of-a-bitching," once inspiring to green troops, seemed to these veterans a crude and obvious pose. Georgie, too, felt his magic had gone. He wrote Beatrice of feeling exhausted, an admission unheard of in the past. His exhaustion was more than physical. "It is hell to be old and passé and know it."

Georgie complained about the Allies' postwar intention to convert Germany into a deindustrialized, agrarian society of no possible threat to world security. To impose such restrictions would ensure economic disaster, he believed, sparking a Communist uprising. As it turned out, the plan to deindustrialize Germany would be abandoned in 1948 when, under George Marshall's European Recovery Program, Germany began receiving billions of dollars in American aid to rebuild its industries for reasons not dissimilar to the one Georgie gave in 1945: "Germany should not be destroyed but rather rebuilt as a buffer against the real danger, which is Bolshevism from Russia."

However, as with his seemingly prescient interpretation of Soviet postwar intentions, Georgie's argument for rebuilding Germany drew more from personal concerns than from geopolitical acumen. A disarmed, pastoral, impoverished Germany would be a useless ally in a war with the Soviet Union, a war he longed to fight because he could imagine nothing else as fulfilling. Extend Germany a helping hand, he proposed; embrace its people as honorable foes turned allies in a new cause. In addition to appealing to his hopes for the future, the arrangement appealed to his romantic sense of the past. Alexander the Great often put rulers he conquered back on their thrones, demanding tribute but not their heads. Ulysses Grant granted generous terms of surrender to Robert E. Lee at Appomattox. Georgie himself had left the Vichy French in power after defeating them in Morocco, trusting in handshakes and champagne toasts to keep his former adversaries peaceable after he moved on to his next campaign.

The distinction between those models of forgiveness and the one he advocated with Germany was the unprecedented level of human atrocity perpetrated by the Nazis. The extent of those atrocities had become known to the world in the spring of 1945 when the first concentration camps were liberated by Allied forces. Georgie saw firsthand the evidence of Nazi brutality when he toured the concentration camps at Ohrdruf Nord and Buchenwald. The sight of thousands of emaciated bodies, living and dead, gave shocking testimony to the mass starvation, torture, and murder conducted there. "Words are inadequate to express the horror of these institutions," he wrote.

His first response was to have his troops visit the camps "to know what kind of people they are fighting." He then directed the local townspeople to be marched past the stacks of corpses and was not surprised nor displeased when the town mayor and his wife went home and hanged themselves. To irrefutably record "the horror details," he brought journalists to the camps "to build up another page of the necessary evidence as to the brutality of the Germans." This was in April. International outrage over these atrocities led to the initiation of criminal proceedings against the perpetrators. Yet by autumn, Georgie's initial reaction of vengeful horror had softened to an unrealistic, even cavalier attitude of forgive and forget. "I am frankly opposed to this war criminal stuff. It is not cricket and is semitic."

The injection of anti-Semitism into his perception of the political dynamics of the occupation signaled his ultimate loss of moral bearings. His position against the deindustrialization of Germany was defensible on the practical grounds of creating a viable buffer to Soviet expansion (though obviously it was not defensible on grounds of Georgie's merely self-interested wish to participate in another war). Too, the summary removal of all mid- and low-level Nazi bureaucrats was at least questionable, as was sending captured German troops to France to rebuild its roads and cities: both policies seemed fair reparation on one hand, legally suspect on the other. Even the U.S. government order, received by Georgie in August, to give Jews "special accommodations" over other displaced persons liberated from Nazi concentration camps was debatable on grounds of fairness to all Hitler's victims. If disagreement with the order failed to recognize the singular horror of the Jewish Holocaust, it nonetheless was shared by many Americans besides Georgie. Yet in his case, when he self-righteously complained "Why not Catholics, Mormons, etc?" his argument was debased by his privately acknowledged anti-Semitism.

His sweeping public pronouncements about due process and fair play and forgiving one's enemies, invoked in the name of "my Anglo-Saxon conscience," in fact only masked his resentment that his career and lifelong pursuit of glory had "petered out" with the war instead of climaxing in some thrilling coronation. Surely someone was to blame for this disappointment. "The more I see of people I regret that I survived the war," he grumbled. Who were these people causing his regret, his cynicism? As Georgie saw it in the first months of occupation, they were just about anyone, whether American, Allied, or German, who might be construed as an enemy of his values and ambitions, "mostly fascists, Communists, and SOB's assorted." But eventually his frequent disparagement of Jews in his diary and private letters indicated that he'd found a new villain.

Several Jews served on Georgie's headquarters staff and never detected any personal bias on his part against them. For his help in tutoring Georgie's son for his West Point reentrance examination, Professor Jacob Silverman got a note from Georgie expressing thanks for Silverman's academic instruction and also for his "psychological influence" on young George IV. Georgie's impression of some Jewish doctors tending the displaced persons in the refugee camps was that they "seemed to be men of very high personal and technical capacity." But he wrote in the same diary entry, "The Jewish type of DP is, in the majority of cases, a sub-human species without any of the cultural refinements of our time. . . . Practically all of them had the flat brownish gray eye common among the Hawaiians which, to my mind, indicates very low intelligence." Such crackpot "ethnology" recalled his analyses of Mexican, Sicilian, and Arab culture and echoed the bigotry his father had espoused years ago, especially in times when Papa's self-esteem was at an ebb.

Adding to Georgie's virulence was his belief that these Jewish DP's, though "lower than animals," were the reason his call for a swift reconciliation with Germany and a subsequent confrontation with the Soviets was being thwarted. As he saw it, on behalf of these shabby and hardly significant Jewish peasants, influential Jews in America, together with "the non-Aryan press," were spreading "a virus . . . of a Semitic revenge against all Germans," leaving the country vulnerable to anarchy, unrest, and Communism. He didn't support the "dismemberment" of Germany, he said, because Germans were "the only decent people left in Europe"—a distinctly minority viewpoint in 1945.

At his news conferences he muttered complainingly about Eisenhower's de-Nazification order while emphasizing how strongly he was following orders. Under his governorship more than 60,000 former Nazis had been removed from office since May; in spending most of his time hunting and traveling, his attitude toward the policy was more indifferent than protesting, willfully ignorant rather than actively subversive. Yet his clear misgivings alerted reporters to a burgeoning conflict between Patton and Eisenhower, and they went after that story in earnest.

Later it would be claimed by Georgie's press officer, Major Ernest C. Deane (and corroborated by correspondent Frank E. Mason of the North American Newspaper Alliance), that three of the reporters at Georgie's news conference of September 22 had worked out a plan to "get" Patton, "plotting at breakfast that morning before the press conference to needle the general and make him lose his temper." If there was indeed such a plan, it isn't hard to see why. His right-wing posturings aside (which in themselves probably won him few fans in the press corps), Georgie's contrived, hard-boiled grandeur invited debunking. He'd dominated Third Army news briefings during the war; confidence in himself as a combat leader had made for an ease in dealing with journalists that no doubt struck many of them as condescending and arrogant. After armistice, he'd maintained his aggressive public persona. However, without the intimidating aura of brute competence that war had conferred on him, this performance appeared increasingly labored and hollow.

Georgie disliked his occupation duties, he was confused by them, he was ignorant of them. He was tired, bitter, and fearful of the future. Most of all, he was alone. His main advocates of recent years had other concerns now. Omar Bradley was in America heading the Veterans Administration; Eisenhower was preparing to leave Europe to become army chief of staff while paying careful attention to his possible future political prospects— certainly neither man cared to grapple with the problems of occupation. Georgie was vulnerable and knew it. He spoke of resigning, of telling everyone to "kiss my ass." But concluding that to quit "would simply discredit me to no purpose," he hung on.

So if some reporters prepared some needling tactics for Georgie's September 22 news briefing—to blow cigarette smoke in his face, to pepper him with twisty questions—it was hardly necessary. In substance, the briefing revealed little that was new: he defended his enforcement of Eisenhower's de-Nazification policy even as he criticized the policy—but his criticism this time was less discreet than in the past. "Something was gnawing his guts," recalled one of Georgie's staff members. "Patton barked out the first things that happened to come into his head. Lunch that noon was a serious affair. Everyone had a notion that the fat was now in the fire."

Georgie reflected on the news briefing later that day with the sluggish foreboding of a boxer who knows he's been hurt. The press always had been on his side, he wrote with rather touching naïveté. "Today there was very apparent hostility. The temerity of the newspaper man in suggesting that he knew more about [de-Nazification] than I do, although I know nothing, made me mad which I think is what they wanted."

Although I know nothing . . . In the past such a candid disclaimer had somewhat redeemed his fascistic-seeming political pronouncements and his carelessness in matters of finance and family relationships. But now, though the spotlight remained on him, the stage on which he stood had changed. The century had seen its second world war, had seen the Holocaust and the atomic bomb. A man in Georgie's position could no longer, as he'd done after slapping the soldiers on Sicily, do "an ostrich act" and hope to evade through charm or professed ignorance or sheepish apology the ramifications of his actions and utterances. At age fifty-nine it was time for him to grow up.

But he was stubborn. At the news briefing he snapped off answers and, in a crucial misstep, didn't disavow his earlier statement likening Nazi Party members to Republicans and Democrats. So incautious was he, Major Deane felt Georgie was deliberately self-destructive. "There is no denying that General Patton," he said, "put himself into the hands of his enemies."

Reports of the briefing, highlighted with his Republican-Democrat comment, appeared nationally in America the next day. Follow-up stories extremely critical of Georgie's management of de-Nazification in Bavaria brought pressure on Eisenhower to relieve his belligerent subordinate. On September 27 Eisenhower informed Georgie of his decision to "transfer" him to the head of Fifteenth Army, a paper army consisting of a small staff writing a military history of World War II. Later Georgie told Beatrice, "I was terribly hurt for a few days but am normal again." Her own thought book account of his firing was brief: "G. relieved from 3d Army thru Eisenhower's cowardice toward press. Crucified and thrown to wolves. Not one voice was raised in his defense."

Georgie's parting ceremonies were held at Third Army headquarters. "Nothing in his dress or bearing reflected the torture of his soul," recalled one observer. " 'All good things must come to an end' was the burden of his brief remarks."

Less than two weeks later, occupation authorities announced that "between 2 and 5 percent" of former German Nazis would be permitted to stay in office lest the society fall into chaos.

Georgie arranged to go home before Christmas. He didn't expect to return to Europe, hoping for a better assignment than the command of Fifteenth Army. Denied that, he would retire from the army to fox hunt, shoot, and sail.

He was due to fly to the States on December 10, a month after his sixtieth birthday. The day before leaving, he went to hunt pheasant near the town of Mannheim on the Rhine River. On the way, his Cadillac limousine was cut off at an intersection by a U.S. Signal Corps truck and struck in its right front quarter. Neither vehicle was traveling fast. Only Georgie was injured.

In typical fashion, he was perched on the edge of the backseat so to better see and be seen. The impact of the collision threw him forward. He cut his forehead on the ceiling light and broke his nose and neck when his head hit the driver's partition. He told one of his companions, General Hobart Gay, "Work my fingers for me." After Gay did so for a moment, Georgie said, "Go ahead, Hap. Work my fingers."

Rushed by ambulance to a military hospital in Heidelberg, Georgie disarmed the hospital staff with his good spirits despite the pain of his scalp wound and broken neck. "Relax, gentlemen," he said, sensing their nervousness at his rank and reputation. "I'm in no condition to be a terror now." And to the physician taking down his medical history, as Georgie mentioned his several concussions and horse kicks in the head: "Do you think it shows?"

The Associated Press telephoned Beatrice with news of the accident. "Critically hurt and paralyzed from neck down," she scribbled in her thought book. "I determined to go to Germany at once." She flew by military plane with Colonel R. Glen Spurling, the army's leading neurosurgeon. They were met at the airport near Heidelberg by a limousine driven, at Georgie's request, by the same driver who'd been at the wheel when Georgie was hurt. It was the best way, Georgie felt, to assure the man that he didn't blame him for what had happened.

He said to Beatrice when she entered his hospital room, "This may be the last time we see each other." She was upbeat, insisting that his doctors were optimistic. They never spoke of death again. Beatrice could take the hard truth, that wasn't the problem. But she expected Georgie to fight and win, and he didn't want to disappoint her. He'd already told his nurses that he was going to die, that he was ready to die.

Doctor Spurling advised him privately that the best Georgie could hope for was a life of "semi-invalidism." For the moment, his condition had to be stabilized, his fractured vertebrae aligned, his strength restored through nourishment and rest. Spurling hoped to move him to a stateside hospital at the end of the month. Georgie observed to the doctor that after surviving steeplechasing, polo, his own clumsy mishaps, and three wars, "This is an ironical thing to have happen to me."

For nearly two weeks he lay immobilized in traction—at times in a head and neck brace, at times with metal hooks inserted into his cheekbones and drawn tight under ten pounds of pressure. A trio of nurses fed him liquid meals like a newborn baby, adjusted his catheter, examined his extremities in vain for hints of movement or feeling. They thought him "cute" when his mood was positive, only slightly "fussy" when he was down; he was a model patient, they said. Beatrice spent her days reading him books and the hundreds of letters and telegrams that poured into the hospital from dignitaries and common folk around the world. Georgie's car accident and subsequent struggle were headline news in America. The criticism he'd received over the past few months was replaced with praise and sympathy.

He had increasing difficulty breathing. His heart beat erratically under the strain of fluid accumulating in his lungs. He had long painful coughing spasms as he tried to clear his chest. Blood appeared in his sputum on December 19, indicating a possible lung embolism. Though continuing to fight for Beatrice's sake, he confided to his nurse that he wished only to sleep. "Why don't they just let me die?" The plaintive question turned to a declaration on December 21. "I am going to die," Georgie told his nurse. "Today."

"Prognosis negative." This was the last report conveyed by the War Department to Bee and Ruth Ellen at their homes in Washington, D.C. On the night of December 21 they each went to bed resigned to the inevitable news of their father's death. The telephone rang at Bee's bedside after midnight. The connection was fuzzy with static—evidently an overseas call. "Hello?" Bee said. She could barely make out the response: "Little Bee, are you all right?" "Daddy?" she said, shaking off sleep. "Daddy?" The line went dead. She immediately dialed the overseas operator to reconnect the line. The operator told her that no call had been placed to Bee's number.

At 2:10 A.M. that same night, Ruth Ellen roused from sleep and glanced across her darkened bedroom to the embroidered bench in front of the bay window. As she described it later, Georgie lay across the bench with his head propped on his arm. He was in uniform. He gave a smile, "his very own," and then was gone. Ruth Ellen checked the time on her alarm clock before lying back down on her pillow. She phoned her sister the next morning. They told each other what had happened to them. "I guess he's dead then," Ruth Ellen said. "Poor Ma," said Bee.

George IV began his Christmas leave from West Point on December 22. At New York's Grand Central Station, before boarding a train to Washington to join his sisters for the holiday, he saw a newspaper boy selling the latest edition. "Patton Dies Quietly in Sleep" was the headline.

On the train George read his father's obituary and of his last hours alive. A memorial service was to be held the next day, with interment to follow on December 24 (George IV's birthday) at the U.S. military cemetery at Hamm, Luxembourg. By Eisenhower's order, all American soldiers who died in Europe during the war were to be buried where they fell—now Georgie was one of them. Beatrice Patton, accompanied by her brother Fred Ayer, who'd joined her in Europe several days earlier, would represent the family at the funeral ceremony.

There were practical reasons—time constraints, travel difficulties—why the Patton children didn't hasten to attend their father's funeral. But future reflection pointed to one unspoken, overriding assumption. Their mother did not wish them to be there. The funeral was Beatrice's last moment with Georgie. She didn't want to share it.

Almost 170 years earlier, Georgie's great-great-great-grandfather, General Hugh Mercer of the Revolutionary War, had determined, in his own words, "to die as I had lived" by refusing to surrender to his British foes at the battle of Princeton. The day after Georgie's death from a pulmonary embolism, his doctor echoed Mercer's words in his medical report. "Patton died as he had lived—bravely."

Yet there are hints, more tantalizing than definitive, suggesting that in his last hours of consciousness Georgie was grappling with other challenges besides the brave acceptance of death. In her thought book, Beatrice only rarely quoted verbatim his words to her as he lay staring at his hospital room ceiling. At one point he interrupted her as she was reading from a volume of military history. "It's too dark," he said. "I mean, too late." She thought he'd momentarily lost his sight, and, not wanting to alarm her, had tried to change his meaning. When he said nothing more, she continued to read. She never remarked on it—and it may only have been a coincidence—but Georgie's utterance echoed the last words of a character in Beatrice's 1936 novel, *Blood of the Shark*. "It's too late," whispers a dying English soldier to the novel's hero, Adam Gordon. "Too dark."

Georgie had had little good to say about the book when it was published; indeed, the period in which Beatrice wrote it saw the worst of his self-destructive behavior and the rockiest time of their marriage. Georgie had virtually total recall of anything he read. Might he have been remembering this snippet from *Blood of the Shark* as he lay dying? Might he, through the passing drift of twelve days' reflection in bed, have recalled those difficult years on Hawaii when he'd so carelessly hurt the people who most loved him? "It's too dark. I mean, too late" poses the question, but can't answer it.

The other significant words Georgie spoke (and Beatrice recorded) were both more and less comprehensible. Spoken as part of some interior dialogue rather than in response to something she said, Georgie said wistfully, "I guess I wasn't good enough." Beatrice took this to signify his disappointment at surviving his last battle rather than being killed in action. Since hearing the tale from Papa when he was a boy, Georgie's cherished paradigm of a desirable end was the death of Confederate General Barnard Bee at the battle of Bull Run in 1861. "There stands Jackson like a stone wall," Bee had exhorted his faltering troops. "Rally behind the Virginians!" Beatrice knew that Georgie seriously regarded the bullet that subsequently pierced General Bee's forehead to be a glorious punctuation on a life well lived, a reward, in short, from God. Georgie's fate, on the other hand— lingering paralyzed in bed, helpless as a child—was surely some kind of rebuke.

When Georgie was twenty he wrote a poem analyzing the thoughts of an ambitious young cadet. The poem, unfinished, began, "His early mind perverted by untruthful literature/He sees a picture of war glorified/And knows not blood is pain and glory but a bubble." It could be said, therefore, that Georgie spent his life trying to deny his youthful intuition that "blood is pain and glory but a bubble." Had he succeeded in that denial, succeeded in spilling blood painlessly and in gaining glory enough to quench his endless thirst for it, one can imagine him dying happy. Yet it appears that he didn't die happy. Rather, in chiding himself that he "wasn't good enough," it appears he died full of introspection and doubt, with a trace, perhaps, of self-revelation.

As a boy, Georgie had been utterly indulged by his parents, his aunt, his sister. In a sense, that condition of pampered childhood was recreated in his Heidelberg hospital room. Nurses tended him, the paternal-like doctor dictated his daily regimen ("Whatever you say goes," Georgie told Spurling), and Beatrice, like Papa and Aunt Nannie years ago, read him military history and, on the day of his death, "Tales of Long Ago" by Arthur Conan Doyle. Yet as a boy, Georgie had eschewed the self-satisfaction such indulgence can cultivate and instead demanded of himself to always aspire, always excel. Even on his deathbed he didn't relent, despite dozens of laudatory telegrams at his feet and any number of well-wishers outside his door. "I guess I wasn't good enough." Such discontent had propelled him from childhood through the length of his life. To invoke it now returned him to childhood and the beginning of his story.

His favorite prayer was taken from Socrates: "All-knowing Zeus; give me what is best for me. Avert evil from me though it be the thing I prayed for; and give me the good, for which, from ignorance, I did not ask." Georgie, from ignorance, often did not ask for the good, did not seek it. But in receiving the chance, despite his personal flaws, to play a great part in destroying one of history's most profane regimes, he was given what was best for him, was given, indeed, the good. His prayer was answered.

After the memorial service, Beatrice accompanied her husband's body by train from Heidelberg to Luxembourg. The train stopped at six city stations along the way where honor guards and local dignitaries stood waiting. At each stop Beatrice addressed the gathered crowds and accepted their commemorative wreaths and flowers. All were impressed by her graciousness. Her personality, wrote Spurling, shone "like a brilliant gem." Like a hard gem, too: at the last moment of making funeral arrangements, Beatrice struck General Bedell Smith, whom Georgie had disliked, from the list of honorary pallbearers and added George Meeks, Georgie's longtime orderly. Now was no time for hypocrisy, she felt.

Under a pouring rain, Georgie was buried at Hamm Cemetery on Christmas Eve morning among many other fallen Third Army soldiers. The white cross bearing his name, rank, and serial number stood in perfect alignment in the ninth row of exactly similar white crosses stretching across the vast cemetery lawn. Two years later his plot would be moved to the front of the cemetery—this was done because tourists visiting his grave were trampling the grass of the surrounding graves.

Today he lies before a low stone wall at the head of the other columns of crosses, a configuration that brings to mind a commander reviewing his troops. Georgie's reaction in 1942 to his troops' designation of "George Patton" as the Torch password perhaps captures what would have been his feelings about the new arrangement at Hamm. "This was not his idea," Beatrice wrote then, "and it pleased him immensely."

She departed Europe immediately after the funeral and arrived in Washington late on Christmas Day. She'd bought her children and grandchildren small gifts and staunchly kept up her cheer through the holidays. "But afterwards," Ruth Ellen wrote, "she was somehow diminished as if she had lost a part of herself. Of course, she had."

☆ ☆ **20** ☆ ☆

The Goddess of Happy Death

BEATRICE wrote in her thought book three weeks after Georgie's death, "The star is gone . . . the accompanist is left behind. There must be a reason, but I pray for understanding." Her next entry began an extended period in which she addressed her late husband directly:

I have just stripped your ribbons from your uniforms to be refitted for George. He will be proud to wear them. Why is it that a beloved one's clothes mean so much? The creases of his body in a coat—and where his legs bend at the groin—it always seems that I must write you what is passing.
    Both girls have played Ouija and it always says "Take care of B—Big B." I could never work it. They may be psychic, being of your blood—I am only your lover—I don't even dream of you at night, and how I wish I could. Perhaps someday.

Beatrice maintained an appearance of good cheer and Yankee perseverance. "The tears run down behind my eyes," she wrote. But others, in addition to her daughters, sensed her depression and tried in their way to uplift her. Her older half-sister Ellen persuaded a skeptical Beatrice to lend her a personal article of Georgie's—a leather glove he'd been wearing at the time of his fatal car accident—with which Ellen's psychic medium, an elderly blind woman Ellen kept on retainer, might contact Georgie in the hereafter. Several séances were held over the glove and over some of Georgie's letters to Beatrice. The items were wrapped unopened in tissue—so the medium didn't know who'd written them. And it was said that she somehow had established herself to be an honest practitioner of her art and not a charlatan. When transcripts of the séances, written down by the old woman's daughter, were sent to Beatrice, Beatrice couldn't resist reading them.

The medium, in a trance, spoke words any grieving lover would long to hear. "This gentleman knew his own mind—loved his wife beyond expression—was happiest when with her and says she is not to miss him—he must progress until they meet again as they surely will." Touching Georgie's wrapped letters, she went on, "He enjoyed physical comforts but took insufficient rest, and, it seems to me, hastened to an end. He has gone on to his reward, and it is better so, his health would have been against him had he lived."

Several details in the transcripts took Beatrice aback. The medium described feeling a touch on her face, a brief, familiar caress—Georgie often had stroked his wife's face when they spoke or sat beside each other or passed each other crossing a room at a cocktail party. And she kept mentioning with apparent confusion the letter B and then "Big B": "I'm talking to Big B—my Big B—Blessed One." Finally, the medium emerged from her first trance with *"Adieu,"* modified in later séances to *"Adio."* As a child, Georgie had picked up snippets of Spanish from Lake Vineyard's Mexican farmhands. As an adult he often waved *"Adios"* in casual partings from his family.

But the interpretation of such things varies with the beholder, and Beatrice, though vulnerable in her bereavement and accustomed, through her association with Georgie and the Pattons, to paranormal attractions, was more upset by the transcripts than comforted. She gave them to Ruth Ellen because she didn't want them in the house. "They make my flesh crawl," she said.

Georgie's death in Europe had sparked what one biographer has termed his "transfiguration." His decline in popularity caused by his various public missteps was reversed in a national upwelling of sympathy during the twelve days he lay dying in Heidelberg. His relief from command of Third Army imparted a tinge of injustice, even tragedy, to the last months of his life. His burial at Hamm with hundreds of his men served to transcend the egotistical bluster that had distanced him from the common soldier. It made him one of them. A casualty of war. Another dead American son.

His skills as a battle commander, never questioned, were lauded as among the finest in American history. Interviews with colleagues, superiors, and his German counterparts left no doubt about his role in the defeat of Hitler's army. Said Field Marshal Gerd von Rundstedt, "Patton was your best." Many U.S. soldiers testified of their affection for him; even those who'd disliked him took a certain pride in having served in his army. Personal reminiscences of him appeared in magazines and newspapers, and his cartoonlike public image acquired new shades of complexity. As military studies of the war were published, his combat style of constant attack was revealed to be far from heedless. Using maneuver and surprise he avoided costly frontal assaults whenever possible, keeping Third Army casualties relatively low. He was a strong critic of the Allies' "terror bombing" of cities such as Berlin, Leipzig, and Dresden. "I do not believe," he wrote, "that this indiscriminate bombing of towns is worth the ammunition, and it is unnecessarily cruel to civilians." He believed that bombing should be directed at "purely military targets."

However, Beatrice continued to believe that his greatness was insufficiently recognized. She sought to burnish his memory with the publication of his war diary. *War As I Knew It* (1947) was a best-seller, though not "one of the great books of the century" as she'd hoped; cleansed of controversy and polished to grammar-book correctness, Georgie's edited prose lacked the crackle of Georgie himself. Beatrice contributed to a Third Army veterans' fund to erect a bronze statue of him in front of the West Point library. She arranged for Douglas Southall Freeman, biographer of George Washington and Robert E. Lee, to write Georgie's biography (Freeman died before he could begin it). She traveled throughout the United States and Europe accepting awards on his behalf and dedicating buildings, streets, parks, and plaques in his name.

A self-described "earthly" person, Beatrice was as concerned with Georgie's immortality in this world as in the next. But before undertaking any of these projects for him, she'd begun a personal project strictly for herself. "Ma took a long time to really work up a hate for somebody," Ruth Ellen recalled, "but when she did, it was to the death." And someone she'd come to hate very much was Jean Gordon, who'd returned from Europe in November.

Since 1936 Beatrice had swallowed her anger at Jean for the sake of family propriety. But just weeks after Georgie's death, she arranged through her brother Fred Ayer to meet her face-to-face in a Boston hotel room. Fred, unaware of why his sister was so darkly intent on this meeting, arrived with Jean ahead of Beatrice. Beatrice entered the room still wearing her outdoor coat and hat. She removed her glove from her right hand and pointed her finger at Jean like a pistol. Fred told Ruth Ellen years later that he'd been appalled by the expression on Beatrice's face and by the steely tone of her voice.

In 1916 Nita Patton wrote her mother that many young officers at Fort Bliss were frightened of Beatrice. Georgie, too, knew that his wife's temper was slow to ignite yet furious in its explosion; despite his dramatic tantrums, the children regarded their mother—composed, taut, and vigilant—as no less formidable than their father. Now Jean learned about Beatrice's temper.

According to Fred Ayer, Beatrice attacked Jean with an old Hawaiian curse that began "May the Great Worm gnaw your vitals and may your bones rot joint by little joint." Fred ran out before she finished. There was so much malevolence in the room, he told Ruth Ellen later, that he couldn't bear to remain.

Evidently one of Beatrice's Hawaiian friends had confided the curse to her years earlier, confided it like a deadly weapon to be used only in extreme situations. Beatrice's social refinement notwithstanding, she'd carried a quirky streak all her life; no doubt it played a part in this strange display with Jean. As to the curse itself, perhaps the best that can be said is that the power of such things lies in the delivery—and Beatrice delivered it with all the virulence she could summon. Within weeks, Jean committed suicide by gas in a friend's New York apartment.

Stories circulated through the family after Jean's death that she left a suicide note declaring, "I will be with Uncle Georgie in heaven and have him all to myself before Beatrice arrives." Such a note would constitute a grimly dramatic touché to Beatrice's curse—but its existence remains only a rumor. It also has been speculated that Jean's suicide may have had nothing to do with Georgie, that she was despondent over a young officer who'd broken off their wartime love affair.

Clearly, however, Beatrice felt sufficiently threatened by Jean to seek, in words, to destroy her. Jean's relationship with Georgie in 1936, followed by their reunion in Europe in 1944, was evidence enough in Beatrice's mind to judge her half-niece to be an opportunistic interloper. Beatrice's resentment may have been defensive. Jean was educated, bright, and amusing. During the war, and for months afterward, she often accompanied Georgie when he entertained guests at his headquarters. Said a fellow Red Cross clubmobile worker of Jean, she "was as witty as he was, and as interested in as many things, including, horses, sailing, and history. In the rather austere and lonely life he led during the war, she was a bright, warm touch, a feminine touch I am sure he needed and appreciated."

Jean told a friend after Georgie's death that she thought it may have been fortunate. "There is no place for him anymore, and he would have been unhappy with nothing to do." The words suggest that Jean had an understanding of him that was insightful and not frivolous, ample reason for his wife to deem her a serious rival. Beatrice, out of love, could forgive Georgie's indiscretion; but Jean she was determined to punish. This punishment accomplished, she moved gracefully into her postwar role of matriarch and eminent widow. Her grace was especially helpful in the period of mourning that followed Jean's suicide. Recalled Ruth Ellen, "Ma was a tower of strength to Jean's mother, her own half-sister, who was devastated by this blow."

George IV graduated from West Point in June 1946 and was commissioned as an infantry lieutenant. Ruth Ellen had a third child. Bee's husband recovered from his war wound and eventually became commandant of cadets at West Point. Beatrice visited her children at their various military stations and often had her grandchildren to stay at her Green Meadows estate. But to her own amazement, she recorded these good times only long after they'd happened. "Indeed there are great gaps," she acknowledged. As often had been the case in her life, her sorrow was expressed by omissions in her thought book, by silence. She still missed Georgie a lot.

She began experiencing recurrences of the heart tachycardia she'd suffered as a young woman. Frightened and in pain during one twelve-hour attack, she consoled herself with the thought (she wrote Georgie afterward) "that the pounding and tripping of my heart was because you were pulling at the bond between us trying to pull me along and help me bump over the road to where you are." During a hike through the grounds of Green Meadows, she came upon an apple tree that had been split by lightning yet had stubbornly clung to life. "So is it with the heart," she wrote, "that, torn asunder, beats on a little while . . . until at last its pulsing ceases—and the future's past." Though her doctor advised her to protect her health, she continued to ride horses and even fox hunt, a sport that once had frightened her. "I am afraid no longer. What I live from now on is extra, and if I get hurt it will not hurt anyone else." Gradually she warmed to this new existence, her afterlife following Georgie's death. "It is a lovely, free feeling," she wrote.

George got married in June 1952. His bride, Joanne Holbrook, was the daughter of a brigadier general and the granddaughter of two army chiefs of cavalry. Wearing lavender chiffon and violets in her hair, Beatrice looked radiant at the wedding. "So like a dolphin, dies the day," Ruth Ellen reflected years later. That is, the yellow-green hues of the Pacific dolphin, a popular game fish, are never so brilliant as just before it breathes its last on the deck of a fishing boat.

War had been raging in Korea since 1950. Bee's husband, Johnnie Waters, a general now, was ordered there soon after her brother's wedding. Bee took the separation hard. Seven years after being reunited with Johnnie after his long imprisonment in Germany, she again was forced to head the household, to wait each day for news from overseas. During the last war, she'd maintained the appearance of coping. Now she faltered. She didn't look well, complained of chest pains, resisted consulting a doctor. Worried, her mother and sister invited Bee to visit them with her two sons. She declined almost defensively.

In October Ruth Ellen was puttering in the backyard of her house in Washington when suddenly a snippet of song popped into her head— "When all the world is old, lads, and all the trees are brown." She began to cry. Her aunt Nita Patton was visiting, and when she came out of the house she asked Ruth Ellen what was wrong. "Something terrible is happening," Ruth Ellen said. Nita nodded. "I feel it, too."

The doctor telephoned early the next day from the Waters' home outside West Point. Bee had died of heart failure. She was forty-one.

Ruth Ellen flew to New York at once. Her mother arrived soon after. "She looked smaller and more transparent than I had ever seen her," Ruth Ellen wrote. "She looked completely defenseless." Their grief only deepened in the next days. Clearing out Bee's things after the funeral, they were stunned to find quantities of alcohol hidden about her bedroom. They hadn't thought she drank at all. They'd thought she was coping okay.

"Swayed by passing breezes but strong in the time of storm" had been Beatrice's earlier description of her elder daughter, a description more hopeful than true, sadly. Now Beatrice murmured over and over, "If only I had known." But Little Bee, it seemed, had not wished to be known. In the future people would speak of her gentleness, her lovely seat on a horse, her affection for her children and husband. But perhaps Ruth Ellen best captured Bee's elusive nature in her observation years later: "It isn't only soldiers who are casualties of war."

*   *   *

After Georgie's death in 1945, letters and telegrams of condolence came to his son almost daily during his last semester at West Point. Strangers asked for mementos of the general. For a while, George accommodated with signatures snipped off letters his father had sent him during the war. As the deluge of requests kept coming, he began forwarding them to his mother to deal with.

Implicit in all this acclaim for his father was the weight of expectation on young George himself. He'd begun to think that he might be "a marked man" in his army career. If he didn't rise high in rank, people would cluck that he'd failed to measure up. If he did rise high, they'd think it was because of his famous name. Suspicious of favoritism, he was reluctant to accept the offer of a superior officer to help him transfer from the infantry service branch to armor. His mother advised him to do it. "No one would help you unless they think you can deliver the goods. *You can.*"

George was a captain teaching small unit tactics at the Armor School at Fort Knox, Kentucky, in early 1953. His pupils were young officers recently back from Korea. They were combat veterans; he, their instructor, was not. Feeling like a fraud, he pressed for assignment to Korea, though his wife was pregnant and the war seemed to be winding down. He had to get into battle. "Our family's different," his mother once had written him. "We have a lot to live up to."

His orders to Korea came through in February. He spent his first night there in Yong Dong Po, north of Seoul. Outside his barracks medical personnel sorted the bodies of American soldiers killed in the recent battle of Pork Chop Hill. "All night long you could hear them trying to identify the bodies. So that kind of unwhetted my appetite."

Action was slow in the first months after he took over a tank company supporting a Korean division. The company held a defensive position in the craggy mountains above the Soyang River Valley. Chinese Communist forces occasionally lobbed mortar fire up the mountain, but otherwise stayed out of sight. A news photographer snapped a picture of George by one of his unit's tanks. "In Father's Footsteps" ran the caption under the picture when it appeared in American newspapers. The tank was an M-46 "Patton."

Toward the end of May, the enemy began to push south, penetrating Korean Army positions and threatening to surround George's company. Heavy mortar fire had blown the tracks off most of his twenty-two tanks, effectively converting them to fixed artillery pieces. Driving in his jeep among these immobilized tanks, he was forced off the road by incoming bombardment. Taking cover in a sandbag bunker, he realized that his radio transmitter had been left behind in the jeep. Mortar rounds exploded around him. He needed that radio, but tried to think of excuses not to retrieve it. No use. He was struck with the image of his father and other Patton ancestors observing him in disappointment. "They seemed to be daring me to cross the road." He took a breath and left the bunker, forcing himself—he didn't know why—to walk instead of run. Just then an explosion rocked the ground behind him. The bunker had taken a direct hit, killing and wounding several men inside. George retrieved the radio.

Enemy infantry attacked within hours, trying to break through and capture the convoy of artillery being evacuated to the south. "In this connection, we piled up over eight hundred Chinese in front of our positions during this three-day battle." The wails of enemy wounded wafted up the ravine after the Chinese broke off their attack. George sent two medics under a white flag to go see if any could be saved. One of the medics was shot by a sniper. George's concern for the enemy's wounded ended there.

Of his first experience of combat: "I felt I'd joined a kind of club. Not better than other people, just different." He got a Silver Star for valor in the engagement. The battalion received a presidential citation.

His wife gave birth to a daughter on July 6. Three weeks later the Korean War ended inconclusively in a cease-fire. "The Forgotten War," it has often been called. George was in Japan on rest-and-recreation leave in September when the Department of the Army contacted him at his Tokyo hotel with news that his mother was dead.

In 1926 Beatrice had a serious fall off a horse. Revived to consciousness by a doctor, she wrote a poem about it afterward:

> Why must you drag me back?
> Death would have been so sweet!
> I gallop through the orchard plied with sunlight
> My blood fast racing,
> The hoofs of all the field pounding accompaniment,
> And then, swift as a lightning flash, the fall—
> And waken in God's arms.

On September 30, 1953, Beatrice would not be dragged back. She tumbled off her horse during a fox hunt near her estate and, according to the autopsy, was dead before she hit the ground, killed by a burst aortic aneurism which, unknown to her children, Beatrice's doctor had warned her about months earlier.

George flew home from Japan. He and Ruth Ellen cremated their mother in accordance with her wish. Beatrice had hoped to have her ashes, she wrote in 1946, "slipped in beside Georgie at Hamm. Then I am disposed of in his great shadow." But only fallen soldiers were permitted to lie in the U.S. military cemeteries in Europe. So her children buried her urn under an elm tree on the Green Meadows property. A large gray boulder marked the spot, on it a small bronze plaque. "I have kept the faith," it read.

Several years later, George, Ruth Ellen, and Ruth Ellen's sixteen-year-old son, Michael, flew to Luxembourg. Ruth Ellen had never seen Georgie's grave. It hadn't seemed important. A human body was merely the soul's ephemeral clothes, she believed. "Love the inmate, not the room," Georgie had taught her long ago. But her son had long wanted to see this place, and on that excuse she and George had undertaken this trip. But they had another reason for coming. They wanted to complete the story.

As the afternoon darkened over the beautiful sad crosses at Hamm, Ruth Ellen stepped to the single cross at the head of the cemetery and removed a brown envelope from her purse. She poured a stream of crumbly white ashes out of the envelope into her palm. As she sifted the ashes through her fingers onto the green grass of Georgie's grave, she recalled a verse from Samuel: "In their death they were not divided: they were swifter than eagles, they were stronger than lions."

Mike, watching her, glanced up to see a large gray cat sitting atop the stone wall behind the grave. He nudged his mother and whispered, "Bast." In the religion of ancient Egypt, the goddess Bast took the form of a cat. Ruth Ellen smiled. Her mother had been interested in mythology ever since her childhood vacation in Egypt, when Beatrice had stolen the mummy's toe. "Bast," she nodded. "The goddess of happy death."

Ruth Ellen, George, and Mike walked out of Hamm's gate just as the cemetery was being closed for the evening. "He knows I never failed him," Beatrice wrote of Georgie the day after he died. Nor had her children failed her.

EPILOGUE

The Pattons

O N THE day of Beatrice's funeral in 1953, the telephone rang at her Green Meadows home. The caller was a Hollywood film producer whose past efforts to enlist Beatrice's help in making a movie about Georgie had been consistently rebuffed. He hoped, in vain it turned out, that her children would be more cooperative.

Just as she'd carried on Georgie's disillusionment with the prying media, so did Ruth Ellen and George, after her death, likewise carry on Beatrice's. Even as a child I was aware of a prevailing fortress mentality whenever they fielded propositions for movie deals and tell-all biographies. The fiercely guarded prize was Georgie's voluminous accumulation of private letters, lectures, articles, and personal diary. In 1964 these papers were donated to the Library of Congress, with public access to be permitted after 1974. In the interim, the historian Martin Blumenson was authorized to examine freely and edit the material for what would become his two-volume study *The Patton Papers* (1972, 1974).

Many of the papers circa World War II had been typed by Georgie's military secretary. In the early 1960s, Ruth Ellen and George learned that the secretary had retained copies of some of these papers and contributed them as a major source for Ladislas Farago's *Patton: Ordeal and Triumph* (1963). They took legal steps against publication until any copyrighted material was excised. Later in the decade, the family learned that Farago's book would be the basis for Twentieth Century-Fox's forthcoming Patton movie. The news was dubiously received. But when the movie came out in 1970, we weren't so high-minded as not to go see it.

I first saw *Patton* at a matinee showing in Manhattan's Times Square when I was twelve years old. The movie recently had opened nationwide and was a popular hit. The theater was packed with what I concluded were the "New York types" I'd heard about in my childhood, people with whom I was advised to be on guard.

For the previous eight months I'd been living at Mineral Wells, Texas, and Fort Rucker, Alabama, remote army posts where my father, George S. Patton IV, had been stationed since coming home from Vietnam in 1969. My family, five kids and our parents, was passing through New York en route to a new army station in Europe. Our layover in the city provided our first opportunity to see *Patton*.

The 1960s were still in full roar in 1970, with no end in sight to the war on the homefront and in Southeast Asia. A hawkish army colonel and his dutifully gung-ho dependents were not exactly the good guys in the view of many Americans. So we kept our heads low, cowed by an irrational fear that, whether as military people or as Pattons, some wild-eyed moviegoer would recognize us and cry, "There they are! Get 'em!" We spoke little to one another, avoided eye contact with strangers, even skipped the popcorn and soda as we hurried to our back-row seats.

The lights went down. An opening shot of a huge American flag confronted us like a blazing sun, rousing the audience to raucous applause. If my family clapped at all, it was belatedly. We were unsure if this patriotic fervor wasn't some sort of inside joke known only to New Yorkers. And we weren't the rah-rah type, having been steeped in the tradition that regard for one's country mainly entails a regard for those killed in its service. In celebrating the flag, a gesture easily vulgarized, we were as circumspect as we would have been before raising a cheer in church.

The applause subsided as George C. Scott, in his Academy Award–winning role as Georgie Patton, appeared on screen in a garishly festooned uniform to give a rallying speech to his troops. The sight of Scott wearing facsimiles of my grandfather's medals in the exact arrangement of a snapshot of Patton displayed in our home briefly popped the illusion for me. But soon I was hooting along with the audience at Patton-Scott's fiery pledge to go through the Nazis "like crap through a goose," and at his derision of war correspondents who "don't know anything more about real battle than they know about *fornicating!*"

The spell was again temporarily broken when my father, seated next to me, leaned over and whispered, "Sounds nothing like him. My old man had a high voice." I'd heard this said before about my grandfather, but at that moment I preferred to believe that Scott's gravelly snarl was pure authentic Patton. So even the intrusion of contrary fact didn't prevent me from slipping once more into a state of suspended disbelief whose last thought before total gape-mouthed immersion was something like "Hey, this picture's got possibilities."

I can still recall the opening bars of *Patton*'s musical score. Pauline Kael, in her *New Yorker* review, pronounced the score banal. It may well be. I'm the least qualified to judge, for the music is bound up with all my impressions of that day, impressions that rather eased themselves after much anxiety, like me into my theater seat, into the passive, big-hearted geniality of someone dazed by a pleasant surprise. I had long been aware of certain pros and cons about being George Patton's descendant. Many people were impressed by it; in the fervent antiwar atmosphere of the time, many were not. Either response seemed to carry an expectation of me to react accordingly with pride or humble apology, though my own attitude fell somewhere in between. Here, in this theater, my ambivalence toward my heritage was acute. It was a relief to discover myself entertained by the movie, its imagery, story, and music drawing me in as just another satisfied customer.

I was four when I saw my first movie ever—in New York City, coincidentally enough, where earlier that same day I and my family had disembarked from a transatlantic crossing aboard the U.S.S. *Independence* after living four years in Germany. America was a brand-new country to me. I was as overwhelmed as any happy immigrant by the traffic and skyscrapers and, from shipboard, that first sight of the Statue of Liberty. My introduction to America was capped off by *The Alamo,* a boisterous shoot-'em-up starring John Wayne as the frontiersman Davy Crockett. Now, at *Patton* almost nine years later, I was watching a movie about another American folk hero, one to whom, after my initial self-consciousness faded, I seemed to have no more personal connection than I had with Crockett.

Late in the movie, during its climactic re-creation of the Third Army's relief of Bastogne during the Battle of the Bulge, I became aware of my father weeping beside me. The weeping was brief. One sniffle, a wipe of his eyes and nose, then a palpable self-composing as he sighed once deeply and refixed his gaze on the screen. That was all, but my concentration was snapped by this sharp reminder that through him I was indeed connected to this General Patton character, and that maybe I was remiss for not affirming that connection with tears.

For the rest of the movie I was achingly alert to any new sniffle or sigh on my father's part, which I might then link with events on the screen in order, like him, to engage them emotionally. Though he didn't weep again, my divided attention through the film's final fade-out put a vivid punctuation on my experience of seeing *Patton.* The movie about his father had touched something inside *my* father; my awareness of this, and my memory of it, was how the movie likewise touched me. Despite the obscuring, myth-making inflation that *Patton* brings to its subject, it led me to consider for the first time in my life that my grandfather was somebody real.

My father did three tours in South Vietnam. On his third tour, in 1968 to 1969, he commanded the Eleventh Armored Cavalry near the Cambodian border. "The Blackhorse Regiment" combined infantry, helicopters, and tanks in a mobile combat machine, and my father plunged himself body and soul into conducting its deadly mission. He twice won the Distinguished Service Cross ("One I deserved, one I didn't") and received a Purple Heart for shrapnel wounds in his abdomen. Recently he has been the regimental association's honorary colonel, and he rarely misses a reunion. During his ten-month stint with the Eleventh Cavalry in Vietnam, he wrote eighty-six letters home to parents whose sons died under his command. He cannot recall that period without being overcome with emotion.

Like his father, he gained some notoriety in the war for his candid passion for his work. "They're a bloody good bunch of killers," he said of his men in the Academy Award–winning Vietnam documentary, *Hearts and Minds.* The press reported that in December 1968 he sent twelve colleagues a Christmas card with a photograph on it depicting the results of an assault on some unfortunate Viet Cong. The photo was rough stuff—blown apart bodies, basically; in color. Its caption read "Peace on earth, good will toward men."

The card caused a minor uproar. My own reaction when I first saw it (I was a sixth grader at the time) was pretty blasé, considering. I'd grown up in an environment where, if not with such graphic pictures, frank, uneuphemized language made as clear as is possible to a noncombatant the horror and exhilaration of battle. (With all the military precedents on both sides of my family, warfare was, simply put, our business—as apt a topic of table conversation as produce might be in a family of grocers, or money in a family of bankers.) For whatever reason, the Christmas card didn't turn my stomach. I had no illusions about Dad's job in South Vietnam.

As for the card's brutally sarcastic caption, "Peace on earth, good will toward men," I am today struck, even impressed, by its defiant rejection of the euphemism so often a part of official descriptions of combat. Our nation's victory in the Persian Gulf in 1991 put a gloss of relative painlessness, from our perspective back home, on the conduct of modern war. But images similar to that on my father's Christmas card no doubt were reprised countless times during the Gulf War, from the missile attacks on Israel and Saudi Arabia to our own air strikes on Kuwait and Iraq. Any such reminder that disturbs us, pains us, and opens our eyes, cannot be a bad thing. That said, my father's reason for sending the card was essentially prankish. Maybe it speaks of war's capacity to dehumanize its practitioners; maybe it speaks of a simple coarseness in his nature. But to me, a sixth grader in 1968, sending out that Christmas card seemed just the sort of outrageous stunt my grandfather might have pulled, and therefore was perfectly cool.

At my school early the next year, I echoed my father's prank when I presented to the class a term report on the country of South Vietnam. In addition to offering observations about its weather ("hot, wet, and wretched") and its people's diet ("in normal times South Vietnam eats very well by Oriental standards"), I discussed the ongoing U.S. incursion there. I illustrated my discussion with pictures clipped from magazines and, for real punch, with some of my father's snapshots.

As I look at these now, I can only believe that my dear teacher must have thought me a very warped child. A photo I'd captioned "What Charlie Does to Us" shows a gutted, smoldering armored personnel carrier; its destruction surely had not been survived by any GI's riding inside it. Another photo ("What We Do to Charlie") depicts a dead Viet Cong naked on his back in the dirt with a fist-sized hole in his neck. This picture and others I'd included in my presentation aren't any more graphic than what today appear regularly in news weeklies and on television. Their impact derives from the fact that they are snapshots, personal, informal keepsakes such as we might take of our travels through exotic places and mail home to people who miss us. A four-color print in a mass-market magazine is removed by several stages from the horror it may portray. A snapshot, like a blurry hand-held video, puts us almost there.

The school I was attending had been founded by Quakers. The pacifist aspect of the Quaker religion was often invoked in our class debates on the morality of the Vietnam War. But rather than serve to chasten or ostracize me, the antiwar sentiments of the school staff engendered, I think, a certain gentle solicitousness of the student whose father was off fighting the war in question. My only conceivable reason for incorporating revolting pictures in my Vietnam show-and-tell was to rebelliously shake off that solicitousness; the only reason, that is, beyond a basic urge to provoke copied from my father, who in turn copied it from his father.

Today, a decade older than Georgie was at the time of his death, my father has little patience for playing the son to the late great World War II general. As Georgie's namesake, my father, in order to pursue his own army dream, was forced to endure a constant association with, and comparison to, his famous father. It was no minor price to pay, and in recent years, after retiring from the service in 1980 as a major general and becoming a farmer in Massachusetts, he has declared it paid in full. Now he is quick to deflect questions about Georgie with the frank admission that he never really knew him. To have heard him suggest this when I was a boy would have shocked me, for he'd seemed to me the ultimate authority on General Patton, and the ultimate reflection of him.

Throughout his career my father sought to strike from his official records any mention of his father. Only while stationed at the U.S. Army Armor Center at Fort Knox in the early 1970s did he willingly immerse himself in Georgie's legacy, taking part in efforts to refurbish the Patton Museum located there. Originally a ramshackle warehouse of Patton memorabilia and a few rusty old tanks, thanks greatly to my father's efforts, the museum today is an elegant memorial both to the history of modern armor and to George S. Patton, Jr. It is as well a memorial to my father's uneasy bond with *his* father. An army career was what they shared instead of time. Accepting this fact, as my father has done, would seem to stand them together as adults shoulder to shoulder as they never stood together in life.

My father's sister Ruth Ellen has undergone a similar detachment from Georgie's burdensome legacy. Almost nine years older than her brother, her recollections of Georgie are more intimate than his; the siblings have rather divided the memories, my father concentrating on the military side, my aunt on the personal. For years she has defended her father against all detractors. But in her late seventies now, she attests almost shruggingly that through much of her youth she didn't especially like him.

As his oldest surviving child, she has fielded countless requests for revelations about his private life and received countless letters from Patton devotees, some requesting a memento, snapshot, or signature, some only expressing admiration. Loyalty to her father became an instinctive reflex before this tide of curiosity about him. To harbor honest ambivalence about him seemed ungrateful and unwelcome.

These days, however, acknowledging her mixed feelings no longer feels disloyal. A daughter's bright shining devotion has assumed a darker, deeper burnish of understanding and acceptance. Georgie was a difficult man, she says; a flawed man; an interesting man. Almost fifty years after his death, her regard for him has assumed the measured devotion between two equals, something chosen and not merely expected. He was a difficult man. Flawed. Interesting. Worth loving.

Shortly before beginning this history, I rented a video of the movie *Patton* and watched it one afternoon. I sat with my son, who was then six, beside me for company and pointed to the television screen. "That's your great-grampa." Unimpressed, he soon squirmed away upstairs. But *Patton* is a long movie, so whenever my son's afternoon wanderings brought him through the TV room he paused and took in a bit of the story before heading out again. How much he absorbed about his ancestor I wasn't sure of, and didn't ask. It would come, or not, in time.

My son returned and climbed in my lap. Together we watched the Third Army's advance on Bastogne during the Battle of the Bulge. It was the point in the movie when I'd heard my father weeping beside me in 1970. The soundtrack subsides to a whisper of snow falling heavily on American troops and vehicles slogging through the Ardennes in December 1944. General Patton observes from a nearby ridge. On impulse he joins the men as they march, putting his arm around one momentarily, slapping another on the back, all of them sharing similar smiles of wonder that he and they are in this together.

Lasting only a few seconds, it is perhaps a contrived Hollywood moment. But it was, for my father, a resonant one. At the time we first watched *Patton,* my father had been back in the States less than a year. He spoke only occasionally of his recent experiences in Vietnam—of the 3,800 soldiers with whom he felt permanently bonded, of the eighty-six dead he would never forget. The movie image of Georgie walking side by side with men he must shortly commit to battle, evoked, my father said later, his own cherished moments of comradeship with his men. It exemplified the essential bond between my father and grandfather, the pride and harrowing accountability that attends the profession they shared.

If my father wept at this image of common experience with his father, perhaps he wept also at its evocation of the personal rapport the two of them never established. That movie scene of Georgie walking in the snow with his soldiers is almost paternal in its depiction of the white-haired general and those boys in their teens and twenties. But Georgie wasn't much of a father to my father. He was distracted, absent, world famous, then dead. How much of a son—given time, given a chance—might my father have been to *him?* Tears in a darkened movie theater mark the question forever unanswerable.

Certainly Georgie would have taken pride in his son's military career. That particular fatherly gratification was not to come to George IV. His sisters' four sons all became career military officers who served with distinction in Vietnam. Nita Patton's sons also became military officers. (Nita saw both David and Peter marry and have Patton grandchildren before her death in 1971.) My father thought he'd produced a contender when George S. Patton V was born in 1955. But my older brother, a lean blue-eyed six-two like his famous grandfather, is mentally retarded. He is a farmer, a horseman, and a Special Olympics champion. He fights and wins battles every day, though not in uniform.

My three other siblings have pursued emphatically nonmilitary careers as a Roman Catholic nun, an actress, and an environmentalist. The last, my younger brother, has, like me, wrestled at times with a feeling of having somehow let down the side by not carrying on the military tradition; we felt this particularly during the Gulf War, when mailing care packages and encouraging letters to our soldiers abroad didn't seem quite the proper destiny of two young Patton brothers. We forget that historically the Patton men were soldiers by necessity, not by choice. Our forebear Hugh Mercer wanted to be a doctor; the eight Patton brothers of Virginia wanted to be lawyers and politicians. But Papa's romantic military dream, and Georgie's embodiment of that dream, cemented the family's sense of itself as born to the profession of arms.

I decided in high school not to attend West Point. Rather than a grand rejection of my heritage, my reasoning focused on basic issues of life-style: I didn't want to cut my hair, didn't want to rise at 5:30 A.M. each day, didn't want to attend school without girls. But as late as my sophomore year of college in 1977 I was still debating whether to become an army officer. My college had thrown out its ROTC program during the Vietnam War, so twice a week I took ROTC courses at a college across town. It wasn't a good experience. My ROTC classmates suspected me, I think, of being some sort of Ivy League mole perhaps researching an undercover satirical piece for some preppy humor magazine. I in turn *acted* like an Ivy League mole, conveying (I'm sure) an attitude that I was there wearing fatigues and cleaning my M-16 as a bit of downtown slumming.

My father was then a two-star general commanding the Second Armored Division (the same division his father commanded before World War II). He invited me to participate in field maneuvers at Fort Hood, Texas, as an anonymous recruit in a tank battalion. He thought a more authentic introduction into military life would help me decide one way or another about pursuing an army career. I agreed reluctantly. I feared that my anonymity would last about two seconds, and I was nervous how enlisted men would react to the general's son playing soldier on their time. It turned out to be one of the greatest experiences of my life.

I was assigned to a scout platoon under the command of a lieutenant just a couple of years older than me. He knew who I was, of course; soon the whole platoon knew. The men couldn't believe I was participating in these maneuvers by choice. "We have to be here," they said. "You don't." Ultimately they seemed more amused than offended by my presence and patiently helped me to integrate into the platoon's daily routine. My ROTC field gear ill-equipped me for the Texas desert, which was hot by day and freezing at night. A black private offered me his scratchy OD blanket, saying he was used to the cold. Displaying a woeful lack of leadership qualities, I accepted his offer gratefully.

This wasn't war. Elements of the division were engaged in war games against one another. The tactical outcome and human toll of artillery strikes, ambushes, night attacks, and forced retreats were decided by field judges driving around in red-flagged jeeps. To be killed meant you had to stay put for twenty-four hours in radio silence—then resurrection, and you could fight on.

On the last day of the maneuvers I was manning an M-60 machine gun mounted in the back of a jeep. My platoon captured a small convoy of supply trucks whose drivers, to my lieutenant's chagrin, refused his order to sprawl facedown on the ground like proper prisoners. This refusal was rather jovial, really. They had no intention of trying to run away. They explained that in the past few days they'd been killed twice and captured once, and frankly were damn sick of it. The lieutenant, who previously had seemed a mild fellow, became furious. He ordered me to train my weapon on the prisoners and to shoot them if they didn't comply. The absurdity of this order escaped him. These were war *games,* after all. My machine gun was loaded with blanks. It escaped the lieutenant, yet, through the sheer force of his rage, it escaped the prisoners, too. Under threat of execution they laid down on the ground. As I stood guard with my harmless gun I admired them all for what struck me as their utterly proper, utterly necessary belief in the deadly seriousness of this exercise. I didn't share that belief, however. And flying back to New England on a plane that evening, I realized I never would.

My son and I watched the end of the *Patton* video. As the credits rolled I propped my chin atop his head, nuzzled it in his hair that I'm told is precisely the texture and color of young Georgie's, and flicked the movie off.

Later my wife told me that in response to a problem vexing him, our son had declared to her that God would take care of it, so why worry. Since ours is not a household where God typically gets this sort of mention, she'd asked him where he'd got that idea. "From Great-grampa, in the movie." I had to smile, for my grandfather's idiosyncratic religious faith is portrayed in *Patton* side by side with his predilection for violence and swagger. Had my son gone outside and begun to shoot up the neighborhood with whatever toy weaponry he owns, it would have seemed a predictable effect of the war movie he'd recently watched. But this reaction was much more in keeping with what I've seen in our ancestry.

The Pattons were an ethereal bunch, God-haunted, often psychic, their eyes turned constantly heavenward, as if scanning for angels or, just as likely, for a thunderbolt headed their way. I harbor none of these traits myself; it seems my son may be more like the Pattons than I am. Then again, I'm forgetting that "The Pattons" is a fiction created by a few ancestors to give their lives and legacies dramatic continuity without which they feared they would vanish. "The Pattons" is an idea. The Pattons are just a family.

SOURCE NOTES

THE MAIN SOURCES for each chapter are listed below with explanatory details. Several books proved of inestimable overall value and will not be listed again. These are: Martin Blumenson's *The Patton Papers*, vols. I and II (1972, 1974); Blumenson's later, more interpretive biography, *Patton: The Man Behind the Legend* (1985); Ladislas Farago's *The Last Days of Patton* (1981); and Ruth Ellen Patton Totten's unpublished *Ma: A Button Box Biography* (1979). A reminiscence by George S. Patton, Jr., "My Father As I Knew Him from Memory and Legend" (1927), and his transcribed interviews of his father, "A Child's Memory of the Civil War" (1927), were also of great value. Many Patton family anecdotes, passed down orally through the generations, were generally recollected by Ruth Ellen Patton Totten and George S. Patton IV. Where possible, I have placed these anecdotes in plausible context by consulting published background histories. All military references were confirmed in *The West Point Military History Series*, Thomas E. Griess, series editor.

Chapter 1. The Contempt of the Proud
The description of the European lineage and arrival in America of Louis and Catherine DuBois is based primarily on records noted in *American Families*, published by the American Historical Society of New York in the

mid-1920s. Though essentially a vanity production of wealthy American families, the book is valuable as a compendium of reminiscences and genealogies that in the years since the book's publication would probably have disappeared. The excerpted slave contract from James Madison to Isaac Hite is taken from *Belle Grove* (1968), published by the National Trust for Historic Preservation.

Chapter 2. To Die As I Had Lived

Hugh Mercer has been the subject of at least three biographies, the first published in 1906, the last, *General Hugh Mercer* by Frederick English, in 1975. Additional information about Mercer's Revolutionary War service was taken from Douglas Southall Freeman's *George Washington*, vol. IV (1948). Descriptions of Robert Patton were based primarily on genealogical research done by Margaret French Patton Jones, a distant relative, in the 1930s and 1940s; her sources included *Virginia and Virginians*, vol. I (1888) by R. A. Brock, and *Sketches of Virginia—Second Series* (1850) by the Reverend William H. Foote. Original papers concerning the illness and death of Nelly Davenport are in the author's possession.

Chapter 3. A Torchlight Procession

The reference to Captain Philip Slaughter is drawn from *A History of St. Mark's Parish, Culpeper County, Virginia* (1877) by the Reverend Philip Slaughter. The career of Congressman John Mercer Patton is recounted in Brock's *Virginia and Virginians*, in Horace Hayden's *Virginia Genealogies* (1979), and in John Pendleton's eulogy to the congressman delivered at the Richmond Circuit Court in November 1858 and transcribed in *American Families*. Descriptions of George S. Patton I were based partly on material in *Virginia Genealogies* and in the remembrance of Patton by his contemporary Charles Walker in the Virginia Military Institute Memorial Volume. Quotations were taken from several family letters of the period, now in the author's possession, and from George Patton's letters on file at the Virginia Military Institute. Information and quotes concerning the Kanawha Riflemen were taken from *The Battle of Scary Creek* (1982) and from the Virginia Regimental Histories Series *22nd Virginia Infantry* (1988), both by Terry D. Lowry.

Chapter 4. Perfectly Resigned

Descriptions of the Scary Creek battle were based on the aforementioned books by Lowry. The Civil War careers of George Hugh Smith and

W. Tazewell Patton are generally recounted in the histories of their respective regiments, *62nd Virginia Infantry* (1988) by Roger U. Delauter, Jr., and *7th Virginia Infantry* (1982) by David F. Riggs. John Mercer Patton's exchange with Stonewall Jackson ("kill them all") was quoted from *Stonewall Jackson: The Legend and the Man* (1959) by Lenoir Chambers. William T. Glassell's Civil War career is recounted in his privately published memoir, *W. T. Glassell and the Little Torpedo Boat "David."* Additional descriptions of George S. Patton I were based on a 1945 piece in *Holland's* magazine, "George S. Patton, Rebel," by Forrest Hull, and a 1984 article in *American History,* "Ancestral Gray Cloud over Patton," by Ashley Halsey. Descriptions of the Gettysburg battle were primarily based on information contained in *The Battle of Gettysburg* by W. C. Storrick, superintendant of guides, Gettysburg National Park Commission. Numerous quotations were taken from family letters in the author's possession.

Chapter 5. The Effects of a General Breakdown

References to the Civil War were drawn from the same sources used in chapter 4.

Chapter 6. The Tin Box

Descriptions of Southern California circa 1866 were primarily based on information contained in *Days of Vintage, Years of Vision,* vol. II (1987) by Midge Sherwood. Quotations from Sue Glassell and George S. Patton II's California letters, on file at the Huntington Library in San Marino, California, were also taken from Sherwood's book.

Chapter 7. Playing Tiger

Quotations from George S. Patton II's speeches delivered at the Virginia Military Institute were taken from originals in the author's possession. Descriptions and some quotations concerning Benjamin Wilson and his family were drawn from Sherwood's aforementioned book, from *B. D. Wilson, Southern California Pioneer* (1946) by M. F. Aitken, and from original letters in the author's possession.

Chapter 8. The Happiest Boy in the World

Descriptions of George S. Patton, Jr.'s early life and education were based in part on interviews with Ruth Ellen Patton Totten and on *The Patton Mind: The Professional Development of an Extraordinary Leader* (1993) by Roger H. Nye.

Chapter 9. Undine and Kuhlborn

Descriptions of the Ayer family and of the early courtship of George S. Patton, Jr., and Beatrice Ayer were based on interviews with Ruth Ellen Patton Totten, and on *The Sarsaparilla Kings* (1993) by Scott C. Steward.

Chapter 10. My Every Slightest Wish

Descriptions and quotations regarding Nita Patton were based on interviews with Ruth Ellen Patton Totten, and on letters and documents in the author's possession. Quotations from Papa Patton's letters were taken from letters in the author's possession and on file at the Virginia Military Institute.

Chapter 11. A Cure for Brittle Bones

Descriptions and quotations regarding Georgie Patton and Beatrice Ayer's courtship and marriage were based on interviews with Ruth Ellen Patton Totten, on letters in the author's possession, and on Beatrice Ayer's scrapbook of clippings and letters of the period.

Chapter 12. We Are Living So Intensely Lately

Descriptions and quotations regarding Nita Patton were based on letters in the author's possession. Background information on Pancho Villa was found in *Pancho Villa and the Columbus Raid* (1949) by Larry A. Harris. Background information on U.S. Cavalry operations circa 1915 was found in *The Story of the U.S. Cavalry* (1953) by John K. Herr and Edward S. Wallace. Family letters and documents in the author's possession were the basis of descriptions of Papa Patton's 1916 Senate campaign. Carmine A. Prioli's *Lines of Fire: The Poetry of General George S. Patton, Jr.* (1991) was helpful in the discussion of Georgie Patton's poetry.

Chapter 13. Talking Blood

Descriptions and quotations regarding Nita Patton, Beatrice Patton, and John J. Pershing were based on letters in the author's possession. Quotations of Georgie Patton's poetry were taken from the aforementioned book by Prioli. Descriptions of the deaths (and aftermath) of Frederick and Ellen Ayer were based on interviews with Ruth Ellen Patton Totten, on the aforementioned book by Steward, and on details recorded in Beatrice Patton's thought book, in the author's possession.

Chapter 14. Faces in the Clouds

Background on AEF operations in World War I was found in John Toland's *No Man's Land: The Last Year of the Great War* (1980). The battlefield exchange between Douglas MacArthur and Georgie Patton was quoted from William Manchester's *American Caesar* (1978). Descriptions and quotations regarding Nita Patton and John J. Pershing were based on letters in the author's possession.

Chapter 15. Au Revoir, Son

Beatrice Patton's impressions of her daughters and husband were quoted from her scrapbooks of the period. Descriptions and quotations regarding Georgie Patton between the wars were based primarily on interviews with Ruth Ellen Patton Totten. The description of the funeral of Papa Patton was based on the recollections of Beatrice Patton Waters as told to Ruth Ellen Patton Totten. Descriptions and quotations regarding Sergeant Joseph Angelo and the Bonus March were based in part on Beatrice Patton's scrapbooks of the period. Descriptions and quotations regarding Georgie Patton and Nita Patton were based on letters in the author's possession and on interviews with Ruth Ellen Patton Totten.

Chapter 16. Hawaiian Legends

Descriptions of Georgie and Beatrice Patton were based primarily on interviews with Ruth Ellen Patton Totten and George S. Patton IV. Critical response to Beatrice Patton's novel *Blood of the Shark* was taken from her scrapbooks of the period. Exchanges between Georgie Patton and Arvin Brown were quoted from letters in the author's possession. References to Everett Hughes and "the researcher," Molly McClellan, who decoded Hughes's wartime diary, were taken from *Parade* magazine's "Intelligence Report" (April 19, 1981) by Lloyd Shearer. Some descriptions of Georgie Patton were quoted from *Before the Colors Fade* (1964) by Frederick Ayer, Jr.

Chapter 17. Torch

Descriptions of Georgie's so-called flashbacks were based on interviews with Ruth Ellen Patton Totten. Descriptions of the relationship of Georgie Patton and George S. Patton IV were based on interviews with the latter. Georgie Patton's exchanges with Arvin Brown about politics and the war in Europe were quoted from letters in the author's possession. Information about Georgie's military studies was provided by the aforementioned book by Nye. Beatrice's impressions of Georgie prior to Operation Torch were

taken from her thought book, as was Georgie's "in case of my death" letter
to her.

Chapter 18. The Fair-Haired Boy

Descriptions of Georgie during his brief tour of the States in 1945 were
based in part on interviews with Ruth Ellen Patton Totten and George S.
Patton IV. Descriptions and quotations regarding Beatrice during World
War II were based primarily on her thought book. The quotation of
Georgie's battle instructions to his officers was taken from *War As I Knew
It* (1947) by George S. Patton, Jr. The excerpt from Georgie's speech to his
enlisted soldiers was taken from *The Unknown Patton* (1983) by Charles M.
Province. Background information on the Hammelburg raid was found in
John Toland's *The Last 100 Days* (1965) and *Patton's Third Army at War*
(1978) by George Forty. The description of the last exchange between
Georgie Patton and his daughters was based on interviews with Ruth Ellen
Patton Totten.

Chapter 19. An Ironical Thing

Descriptions and quotations regarding Beatrice and Georgie Patton
shortly before his death were taken from Beatrice's thought book. Descriptions of events in the lives of Georgie Patton's children during the time of
his death were based on interviews with Ruth Ellen Patton Totten and
George S. Patton IV.

Chapter 20. The Goddess of Happy Death

Incidents involving Beatrice Patton and her family in the years following
Georgie Patton's death were based in part on interviews with Ruth Ellen
Patton Totten, George S. Patton IV, John K. Waters, Jr., and George Patton
Waters.

ACKNOWLEDGMENTS

O N THANKSGIVING morning 1993, Ruth Ellen Patton Totten passed away at age seventy-eight. My aunt possessed unmatched insight into the life and character of her father, George S. Patton, Jr., and this book could not have been written without her support and participation. Her deep interest in history led her, as a young girl, to interview many of her elderly relatives about their lives and memories, forging a link to earlier generations that otherwise would have been lost. The tales Ruth Ellen recorded in her childhood notebooks, the genealogical research she conducted throughout her life, and our many hours of discussions together, are the raw material of this book. I am indebted to her for allowing me to carry on what she always considered to be her life's work: telling the story of our family.

My father was immensely helpful in clarifying matters of military history and in helping me to understand the complex personalities of his parents. Thanks also to my mother, siblings, and assorted relatives for their assistance and encouragement along the way. And thanks to Richard Marek, Jim Wade, Harvey Klinger, and Scott Steward.

Finally, I offer my deepest thanks and love to my own family, Tom and Chris Zawacki, Robert and James Patton, and above all to my wife, Vicki, without whom this book would not have mattered, much less have been completed.

INDEX